Leading Student Assessment

STUDIES IN EDUCATIONAL LEADERSHIP

VOLUME 15

SCOPE OF THE SERIES

Leadership we know makes all the difference in success or failures of organizations. This series will bring together in a highly readable way the most recent insights in successful leadership. Emphasis will be placed on research focused on pre-collegiate educational organizations. Volumes should address issues related to leadership at all levels of the educational system and be written in a style accessible to scholars, educational practitioners and policy makers throughout the world.

The volumes – monographs and edited volumes – should represent work from different parts in the world.

For further volumes:
http://www.springer.com/series/6543

Charles F. Webber • Judy L. Lupart

Editors

Leading Student Assessment

 Springer

Editors
Charles F. Webber
Faculty of Human, Social and Educational
Development
Thompson Rivers University
900 McGill Road
Kamloops, British Columbia
Canada, V2C OC8
cwebber@tru.ca

Judy L. Lupart
Department of Educational Psychology
University of Alberta
Edmonton, Alberta
Canada, T6G 2G5
judy.lupart@ualberta.ca

ISBN 978-94-007-1726-8   e-ISBN 978-94-007-1727-5
DOI 10.1007/978-94-007-1727-5
Springer Dordrecht Heidelberg London New York

Library of Congress Control Number: 2011938107

Printed on acid-free paper

Springer is part of Springer Science+Business Media (www.springer.com)

Contents

About the Editors

Charles F. Webber is Professor and Dean in the Faculty of Human, Social, and Educational Development at Thompson Rivers University in British Columbia, Canada. His current research focuses on the influence of school leaders on student achievement and on cross-cultural leadership development, including technology-mediated leadership development. During his career as an educator he has served as a classroom teacher, curriculum consultant, principal, professor, associate dean, and dean. His work appears in national and international journals and he has served as an invited presenter in conferences, seminars, and workshops in North America, Europe, Asia, Africa, the Middle East, New Zealand, and Australia. He was the founding editor of the *International Electronic Journal for Leadership in Learning* published by the University of Calgary Press, and he is the past academic editor of the *Educational Forum*, a scholarly journal published by the American educational honor society *Kappa Delta Pi* based in Indianapolis.

Judy L. Lupart is Professor and Canada Research Chair in Special Education, beginning January 2003, in the Department of Educational Psychology at the University of Alberta. She has served as the Founding Director of the University of Calgary Centre for Gifted Education, and the Founding Editor of the journal *Exceptionality Education Canada*. Her research, publication, and teaching interests include inclusive education and school transformation; cognition, transfer, and educational applications; learning disabilities, giftedness, and at-risk learners; and girls, women, and achievement.

About the Contributors

Nola Aitken is a Professor in the Faculty of Education at the University of Lethbridge. Nola was a schoolteacher for over two decades before working as a Test Development Specialist for the Mathematics Provincial Achievement Program at Alberta Education. Since her 5-year term at Alberta Education, Nola has been teaching and researching student assessment in undergraduate and graduate programs, mathematics education, and Native ways of knowing mathematics at the University of Lethbridge.

John O. Anderson is Professor and Chair of the Department of Educational Psychology and Leadership Studies at the University of Victoria. He teaches and researches in the area of educational measurement and large-scale student assessment.

Dale Armstrong held a variety of positions with Edmonton Public Schools, including teacher, science consultant, assistant principal, principal, and Director of Student Assessment. He completed his graduate studies in curriculum and instruction at the University of Oregon and pursued independent study with U.S. assessment experts Grant Wiggins, Jay McTighe, and Richard Stiggins. He was instrumental in the formation of the Alberta Assessment Consortium and served as the chairperson for 4 years. Dale was a sessional lecturer at the University of Alberta, teaching a course in Assessing, Evaluating, and Communicating Student Learning in the Faculty of Education. Dale coauthored two articles on curriculum alignment and has been involved in the writing of four publications produced by the Alberta Assessment Consortium. As a private consultant, he facilitated many workshops throughout Alberta, British Columbia, the United States of America, and Singapore. Dale was a coauthor of the original submission of the chapter included in this book. However, he passed away in October 2008 before the final submission was completed. He is recognized as coauthor to acknowledge his part in the original submission, as well as the tremendous contribution he made to the work of the Alberta Assessment Consortium since its inception in 1993.

Sherry Bennett is the Executive Director of the Alberta Assessment Consortium (AAC). Her career in education has included the roles of music specialist, elementary generalist, curriculum coordinator, and consultant. Prior to assuming her role as Executive Director, Sherry was involved with a variety of AAC projects as a developer, reviewer, author, and workshop facilitator, presenting assessment workshops throughout Alberta as well as in the Northwest Territories and Singapore. She completed a 2-year secondment in the Faculty of Education at the University of Alberta, teaching undergraduate education courses and mentoring student teachers. Sherry has authored a variety of student, teacher, and professional development materials to support Alberta programs of study. In her current role, she guides the development of classroom assessment materials, professional development resources, and publications to enhance the building of assessment capacity in Alberta.

Jim Brandon is an Assistant Professor and the Director of Professional Programs at the University of Calgary. He is a past president of the College of Alberta School Superintendents and its former Director of Leadership Capacity Building. Jim served a total of 23 years in the superintendency of two Alberta school districts, worked as a principal for nine years and as a vice-principal for four. Teaching secondary social studies was his primary focus during his classroom years.

Susan M. Brookhart is an independent educational consultant based in Helena, Montana, and a Senior Research Associate in the Center for Advancing the Study of Teaching and Learning in the School of Education at Duquesne University. Sue's interests include the role of both formative and summative classroom assessment in student motivation and achievement, the connection between classroom assessment and large-scale assessment, and grading. She is author or coauthor of 9 books and over 50 articles on classroom assessment, teacher professional development, and evaluation. She serves on the editorial boards of several journals.

John Burger is the Director of Schools for the Rocky View School Division, located in Airdrie, Alberta, Canada. His current research focuses on educational leadership development, data-informed decision making within critically reflective leadership models, development of balanced and holistic student assessment models, and value-added data models to inform program evaluation and development within networked school jurisdiction and state/provincial-level applications. Additional interests include teacher education reform, top-down/bottom-up accountability, and high school completion supports.

Sandy Heldsinger has extensive experience in educational assessment and measurement. She coordinated the full cohort testing program in Western Australia which involved the assessment of approximately 80,000 students; she worked as a research officer at the University of Cambridge Local Examinations Syndicate (UCLES); and she was employed by the University of Western Australia where she lectured in Educational Assessment, Measurement, and Evaluation and was involved in a number of extensive research projects. Sandy is currently employed at the Association of Independent Schools, Western Australia, as the manager of several

Australian Federal Government school initiatives. Sandy's doctoral thesis examined the process of pairwise comparison in educational standard setting exercises.

Joan Jeary is semi-retired and continues to practice as an Educational Psychologist in Alberta, Canada. Joan has many years of experience as a teacher, school psychologist, and school and district administrator. Immediately prior to retirement, Joan served as Director of the University of Calgary Applied Educational and Psychological Services and was employed as an Assistant Professor in the Faculty of Education at the University of Calgary.

Ken Leithwood is Professor of Educational Leadership and Policy at OISE/ University of Toronto. His most recent books include *Distributed Leadership According to the Evidence* (Routledge 2008), *Leading with Teachers' Emotions in Mind* (Corwin 2008), and *Turnaround School Leadership* (Jossey Bass 2010). Professor Leithwood is the recent recipient of the University of Toronto's Impact on Public Policy award and a Fellow of the Royal Society of Canada.

Marla W. McGhee is Associate Professor of Educational Leadership at Texas Christian University. She received her Ph.D. from the University of Texas at Austin. She has conducted research and worked in public schools for over two decades, serving as a teacher, an elementary principal, a secondary principal, a curriculum area director, and a district-wide director of professional development.

Lionel (Skip) Meno is Professor of Education and former Dean at San Diego State University. He received his Ed.D. in Educational Administration from the University of Rochester, and was at the forefront of educational reform in New York and Texas. He has consulted widely throughout the United States.

Anna Nadirova is a Senior Research Officer in the People and Research Division of the Alberta Department of Education in Alberta, Canada. Anna acts as the data steward for the division. Her research interests include comprehensive data analysis and practical applications at the state/provincial, jurisdiction and school levels, statistical methodology, education workforce development, student assessment, program evaluation, and effects of educational and external environments on student achievement and high school completion.

Sarah W. Nelson is Associate Professor of Education at Texas State University–San Marcos. She received her Ph.D. in Educational Administration from the University of Texas at Austin. She has conducted research in international leadership, social change efforts, and multicultural education.

Jean L. Pettifor is an Adjunct Professor at the University of Calgary and a Past President of the Psychologists Association of Alberta, the College of Alberta Psychologists, and the Canadian Psychological Association. Provincially, nationally, and internationally she has received many awards for her lifetime contributions, the most recent award being the Honorary Doctor of Laws degree from Athabasca University in 2009. She continues to promote value-based ethical decision making across a wide range of applications.

Marsi Quarin-Wright is the Vice-Principal of Ecole Percy Pegler Elementary School in Okotoks, Alberta. She has worked with Foothills School Division for the past 16 years as a teacher, learning coach and member of the Foothills Assessment Specialist Team. Marsi is graduate of the University of Lethbridge MEd and BEd programs and holds an Early Childhood Certificate from Lethbridge Community College.

Donald H. Saklofske is a Professor in the School and Applied Child Psychology program, Faculty of Education, University of Calgary where he recently completed his term as Associate Dean, Research. He will be moving to the Psychology Department at the University of Western Ontario next year. His books, chapters, and journal articles focus on intelligence, personality, individual differences, and psychological and educational assessment.

Vicki L. Schwean is Professor and Dean of the Faculty of Education at the University of Western Ontario. She previously held appointments as Professor and Vice Dean in the Faculty of Education, University of Calgary. She has also served in other senior leadership positions at the University of Calgary and the University of Saskatchewan. Her research and publications focus on socio-emotional resilience, psychological assessment, and psychosocial disorders.

Shelleyann Scott is an Associate Professor in Educational Leadership at the University of Calgary's Faculty of Education. Her experience spans the contexts of business, government, and medical research. She is an experienced tertiary and secondary educator. Her research interests include the establishment and evaluation of professional development; the use of information communication technology to support ongoing reflection and learning for educators and students; instructional strategies; and student assessment. Shelley has authored and coauthored numerous scholarly publications and is a reviewer for the *Educational Forum*.

Charles L. Slater is Professor of Educational Leadership at California State University–Long Beach. He received his Ph.D. in Curriculum and Instruction from the University of Wisconsin. He has been a superintendent of schools in Massachusetts and Texas. He conducts research on leadership and teaches in Mexico.

John Venn is a Professor in the College of Education and Human Services at the University of North Florida in Jacksonville. John currently serves as a Research Associate for the Florida Institute of Education at the University of North Florida where he is helping to adapt a literacy curriculum to meet the needs of young children with disabilities. John is the author of *Assessing Students with Special Needs, Fourth Edition* (Merrill/Prentice Hall 2007). He has written numerous articles, test reviews, book chapters, and professional materials on assessment and related topics. His research interests include classroom-based assessment, curriculum-based measurement, and developmental assessment.

Chapter 1
Taking Stock of Here and Now

Judy L. Lupart and Charles F. Webber

Introduction

Student assessment has been a cornerstone of educational practice for decades, and in recent years, a great deal of controversy has surrounded the assessment of children's abilities and achievements. Students and classroom teachers are the key players in the multiple activities and processes associated with student assessment; however, parents, administrators, university faculty, and government officials have assumed an increasingly prominent role as accountability efforts and educational change movements have taken hold. Despite the many advances we have seen there is a growing sense that current practice, policy, and research can be improved significantly. Before we can move ahead to building a more dynamic and effective framework for student assessment, it is essential to have a clear and comprehensive understanding of the field as it is currently configured. The purpose of this text is to provide readers with just such an overview.

Specifically, we aim to provide practitioners, policy makers, researchers, and university teacher preparation faculty with a comprehensive, current overview of the state and art of student assessment. It is our hope that the chapters in the present volume make a unique contribution to the field of student assessment by speaking more broadly and directly to the relevant concerns and issues. We are optimistic that as a result of reading this book, readers will be able to consolidate their own thinking and practice in the area.

J.L. Lupart (✉)
Department of Educational Psychology, University of Alberta,
Edmonton, AB, Canada
e-mail: judy.lupart@ualberta.ca

C.F. Webber
Faculty of Human, Social, and Educational Development,
Thompson Rivers University, Kamloops, BC, Canada
e-mail: cwebber@tru.ca

C.F. Webber and J.L. Lupart (eds.), *Leading Student Assessment,*
Studies in Educational Leadership 15, DOI 10.1007/978-94-007-1727-5_1,
© Springer Science+Business Media B.V. 2012

Our contributing authors represent a wide spectrum of expertise and scholarship, and subsequent chapters have been organized into four pertinent themes: (a) Leadership, (b) Fairness and Equity in Assessment, (c) Factors Influencing Student Assessment, and (d) Assessment in the Classroom. We believe that these four themes encapsulate the broad range of contemporary knowledge and research within the field of student assessment. Each of the chapters within the theme areas provides a unique but complementary perspective germane to the general theme, and collectively, the works give us the opportunity to advance our knowledge greatly. Some of the key questions we address in this text include:

1. What are the barriers that practitioners face in insuring quality assessment?
2. What do school leaders need to know to be successful in improving student performance?
3. How do funding policies and decisions that relate to assessment help students?
4. Are differences in ethnicity, culture, language, and ability of students a deterrent to "fair" assessment practice in a society that is ever increasing in diversity and globalization?
5. Is large-scale assessment information about student performance sufficient?
6. Are informal assessment processes and procedures reliable and valid?
7. Is there sufficient incorporation of research findings into student assessment and practice?
8. How can we ensure that classroom and external assessment practices are balanced and optimal?
9. What does student voice add to student assessment practice and achievement?
10. Can we isolate the factors that are predominant in the overall goal of improving student achievement?

The questions we have posed are all worthy of closer examination, and these will be addressed throughout in the general text. In the following sections of this chapter, a brief summary of the contributing chapters is presented, followed by a discussion of the challenges and insights that are salient. The chapter concludes with a stratagem to take the field of student assessment from where it is toward groundbreaking new ways of capturing and advancing the best of our knowledge and experience.

Leading Student Assessment from Here

Leadership

Any student assessment program within the classroom, school, and district can be substantially challenged or augmented by the quality and style of leadership that is provided. Chapter 2 leads the discussion with the assertion that the role of the school leader or principal is vital to general school improvement and significant to student achievement in particular. Although a strong link between large-scale assessment and principal-lead student performance improvement has often been touted as a profound strategy in the school accountability movement, Leithwood argues that these positive assumptions are flawed. Following a detailed presentation of the various challenges principals are faced with as they orchestrate endeavors to improve student performance, he concluded that large-scale assessment results have minimal practical relevance for both school leaders and classroom teachers. Instead, Leithwood advocates for more informal teacher collected information about what causes students to achieve at the levels they do and the school features that promote greater student success. Principals who are knowledgeable about the dubious contribution of large-scale assessments could improve student performance results more dramatically through the adoption of "robust, systematically collected information" to achieve evidence-based decision making and instructional improvement.

Chapter 3 provides a detailed overview of the accountability efforts in the USA aimed toward significant improvement in student achievement. Currently, there is a strong connection between student assessment and large-scale, centralized, high-impact testing. Positive outcomes of this process, initiated in 1981, include the alignment of mandated testing and compulsory academic standards set by the state, criterion-referenced assessments linked to the state curriculum, and the measurement of achievement of all students along with the disaggregation of results by ethnicity, gender, students in poverty, English language learners, and students with special needs and programs. Negative outcomes for high-stakes testing include the widespread practice of curriculum narrowing, increased hours in the school day allocated to exam preparation, and a sharp increase in student dropout rates. These factors have lead to multiple strands of misplaced accountability, leading focus away from actual student learning. Slater (2011) concludes his chapter with several insights for improving current systems of student assessment through strategies such as the creation of a learning culture in the schools and using multiple perspectives that place teachers and school leaders more centrally into the dialogue.

Chapter 4 add to the discussion with a provincial example of applying a framework of analysis to existing assessment practice. Taking an *assessment for learning stance*, this chapter summarizes a comprehensive conceptual framework representing the perceived ideal relationships among educational research, policy, and practice. A series of nine standards, based on analysis and review of the current research, are put forth as a way to capture relevant knowledge on teaching, leadership, professional learning, and educational policy research and practice. This framework is then linked to nine assessment levels, the first four captured in a representative School Division of approximately 7,000 students, 400 teaching staff, and 25 schools. The remaining five levels of assessment are applied through the lens of existing provincial policy and initiatives. The discussion is completed with the presentation of four paradoxes that emerged from the overall analysis and are put forth as a possibility for a new and improved framework for the province.

Fairness and Equity in Assessment

One of the most promising areas in student assessment in the past few decades is increased attention and development in creating assessment practices that are both fair and equitable. Pettifor and Saklofske (2011) begin the discussion with an overview of general contemporary issues relating to student assessment, primarily in North America, as a backdrop to a comprehensive presentation of issues pertaining to fair assessment practice in Canada. In the classroom context, the development and selection of assessment methods are highlighted, as is the importance of teacher implementation of these in accordance with *Standards for Teacher Competence in Educational Assessment of Students* (1990). From developing and choosing methods for assessment to collecting assessment information, scoring and interpreting results, and reporting assessment findings, attention to fairness and equity must prevail. Similarly, the *Principles for Fair Student Assessment Practices for Education in Canada* (Centre for Research in Applied Measurement and Evaluation 1993) has particular relevance for assessments produced external to the classroom, specifically for standardized assessment measures. A model for ethical decision making is presented, merging ethical language and concepts with good practice, and is offered as a "means of enhancing the effectiveness of fair educational assessments in serving the learning needs of students" (p. 12).

School psychologists have much to do with student assessment although their role is often misunderstood in the educational field. Jeary and Schwean (2011) clarify the important contribution school psychologists make by calling attention to their unique foundational expertise in psychological processes underlying learning and behavior, particularly for students with the most challenging needs. Multifaceted tools and approaches are used to gather information from relevant family, classroom, school district, and community contexts. Standards for training and practice across North America have been set out by the Canadian Psychological Association (2011) and the National Association of School Psychologists (2000) in 11 domains spanning diverse areas such as data-based decision making and accountability, instructional interventions to collaboration, and consultation. Pressures to respond to a multitude of factors that are known to adversely affect student development in all areas have foreshadowed the creation of new wraparound models such as the *Systems of Care* approach.

Chapter 7 presents a conceptual model for assessing students with special needs that includes four key steps: screening, identifying, intervening, and measuring progress. He takes a critical look at issues, first associated with formal assessment and students with special needs. Fairness in testing emerges as a fundamental consideration in that test administration and interpretation can be significantly biased if the unique needs of the student are not addressed. Moreover, the educational accountability movement and associated expectations for improving student achievement place additional demands on teachers to teach test taking and to develop their knowledge and skills in linking these assessments to instructional decision making. In a similar vein, informal assessment of students with special needs is often cast in a negative light for many teachers who may not have the background and training to conduct the high-quality assessment that these challenged students require. Directly related to this are issues of knowledge and expertise surrounding validity and reliability standards for informal assessment of students with special needs. Finally, Venn (2011) captures the complexities of making appropriate testing accommodations and accurate determination of test modifications and alternative assessments for students with special needs. Universal design for assessment may hold particular promise for the future.

Factors Influencing Student Achievement

One of the most challenging areas associated with student assessment is the identification of those factors that impact significantly on levels of student achievement and, if possible, setting out the interventions that will improve student achievement. Chapter 8 asserts that it is widely accepted that "our understanding of the empirical relationships between student, home and school correlates of learning outcomes is not well developed." Policy makers in education are continuously interested in finding the critical school system traits that impact positively on school outcomes. Research has helped to map the key factors, such as teacher and school traits and curriculum and instruction, as being significantly related to student achievement; however, the relationships can vary substantially from grade to grade, one school to the next, and even across subjects. Anderson describes a study examining the relationship between student socioeconomic status and mathematics achievement that utilizes hierarchical linear modeling. The secondary data analysis carried out is from two large-scale assessment programs. Findings confirm the need to avoid universal generalization due to the multi-levels of consideration that such results need and the immense complexity of identification of the underlying context of factors that influence the results. To be of real value for policy makers, future large-scale assessment studies need to be reconceptualized into long-term research studies.

Burger and Nadirova (2011) add to the discussion through a detailed presentation of the Grade Level Achievement (GLA) program currently implemented in Alberta schools. The GLA is teacher reported and based upon their judgment of students' academic progress for the full range of classroom assessment carried out in a given subject area over the entire school year or term. Alberta Education gathers this data annually and compares it with the results of the provincial achievement tests to ensure a more balanced and comprehensive examination of factors affecting student achievement. This program takes a bold step in paving the way toward more meaningful assessment-related information for the school, district, and government. Moreover, it goes beyond traditional parameters "to help inform and engage students and parents in the learning process, and to evaluate the achievement of different populations of students to ensure that their learning needs are better understood and met."

Chapter 9 groundbreaking insight into the importance of placing the student at the center of any assessment, classroom, or external. She is especially convincing in the assertion that students have for too long been the recipients of others' decision making, even though assessment results often have far-reaching impacts for the student. Not only does it make sense to have students become more aware of the purposes of all types of assessment they are expected to participate in but also to involve the students in the actual design and evaluation of assessment initiatives within the classroom and beyond. Knowing more about the perceptions of students concerning this important element of classroom practice and provincial reporting is fundamental to the development of new tools and procedures aimed at maximizing the learning potential and achievement of all students, including those who are most challenged in their learning.

Assessment in the Classroom

The knowledge base for this segment of assessment practice is by far the largest and fastest growing and consequently is difficult to capture in just one subsection. The three chapters included here are representative of the robust and dynamic changes currently available in the burgeoning literature on classroom assessment. Chapter 11 targets a key component in effective formative classroom assessment practice (i.e., teacher feedback). Brookhart contends that there is ample support for the connection between good external feedback provided by informed teacher practice and learning that is internally regulated by the student. In addition to the cognitive benefits of establishing this form of reciprocal teacher/student interaction, there are considerable positive motivational rewards as students take on increasingly greater control over their learning. Research literature support is presented for numerous aspects of teacher feedback, including timing, amount, mode, etc. Concluding remarks focus on the importance of teachers knowing the full spectrum of choices they have when providing student feedback and how administrators and policy makers need to provide the appropriate professional development opportunities in this area.

Chapter 12 is complementary to Chapter 11 in that the focus is on ways to support assessment practice in the classroom; specifically, she advances a strong case for why teacher observation is at the core of this process. Three concepts (i.e., continuum, latent, and manifest ability) are defined, and several examples of formal and informal assessment are presented to demonstrate ways teachers can refine practice for deeper understanding of student development and growth. Throughout the discussion, Heldsinger cautions educators to avoid interpreting common dichotomies such as formative/summative and norm-/criterion-referenced in assessment as fundamental. Instead, she argues through example how "careful scrutiny and articulation of the qualitative differences amongst students performances, provides precision of assessment along the continuum," illustrating that indeed dichotomies are merely a matter of emphasis.

Chapter 13 extends the discussion through presentation of an elaborate assessment model, field developed by practitioners representing the Alberta Assessment

Consortium (AAC). A series of question-led steps surrounding the four critical elements of planning for assessment, assessing, evaluating, and communicating student learning is presented as a practical guide for teachers to use in their everyday classroom assessment practice. Drawing from the diverse and ongoing professional development activities and experience of the AAC, Bennet and Armstrong make a very strong case for continuous and supported involvement of classroom teachers as the most important observers and learning mentors of students. This unique learning partnership between students and their classroom teacher is pivotal in ensuring possibilities for maximizing the achievement of all students. The AAC model serves as one salient example of how practitioners can work collaboratively to configure student assessment practices to maximize student learning in the classroom.

In summary, from the delineation of the four subthemes and a brief account of the respective contributions of individual chapters, we have been able to discern a number of challenges that appear to be at the forefront in the field of student assessment.

Challenges Here and Now

Establishing Coherence

Several references point to a need for greater coherence in the direct and indirect approaches to school improvement and student assessment. For example, Leithwood (2011) asserts that this means creating ways to improve the organizational conditions that support productive school improvement efforts. This possibly could be complemented through the implementation of new ways to estimate progress and the determination of how to sustain continuous improvement. In support, Slater (2011) suggested that greater coherence among government policies and assessment practices would be a fruitful area to develop. As Anderson (2011) has noted, efforts must be directed toward the understanding of the empirical relationships among student, home, and school correlates of learning outcomes. Moreover, an understanding of relationships among school system traits, the outcomes of schooling, and policy development is crucial to any effort to promote greater coherence.

In addition to the consideration of general approaches to student assessment, especially as it pertains to the perceived lack of evidence to connect school improvement to the use of high-stakes tests as accountability measures, Venn (2011) has leveled strong caution for practices that do not provide appropriate accommodations or alternatives for students with special needs. Any viable school improvement approach having to do with student assessment must incorporate ways for students with special needs to demonstrate the full extent of their learning before overall coherence in student assessment can be established.

Knowing Enough

A common thread in several of the chapters is the challenge of ensuring that there is sufficient knowledge and skills necessary for optimal student assessment on the part of classroom teachers as well as school and community leaders. For the latter, Venn (2011) raises particular concern as it is commonly believed that large-scale assessments can be used in ways that result in improved schools. Indeed, Leithwood (2011) is a strong advocate for helping teachers intensify their role in student assessment as a means of supporting students to reach high standards of achievement. Moreover, he sees this kind of teacher involvement as an ideal strategy to compensate for the critical limitations of large-scale assessment data in determining the current status of student learning. Added to this, Pettifor and Saklofske (2011) have noted that competent practice is an ethical requirement because incompetent practice results in harm to others.

According to Heldsinger (2011), there are serious concerns over this issue in that efforts made to obtain measurement, in the classical definition of the term, require specialist knowledge, and teachers do not typically have the expertise nor the time to devise assessment that provides measurement. Such expertise might require, for example, an understanding of the concept of error of measurement (Pettifor and Saklofske 2011) or the need to understand terminology that may have different meanings in different settings (e.g., standards; Slater 2011). Not knowing enough puts the classroom teacher and educational leaders in a very awkward position when they are asked to respond to the absence of robust evidence about the causes of students' current performance (Leithwood 2011). Other factors can lead to misplaced accountability, for example, when higher and low SES school results are compared as if there were no SES differences (Slater 2011). Knowing enough, it appears, is a state most schools and communities are still striving to achieve.

Recognizing Mistakes

It isn't often that educators, administrators, and/or researchers admit that there may have been mistakes that were inadvertently overlooked in student assessment practices or in any other area associated with student learning. It is interesting to note that such missteps are often surprisingly well recognized in everyday practice, even though an issue may not be addressed in publications. Our contributors have been helpful in making some first steps at identifying some of the more salient mistakes. Leithwood (2011) admonishes that there is a tendency for educators to dismiss large-scale assessments information when it does not fit with their own assessments. Since not knowing is not an option, every effort should be made to clarify and assist teachers to use all the available assessment information sources.

Slater (2011) contends that in regard to high-stakes testing, there is a serious need to avoid an over emphasis on public perception and instead focus on best practices. Caution and discretion are emphasized for two practices now rampant in

American schools: (a) overusing instructional time to prepare students for examinations, and (b) narrowing the curriculum to subjects and content covered on high-stakes testing. Both Brookhart (2011) and Anderson (2011) make a very strong case for incorporating robust research findings into classroom and community assessment practice and procedures. Leithwood (2011) directs us to consider ways to overcome common errors in human judgment as a significant factor here. He is further critical of the many delays that are typically evident in reporting results, especially large-scale assessments. Adding to the discussion, Jeary and Schwean (2011) identify many of the unique contributions that support professionals, such as school psychologists, can bring to the overall student assessment program that may be mistakenly underutilized.

Achieving Transparency and Authenticity

The research literature over the past decade has revealed, quite convincingly, that if we want to optimize schooling, students need to be aware of their own learning goals and expectations for assessment. Heldsinger (2011) suggests that "Teachers continually place students in situations that allow them to observe students' underlying or latent ability, that is to make their ability manifest." As Aitken (2011) has very aptly demonstrated, including the voice of the student in all phases of student assessment is essential, and engaging teacher and student in partnership with a focus on improving student learning moves student assessment much closer toward the goal of achieving transparency and authenticity (Bennet and Armstrong 2011).

Despite the evidence yielded by recent research, Pettifor and Saklofske (2011) have ascertained that taking the typical classroom into consideration, there appears to be a dire need for improvement in this area. Making reference to student perceptions of assessment as "another unknown or black hole," they stress that students should be provided with sufficient opportunity to demonstrate the knowledge, skills, attitudes, or behaviors being assessed. Students should feel that they know the content to be tested, and they should have a good idea as to how the assessment will be scored and evaluated.

Addressing Diversity

Students come to school with a wide array of learning characteristics and needs, and over the past 50 years, the reality of ever increasing student diversity in the general education classroom has been a considerable challenge, particularly for student assessment purposes. For example, Burger and Nadirova (2011) report that factors such as gender, birth month, and family mobility all have an impact on student achievement. Students who have physical, behavioral, or cognitive disabilities, and many others from dysfunctional families and economically disadvantaged or culturally different backgrounds, do not easily fit into the typical school classroom and/or culture. The press for greater accountability, often through high-stakes assessment, can have far-reaching negative consequences for students with exceptional needs (Venn 2011). At a time when there is much rhetoric about creating inclusive schools, students who are on the margins are seen to be increasingly at risk for experiencing failure. Venn (2011) has outlined many shortcomings in formal and informal assessment practices for students with special needs, and despite our efforts to make accommodations and provide equitable alternatives, our most vulnerable students continue to struggle in systems that fail to seriously address issues associated with student diversity. Moreover, Pettifor and Saklofske (2011) assert that schools often face dilemmas that involve cultural diversity and that these are among the more difficult to resolve in ways that respect all parties.

Heldsinger (2011) maintains that student ability is best conceptualized in terms of a continuum and that assessment processes can be devised to represent the full range of skills and understandings of the underlying developmental continuum. Accordingly, it should be possible to construct tests that reveal "information about the underlying developmental continuum and information about students' ability in relation to that developmental continuum." In any case, it remains clear that the problem of adequately addressing the issues of student diversity in assessment is serious and warrants considerable attention in the future.

Insights That Really Matter: The Old Chestnuts

Accepting that there are significant and complex challenges concerning student assessment that need to be addressed, it is important to acknowledge the practices and understandings that have been successful. A review of the chapters contained in this volume resulted in six areas of particular salience.

Large-Scale Assessments Have Value

Although much controversy surrounds large-scale and/or high-stakes assessment, there is sufficient evidence to indicate that there is value in continuing with the practice. Perhaps most central to the dissenting views is the fact that the issues are multifold and complex. Interpreting all relevant factors requires considerable expertise; unfortunately, many if not most, educators and educational leaders do not typically have the necessary statistical and technical background or experience. Researchers who have the expertise to weigh out the advantages and drawbacks (Anderson 2011) continue to endorse these programs. Slater (2011) has provided a comprehensive analysis of the US experience, and he outlines several factors that support the research, from providing public access to results to ensuring curriculum consistency and coherence. From the field, educational leaders such as Brandon and Quarin-Wright (2011) assert that external assessments are a necessary mechanism for building confidence in the provincial school system.

One Size Does Not Fit All

With so much emphasis on school accountability and raising the achievement levels of our students, it is possible that undue focus has been directed at large-scale and external assessment. Consequently, we may be fixated on the quest for the "perfect" assessment tool, although this may be an impossible goal. Indeed, Anderson (2011) noted "the relationships of student and school characteristics to educational performance as measured by mathematics achievement are complex and they do not lend themselves to universal generalization." Any student assessment program must consider the full range of assessment data, especially classroom assessment. Heldsinger (2011) has argued in support of this notion in her suggestion of a conceptual framework based on a developmental continuum. In light of the dramatic increases in student diversity, it seems that student assessment efforts need to be redirected toward student-centered approaches to ensure that there is an appropriate balance in our assessment programs.

Understanding Takes Time

There is no quick fix for the multiple issues and problems that are associated with student assessment. Anderson (2011) has indicated a need to allow incrementally expanding understandings of the complex and dynamic systems that our schools are. In a time when resources, human and financial, are limited, there is a tendency to want fast track solutions to complex problems; however, pursuing this course is not only inefficient but also ineffective. Anderson (2011) has cautioned that "variation is to be anticipated: one school to another, one province to another, one grade to another, and one achievement data base to another." Further, Leithwood (2011) urges educational leaders to focus on long-term trends. The "patchwork quilt" approach to student assessment that characterizes many current jurisdictions needs to be redirected to create a solid foundation of knowledge and practice upon which future efforts can be built.

Research Matters

It might be considered obvious to state that student assessment should be based on information that is research derived and trustworthy. In reality, there are still widespread concerns about the lack of such a consolidated knowledge base in our systems. Leithwood (2011) has warned that actually improving student performance requires information of a very different order, without which school leaders may experience limited success. Large-scale assessments tell only part of the story, and Leithwood is adamant that robust, systematically collected information, such as teachers' assessments, provide the best clues for instructional improvement.

Brandon and Quarin-Wright (2011) has highlighted the importance of basing standards, policies, and practices on research for province-wide student assessment initiatives. To effect progress, he asserts, stakeholder groups need to strive for common ground filtered through dispassionate consideration of the best available evidence. At the level of the individual school, Leithwood (2011) has noted that those that are highly efficacious are the ones where teachers have accepted responsibility for their students' learning. Typically, this means working in a deliberate, research-driven manner to bring forward the underlying social, affective, and cognitive causes of individual student achievement. The research on teacher feedback described by Brookhart (2011), for example, is prototypical of how this can be achieved. In the context of maximizing student learning, the quality of teacher feedback can significantly improve internal regulation of learning.

Proactive Trumps Reactive

Anyone who has been involved in student assessment, particularly at the school level for at least a decade, has no doubt recognized that trends come and go, and more often initiatives are put in place as a reaction to each new crisis. Calls for accountability, criticism of the test instruments, perceived failure of schools to increase provincial achievement scores, and infighting between stakeholder groups are just some of the issues that seem to surface with regularity. The collective chapters in this text provide some excellent proactive approaches concerning theory and practice of student assessment in the classroom and beyond. Beginning with the area of assessment leadership, there is a strong indication that external assessments, while valued and perceived as being important to the emergent theory and practice in student assessment, are falling short of expectations. Most programs, it would seem, tend to operate in the absence of any clearly articulated parameters, and more importantly, linkages to the other elements of student assessment, particularly classroom assessment, have not been adequately designed and developed.

Consequently, leaders responsible for guiding, implementing, interpreting, and evaluating the full range of student assessment programs and results at all levels including school, district, and government need to formulate new ways of bringing these important elements together. As a logical start, it would seem that leaders from these three levels need to combine their knowledge and practice to ensure maximum yield of data sources and relevant information. This would require, at a minimum, strategic meetings where examination of current practices, relevant research, and theory on students' assessment take place to ensure that all new approaches are compatible and connected with each other level of innovation. Top-down and bottom-up approaches need to be more carefully planned and meshed to ensure that large-scale assessment results are complementary to the ongoing classroom and special needs assessment.

In summary, it is clear that future direction in student assessment transformation must go beyond simple tweaking of systems and procedures that are in place.

Instead, the confining boundaries that are currently limiting the possibilities for groundbreaking new approaches will need to be shattered and reconstructed. In what follows, a brief description of what that process might look like is presented, and these foundations will be outlined in the concluding chapter of this text.

From Here to Boundary Breaking

The field of student assessment has been well served by documents and policies that identify the basic principles that underlie good student assessment practice. A first step toward boundary breaking is to review the existing principle frameworks that are commonly adhered to. Pettifor and Saklofske, Jeary and Schwean, and Venn (2011) all contribute to this concept of *principle analysis*.

Following principle analysis, the *purposes* for all aspects of student assessment need to be reviewed. Different types of assessment are typically aligned with specific purposes, and several of our authors including Pettifor and Saklofske, Jeary and Schwean, Heldsinger, Leithwood, and Venn (2011) have noted that there can be a wide range of purposes. Pettifor and Saklofske (2011) describe this component as a "process of obtaining the kind and amount of good information needed to make informed decisions that will guide subsequent practice."

The next step along the pathway to boundary breaking is couched in the combination of divergent and convergent processes of *creative thinking* and *realism*. Consideration of the realities and, at times, limitations that the day to day school operations can have on student assessment policy and practice is essential; however, there should be equal or greater consideration given to possibilities beyond the status quo. To achieve this goal, Leithwood and Jeary and Schwean (2011) promote creative thinking possibly within a school improvement and/or psychological perspective framework.

Solution detection proceeds from creative thinking and realism substeps described above. Strategies for navigating this element can be directed toward multiple levels of action including: (a) defining a goal state (Leithwood 2011), (b) drawing from research and theoretical databases in psychology (Jeary and Schwean 2011), and (c) using widely accepted developmental models to explain learning and cognitive growth (Heldsinger 2011).

The logical follow-through after solution detection is to create a kind of solution pathway (Leithwood 2011) or orderings of skills and understandings (Heldsinger 2011) through a process of *mapping*. Jeary and Schwean (2011) describe this process as "unraveling problem dimensions using sophisticated models which can be used to navigate through a sea of complex human data and to provide a simple but useful map of the interaction between people factors and aspects of their living/learning environments."

The final and perhaps most important element for advancing to "boundary breaking" in student assessment is achieved through a process referred to as *possibilizing*. As Webber and Robertson (1998, 2002) have described it, the notion captures a dynamic sense of seeking out cognitive dissonance by creating opportunities to question and imagine alternatives. Through critical review of the heretofore accepted, the goal is to push the edges of beliefs and practices to new heights and perhaps even the growth of a new and bold counterculture in student assessment.

In conclusion, this introductory chapter has been set forward to situate the subsequent chapters into a framework for moving toward *boundary breaking* as an important and necessary goal state for future student assessment practice. Readers have been party to a brief overview of the salient information emerging from each of the chapters of our contributing authors. Out of this process, it was possible to identify four foundational themes of *leadership, fairness and equity, factors influencing student achievement*, and *assessment in the classroom*. Following a synthesis and analysis of the content within the four foundational themes, we identified a number of significant challenges associated with student assessment that are predominant in our schools. Recognizing that many aspects of traditional student assessment are fundamental and necessary to any future conceptualization of the field, we felt it was important to also identify the valued and timeless insights that have emerged from our past and contemporary student assessment knowledge base. With the future goal state of *boundary breaking* in mind, we carved out a series of steps that we believe are central to any serious attempt at making a fundamental change in student assessment. Beginning with a review of student assessment principles and purposes, then on to divergent and convergent processes of creative thinking and realism, we have the basis for the next step in the process, which is solution detection. Once we have exhausted the multiple choices needed, we can set out possible directions for positive change through mapping. The final step of possibilizing takes us up to and beyond what is known and practiced currently. Drawing from the concepts, knowledge, research, and theory presented in the chapters, we believe it is within our sights to imagine and, more importantly, to envisage a fundamental transformation in student assessment. Achieving this means springboarding to uncharted territory in our policies, practices, research, and theory. To this end, the final chapter in this text will describe in full detail what it will take to answer the questions first posed at the beginning of this chapter. It is our hope that the concluding chapter will chart a course for the future in the field of student assessment.

References

American Federation of Teachers. (1990). *Standards for teacher competence in educational assessment of students*. Washington, DC: American Federation of Teachers, National Council on Measurement in Education, and National Educational Association.

Canadian Psychological Association. (2011). Hicengene (regulation) of the procture of psychology. Ottawa: Canadian psychological Association.

Centre for Research in Applied Measurement and Evaluation. (1993). *Principles for fair student assessment practices for education in Canada*. Retrieved from http://www.education.ualberta.ca/educ/psych/crame/files/eng_prin.pdf

National Association of School Psychologists. (2000). Standards for training and field placement programs in school psychology. Bethesda, MD: National Association of school psychologist.

Robertson, J. M., & Webber, C. F. (2002). Boundary-breaking leadership: A must for tomorrow's learning communities. In K. Leithwood & P. Hallinger (Eds.), *Second international handbook of educational leadership and administration* (pp. 519–556). Dordrecht, the Netherlands: Kluwer Academic Publishers.

Webber, C. F., & Robertson, J. (1998). Boundary breaking: An emergent model for leadership development. *Educational Policy Analysis Archives*, 6(21). Retrieved November 15 2004 from http://epaa.asu.edu/epaa/v6n21.html

Chapter 2
School Leadership, Evidence-Based Decision Making, and Large-Scale Student Assessment

Kenneth Leithwood

Current preoccupations with student assessment data have their roots in the demanding external accountability policies imposed on schools beginning in the early to mid 1990s. These policies have dramatically reshaped the responsibilities of school leaders. In almost all contemporary school systems those in formal leadership roles, particularly principals, are now held directly accountable for improvements in the performance of their students. The consequences of failure for principals range from mildly negative (pressure from district administrators, dissatisfaction from some parents) to career threatening (removal from the position), depending on the specific policy and district context in which principals find themselves. Large-scale assessment results are the primary, often the only, instruments used for such accountability purposes. It should not be surprising, then, to find school leaders looking to the results of such tests for clues to assist them in their school improvement task. Just how likely is it, however, that large-scale assessment data will provide such clues?

Typically the brainchild of policy makers, large-scale assessments, according to McDonnell's (2005) review, are expected to accomplish a wide range of purposes. In addition to the accountability they impose on principals and other educators, policy makers expect large-scale assessments to:

- Provide current status information about the system.
- Help with instructional decisions about individual students.
- Bring greater curricular coherence to the system.
- Motivate students to perform better and parents to demand higher performance.
- Act as a lever to change instructional content and strategies.
- Certify the achievement or mastery of individual students.

K. Leithwood (✉)
Ontario Institute for Studies in Education, University of Toronto, Toronto, ON, Canada
e-mail: kenneth.leithwood@utoronto.ca

C.F. Webber and J.L. Lupart (eds.), *Leading Student Assessment*,
Studies in Educational Leadership 15, DOI 10.1007/978-94-007-1727-5_2,
© Springer Science+Business Media B.V. 2012

This is an astonishingly broad range of purposes, several of which are near and dear to the hearts of improvement-minded school leaders (e.g., help with instructional decisions about individual students). But as McDonnell (2005) pointed out, efforts to use the same test for multiple purposes will often run afoul of standards considered vital by the measurement community. Invoking such standards established by the American Educational Research Association (2000), McDonnell described,

> the need to base high stakes decisions on more than a single test; validated tests for each separate use; and [provision of] adequate resources for students to learn the content being tested (p. 46).

Very few large-scale assessments come close to meeting these standards, an inauspicious point of departure for considering their use by school leaders.

While current expectations of school leaders roughly parallel the expectations of leaders in most organizations—"improve the bottom line"—we need to acknowledge the uniquely demanding nature of this mission for school leaders. Student and family background variables are widely believed to account for more than half of the variation across schools in student achievement. Indeed, the best evidence currently available (e.g., Creemers and Reetzig 1996) suggests that of all variables within the school, those ostensibly under the direct control of principals collectively explain 12–25% of the variation in student achievement.

The implication of this evidence about the proportion of student achievement, explained by what schools do directly, indicates that successfully improving student performance depends on school leaders exercising enormous leverage over the variables which they are able to influence, leverage likely to depend on exceptionally sensitive information about students' learning and how it might be improved. What do school leaders need to know to be successful in improving student performance in their schools? Is large-scale assessment information about the performance of their students sufficient? If not, what else would be helpful? Just how large a proportion of what leaders need to know is captured by large-scale assessment information about their students' performance?

This chapter grapples with these questions as a means of widening the conversations, now underway in many educational jurisdictions, about evidence-based decision making (Earl 2001), what this means for principals and for their role in advocating for evidence-based decisions on the part of their school colleagues. The argument I develop in the chapter is as follows:

> Evidence about student performance is clearly essential for school leaders to successfully carry out their school improvement task. But such information provided by large-scale assessment is often fraught with limitations and is always woefully insufficient. Actually improving student performance also requires information of a very different order, and the absence of this information in most schools greatly diminishes school leaders' chances of success.

This argument is developed through the examination of five challenges facing school leaders in their efforts to improve the performance of their students:

- Compensating for the critical limitations of large-scale assessment data in determining the current status of student learning.
- Estimating progress and sustaining continuous improvement.

- Responding to the absence of robust evidence about the causes of students' current performance.
- Improving the organizational conditions that support productive school improvement efforts.
- Overcoming common errors in human judgment.

Challenge One: Compensating for the Critical Limitations of Large-Scale Assessment Data in Determining the Current Status of Student Learning

What are the challenges for leaders attempting to use such measures? Typically part of national, provincial, or district student testing programs, these measures have three well-known limitations for leaders: A narrow focus, unknown local reliability, and significant delays in the reporting of results.

Narrow Focus

Most large-scale testing programs confine their focus to math and language achievement with occasional forays into science. Only in relatively rare cases have efforts been made to test pupils in most areas of the curriculum, not to mention cross-curricular areas such as problem solving (see Saskatchewan for an exception on this) or teamwork. Technical measurement challenges, lack of resources, and concerns about the amount of time for testing explain this typically narrow focus of large-scale testing programs.

This means, however, that evidence of a school's impact on student achievement using these sources is evidence of effects on pupils' literacy and numeracy. Even when testing programs are expanded, as in the case of Alberta's addition of science and social studies in Grade 9, they almost never come close to reflecting the full range of important cognitive, social, and affective goals reflected in the school system's curriculum policies. So the contribution of schools to individual students and to society, more generally, is always underestimated by these large-scale testing programs, typically by a huge margin. The consequences of such underestimation are much more than technical. Such consequences include the potentially serious erosion of parent and community support for public schooling, an erosion felt first at the local school level—what gets measured gets valued.

The implication of this challenge for school leaders is twofold. First, school leaders will need to adopt additional assessments in their schools, assessments designed to measure a larger proportion of the goals their schools aim to develop among their students. Leaders moving in this direction, second, will need to assume an educative role with parents and community members, helping them to appreciate the value of this larger range of goals for their children.

Lack of Reliability at the Local Level

Lack of reliability at the school and classroom level is a second limitation of many large-scale testing programs. Most such programs are designed to provide reliable results only for quite large groups of pupils; results aggregated to national, state, or district levels are likely to be reliable (Heubert and Hauser 1999). This also may be the case for the aggregated results of student performance in relatively large schools, but not for performance results disaggregated by student groups or categories as required in the US *No Child Left Behind* legislation. As data are disaggregated, or the number of pupils diminishes, as in the case of a classroom, single school, or even a small district or region, few testing systems claim to even know how reliable are their results (e.g., Wolfe et al. 2004).

The likelihood, however, is that they are almost certainly not very reliable, thereby challenging their diagnostic value to school leaders and their staffs. Indeed Wilson (2004) has argued that the testing community has paid insufficient attention to the central place of classrooms in assessing student performance. This lack of reliability warrants restricting the analysis of large-scale assessment results to data aggregated above the level of the individual school or leader—in direct opposition to virtually all the systems of school reporting in most British, Canadian, and American contexts.

Delays in Reporting Results

To the three technical limitations of large-scale testing programs discussed above, most school leaders would quickly add "lack of timely reporting of results." It is by no means unreasonable for teachers and principals to complain that the test performance of students, collected in the spring of the year but not made available to them until the fall, lack diagnostic currency for their instructional and school improvement purposes. While many jurisdictions now aim to reduce this reporting lag, it remains a common problem.

For instructional and school improvement purposes, testing ideally would occur in the very early fall with results available to schools by mid-fall, at the latest. The fact that this is unlikely to happen anytime soon simply reinforces the value of schools adopting their own measures of student achievement, in addition to participating in large-scale assessments.

School leaders wanting reliable evidence about student performance in their schools and classrooms will usually have to supplement large-scale test results by administering additional (valid) assessments known to provide reliable estimates of individual student performance. They would also be advised to educate their staffs and communities about the reasons for selecting measures of achievement in addition to those provided by large-scale assessments.

Challenge Two: Estimating Progress and Sustaining Continuous Improvement

Monitoring the extent to which a school improves the achievement of its pupils over time is a much better reflection of a school's and a leader's effectiveness than is the school's annual mean achievement scores. Many educational systems now acknowledge this to be the case, even though year-over-year comparisons have been the norm until recently, as illustrated by the "adequate yearly progress" targets established for most principals working in compliance with the US *No Child Left Behind* legislation. Technically speaking, however, arriving at a defensible estimate of such change is difficult. Simply attributing the difference between the mean achievement scores of this year's and last year's pupils on the province's literacy test to changes in a school's effectiveness overlooks a host of other possible explanations:

- Cohort differences: This year's pupils may be significantly more or less advanced in their literacy capacities when they entered the cohort. Such cohort differences are quite common.
- Test differences: While most large-scale assessment programs take pains to ensure equivalency of test difficulty from year to year, this is an imperfect process and there are often subtle and not-so subtle adjustments in the tests that can amount to unanticipated but significant differences in scores.
- Differences in test conditions: Teachers are almost always in charge of administering the tests and their class's results on last year's tests may well influence the nature of how they administer this year's test (more or less leniently) even within the guidelines offered by the testing agency.
- External environment differences: Perhaps the weather this winter was more severe than last winter and pupils ended up with six more snow days—six fewer days of instruction—or a teacher left half way through the year, or was sick for a significant time.
- Regression to the mean: This term is used by statisticians to capture the highly predictable tendency for extreme scores on one test administration to change in the direction of the mean performance on a second administration. So schools scoring either very low or very high in a year can be expected to score extremely less during the next, quite aside from anything else that might be different.

To demonstrate the powerful effects that these and related factors have on a school's performance over time, my colleagues and I have recently examined the achievement trajectories of all elementary schools in Ontario for which Educational Quality and Accountability Office (EQAO) Grade 3 reading scores were available (we will be undertaking the same examination of scores in other content areas, as well). We examined the achievement trajectories of these schools over three annual testing cycles (2004–2005, 2005–2006, and 2006–2007). For each of these years, a school's performance could stay unchanged or stable (S), decline (D), or increase (I). A "continuous improvement" trajectory would, of course, consist of increased achievement over each year for 3 years (III). Results are summarized in Table 2.1.

Table 2.1 Patterns of school performance in Ontario schools (2004–2007)

Pattern of change (3 years)[a]	Number of schools	Percent of schools
DSS	1	.0
DSD	7	.2
DSI	29	.8
DDS	5	.1
DDD	23	.6
DDI	175	4.6
DIS	33	.9
DID	341	8.9
DII	353	9.2
ISS	3	.1
ISD	14	.4
ISI	27	.7
IDS	17	.4
IDD	143	3.7
IDI	536	14.0
IIS	28	.7
IID	407	10.7
III	284	7.4
Total	2,494	65.3

[a]S stable/unchanged; D decreased; I increased

The left column of the table indicates that 18 possible achievement patterns were actually found among the schools in the province. The next column of Table 2.1 indicates that no single pattern of the 18 possibilities represented more than 14% of the schools (IDI) and only 7.4% of schools in the province demonstrated a continuous improvement pattern (III). The other most common patterns were IID (10.7%), DII (9.2%), and DID (8.9%). Combining the results for the two most positive patterns (DII and III) captures about 16% of the province's schools.

To add further meaning to these results, individual patterns of achievement have been clustered into six broader trajectories:

*   *Temporary success*: This broad pattern consists of an increase in student performance the first year (2004–2005) followed by 2 years of either no change (S) or decreased performance (ISS, IDD, IDS, and ISD). This pattern encompassed 4.6% of the province's schools.
*   *Temporary failure*: This pattern consists of a decrease in performance in the first year followed by stable or increased performance over the next 2 years (DIS, DSI, DII). About 11% of the schools fell into this pattern.
*   *Longer term success*: Keeping in mind that we are working with only 4 years of data (three annual cycles of change), this pattern consisted of increased performance the first year followed by steady or increased performance in the subsequent 2 years (III, ISI, IIS). Approximately 9% of schools reflected this pattern.
*   *Longer-term failure*: Schools demonstrating this pattern had decreased performance the first year followed by 2 years of either stable or decreased performance. Fewer than 1% of the province's schools fit this pattern.

- *No predictable direction*: The performance of almost a quarter (23%) of schools in the province demonstrated this pattern (DID and IDI).
- *Running out of steam*: More than 10% of the province's schools fit this pattern, one that entailed 2 years of increased performance followed by a third year of decline (IID).
- *Finally catching a break*: A pattern consisting of 2 years of decline followed by a year of increased performance described the achievement trajectory in 4.6% of the schools in the province (SSI, DSI, DDI, and SDI).

These results indicate quite clearly that when large-scale assessment results are the criterion by which school improvement is measured, such improvement is a very bumpy road for most schools. *No predictable direction* is the pattern of change evident for by far the largest group of schools. *Long-term success* is a pattern evident among only 9% of schools, with the most desirable subpattern, "continuous improvement" (III), reflected in just 7.4% of the cases.

Linn (2003) has demonstrated with data from other educational jurisdictions that the challenges in estimating change from cross-sectional data, so clearly illustrated with our Ontario data, become less severe as change is traced over 3 or 4 years. It is the conclusions drawn from simply comparing this year's and last year's scores that are especially open to misinterpretation. While our Ontario results support (weakly) Linn's advice on this matter, they also suggest that even a longer time-frame horizon may provide conflicting inferences about the direction of student performance in a school.

The lesson for school leaders here is at least to focus on long-term trends (3, 4, or more years) in their schools' performance and not to be especially impressed or alarmed with changes in annual performance. Current efforts to develop systems for tracking the progress of individual students throughout their school careers could go a long way toward assisting school leaders in estimating the effects of their efforts to improve student achievement and compensating for the erratic long-term trends reflected in the Ontario data. School leaders should also be aware that, rhetoric aside, the concept of "continuous improvement," measured through the use of large-scale assessment results, is a rarely reached goal, and when it does appear it may not be of their own making, anyway.

Challenge Three: Responding to the Absence of Robust Information About the Causes of Students' Current Performances

Let's temporarily assume that the challenges described above have been addressed in some fashion. At minimum, for example, the report of large-scale assessment results provided by the province to the school is reliable and sufficiently broad to reflect the school's priorities for teaching and learning. Now the school has a reasonable estimate of the status of student learning in key areas of the curriculum. In some of these areas, students seem to be doing very well indeed, but there is clearly room for improvement in others. Perhaps, for example, the reading comprehension scores of

Grade 6 students are significantly below both the district mean as well as the level achieved by students in other schools in the district serving similar populations.

What now? To explain this third challenge for principals and teachers, I adopt a view of school improvement as a "problem" defined along the lines suggested by cognitive psychologists (e.g., Fredericksen 1984; Gagné 1985), as:

- A current state: For the school staff, this state is at least partly addressed by student assessment data.
- A goal state: This state is often clarified through some school improvement planning process in which the aspirations for students are clarified and some consensus among stakeholders on their importance is reached.
- Operators or solution paths: Strategies for transforming the current state into the goal state, likely to be ambiguous in the case of most school improvement problems.

The value or impact of school improvement solution paths selected by school staffs will typically depend on how well they account for the causes of their students' current achievement status. A recent case study by Timperley (2005) nicely illustrates how this element of problem solving was addressed in one elementary school. This case likely captures a form of "best practice" in comparison with other current approaches to this element of school improvement problem solving. Over several years, those leading the literacy initiatives in this school moved from engaging groups of teachers in discussions of assessment results, aggregated at the school and classroom levels, to discussions of such results disaggregated to the individual student level.

Timperley (2005) found dramatically different causal explanations for inadequate results invoked by teachers under each of these two conditions. High levels of data aggregation were associated with external-to-the-school teacher explanations (e.g., the children are from poor families and receive little support for literacy development in the home). Reports of individual student results were associated with much more reflection by teachers about their own instructional practices and how those practices should be altered.

Most of us will agree that such a shift in teachers' causal musings is a good thing. At least these teachers began to consider what they might do to improve their students' literacy skills rather than viewing the development of such skills as beyond their control. But the value of these teachers' reflections on their own practices depended entirely on their own sense-making capacities, the accuracy of their knowledge about their students, the sophistication of their own knowledge about how literacy develops, and the nature of effective literacy instruction. We might reasonably assume, under these circumstances, that the outcome would be highly variable across any group of teachers, a variability that might be reduced in the context of a collaborative school culture. But we should also expect a high degree of variability across schools with collaborative cultures because of significant differences in the collective instructional expertise of staffs.

The central point of this discussion is that, whether working in schools with isolated or collaborative cultures, teachers and school leaders almost always have to rely on their own often rich, but highly personal, situation-bound, and unsystematic evidence to explain the causes of the student achievement data with which they are confronted. And as the evidence synthesized by Nisbett and Ross (1980) many years ago indicates, peoples' causal explanations cannot extend beyond what people already know.

Responding usefully to this challenge entails working with staffs in a much more deliberate manner to surface the underlying social, affective, and cognitive causes of individual student achievement. The results of such activity will be a different order of evidence than the formative evidence suggested by Black and Wiliam (2004), for example. While school leaders often invite consultation around their school-improvement processes, such consultation rarely consists of help in diagnosing the challenges individual students are facing in improving their own learning. Such information, however, could serve a pivotal role in determining much of what goes into a school improvement plan.

Challenge Four: Improving the Organizational Conditions That Support Productive School Improvement

Direct and Indirect Approaches to Improvement

School leaders and their colleagues work at increasing the performance of their students in two distinct ways. These two routes to improvement are reflected reasonably well in the literatures now associated with *school improvement*, on the one hand, and *school effectiveness*, on the other (see Creemers 2007 for a recent explanation of this distinction). The school improvement literature concerns itself with often carefully planned processes intentionally aimed at accomplishing more or less specific outcomes. In this literature, school leaders typically occupy the foreground of the action and are portrayed as responsible for ensuring the development and implementation of school improvement processes (Silins and Mulford 2007).

The effective schools literature describes features of the school organization associated with greater than average impacts on student achievement. In this literature, "strong" school leadership is one of from 5 to 12 "correlates" of schools whose students perform beyond expectation (Teddlie and Stringfield 2007). While school leaders are not relegated to the background in this literature, their importance is balanced with the influence of at least a handful of other organizational features or conditions such as "safe and orderly culture" and "high expectations for student achievement" (e.g., Sackney 2007).

The second challenge described above reflects the planned and goal-driven nature of efforts which are the focus of the school improvement literature. The challenge taken up in this section is more reflective of the effective schools literature. Improving the organizational conditions that support school improvement acknowledges the often indirect nature of leadership effects and aims to build an organization in which powerful practices are nurtured in both explicit and quite subtle ways. This means creating conditions in the school which increase the likelihood that staffs will have both the will and skill to engage in effective practice, irrespective of intentional direction and action on the part of school leaders.

A large proportion of leadership effects research is conducted from this perspective, with promising conditions for improving student learning, assuming the role of "mediators"; these are conditions over which leaders have some direct influence and which, in turn, have a direct and significant effect on what and how well students learn. Such research assumes that "leadership" entails the exercise of influence, as reflected, for example, in a widely accepted definition of leadership:

> the ability of an individual to influence, motivate, and enable others to contribute toward the effectiveness and success of the organizations of which they are members (House et al. 2004, p. 15).

The Indirect Approach Illustrated

The challenge facing school leaders when they are working on the improvement of their schools in this indirect way is to identify the most promising "links in the chain" connecting what they do (their influence) to the performance of students. Figure 2.1 illustrates the way in which leadership effects on student learning have often been explored over the past two decades (e.g., Leithwood et al. 2006, 2004). This figure acknowledges the assumption, alluded to above, that leadership effects on students are largely, though not exclusively, indirect (Hallinger and Heck 1996; Pitner 1988). Leaders' indirect effects depend on the extent and nature of their influence on key variables or conditions (the mediators in Fig. 2.1) that are alterable through the direct intervention of leaders and which themselves have the power to directly influence the learning experiences of students.

Leaders' effects not only depend on the influence they exercise on these mediating variables, however. Such effects are either dampened or enhanced by what are often considered to be context variables (the moderators in Fig. 2.1). Student socioeconomic status (SES) is often used as a proxy for these variables. But specific features of students' family cultures, such as parental expectations for student success, respect for teachers, provision of a supportive environment in the home for school work, adequate nutrition, and the like, are the conditions that shape the social and intellectual "capital" which students bring to school and determine so much of what they learn (Walberg 1984).

School leader practices have been described in many ways. By way of illustration, however, there is considerable evidence at this point suggesting that the repertoire of almost all successful school leaders includes sets of specific practices aimed at establishing directions for their organizations, helping their colleagues build the capacities they will need to accomplish those directions, continually refining the design of the organization to facilitate teachers' work, and managing the instructional program in their schools (Leithwood and Riehl 2005; Leithwood et al. 2006).

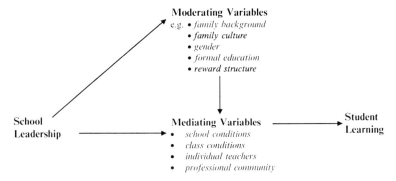

Fig. 2.1 How school leadership influences student learning

Figure 2.1 points in a general way at some of the most critical knowledge school leaders need, beyond knowledge of the status of their students' learning, if they are to be successful in improving such learning. This is knowledge about both mediators and moderators of their influence. Leithwood and Levin's (2005) recent review of leadership research identified some 11 school-level mediators, 6 classroom-level mediators, and 11 mediators concerned with teachers that have been included in recent leadership effects research. For illustrative purposes, the remainder of this section discusses three of these mediators of leadership effects on student learning—academic press, trust, and collective teacher efficacy. For each mediator, the evidence which would justify leaders' attention to it is summarized, as well as the advice to leaders provided by such evidence about how to increase the impact of that mediator on student learning.

Academic Press

This is a school-level mediator. In schools with significant degrees of academic press, administrators and teachers set high but achievable school goals and classroom academic standards. They believe in the capacity of their students to achieve and encourage their students to respect and pursue academic success. School administrators supply resources, provide structures, and exert leadership influence. Teachers make appropriately challenging academic demands and provide quality instruction to attain these goals. Students value these goals, respond positively, and work hard to meet the challenge.

Research on effective schools identified academic press as one important correlate of effective school climate and linked it with student achievement as early as the late 1970s and early 1980s. Of the more than 20 empirical studies of academic press which have been published since about 1989, by far the majority have reported significant, positive, though moderate relationships between academic press and student achievement, most often in the area of math, but extending to other subjects such as writing, science, reading, and language, as well. academic press is described as explaining almost 50% of the between-school variability in mathematics and reading in Goddard, Sweetland, and Hoy's (2000) study, for example, after controlling for the effects of students' family backgrounds. Most of the evidence suggests that a school's academic press makes an especially valuable contribution to the achievement of disadvantaged children.

Academic press is one of the more malleable conditions for leadership intervention and a small number of studies have provided some guidance on the practices likely to increase a school's academic press (e.g., Alig-Mielcarek 2003; Jacob 2004; Jurewicz 2004). Included among those practices are the following:

- Promoting school-wide professional development.
- Monitoring and providing feedback on the teaching and learning processes.
- Developing and communicating shared goals.
- Being open, supportive, and friendly.
- Establishing high expectations.
- Not burdening teachers with bureaucratic tasks and busy work.
- Helping to clarify shared goals about academic achievement.
- Grouping students using methods that convey academic expectations.
- Protecting instructional time.
- Providing an orderly environment.
- Establishing clear homework policies.
- Monitoring student performance in relation to instructional objectives.
- Base remediation efforts on the common instructional framework.
- Requiring student progress reports to be sent to the parents.
- Making promotion dependent on student mastery of basic grade level skills.

Teacher Trust in Colleagues, Parents, and Students

An individual-level teacher mediator, trust is conceptualized in many different specific ways (e.g., Dirks and Ferrin 2002). But almost all efforts to clarify the nature of trust include a belief or expectation, in this case on the part of most teachers, that their colleagues, students, and parents support the school's goals for student learning and will reliably work toward achieving those goals. Transparency, competence, benevolence, and reliability are among the qualities persuading others that a person is trustworthy. Teacher trust is critical to the success of school improvement initiatives and nurturing trusting relationships with students and parents is a key element in improving student learning. (e.g., Lee and Croninger 1994).

Trust remains a strong predictor of student achievement even after the effects of student background, prior achievement, race, and gender have been taken into account in some recent studies of trust in schools. Goddard (2003) argued that when teacher–parent and teacher–student relationships are characterized by trust, academically supportive norms and social relations have the potential to move students toward academic success. Results of a second study by Goddard and his colleagues (2001) provide one of the largest estimates of trust effects on student learning. In this study, trust explained 81% of the variation between schools in students' math and reading achievement.

Principal leadership has been highlighted in recent evidence as a critical contributor to trust among teachers, parents, and students (e.g., Bryk and Schneider 2003). This evidence suggests that principals engender trust with and among staff and with both parents and students when they:

- Recognize and acknowledge the vulnerabilities of their staff.
- Listen to the personal needs of staff members and assist as much as possible to reconcile those needs with a clear vision for the school.
- Create a space for parents in the school and demonstrate to parents that they (principal) are reliable, open, and scrupulously honest in their interactions.
- Buffer teachers from unreasonable demands from the policy environment or from the parents and the wider community.
- Behave toward teachers in a friendly, supportive, and open manner.
- Set high standards for students and then follow through with support for teachers.

Collective Teacher Efficacy

Also a teacher-level mediator, collective teacher efficacy (CTE) is the level of confidence a group of teachers feels about its ability to organize and implement whatever educational initiatives are required for students to achieve high standards of achievement. The effects of efficacy or collective confidence on performance are indirect through the persistence it engenders in the face of initial failure and the opportunities it creates for a confident group to learn its way forward (rather than giving up).

In highly efficacious schools, evidence suggests that teachers accept responsibility for their students' learning. Learning difficulties are not assumed to be an inevitable by-product of low SES, lack of ability, or family background. CTE creates high expectations for students as well as the collectively confident teachers. Evidence suggests that high levels of CTE encourage teachers to set challenging benchmarks for themselves, engage in high levels of planning and organization, and devote more classroom time to academic learning. High CTE teachers are more likely to engage in activity-based learning, student-centered learning, and interactive instruction. Among other exemplary practices, high CTE is associated with teachers adopting a humanistic approach to student management, testing new instructional methods to meet the learning needs of their students, providing extra help to students who have difficulty, displaying persistence and resiliency in such cases, rewarding students for their achievements, believing that their students can reach high academic goals, displaying more enthusiasm for teaching, committing to community partnerships, and having more ownership in school decisions.

While the total number of well-designed studies inquiring about CTE effects on students is still modest (about eight studies), their results are both consistent and impressive. This relatively recent corpus of research demonstrates a significant positive relationship between collective teacher efficacy and achievement by students in such areas of the curriculum as reading, math, and writing. Furthermore, and perhaps more surprising, several of these studies have found that the effects on achievement of CTE exceed the effects of students SES (e.g., Goddard, Hoy, & Woolfolk Hoy 2000) which, as we have already indicated, typically explains by far the largest proportion of achievement variation across schools. High CTE schools also are associated with lower suspension and dropout rates as well as greater school orderliness (Tschannen-Moran and Barr 2004).

There are two sources of insight about how leaders might improve the collective efficacy of their teaching colleagues. One source is the theoretical work of Albert Bandura, clearly the major figure in thinking about CTE. His work, now widely supported empirically, identified a number of conditions which influence the collective efficacy of a group: opportunities to master the skills needed to do whatever the job entails, vicarious experiences of others performing the job well, and beliefs about how supportive is the setting in which one is working. Leaders have the potential to influence all of these conditions, for example, by:

- Sponsoring meaningful professional development.
- Encouraging their staffs to network with others facing similar challenges in order to learn from their experiences.
- Structuring their schools to allow for collaborative work among staff.

A second source of insight about how leaders might improve the collective efficacy of their teaching colleagues is the small number of studies that have inquired about the leadership practices which improve CTE. For the most part, these have been studies of transformational leadership practices on the part of principals. Evidence from these studies demonstrates significant positive effects on CTE when principals:

- Clarify goals by, for example, identifying new opportunities for the school, developing (often collaboratively), articulating and inspiring others with a vision of the future, promoting cooperation and collaboration among staff toward common goals.
- Offer individualized support by, for example, showing respect for individual members of the staff, demonstrating concern about their personal feelings and needs, maintaining an open door policy, and valuing staff opinions.
- Provide appropriate models of both desired practices and appropriate values ("walking the talk").

The three mediators of leadership effects on student learning discussed in this section, like a large proportion of the larger set identified by Leithwood and Levin (2005) have two qualities in common worth further attention. They are properties of the group and they are "soft"—sociopsychological states rather than bricks and mortar—money, contracts, or teaching materials. Both of these qualities make them quintessentially suitable for the attention of school-level leaders and their school improvement efforts. Those leaders physically in the school can act in ways that are more sensitive to the underlying beliefs, values, and emotions from which these school conditions spring. Furthermore, there is little dependence on resources controlled largely outside the school in order to nurture the development of conditions.

Leaders need to know, in sum:

- Which of a wide array of potential mediators should be a priority for their attention and effort.
- What the status is of each of these mediators in their schools.
- What they can do to improve the condition of each of these high priority mediators in their schools.

Challenge Five: Overcoming Common Errors in Human Judgment

The challenge described in this section is one that school leaders frequently encounter. One manifestation of this challenge is the tendency for some teachers to quickly dismiss the results of large-scale assessment information about their students' performance when it deviates significantly from the results of their own assessments. This makes it very difficult for school leaders to engage their staffs in serious deliberations about how to interpret and use large-scale assessment information in their schools. The information, from their teachers' perspective, is largely invalid. Our analysis of the challenge, of which this is an instance, draws heavily on a strand of psychological research with roots that can be traced back more than 150 years, but one which acquired significant empirical traction beginning in the 1970s thanks to the efforts of such scholars as Nisbett and Ross (1980) and Kahneman et al. (1982).

This challenge, to be clear at the outset, is unique neither to administrators and teachers nor to the processes they use to make sense of large-scale assessment results, in particular. It is a pervasive challenge confronted whenever judgements are being made under less than "certain conditions," which is very often. Necessarily inferential in nature, judgements under uncertainty often fall prey to the kinds of errors that scientists have worked hard to develop methods for avoiding in their own work. These methods, suitably adapted to everyday judgment and choice, serve as the standards for determining whether or not a person or group, acting as "intuitive scientists" (Nisbett and Ross 1980), has committed errors in judgment.

Over a period of about 10 years, from the mid 1980s to the mid 1990s, my colleagues and I studied the judgment and problem-solving processes of educational administrators (principals and superintendents) in an effort to identify differences between expert and typical administrators (e.g., Leithwood and Steinbach 1995). Some of those studies were framed by concepts drawn from research on human judgment carried out by the authors cited above, among others. These studies were aimed at determining the extent to which differences in the expertise of school administrators could be accounted for by the types and incidence of errors made in their judgment processes. Our evidence suggested that such differences did account for significant variation in administrators' expertise and illustrated the nature of this variation.

Table 2.2 Errors in human judgment applied to evidence about student achievement

Types of errors	Example in context of large-scale assessment results
1. Overweighting vividness in interpreting the problem	Discount statistical information about student achievement in favor of own case-based impressions
2. Generalizing from a small or biased sample	Allow experiences with small group of students to overwhelm judgements about what to do with other students
3. Failure to see that a situation is unique or different from others in the past	Discount the need for changes in instruction due to changes in student cohort
4. Failure to determine actual causes of problem. (The previous section provided an extended treatment of this error)	Move directly from report of student achievement to instructional strategies without considering causes of failure
5. Failure to modify a single approach or strategy in light of situational features	Continue "tried and true" instructional strategies in face of significant changes in student population
6. Use of theories and schemas that do not accurately represent reality	Schools cannot compensate for challenges to student learning caused by family background

The left column of Table 2.2 lists those cognitive errors identified by Nisbett and Ross (1980) which were included in one of our studies of leadership expertise (Stager and Leithwood 1989). The right column provides examples of how each category of error, on the part of either teachers or school leaders, might manifest itself in the context of responding to large-scale assessment results. Six types of errors are included in the table: overweighting vividness in setting priorities or interpreting the problem; generalizing from a small or biased sample; and four errors that have in common the overuse or misuse of one's existing theories, knowledge structures, or schemas. Error 4 was the focus of Challenge Two (above) so it is not discussed any further here.

Overweighting Vividness in Interpreting the Problem

This error consists of the tendency to ignore very robust data about student achievement in statistical form in favor of much more immediate, vivid, and multidimensional impressions. Typically, these will be impressions gleaned from observing students in one's own class, in the case of teachers, or in the last class you visited, in the case of principals. Such data are vivid because they have real people attached to them. This error might lead to an assertion such as "these tests are not sensitive enough to capture what our students really know."

School leaders and teachers repeatedly demonstrating this error in response to large-scale assessment results will benefit from opportunities to develop a better understanding of basic concepts (e.g., standard deviation, scale reliability) used in summarizing data in statistical form. The goal, in this case, is to create vividness where it does not exist by giving people the tools to "see it" in a form different from what they have been are used to. Many school leaders will benefit from these same opportunities.

Generalizing from a Small or Biased Sample

This error will sometimes become evident in the tendency for teachers to generalize to the whole class or the whole school the performance of those students with whom they are most familiar. This error does not arise from vividness but from insensitivity to the wide variation found in larger populations on most matters. School leaders will need to provide targeted opportunities for teachers prone to improve their understanding of the pitfalls of generalizing from small samples.

Failure to See That a Situation Is Unique or Different from Others in the Past

Teachers and school leaders who are expert at what they do are less prone to this error than are their less expert counterparts. Nevertheless, both the fast-paced nature of the world they work in and the automaticity that is part of becoming expert in one's field leave even experts at risk of this error. Both fast pace and automaticity press teachers and administrators confronted with new problems to search for similarities with problems they have experienced and solved in the past. The detection of similarities will trigger well-rehearsed solutions, thereby reducing the cognitive demand required for a response.

This error might easily creep into the responses of principals and teachers examining the aggregated mean results of their students' performance on this year's large-scale assessment. Should such aggregated results mirror, or be very similar to, the aggregated mean results of last year's assessment, it would be easy for them to conclude that nothing has changed and to give the data no further thought. In fact, the aggregated results might well mask significant differences from last year on the part of some groups of students. Results for the small cohort of ESL students, for example, might have fallen dramatically while the results for all other students has crept forward just enough to keep the average level of achievement unchanged. Too bad for the ESL students!

This is a remarkably difficult error for school leaders and their staffs to avoid for the reasons already mentioned (automaticity and fast-paced context). It requires at least constant vigilance on the part of leaders and a willingness to ask questions of staff which will, at the time, seem only to slow down decision making and create more work. This likely demands an exceptionally reflective disposition on the part of school leaders and a willingness to foster such a disposition among teachers.

Failure to Modify a Single Approach or Strategy in Light of Situational Features

This error may occur even when people acknowledge unique features of the problem they are facing in comparison with problems they have addressed in the past. This error entails acting on the assumption that one's typical or previously used solutions will be suitable or powerful enough to succeed anyway. So school staffs may acknowledge, for example, that the new curriculum guidelines issued by the province place much greater emphasis on students' own knowledge construction while, nevertheless, also maintain that their current forms of instruction, premised on a very different model of how students learn, will still be suitable.

Returning to an earlier example, suppose the same school staff faced with unchanged year-over-year aggregated mean large-scale assessment results were eventually persuaded to disaggregate the data and found the problem with their ESL students. If they then decided to continue with their "tried and true" instructional strategies, they would be guilty of this error. To reduce the incidence of this error, school leaders will need to ask their colleagues uncomfortable questions about the justification for continuing practices that seem unlikely to be productive in changed circumstances.

Making Use of Theories or Schemas That Do Not Accurately Represent Reality

This error is very well illustrated by the results of a recent analysis conducted in Australia (Mulford et al. 2007). The study compared a large sample of elementary and secondary school principals' estimates of how well their students were achieving in literacy and numeracy with students' actual scores on state tests; student success was classified, for this purpose, as low, medium, or high. Results of this study pointed toward a strong tendency for principals of schools whose actual student scores were low and medium to significantly overestimate the success of their students (74% overestimated for primary and 71% for secondary), in some cases by two levels (16% for primary and 30% for secondary).

A larger proportion of principals of schools whose students were actually high achieving (86% primary and 63% secondary) estimated such achievement accurately. These results, however, cannot be interpreted to suggest that principals of higher achieving schools are more accurate in their assessments, only that the tendency of principals to be "optimistic" about their school's success had a greater chance of reflecting reality in high performing schools. The errors in principals' estimates of their students' success, it should be noted, occurred in a policy context which makes test scores on state exams widely available to schools and encourages their use!

The cognitive error which surfaced in this study also reflects evidence summarized by Nisbett and Ross (1980) indicating that peoples' beliefs and behaviors have a tendency to become aligned over time even when they start off being very different. Arguably, principals are under pressure from many sources to be cheerleaders for their schools. After months or years of defending or justifying the quality of their school programs, they may well begin to believe the justification—even if that was not the case at the outset.

Avoiding this error likely requires a high level of metacognitive control on the part of the principal. In its absence, principals will lose the critical edge they need to continue moving their school forward. This is one explanation for the widespread belief in many organizations that leaders should not remain in the same position beyond 6 or 7 years (Gabarro 1987).

Conclusion

The overwhelming motivation for developing large-scale assessment programs has been the desire to hold schools more publicly accountable. I accept the need for some form of external accountability for schools and have not attempted, myself, to offer a better solution than large-scale assessment programs. My concern in this chapter has been with the proliferation of purposes for large-scale assessments that have occurred over time, and in particular, the claim that the results of such assessments are powerful sources of insight for those in schools, such as school leaders, aiming to improve student performance. The skeptics among us might be inclined to the view that this proliferation of purposes is little more than an attempt to justify the expenditure of sizeable public monies and the enormous opportunity costs associated with the student, teacher, and administrator time these assessments consume.

Most public opinion polls, nevertheless, suggest very high and stable levels of support for large-scale student testing programs (e.g., Livingstone et al. 2001, 2003). These same polls also indicate that very few respondents have much understanding of what such testing entails, the technical limitations of what they produce, and the collateral outcomes which often result. With such blind support, there is little incentive among assessment advocates to do anything but continue. Like it or not, school leaders will have to deal with the results of large-scale assessments, "warts and all," in the foreseeable future. So my purpose in this chapter has been to unpack a series of challenges faced by improvement-oriented school leaders when confronted with the results of large-scale assessments for their schools.

Adopting a cognitive psychological perspective, I framed the student performance improvement task as an ill structured problem—ill structured because of the uncertain nature of the "solution paths" between a current state (the current level of student performance in one' school) and a goal state (the desired, and no doubt, higher, level of such performance). With this perspective on the improvement task of school leaders, the chapter asked in what ways the results of a typical large-scale assessment could be helpful. It is reasonable to expect that assessment results, as a minimum, would help school leaders and their staffs understand the current state of student learning in their schools. But large-scale assessments actually have very limited potential for this very important purpose because of the narrow set of student outcomes they measure, their unknown reliability at the school and classroom levels, difficulties in using such data for tracking changes in student performance over time, and the large time lags between collecting and reporting results. These unhelpful features of large-scale assessment programs, furthermore, are as serious a compromise to their value in determining whether a desired state of student performance has been reached as they are in determining the current state.

Beyond pointing out these limitations of large-scale assessments, the chapter described several other critical challenges that school leaders face in their efforts to improve their students' performance. Two of these challenges can only be addressed with information that most teachers and school leaders acquire through informal and almost always unsystematic means, at best. This is information about the causes of students' current levels of achievement and the status of those conditions in the school which nurture and support its improvement efforts. We need to move past the view that information about the status of students' achievement is the only information needed for school improvement purposes. School leaders desperately need robust, systematically-collected information about those other features of their schools that account for student achievement if their success is to approximate the aspirations of our current policies.

This chapter, in sum, has argued that most large-scale assessment results are of quite limited practical use to school leaders and their teacher colleagues in their efforts to improve their students' performance. Such results, for example, might just as easily misrepresent, as accurately capture, current levels of achievement in modest-sized schools and in virtually all classrooms. Evidence about multi-year achievement patterns across Ontario schools indicated just how uneven is the trajectory of improvement in school performance when Ontario's large-scale assessment program is the yardstick for measuring that performance. Admittedly, schools occasionally do face circumstances with the documented potential to quickly and dramatically alter the quality of their students' educational experiences. Principal succession is one of these circumstances (MacMillan 2000); a high rate of teacher turnover with immediate effects on teacher quality is another. But these are occasional rather than frequent circumstances faced by schools and certainly do not occur sufficiently often in most schools to account for the bumpy trajectories of achievement found in the Ontario data. Changes in the quality of education provided to students by most schools, most of the time, are better described as gradual and highly incremental. Ironically, reformists wring their hands about such slow and incremental change in schools, on the one hand, yet are willing to accept large-scale assessment evidence of dramatic short term achievement increases and decreases at face value, on the other.

In the face of their large-scale assessment results, school leaders often feel like technically naïve, statistics virgins, struggling to unlock some powerful new insight buried in the numbers, if only they understood them. The sense of guilt produced by these feelings of inadequacy is not warranted, however. Similarly, there is a substantial literature that is quite critical of teacher assessment practices while arguing for an increase, on teachers' parts, in the skills and understandings more closely associated with the technology of large-scale assessments. This seems like a classic case of "the pot calling the kettle black." Certainly many teachers could benefit from additional understandings about test and measurement concepts. But this would not be of a different magnitude than the additional understandings needed by those promoting the use of large-scale assessment results for school improvement purposes. As it stands now, teachers have no reason to apologize for their own assessment efforts in the face of the huge challenges still to be addressed by the designs of most large-scale assessment programs (see the 2005 annual yearbook of the *National Society of Education* for much more on this). Flaw for flaw—and I claim only impressionistic evidence here—most teachers' assessments seem likely to provide better clues for instructional improvement than do most large-scale assessment results. Those of us who are members of the research and policy communities should be much more forthright with teachers and administrators about the limitations of large-scale assessments for school improvement purposes.

References

Alig-Mielcarek, J. M. (2003). *A model of school success: Instructional leadership, academic press, and student achievement.* Unpublished doctoral dissertation, Ohio State University, Columbus, OH.

American Educational Research Association. (2000). Position statement of the American Educational Research Association concerning high-stakes testing in preK-12 education. *Educational Researcher, 29*(8), 24–25.

Black, P., & Wiliam, D. (2004). The formative purpose: Assessment must first promote learning. In M. Wilson (Ed.), *Towards coherence between classroom assessment and accountability (103rd yearbook of the national society for the study of education)* (pp. 20–50). Chicago, IL: University of Chicago Press.

Bryk, A. S., & Schneider, B. (2003). Trust in schools: A core resource for school reform. *Educational Leadership, 60*(6), 40–44.

Creemers, B. (2007). Educational effectiveness and improvement: The development of the field in mainland Europe. In T. Townsend (Ed.), *International handbook of school effectiveness and improvement* (pp. 223–241). Dordrecht, the Netherlands: Springer.

Creemers, B. P. M., & Reetzig, G. J. (1996). School level conditions affecting the effectiveness of instruction. *School Effectiveness and School Improvement, 7*(3), 197–228.

Dirks, K. T., & Ferrin, D. L. (2002). Trust in leadership: Meta-analytic findings and implications for research and practice. *Journal of Applied Psychology, 87*(4), 611–628.

Earl, L. M. (2001). Data, data everywhere (and we don't know what to do): Using data for wise decisions in schools. In P. de Broucker & A. Sweetman (Eds.), *Towards evidence-based policy for Canadian education* (pp. 39–51). Kingston, ON: John Deutsch Institute for the Study of Economic Policy, Queen's University.

Fredericksen, N. (1984). Implications of cognitive theory for instruction in problem solving. *Review of Educational Research, 54*(3), 363–407.

Gabarro, J. J. (1987). *The dynamics of taking charge.* Boston, MA: Harvard Business School Press.

Gagné, E. D. (1985). *The cognitive psychology of school learning.* Boston, MA: Little, Brown and Co.

Goddard, R. D. (2003). Relational networks, social trust, and norms: A social capital perspective on students' chance of academic success. *Educational Evaluation and Policy Analysis, 25*(1), 59–74.

Goddard, R. D., & Goddard, Y. L. (2001). A multilevel analysis of the relationship between teacher and collective efficacy in urban schools. *Teaching and Teacher Education, 17*(7), 807–818.

Goddard, R. D., Hoy, W. K., & Woolfolk Hoy, A. (2000). Collective teacher efficacy: Its meaning, measure and impact on student achievement. *American Educational Research Journal, 37*(2), 479–507.

Goddard, R. D., Sweetland, S. R., & Hoy, W. K. (2000). Academic emphasis of urban elementary schools and student achievement in reading and mathematics: A multi-level analysis. *Educational Administration Quarterly, 36*(5), 683–702.

Hallinger, P., & Heck, R. (1996). Reassessing the principal's role in school effectiveness: A review of empirical research, 1980–1995. *Educational Administration Quarterly, 32*(1), 5–44.

Heubert, J., & Hauser, R. (Eds.). (1999). *High stake tests: Testing for tracking, promotion and graduation.* Washington, DC: National Academic Press.

House, R., Hanges, P., Javidan, M., Dorfman, P., & Gupta, V. (2004). *Culture, leadership and organizations: The Globe study of 62 societies.* Thousand Oaks, CA: Sage.

Jacob, J. A. (2004). *A study of school climate and enabling bureaucracy in select New York City public elementary schools.* Unpublished doctoral dissertation, University of Utah, Salt Lake City, UT.

Jurewicz, M. M. (2004). *Organizational citizenship behaviors of middle school teachers: A study of their relationship to school climate and student achievement.* Unpublished doctoral dissertation, College of William and Mary, Williamsburg, VA.

Kahneman, D., Slovic, P., & Tversky, A. (Eds.). (1982). *Judgement under uncertainty: Heuristics and biases.* Cambridge, UK: Cambridge University Press.

Lee, V. E., & Croninger, R. G. (1994). The relative importance of home and school in the development of literacy skills for middle-grade students. *American Journal of Education, 102*(3), 286–329.

Leithwood, K., Day, C., Sammons, P., Harris, A., & Hopkins, D. (2006). *Successful school leadership: What it is and how it influences pupil learning.* London, UK: DfES. Available at http://www.dfes.gov.uk/research/data/uploadfiles/RR800.pdf.

Leithwood, K., & Levin, B. (2005). *Assessing school leader and leadership programme effects on pupil learning* (RR662). Department for Education and Skills (DfES).

Leithwood, K., & Riehl, C. (2005). What we know about successful school leadership. In W. Firestone & C. Riehl (Eds.), *A new agenda: Directions for research on educational leadership* (pp. 22–47). New York, NY: Teachers College Press.

Leithwood, K., Seashore Louis, K., Anderson, S., & Wahlstrom, K. (2004). *How leadership influences student learning: A review of research for the Learning from Leadership Project.* New York, NY: The Wallace Foundation.

Leithwood, K., & Steinbach, R. (1995). *Expert problem solving processes: Evidence from principals and superintendents.* Albany, NY: SUNY Press.

Linn, R. (2003). Accountability: Responsibility and reasonable expectations. *Educational Researcher, 32*(7), 3–13.

Livingstone, D. W., Hart, D., & Davie, L. E. (2001). *Public attitudes towards education in Ontario 2000: The 13th OISE/UT Survey.* Toronto, ON: Ontario Institute for Studies in Education, University of Toronto.

Livingstone, D. W., Hart, D., & Davie, L. E. (2003). *Public attitudes towards education in Ontario 2002: The 14th OISE/UT Survey.* Toronto, ON: Ontario Institute for Studies in Education, University of Toronto.

Macmillan, R. (2000). Leadership succession, cultures of teaching and educational change. In N. Bascia & A. Hargreaves (Eds.), *The sharp edge of educational change: Teaching, leading and the realities of reform* (pp. 52–71). London, UK: Routledge/Falmer.

McDonnell, L. M. (2005). Assessment and accountability from the policy maker's perspective. In J. Herman & E. Haertel (Eds.), *Uses and misuses of data for educational accountability and improvement (104th Yearbook of the National Society for the Study of Education)* (pp. 35–54). Malden, MA: Blackwell.

Mulford, B., Kendall, D., Edmunds, B., Kendall, L., Ewington, J., & Silins, H. (2007). Successful school leadership: What is it and who decides? *Australian Journal of Education, 51*(3), 228–246.

Nisbett, R., & Ross, L. (1980). *Human inference: Strategies and shortcomings of social judgment.* Englewood Cliffs, NJ: Prentice-Hall.

Pitner, N. (1988). The study of administrator effects and effectiveness. In N. Boyan (Ed.), *Handbook of research on educational administration* (pp. 99–122). New York, NY: Longman.

Sackney, L. (2007). History of the school effectiveness and improvement movement in Canada over the past 25 years. In T. Townsend (Ed.), *International handbook of school effectiveness and improvement* (pp. 167–182). Dordrecht, the Netherlands: Springer.

Silins, H., & Mulford, B. (2007). Leadership and school effectiveness and improvement. In T. Townsend (Ed.), *International handbook of school effectiveness and improvement* (pp. 635–658). Dordrecht, the Netherlands: Springer.

Stager, M., & Leithwood, K. (1989). Cognitive flexibility in principals' problem solving. *Alberta Journal of Educational Research, 35*(3), 217–236.

Teddlie, C., & Stringfield, S. (2007). A history of school effectiveness and improvement research in the USA focusing on the past quarter century. In T. Townsend (Ed.), *International handbook of school effectiveness and improvement* (pp. 131–166). Dordrecht, the Netherlands: Springer.

Timperley, H. S. (2005). Distributed leadership: Developing theory from practice. *Journal of Curriculum Studies, 37*(6), 395–420.

Tschannen-Moran, M., & Barr, M. (2004). Fostering student achievement: The relationship between collective teacher efficacy and student achievement. *Leadership and Policy in Schools, 3*(3), 189–209.

Walberg, H. (1984). Improving the productivity of America's schools. *Educational Leadership, 41*(8), 19–27.

Wilson, D. (2004). Assessment, accountability and the classroom: A community of judgment. In D. Wilson (Ed.), *Towards coherence between classroom assessment and accountability (103rd Yearbook of the National Society for the Study of Education)* (pp. 1–19). Chicago, IL: University of Chicago Press.

Wolfe, R., Childs, R., & Elgie, S. (2004). *Final report of the external evaluation of the EQAO's assessment process.* Toronto, ON: Ontario Institute for Studies in Education, University of Toronto.

Chapter 3
Lessons Learned: The Promise and Possibility of Educational Accountability in the United States

Charles L. Slater, Marla W. McGhee, Sarah W. Nelson, and Lionel "Skip" Meno

The authors review the promise and possibility of educational accountability and revisit fundamental questions. To whom should schools be accountable and for what? They recommend real-world standards for a broad curriculum, measures to keep students in school, and an assessment system that provides data for teachers to help students to learn. The goal is the development of a learning and assessment culture in each school that is characterized by democratic participation, debate, and dialogue.

Improving and reforming education has been on the national forefront for some time in the United States. In August 1981, the then Secretary of Education, Terrell Bell, assembled the National Commission on Excellence in Education to prepare a report on educational quality in America. In a letter to the secretary, Chairperson David Gardner wrote,

> The Commission deeply believes that the problems we have discerned in American education can be both understood and corrected if the people of the country, together with those who have public responsibility in the matter, care enough and are courageous enough to do what is required. (National Commission on Excellence in Education 1983).

C.L. Slater (✉)
California State University – Long Beach, Long Beach, CA, USA
e-mail: cslater@csulb.edu

M.W. McGhee
Texas Christian University, Fort Worth, TX, USA

S.W. Nelson
Texas State University – San Marcos, San Marcos, TX, USA

L. "Skip" Meno
San Diego State University, San Diego, CA, USA

C.F. Webber and J.L. Lupart (eds.), *Leading Student Assessment*,
Studies in Educational Leadership 15, DOI 10.1007/978-94-007-1727-5_3,
© Springer Science+Business Media B.V. 2012

Fueled by testimony about international achievement rankings, performance on standardized batteries, concerns regarding required remediation of postsecondary students, and the need for a more highly skilled work force, the Commission offered a set of recommendations to the Secretary and the American people. These included improved graduation requirements, more-rigorous standards for college admissions, increased time for learning through lengthening the school day and expanding the school year, a focus on improved teaching, and greater responsibility for leadership and fiscal support.

Eleven years after the release of *A Nation at Risk*, education again received national attention when a piece of sweeping federal legislation was signed into law—P.L. 103–227, Goals 2000: Educate America Act. "Goals 2000 establish[ed] a framework in which to identify world-class academic standards, to measure student progress, and to provide the support that students may need to meet the standards" (Summary of Goals 2000). Eight national education goals were stated in the Act:

By the year 2000—

1. All children in America will start school ready to learn.
2. The high school graduation rate will increase to at least 90%.
3. All students will leave grades 4, 8, and 12, having demonstrated competency over challenging subject matter including English, mathematics, science, foreign languages, civics and government, economics, the arts, history, and geography, and every school in America will ensure that all students learn to use their minds well, so they may be prepared for responsible citizenship, further learning, and productive employment in our nation's modern economy.
4. United States students will be first in the world in mathematics and science achievement.
5. Every adult American will be literate and will possess the knowledge and skills necessary to compete in the global economy and exercise the rights and responsibilities of citizenship.
6. Every school in the United States will be free of drugs, violence, and the unauthorized presence of firearms and alcohol and will offer a disciplined environment conducive to learning.
7. The nation's teaching force will have access to programs for the continued improvement of their professional skills and the opportunity to acquire the knowledge and skills needed to instruct and prepare all American students for the next century.
8. Every school will promote partnerships that will increase parental involvement and participation in promoting the social, emotional, and academic growth of children (Goals 2000).

The Act was instrumental in launching a national standards movement to identify what students should know and be able to do in a variety of disciplines as successful citizens in the twenty-first century.

Up to this point, national initiatives did not have a significant impact on widespread mandated student testing. However, that started to change in the late 1990s when interest in assessment on a national level began to be more broadly discussed and considered. Since 1969, the National Assessment of Educational Progress (NAEP), commonly known as the nation's report card, had been administered on a voluntary basis to random samples of students in states that chose to participate in the biannual testing (Institute for Education Sciences 2009). Authorized by Congress, funded through the US Department of Education (USDE), and administered by the National Center for Education Statistics (NCES), NAEP targets reading, writing, mathematics, science, US history, geography, civics, the arts, and foreign languages at grades 4, 8, and 12. In 1998, the commissioner of NCES assembled a task force of educational policymakers and practitioners from around the country to generate strategies intended to compel all states and jurisdictions to participate in NAEP testing in the year 2000. And in the 2000 presidential race, "both major-party Presidential hopefuls ... endorsed in principle the idea of upgrading the NAEP to a high-stakes measuring rod for distributing financial rewards to states that meet accountability standards" (Holland 2000, p. 1).

The nationally televised presidential debates, however, truly foreshadowed the advent of mandated individual student testing promoted from the highest levels of American government. When addressing a question regarding public education, Vice President Al Gore "referred to testing no fewer than five times in his first brief response" (Waite et al. 2001, p. 188). Then Governor of Texas, George W. Bush, followed by stating,

He says he's for voluntary testing. You can't have voluntary testing. You must have mandatory testing .... That's a huge difference. Testing is the cornerstone of reform. You know how I know? Because it's the cornerstone of reform in the State of Texas .... (Commission on Presidential Debates 2000)

The No Child Left Behind Act (NCLB) was signed into law on January 8, 2002, and significantly expanded the federal role in education (US Department of Education 2009a). Schools are held accountable to improve educational achievement through annual testing, academic progress, school report cards, and teacher qualifications. The legislation promotes the use of scientifically based research to improve instruction, particularly in the area of reading through the Reading First and Early Reading First programs (US Department of Education 2009b, c). According to the ED.gov website, "Under No Child Left Behind, states and school districts have unprecedented flexibility in how they use federal education funds" (http://www.ed.gov/nclb/overview/intro/4pillars.html). The law also claims to offer more choices and control for parents, allowing them to transfer their children out of schools if they are not performing well, and provides supplemental educational services, when warranted, such as tutoring and summer learning opportunities.

NCLB requires annual testing of at least 95% of students at each school in grades 3–8 in reading and mathematics. In addition to overall scores, data are compiled on students from low-income families, students from different racial groups, those with disabilities, and English language learners. The tests are aligned with state academic standards. Students as a whole and all student groups must make adequate yearly progress (AYP).

Schools with a high concentration of students from poor families receive what are called Title I funds from the federal government (US Department of Education 2009d). Title I schools that fail to meet targeted goals 2 years in a row must offer students a choice of other public schools to attend. After 3 years, students must be offered supplemental educational services. All students must reach a minimum level of proficiency by 2013. Moreover, states and districts report student achievement for all groups, and Title I schools complete a public report. Additionally, all teachers must meet the definition of highly qualified, and Title I paraprofessionals must have at least 2 years of postsecondary education or pass an evaluation. Schools are also expected to provide quality professional development experiences for teachers and paraprofessionals. Six years after being signed into law, NCLB continues to loom large at state levels of education with US Department of Education officials strictly monitoring and controlling the flow of federal aid based on compliance with expectations.

Positive Outcomes of Accountability Systems

Student assessment in the United States is now associated with large-scale, centralized, high-impact testing. This approach, even with its downfalls, has been instrumental in reshaping some of education's more haphazard practices. For example, before the advent of state standards and curriculum objectives associated with accountability systems and testing, course expectations and content varied greatly with the responsibility for curriculum development often falling to individual schools or school districts. Before this attention to curriculum standards, some teachers were expected to instruct courses for which no curriculum had been established. In the absence of guiding documents, it was not uncommon for a textbook to fill the learning objectives, curricular gap. Mandated tests in many places are now aligned with state-prescribed academic standards and expectations. And, norm-referenced tests have been replaced with criterion-referenced assessments correlated to the state curriculum guidelines.

One of the most significant yet controversial changes associated with educational accountability systems has been to disaggregate and report results by student group. Prior to the implementation of this practice, the achievement of minority students, such as African-Americans, Hispanics, and low-socioeconomic students, was often lost or hidden amid overall test results that were not uniformly reported (Hilliard 1991, 1998). Achievement is now measured for all students in a school and disaggregated by ethnicity, gender, students in poverty, English language learners, and special program students. The gap between majority–minority achievement is being publicly targeted, and closing this performance gulf has become the driving purpose of the accountability movement.

Through these reporting systems, teachers, principals, and superintendents have access to consistent sets of student performance data. Educators have become informed about individual student performance as it relates to testing and often use this information to make instructional decisions such as which areas of the curriculum need greater emphasis and which students are eligible for additional support. Moreover, many of these reports are now available to the public via state and district websites, allowing parents, community members, and other interested parties to become more knowledgeable about their public schools.

Unintended Consequences of Educational Accountability

Although several notable outcomes can be attributed to the implementation of educational accountability systems, there have also been a number of unintended consequences that deserve to be mentioned here. Assessment (a core feature of most accountability programs) is a critically important aspect of schools and learning, but there is a distinct difference between assessing and purely "testing." *Assess* comes from the Latin *assidere*, which means to "sit by." This definition implies that assessment can be considered an opportunity to guide or inform and could be carried out in a variety of ways, only one of which might include paper–pencil testing. However, more *authentic* forms of assessment, so named because they emulate actions associated with an assessed field or discipline, seem to be losing out to standardized tests, due, in part, to cost, which is substantially lower for mechanically scored standardized batteries (Kornhaber 2004). If not used with care, this type of testing—commonly associated with accountability systems—can drive schools and educators toward what is objectively testable and away from more complex teaching and learning goals. Kornhaber called this approach to school improvement an application of "the theory of test-driven reform" (p. 51).

Educational decision and policy makers have insisted on this form of assessment because they think it addresses a range of educational dilemmas. The first step associated with this theory is to publicly spell out higher standards. To find out whether the standards are being met, students are tested. In order to motivate teachers and students, test results are attached to sanctions or rewards. "Under NCLB, all states are now required to adhere to this theory.... The underlying logic ... is clear, but it is important to consider how well it plays out in practice" (Kornhaber 2004, p. 52). The unanticipated consequences that follow are examples of how comprehensive accountability systems, with a test-driven core, can sometimes harm the very students the system purports to benefit.

Curriculum Narrowing

Besides increasing a propensity toward objective testing, accountability systems can heavily influence the organization and delivery of curriculum. In the state of Texas, for example, a rewrite of the curriculum standards caused the arts, health, physical education, technology applications, and second languages to no longer be considered part of the central required curriculum as they were relegated to "enrichment" status. This reduction in the number of curriculum areas placed more direct focus on the subjects that were to be tested as part of the annual accountability program. And, within those subjects, a further narrowing was detected. For example, educational researchers have found that some targeted students are taught only the genres of writing that are annually tested rather than being exposed to a full range of writing aims and modes (McNeil 2000). Clearly, the emphasis in some schools has moved away from teaching a comprehensive, well-rounded curriculum to testing specific objectives.

Related to curriculum narrowing and paring down is the practice of placing particular students in preparation classes to ready them for taking the test. This sometimes means altering the student's schedule and reducing the number of elective classes a learner may take. In these classes, students are taught test-related strategies rather than being exposed to an enriched, high-level curriculum.

> Gaming techniques include teaching test-taking skills, such as how to bubble in an answer sheet as quickly as possible or how to eliminate choices. Both of these may be useful on a test but have exceedingly little to do with actually learning disciplinary skill or content. (Kornhaber 2004, p. 57)

Another way curriculum is being shaped by accountability testing is the de-emphasis or suspension of some subject areas. Language arts and math have been tested regularly on state assessments for some time, while subjects such as science and social studies have been more recently added. When social studies and science were not part of the regularly tested curriculum, it was not uncommon to hear reports from the field regarding teachers being instructed not to teach these subjects or to greatly reduce instructional time in these areas, focusing instead on curriculum areas that would be annually tested. Untested subjects like the arts, physical education, and music have been known to completely disappear from the instructional day until the testing period has passed. So, too, have field excursions, work in the library media center, and other activities not believed to support or promote passage of state exams.

The Redirection of Instructional Time

As accountability system pressures increase, balancing effective instructional practice with test preparation is an increasing challenge for educators. There is legitimate concern about how class time actually is being used, as more and more of the school day seems to be focused on exam preparation rather than on student learning. Numerous documented cases and anecdotes from the field support this premise, so much so that policymakers have taken action to refocus schools on their primary mission of teaching and learning. In North Carolina, the Senate Education Committee approved a bill to limit to five the number of days that students take standardized exams (Associated Press 2003). Texas lawmakers also passed a bill that limits to 10% the number of instructional days a district can utilize for test practice. Professional organizations are also getting involved. One example is in the Austin

Independent School District in Texas where Education Austin, a local union, encouraged teachers to log, on a daily basis, the percentage of instructional time spent on testing or test preparation (Education Austin 2007).

Test preparation itself has taken on the status of a course in the curriculum. McNeil (2000) explained that test practice sheets, test-taking skills, and practice tests are competing for precious instructional time in many schools. The more pressure there is to raise scores, the more emphasis is placed on the test and the less on other activities. This test preparation takes a significant amount of time in the school day and may not be making much difference in outcomes. In a recent study of 41 districts across the state of Texas, 63% of superintendents reported requiring students to practice for accountability exams by participating in a mandated benchmarking protocol. Investigators found that, in some cases, students were spending up to 35 days or 7 weeks practicing for accountability system-related examinations. What is even more troubling, though, is that the time spent in benchmark testing yielded almost no benefit on test results; in mathematics no improvement was found, and in reading the impact was small (6%) (Nelson and McGhee 2004; Nelson et al. 2007b).

Disaggregating data by income and ethnic groups was intended to draw attention to students who were not well served by public schools. But rather than receiving additional resources and a more enriched curriculum from better-qualified teachers, students from poor families and students of color may be receiving a test preparation program.

Darling-Hammond (1994) put assessment in context. She set fairness as the first criterion. Rather than penalize or disadvantage students, tests should result in positive consequences for teaching and learning (consequential validity). We should at least ask how testing affects the teaching learning process and whether it promotes higher-order thinking skills and long-term changes. Testing should be part of broader reform efforts and support professional and organizational development. Test results should inform and improve rather than sort and rank.

Testing can lead to tracking of students. What may start as a temporary arrangement to prepare students who need extra help for the test can gradually become a more time-consuming portion of curriculum for students with lower-level skills. Such students may also be taught by teachers with less seniority and experience. They are also more likely to be retained and suffer long-term academic consequences (Shepard and Smith 1986).

Glasser (1990) offered a similar list of criteria that depart from previous uses of standardized tests. The tests should survey possibilities for student growth and allow students to judge their own work. They should represent meaningful tasks and a broad range of skills and knowledge.

Pushing Students Out

McNeil et al. (2008) offered the most sweeping indictment to date of high stakes accountability. They reported that while Texas has publicly reported gains in test scores, students were dropping out of school in ever-increasing numbers. The accountability system itself forced schools to push out students who would not do well on state tests.

The Texas Education Agency permits high schools to remove students from the dropout list for a variety of reasons. For example, if students say they are transferring to another school or planning to take the GED, they are not counted as dropouts. Thus, the official dropout rate is 2–3% per year. Yet, the attrition between grades 9 and 12 runs over 50% in the urban school district McNeil et al. (2008) studied, and the rate was higher for Latino and African-American students. The authors described a system by which schools retain students in grade 9 so that they do not take the state test in grade 10. Some languished in grade 9 until they finally dropped out of school. Elementary school test scores showed improvement, but the gains were lost when students faced the demands of middle and high school curricula.

Heilig and Darling-Hammond (2008) used the same sample as McNeil et al. (2008) to demonstrate how incentives can be perverted from their original intent. Some school districts have tried to obtain higher test scores by testing fewer students at the elementary level and pushing out students at the high school level. Heilig and Darling-Hammond asked, "Do policies that reward and sanction schools and students based on test scores improve achievement and the quality of education for all or most students?" (p. 75), and wondered if it is possible to create a high-stakes system that does not encourage schools to sacrifice the good of some students to obtain higher test scores to enhance the school rating.

Accountability Reconsidered

In announcing passage of legislation to establish a national system for accountability, President Bush stated,

> There is no greater challenge than to make sure that every child—and [I] mean every child, not just a few children—every single child—regardless of where they live, how they're raised, the income level of their family, every child receive a first-class education in America. (Bush 2002, p. 1)

Such a proclamation suggests that NCLB was designed to address all of the many factors that inhibit education for democracy. References to school location, family income, and approach to parenting imply that societal factors beyond the school walls play a role in educational success and would be addressed. Within this same speech, however, the focus of reform was narrowed, and two notions become clear: (a) While interest in educational improvement may be widespread throughout all levels of government, the responsibility rests squarely on the shoulders of educators and families, and (b) educational success entails proficiency on a narrow set of academic standards. According to Bush, "Every school has a job to do. And that's to teach the basics and teach them well" (p. 3). He went on to explain that when schools fail to meet this expectation, parents have a right and a duty to take their children to another school.

Misplaced Accountability

This legislation specifies a narrow definition of educational success, and responsibility for success is misplaced. This misplaced accountability occurs in two ways. First, a person or organization can become accountable to the wrong entity, usually as the result of reward or sanction. Lawmakers, for example, are often thought to be more accountable to the lobbyists who finance political campaigns than to their constituents (Center for Responsive Politics 2009). A second form of misplaced accountability results when a person is held accountable for something over which he or she has little or no control. Comparing mortality rates of trauma centers to those of specialized hospitals is an example of this kind of misplaced accountability. Trauma centers may be able to reduce mortalities through improved practice, but the only way to match the mortality rate of specialized hospitals is to stop admitting the most critically injured patients. In education, misplaced accountability occurs when test scores of schools in advantaged areas are compared to those of schools with fewer resources and less community support.

Accountable to Whom?

Both types of misplaced accountability are visible within the current system. The first is seen in a shift in the focus of accountability. The stated intent of NCLB is to ensure schools are accountable to the students and families they serve, particularly students who have historically not been well served in public schools. Yet, because the system relies heavily on rewards or punishments attached to standardized test scores, schools have become more accountable to public perception than the students they teach. This form of misplaced accountability is why some schools have eliminated a full, rich curriculum in favor of one that emphasizes tested subjects (McNeil 2000), why allocation of tutoring services is based on how likely tutoring is to help a student pass an accountability test rather than on how much help a student needs (Nelson et al. 2007a), and why school counselors will encourage certain students to leave school early and get a GED (Valenzuela 1999).

Accountable for What?

The second type of misplaced accountability has arisen from the centralization of decision making that has occurred under NCLB. Increasingly, in the name of accountability, policymakers at all levels are moving to limit the authority of those who are closest to the classroom. Several school districts have required teachers to use prescriptive instructional guides and monitor them to ensure compliance. School principals have adopted commercially packaged school improvement programs to obtain funding for their schools. Parents have to contend with limited intervention strategies or risk having their child retained. And yet, those who call for accountability and who make such decisions end up with none of the responsibility if things go wrong. The president can sign NCLB but place all responsibility for improvement on teachers and administrators who have had no hand in deciding it (Epstein 2004).

Additionally, misplaced accountability results from the accountability system being concerned only with what occurs within the school system itself, ignoring the many other factors that affect education. Rothstein (2004) made a persuasive argument that schools alone will not be able to address the issue of educational inequity. While acknowledging there is much that schools can and should do to improve educational outcomes, Rothstein submitted that the roots of inequity are planted outside the school. The achievement gap, he asserts, may be exacerbated in schools, but it is not created there; it is created by the differences in circumstance among children from birth to age 5, in the hours before and after school, and during summer months when school is closed. For some children, these are times of enrichment and extended learning. For others, they are times of uncertainty and fear, times of hunger, and times of shouldering adult responsibilities. Such differing circumstances naturally create differing outcomes. To expect schools alone to redress them is, indeed, misplaced accountability.

Ladson-Billings (2006) described the educational debt that has accumulated from repeated denial of equal educational opportunity. Redressing this educational debt will require an expanded notion of accountability, one that includes not only educators but also policymakers and corporations that have had a hand in creating the conditions of educational inequity (Rothstein 2004).

Recommendations

High stakes accountability began with significant accomplishments. It specified standards for learning and created a more consistent, organized curriculum. Criterion-referenced testing provided a more fair assessment of objectives than norm-referenced testing. Data were available to use for decision making and were disaggregated to focus attention on all groups in the school. Figure 3.1 illustrates these contributions as well as recommendations to overcome unintended consequences.

Real-World Standards for a Broad Curriculum

The curriculum must be broadened, not narrowed, to reflect the demands of the real world. Standards are now commonplace in all states. Rather than seeing these standards as settled, dialogue and debate should be increased. Currently, the standards have great breadth with little depth. The grade 4 social studies curriculum in Texas, for example, contains 79 separate objectives (Texas Education Agency 1998).

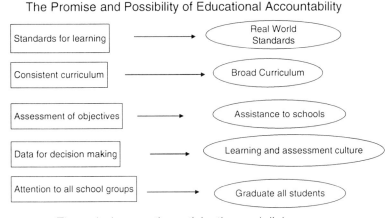

The Promise and Possibility of Educational Accountability

Standards for learning	→	Real World Standards
Consistent curriculum	→	Broad Curriculum
Assessment of objectives	→	Assistance to schools
Data for decision making	→	Learning and assessment culture
Attention to all school groups	→	Graduate all students

Through democratic participation and dialogue

Fig. 3.1 The promise and possibility of educational accountability

The use of standards can be likened to touring Europe in 3 days, creating a situation in which the traveler would be hard pressed to discuss anything about the countries visited.

The question not addressed is this: What do successful adults do? Performance-based assessments prior to graduation should examine students on the basis of what is expected from them as workers, citizens, and competent adults. Eisner (2001) described accountability as an effort to systematize, standardize, and "tidy up a messy system" (p. 367). Student outcomes may be specified with little debate, justification, or clarification of conflicts between them. Kohlberg and Mayer (1972) called this a "bag of virtues." Outcomes are not necessarily related to child development, and their worth is not given extensive consideration.

Eisner (2001) asked, "Can we widen what parents and others believe to be important in judging the quality of our schools?" (p. 372). A broad view of the goals of education would suggest that students should not only be able to read, write, and do mathematics, but they should be problem solvers, active citizens, speakers of two languages, artists, musicians, athletes, and people who reflect, listen, and speak with care (Slater 2005).

A balanced curriculum means that time will be allotted for a variety of studies related to what is important for life and work. Legislative efforts to restrict time spent in testing may be a necessary short-term step, but the overall system should be designed to encourage breadth and depth in the curriculum.

Keeping Students In

The most troubling unintended consequences of high-stakes testing have been the exclusion of some students from testing at the elementary level and the apparent increase in dropouts at the high school level. No one wants a system that is not open and fair. The fundamental purpose is to improve education for all and reduce or eliminate the achievement gap.

The most common approach to address the issue of students being pushed out in order to create favorable test results is to work to close the loop holes and strive for a system with incentives that do not have negative consequences. But as long as the tests carry high stakes that can determine whether a principal keeps a job or a school stays open, educators will be tempted to balance the scales to avoid punishment even if some students are pushed out. State education departments strive to stay one step ahead. Like the Internal Revenue Service, they constantly strive to find ways to prevent schools from cheating and getting around the intent of the system.

From Punishment to Assistance

Formative assessment and the use of rubrics in a developmental approach can help state school systems to move from punishment to assistance. Schools have difficulty making use of large-scale assessment data to improve achievement if the system is designed primarily for centralized accountability. Leithwood (2008) explained the importance of formative assessment of schools. Rather than just looking at inputs and outputs, formative assessment examines what is going on within the system. Teachers can look at the process through which students are learning. Students need to examine their own work. "Opportunities for pupils to express their under-standing should be designed into every piece of teaching, for this will initiate the interaction through which formative assessment aids learning" (Black and Dylan 1998, p. 143).

The classroom techniques of formative assessment include questioning with adequate wait time, grading with comments on what was done well and what needs improvement, opportunities for students to respond, peer assessment, and self-assessment (Black et al. 2004). These techniques might equally well be applied to schools. Too often test results are only used to rate schools as either adequate or inadequate. It would be more helpful to specify what needs improvement and to provide time for schools to respond.

Summative scores without formative comments can lead to an atmosphere of fear. A cornerstone of Deming's model of continuous improvement was to drive out fear (Dobyns and Crawford-Mason 1991). People can improve constantly and for-ever if they are given the freedom to set their own goals and are free of the threat of punishment.

Heldsinger (2008) advocated formative assessment through developmental rubrics for classroom use with students. Teachers carefully observe students from a developmental perspective. Then they involve students in the design of the rubric and make sure that they understand what is expected.

In the same way, teachers could engage in action research to develop school rubrics that correspond to stages of improvement. Expectations would be set for each stage, and results could be monitored for success. When accompanied by honest and thorough self-assessment, evaluation decisions can lead to significant change.

Development of a Learning and Assessment Culture

Shepard (2000) outlined a constructivist approach to classroom assessment that is consistent with the use of standards. However, she said that the standards movement has incorporated external testing with rewards and punishments that are hostile to thoughtful classroom assessment practices.

It is not enough to object to high-stakes testing. Schools need to rethink their assessment practices to move away from testing to meet others' requirements and ask, "Could we create a learning culture where students and teachers would have a shared expectation that finding out what makes sense and what doesn't is a joint and worthwhile project, essential to taking the next steps in learning?" (Shepard 2000, p. 10). This learning culture would respect the learner and include assessment that comes at the middle as well as the end of instruction. Teachers would engage in discussion to determine prior knowledge, and offer feedback that ignores insignificant errors, forestalls others, and only occasionally intervenes. Students would self-assess and, consistent with the standards approach, the criteria for learning would be transparent.

An Accountability Model

Almost every state has implemented top-down accountability. Nebraska is an exception. It has developed a distinctly different system of assessment called School-based, Teacher-led Assessment and Reporting (STARS; Gallagher 2007, 2008). Democratic deliberation and informed decisions in the hands of teachers are what make the system different. It starts on the school level. This way of thinking is different from teacher compliance. It runs counter to what has been called scientifically based research, not because it does not include experimentation and rigorous attention to data but because it is decentralized and provides a variety of context-based approaches. The state report card promotes "ratings," not "rankings." The data are not reduced to a single number.

STARS requires each district to adopt state standards or develop local standards that are equal to or exceed state standards. Each district then develops a plan for assessing their standards based primarily on locally developed criterion-referenced tests which were unique to that district.

The argument here is not that all states should adopt the Nebraska approach. Rather, along with efforts to implement accountability, there should be more attention to lessons learned, multiple perspectives, and democratic participation.

Democratic Participation

The best data will not yield decisions, nor will it automatically improve school performance. Decisions and improvement depend on human judgment. We cannot remove error, but we can make it less likely. One of the key ingredients is trust. Leithwood (2008) identified trust and collective teacher efficacy as key mediating variables of leadership. The principal has a major role in creating an atmosphere in which teachers can express opinions in an atmosphere of healthy debate. The principal, in turn, is part of a larger system that can either encourage or discourage open discussion.

With pressure to increase test scores quickly, there is a tendency to feel that there is no time for discussion. Debate and divergent views give way to a centrally determined approach. McNeil (2000) argued that accountability discourse is closed; only technical questions are permitted. Some educators may not know of any questions to ask because they only have experience of the current high-stakes testing.

What is not examined is the quality of conversation in the classroom, the faculty meeting, or the board meeting. Teachers can be isolated with little voice about what will be tested or how to go about making improvements based on data. Students may adopt an instrumental approach and only want to know what they need to do to earn a grade. Intellectual life, on the contrary, requires risk-taking, exploration, uncertainty, and speculation. An alternative to accountability would be a philosophy that emphasizes questions over outcomes, multiple perspectives rather than one right answer, connections across disciplines, applications to community life, cooperative work, and service learning.

Schön (1983) expressed this philosophy in terms of reflection in action, which he contrasted with technical rationality. He opposed the firmly bounded, scientific, and standardized approach of technical rationality and said, "It is striking that the dominant model of professional knowledge seems to its proponents to require very little justification" (p. 30). Those who follow the technical rational model are inattentive to data and questions that fall outside of their paradigm.

Reflection in action depends on the practice of teachers and what they know from their experience. It turns thought back on action and on the knowing which is implicit in action. Schön (1983) described teachers' tacit knowledge in this way:

> There are actions, recognitions, and judgments which we know how to carry out spontaneously; we do not have to think about them prior to or during their performance.
> We are often unaware of having learned to do these things; we simply find ourselves doing them. In some cases, we were once aware of the understandings which were subsequently internalized in our feeling for the stuff of action. In other cases, we may never have been aware of them. In both cases, however, we are usually unable to describe the knowing which our action reveals. (p. 54)

Conclusion: The Need for Dialogue

We have argued for discussion of standards that promote a broad curriculum and an accountability system that emphasizes assistance over punishment to encourage schools to keep students until they graduate. A developmental approach for schools in need of improvement, whole-school formative assessment, a school-wide learning and assessment culture, and democratic participation are some of the ways to address the unintended consequences of NCLB. Continued improvement will depend on dialogue at all levels of education.

Accountability has required discipline and focus. Educators adopted a common language of testing and accountability. Broader questions of purpose were suspended. Progress can come from new paradigms, but they can also restrict thinking and confine education to narrow possibilities. One paradigm cannot capture all truth. Counter perspectives are essential for continued understanding.

This paper has been a plea to consider what is not in the accountability paradigm. One way of thinking has come to dominate the field. We need multiple perspectives and dialogue. The quality of conversation is directly related to whether we will achieve worthwhile aims with students. If the accountability system requires blind adherence or, worse, if we fail to see other ways of setting and assessing goals, progress in education will be impeded.

Vigorous debate and critical discussion are essential to progress on all levels of education from the school house to the state house to Congress. We need those who will carry the banner of standards and accountability, and we need what Carl Glickman (2004) has called the loyal opposition to question and present alternatives.

References

Associated Press. (2003, May 8). *Bill would limit elementary testing days.* Retrieved October 16, 2004, from http://www.journalnow.com/servlet/Satellite?pagename=WSJ%2FMGArticle%2F WSJ_BasicArticle&c=MGArticle&cid=1031769526146

Black, P., & Dylan, W. (1998). Inside the black box: Raising standards through classroom assessment. *Phi Delta Kapan, 80*(2), 139–148.

Black, P., Harrison, C., Lee, C., Marshall, B., & Dylan, W. (2004). Working inside the black box: Assessment for learning in the classroom. *Phi Delta Kappan, 86*(1), 9–21.

Bush, G. W. (2002, January 8). *President signs landmark no child left behind education bill.* Retrieved May 22, 2008, from: http://www.whitehouse.gov/news/releases/2002/01/20020108-1.html

Center for Responsive Politics. (2009). *Centre for responsive politics.* Retrieved August 9, 2009, from http://www.opensecrets.org/

Commission on Presidential Debates. (2000, October 3). *Unofficial debate transcript.* Retrieved May 18, 2008, from http://www.debates.org/pages/trans2000a.html

Darling-Hammond, L. (1994). Performance-based assessment and educational equity. *Harvard Educational Review, 64*(1), 5–31.

Dobyns, L., & Crawford-Mason, C. (1991). *Quality or else.* New York: Houghton Mifflin.

ED.gov website http://www.ed.gov/nclb/overview/intro/4pillars.html

Education Austin. (2007). *Legislature's 10% cap could mean relief: Putting the lid on overtesting in AISD.* Retrieved August 9, 2009, from http://www.steamybowl.com/ea/legislatures10cap.pdf

Eisner, E. W. (2001). What does it mean to say a school is doing well? *Phi Delta Kappan, 82*(5), 367–372.

Epstein, N. (2004). *Who's in charge here? The tangled web of school governance and policy.* Denver, CO: Education Commission of the States.

Gallagher, C. W. (2007). *Reclaiming assessment: A better alternative to the accountability agenda.* Portsmouth, NH: Heinemann.

Gallagher, C. W. (2008). Democratic policy making and the arts of engagement. *Phi Delta Kappan,* *89*(5), 340–346.

Glasser, W. (1990). *The quality school: Managing students without coercion.* New York, NY: Harper & Row.

Glickman, C. (2004). *Letters to the next president: What we can do about the real crisis in public education.* New York: Teachers College Press.

Goals. (2000). *Educate America Act of 1994.* Retrieved August 27, 2011 from http://www2.ed. gov/legislation/GOALS2000/TheAct/index.html

Heilig, J. V., & Darling-Hammond, L. (2008). Accountability Texas-style: The progress and learning of urban minority students in a high-stakes testing context. *Educational Evaluation and Policy Analysis, 30*(2), 75–110.

Heldsinger, S. (2008). *Using a measurement paradigm to guide classroom assessment processes.* Presentation at the International Perspectives on Student Assessment Lecture Series, University of Calgary and University of Alberta, Canada.

Hilliard, A. G. (1991). Do we have the *will* to educate all children? *Educational Leadership, 49*(1), 31–36.

Hilliard, A. G. (1998). The standards movement: Quality control or decoy? *Rethinking Schools: An Urban Educational Journal Online, 12*(4).

Holland, R. (2000, June). *NAEP becoming an offer states can't refuse: 'Godfather' strategy usurps state sovereignty.* School Reform News: The Heartland Institute. Retrieved May 18, 2008, from http://www.heartland.org

Institute for Education Sciences. (2009). *National assessment of educational progress: The nations report card.* National Center for Educational Statistics, US Department of Education. Retrieved August 9, 2009, from http://nces.ed.gov/nationsreportcard/

Kohlberg, L., & Mayer, R. (1972). Development as the aim of education. *Harvard Educational Review, 42*(4), 449–496.

Kornhaber, M. (2004). Appropriate and inappropriate forms of testing, assessment, and account-ability. *Educational Policy, 18*(1), 45–70.

Ladson-Billings, G. (2006). The Education Debt. *Educational Researcher, 35*(7), 3–12.

Leithwood, K. (2008, February). *School leadership, evidence-based decision making and large-scale assessment.* Lecture at the International Perspectives on Student Assessment Lecture Series, University of Calgary.

McNeil, L. M. (2000). Creating new inequalities: Contradictions of reform. *Phi Delta Kappan, 81*(10), 729–734.

McNeil, L. M., Coppola, E., Radigan, J., & Vasquez Heilig, J. (2008). Avoidable losses: High-stakes accountability and the dropout crisis. *Education Policy Analysis Archives, 16*(3), 1–45.

National Commission on Excellence in Education. (1983). *A nation at risk: The imperative for education reform.* Washington, DC: Government Printing Office. Retrieved May 18, 2008, from http://www.ed.gov/pubs/NatAtRisk/index.html

Nelson, S., & McGhee, M. (2004). *Time off task: How test preparation is siphoning instructional time for students of color and students of poverty.* Paper session presented at the annual meeting of the University Council for Educational Administration, Kansas City, MO.

Nelson, S., McGhee, M., Meno, L., & Slater, C. L. (2007a). Fulfilling the promise of educational accountability: A unique perspective. *Phi Delta Kappan, 88*(9), 702–709.

Nelson, S., McGhee, M., Reardon, R., Gonzales, K., & Kent, C. (2007b). *Supplanting teaching with testing: Does it raise test scores?* Paper session presented at the annual meeting of the University Council for Educational Administration, Alexandria, VA.

Rothstein, R. (2004). *Class and schools: Using social, economic, and educational reform to close the black-white achievement gap.* New York: Teachers College Press.

Schön, D. A. (1983). *The reflective practitioner: How professionals think in action.* New York: Basic Books.

Shepard, L. A. (2000). The role of assessment in a learning culture. *Educational Researcher, 29*(7), 4–14.

Shepard, L., & Smith, M. L. (1986). Synthesis of research on school readiness and kindergarten retention. *Educational Leadership, 44*(3), 78–86.

Slater, C. L. (2005). What does it mean to be an educated person? *The School Administrator, 8*(62), 56.

Summary of Goals. (2000). *Educate America Act.* Retrieved August 27, 2011 from http://www.ncrel.org/sdrs/areas/issues/envrnmnt/stw/sw0goals.htm

Texas Education Agency. (1998, September 1, 1998). *Chapter 113. Texas essential knowledge and skills for social studies. Subchapter A. Elementary.* Retrieved August 9, 2009, from http://ritter.tea.state.tx.us/rules/tac/chapter113/ch113a.html#113.6

US Department of Education. (2009a). *No child left behind.* Retrieved August 9, 2009, from http://www.ed.gov/nclb/landing.jhtml

US Department of Education. (2009b). *Reading first.* Retrieved August 9, 2009, from http://www.ed.gov/programs/readingfirst/index.html

US Department of Education. (2009c). *Early reading first.* Retrieved August 9, 2009, from http://www.ed.gov/programs/earlyreading/index.html

US Department of Education. (2009d). *Title I – Improving the academic achievement of the disadvantaged.* Retrieved August 9, 2009, from http://www.ed.gov/policy/elsec/leg/esea02/pg1.html

Valenzuela, A. (1999). *Subtractive schooling: U.S. Mexican youth and the politics of caring.* Albany, NY: State University of New York Press.

Waite, D., Boone, M., & McGhee, M. (2001). Last volley in the culture wars? A critical sociocultural view of accountability. *Journal of School Leadership, 11*(3), 182–203.

Chapter 4
Student Assessment Policy and Practice in Alberta: An Assessment for Learning

Jim Brandon and Marsi Quarin-Wright

Introduction

This chapter examines student assessment policy and practice within the context of the 2009 *Alberta Student Assessment Study* (ASAS) (Webber et al. 2009). At a time of unprecedented interest in student assessment, we explore the degree to which educational policy and practice in the Canadian province of Alberta reflect the best available research evidence in each of the ASAS's four focus areas: (1) quality teaching, (2) educational leadership, (3) professional learning, and (4) education policy. From our perspectives as practice-based researchers, we aim to gage aspects of contemporary assessment policy and practice through an *assessment for learning* approach for the purpose of enhancing educational policy and practice.

The chapter is divided into four parts. A general overview of our foundational assumptions is followed by an explanation of the nine research-informed standards featured in our conceptual framework. These standards are then used in two *formative assessments*. We first look at assessment practice before applying the standards to selected Alberta provincial policies. Discussion and implications are framed by the four major goals of the ASAS:

1. Define optimal assessment theory and practice relative to:

    (a) Curricular learning outcomes and performance standards and reporting of levels of achievement within grade.

J. Brandon (✉)
University of Calgary
e-mail: jbrandon@ucalgwy.ca

M. Quarin-Wright
Foothills School Division, High River, AB, Canada
e-mail: quarin-wrightm@fsd38.ab.ca

C.F. Webber and J.L. Lupart (eds.), *Leading Student Assessment*,
Studies in Educational Leadership 15, DOI 10.1007/978-94-007-1727-5_4,
© Springer Science+Business Media B.V. 2012

(b) How external tests and classroom-based assessment of student achievement can be optimally used to inform decisions regarding student program needs and, when aggregated upwards, decisions at the school, jurisdiction, and provincial levels of decision-making relating to improving learning opportunities for students.

2. Describe how educational leadership can be strengthened to facilitate more effective classroom assessment and accurate and meaningful reporting of assessment information, including grade level of achievement, to parents and to Alberta Education.
3. Identify professional development models that are needed to build and enhance capacity in the area of classroom assessment (of, for, and as learning) in Alberta schools.
4. Consider the question, "where do we go from here" in developing a holistic framework for classroom assessment for the province and provide recommendations based on what is learned from the preceding questions and areas of inquiry. Our conclusion conveys four student assessment paradoxes in response to the ASAS Goal Four question: "where do we go from here in developing a holistic framework for classroom assessment for the province?" These paradoxes suggest ways in which educational policymakers and practitioners can begin to move past solidified perspectives and contested views to improve policy and practice.

Conceptual Framework

This section highlights the conceptual underpinnings and assumptions that guide this assessment for learning. Figure 4.1 is an idealized representation of relationships among educational research, policy, and practice. The outer circle indicates that (a) education research should inform both policy and practice, (b) research-informed policy should influence practice, and (c) the contextualized realities of educational practice should inform both research and policy. The pyramid within the

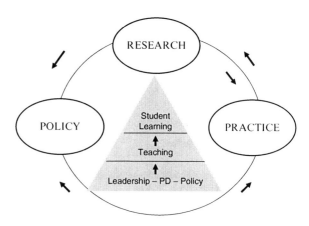

Fig. 4.1 Conceptual framework

Fig. 4.2 Assessments for
policy and practice learning

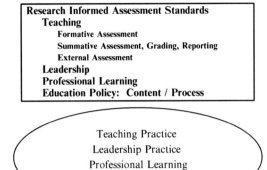

circle suggests ways in which policy, leadership, and professional learning indirectly impact student learning. Our assessment for learning approach is portrayed in Fig. 4.2. Areas in which research-informed standards have been developed are shown in the upper rectangle. The degree to which current practice and selected provincial policies reflect the best available evidence in selected areas of policy and practice is illustrated in the oval at the bottom.

Our conceptual framework models effective assessment practice. We first provide images of research-informed policy and practice. These images are then used as standards for our assessment for learning. The design parallels effective classroom assessment wherein clearly delineated learning targets or learner outcomes are the starting points for student assessment.

Assessment Standards

Effective assessment starts with a clear vision of what is to be assessed. As Stiggins and Chappuis (2005) make evident, "We can't dependably assess that which we have not defined" (p. 2). Each of the assessment standards presented in this section is designed to create a clear picture of evidence-based policy or practice that will subsequently be used in the assessment for learning sections below. We begin with the general theoretical stance that shapes the development and use of our standards. In separate subsections, we then move into descriptions of the standards and the evidence upon which each is based.

The advice of two scholars has been helpful in the formulation of our standards. Marzano advocated for "lean and mean standards that are specific and non-redundant" (as cited in Scherer 2001, p. 4). Darling-Hammond (1994) observed:

> Standards are useful only to the extent that teachers can use them to build their own knowledge and understanding of what helps students learn… it is the process of using a set of images about teaching and learning to deepen one's own understanding and that of the teachers and students with whom we work that makes standards useful in any way (p. 10).

Table 4.1 A research-informed image of quality teaching

Quality teaching as situated, collective expertise-in-action that
• Is contingent on the dynamic interplay of content, teacher, learner, and context
• Involves professional commitment to collegial practice and reflection over time
• Accesses scientific and artistic pedagogic tools in a fluent, seamless, holistic, and constantly evolving pattern of practice

Just as Darling-Hammond sees merit in "using a set of images… to deepen understanding" in teaching, it is our desire to use research-informed images to deepen our understanding of student assessment policy and practice.

Standard One: Quality Teaching as Situated, Collective Expertise-in-Action

In our view, any discussion of classroom assessment needs to understand assessment as an aspect of teaching. Our first assessment standard is expressed through the image of *quality teaching as situated, collective expertise-in-action*. This notion is based on our reading of leading authors in this field (i.e., Bennett and Rolheiser 2001; Danielson 1996; Darling-Hammond 1994, 1999, 2001; Darling-Hammond and Sclan 1992; Fullan 2003; Marzano et al. 2001; Organization for Economic Co-operation and Development 1994; Stigler and Hiebert 1999; Stronge 2002).

That quality teaching is situated in a given context is noted in several studies. Darling-Hammond and Sclan (1992) promoted conceptions of teaching as "informed judgment" rather than as "mastery of simple routines." Emphasis on the former takes "a reflective teaching orientation stimulated by attention to teachers' individual contexts and felt needs" rather than emphasizing the "production of specific teacher behaviors thought to represent effective teaching" (Darling-Hammond and Sclan 1992, p. 15) (Table 4.1).

The idea of *expertise-in-action* is a significant component of quality teaching. Fullan (2003) indicates that the future of teaching rests in the notion of "through informed professional judgment" (p. 7). Stronge (2002) supported this view of dynamic expertise and noted that the "teacher must have sufficient knowledge of content, of pedagogy, of context, and of students to appreciate the intricacies that are bound up in the teaching and learning process" (p. 63). Lieberman and Miller (1999) painted a picture of pedagogy that goes beyond a mere set of technical skills by constructing good teaching as "a complex array of values, knowledge, experience, intuition, and commitment to improve" (p. 63). Darling-Hammond (1994) noted that "teaching is intense activity, that it requires juggling of subject matter, cognitive goals, social goals; management of time, materials and equipment; and the needs and responses of individual students" (p. 18). These observations also underline the situated aspect of the standard.

Table 4.2 A research-informed image of formative assessment

Formative assessment as a key aspect of teaching and learning that provides students with clear pictures of progress and how to improve – during the learning process by
• Utilizing ongoing descriptive and encouraging feedback to support learning
• Fostering student involvement in, reflection on, and ownership of the learning process
• Providing feedback to inform instruction

The collective aspect of the standard's conception of quality teaching has only recently appeared in the literature. Bennett and Rolheiser (2001) call for extended professional learning leading to "collectively conscious instructional intelligence" or expert teacher "intuition informed by experience combined with the experience and research of others" (p. 46). Fullan (2003) advocated "collective deliberations focusing on continuous improvement" (p. 6). Similar research support for the fundamental importance of the collective improvement of teaching is found in the work of Elmore (2000, 2002, 2004), Marzano et al. (2001), and Stigler and Hiebert (1999).

The standard development approach employed is similar to the processes utilized by educational organizations, such as the Committee on Standards for Educational Evaluation (Sanders 1997). Our Standard One was first written in draft form based upon a review of applicable research (Brandon 2005). The standard was then provided to others for review, and alterations were made based upon the feedback received. Evolutionary refinements were made through reflection and consideration of new insights gleaned from ongoing reading in this content area. The same approach was used in the development of Standards Five, Eight, and Nine below.

Standard Two: Formative Assessment as Generative and Informative Teaching

Our second assessment standard is expressed through the image of *formative assessment as generative and informative teaching*. The image's first indicator underlines the importance of providing students with a clear picture of progress and how to improve during the learning process. Students need to know where they are in relation to where they are going in their learning. This is achieved through the teacher's skillful use of ongoing, descriptive, and encouraging feedback. In our conception, formative assessment is a key aspect of generative and informative teaching that fosters student involvement in, reflection on, and ownership of the learning process.

A strong body of research supports the concepts expressed through this standard. Black and Wiliam (1998), Chappuis and Chappuis (2007), Chappuis et al. (2005), Costa and Kallick (2004), Marzano (2006), and Tomlinson (2007) are among the chief works consulted in the construction of this image of formative assessment (Table 4.2).

Table 4.3 A research-informed image of summative assessment, grading, and reporting

Summative assessment, grading, and reporting that provide students and their parents with clear pictures of achievement in relation to learning outcomes in the Program of Studies or in an Individual Program Plan – at the end of a learning episode

- Provides consistent, accurate, and outcome-referenced descriptions of learning
- Based upon informed professional judgment using varied assessment tools to show best available evidence of learning
- Fosters student involvement in, reflection on, and ownership of the learning process

We first drafted the standard in early January of 2008 based upon our review of the assessment literature noted above. Early drafts were discussed and refined through conversation with several school-based leadership colleagues and with those in the Foothills School Division System Leadership Team. The standard later evolved into one of three components of a College of Alberta School Superintendents (CASS) position on Research-Informed Student Assessment. Minor adjustments were made in consultation with the CASS Provincial Executive in early April 2008. The three assessment standards were circulated to all 258 CASS members and were adopted by at the Annual General Meeting on April 25, 2008.

Standard Three: Summative Assessment, Grading, and Reporting as Consistent, Accurate, and Outcome – Referenced Descriptions of Learning

This third assessment standard is expressed through the image of *summative assessment, grading, and reporting as consistent, accurate, and outcome – referenced descriptions of learning.* Similar to the evidence on formative assessment, it is imperative to provide students and their parents with clear pictures of achievement in relation to learning outcomes in the Program of Studies or in an Individual Program Plan. In the case of summative assessment, the picture of achievement in relation to learning outcomes is communicated (by letter, symbol, number, or statement) at the end of a unit, term, or school year. Consistent and accurate professional judgments must be informed through the application of appropriate and varied assessment tools to show the best available evidence of learning. The literature supports focusing on what the student knows and is able to do in relation to clearly identified learning targets. Such an approach fosters student involvement in, reflection on, and ownership of the learning process (Table 4.3).

The educational literature and research vein upon which this standard is based is represented by the work of several authors (i.e., Davies 2000; Marzano 2006; O'Connor 2002, 2007; Reeves 2007). The standard drafting process for Standard Three was the same as for Standards Two and Four.

Table 4.4 A research-informed image of external assessment

*External assessments as complementary outcome – referenced descriptions of learning that
provide snapshots of achievement in relation to a significant portion of the outcomes of the
Program of Studies*
- Provide data over time to aid policymaking and curriculum development
- Provide data over time to be used in combination with classroom, school, and jurisdiction data
  to inform longer-term instructional, school, and system improvement planning
- One of many assessment tools to inform professional judgment in relation to summative
  assessment, grading, and reporting

Table 4.5 Percent of Program of Studies outcomes covered in provincial examinations

Course	Grade 3	Grade 6	Grade 9	Grade 12
English language arts	70	66	69	75
Social studies		74	83	
Social studies 30				75–80
Social studies 33				80–85
Mathematics	95	83	88	85–95
Science/sciences		70	73	65

Source: Alberta Education, Accountability and Reporting Division (November 2007)

Standard Four: External Assessment as Complementary Outcome – Referenced Descriptions of Learning

Our final assessment standard is expressed through the image of *external assessment as complimentary outcome – referenced descriptions of learning* (Table 4.4).
External assessments, such as the Alberta Diploma Examinations and the Provincial
Achievement Tests, provide snapshots of achievement in relation to a significant
portion of the outcomes in the Program of Studies (see Table 4.5). The image's first
indicator underlines that a primary benefit of external exam is to policymakers and
curriculum developers. Results over time provide data that are useful for policy
development and program review. A second value of external assessment is the
provision of data to inform longer-term instructional, school, and system improvement planning. The final descriptor calls for use of external assessment as one additional tool at the disposal of the teacher to inform professional judgment in relation
to summative assessment, grading, and reporting.

A number of authors were studied in the development of this standard (e.g.,
Davies 2000; Marzano 2006; O'Connor 2002, 2007; Reeves 2007). As in the drafting
of Standards Two and Three, this evidence-based image was adopted by CASS at its
Annual General Meeting on April 25, 2008, following considerable discussion at
the local and provincial levels.

Table 4.6 A research-informed image of professional learning

Professional learning as coherent, incremental capacity building that

- Expects and nurtures staff learning within a community of professional practice
- Integrates ongoing opportunities for reflection, professional dialogue, and continuous pedagogic learning in – or directly related to – the school setting
- Gradually improves student learning, increases teacher efficacy, and builds school capacity

Standard Five: Professional Learning as Coherent, Incremental Capacity Building

To examine the "professional development models that are needed to build and enhance capacity in the area of classroom assessment" as outlined in the fourth goal of the ASAS, we utilize the image of *professional learning as coherent, incremental capacity building*. Several works were instrumental in developing this standard (i.e., Elmore 2002; Fullan 2001a, b, 2003; Guskey 2000, 2003; Lieberman and Miller 1999; Richardson 2003; Sparks 2002; Stigler and Hiebert 1999) (Table 4.6).

One major idea in this image of research-informed professional learning is coherence. The standard's first indictor is that the learning of all staff and students is both expected and nurtured in the context of community of professional practice. Learning communities help in the development of coherence, as observed by Lieberman and Miller (1999), in that they are "organizational forms that provide for support and pressure" (p. 72). "Professional learning is most powerful," they further elaborated, "when it occurs as a result of one's being a member of a group of colleagues who struggle together to plan for a given group of students, replacing the traditional isolation of teachers from one to another" (p. 62). Fullan (2001a) called for program coherence to avoid "too many disconnected, episodic, piecemeal, superficially adorned projects" (p. 109).

Incremental staff learning is the second main component. Sparks (2002) indicated that "powerful forms of professional development engage teachers in the continuous improvement of their teaching" through "training, coaching, critical friends and other reflective processes" (pp. 10–14). Fullan (2001b) supported "learning in the setting where you work, or learning in context" because it has the "greatest payoff" (p. 126). Lieberman and Miller's (1999) *growth-in-practice* idea reflects the need to rebalance the content of teacher learning to include more of what they refer to as "'inside knowledge' – by teaching and picking up ideas from fellow teachers and trying them out in their classroom," what Schon (1987) called "an epistemology of practice that takes fuller account of the competence practitioners… display in situations of uncertainty, complexity, uniqueness, and conflict" (p. 63). Stigler and Hiebert (1999) came to a similar conclusion that improvement will be continual, gradual, and incremental because "teaching is a system deeply embedded in the surrounding culture of schools" (p. 132). Incremental staff learning is integrative and provides ongoing opportunities for teacher reflection, professional dialogue, and continuous pedagogic learning in – or directly related to – the school setting.

Table 4.7 A research-informed school leadership standard – the PQPG

The school principal is an accomplished teacher who provides quality leadership in the provision of optimum learning and development for all students in the school
1. Fostering effective relationships
2. Embodying visionary leadership
3. Leading a learning community
4. Providing instructional leadership
5. Developing and facilitating leadership
6. Managing school operations and resources
7. Understanding and responding to the larger societal context

The third key concept within this standard is capacity building. Fullan (2003) observed, "it takes capacity to build capacity" (p. 7). To Glickman et al. (2001), we must "return wisdom, power, and control to both individuals and the collective staff in order for them to become true professionals" (p. 56). Guskey's (2000) insight was that "change in teacher attitudes and beliefs occur only after teachers changed their practices and they begin to see the results of these changes in terms of student outcomes" (p. 68). Stigler and Hiebert (1999) made a similar point:

> Teaching is a system built from all elements of the local context: teacher, students, curriculum, and so on. Improving the system requires taking all of these elements into account... Teaching is unlikely to improve through researchers' developing innovations in one place and then prescribing them for everyone. Innovations can be spread around the country, but only by trying them out and adjusting them again and again as they encounter different kinds of classrooms (p. 133).

The final indicator ties staff learning to three key results: the gradual improvement of student learning, an increase in teacher efficacy, and enhanced school capacity. This standard was originated through the same approach described in the development of Standards One, Eight, and Nine (Brandon 2008).

Standard Six: Principal Quality Practice Guideline

The next standard used in our analysis is Alberta's *Principal Quality Practice Guideline* (PQPG). Table 4.7 presents the standard's seven leadership dimensions. The descriptors, which provide detailed expectations related to each leadership dimensions, are detailed in the complete document (Alberta Education 2008).

The PQPG development process was led by an active stakeholder advisory committee, which referred to the research-informed positions on the principalship developed by the Alberta School Boards Association, Alberta Teachers' Association, CASS, Interstate School Leaders Licensure Consortium, and Alberta Home and School Councils' Association. The committee, which began its work in the spring of 2005, found that the research literature and Alberta Education partners agreed that individuals designated as principals require a broad repertoire of competencies

Table 4.8 A research-informed system leadership standard – the CPS

The CASS member is an accomplished leader and teacher who ensures that each student is provided with the opportunity to achieve optimum learning

1. Visionary leadership
2. Instructional leadership
3. Human resource leadership
4. Ethical leadership
5. Effective relationships
6. Organizational leadership and management
7. External influences on education
8. Chief executive and chief education officer leadership

to successfully fulfill their complex and critical roles within the education system. A first draft of the practice standard was completed in early 2006.

In the fall of 2006, focus group meetings were held across the province to provide opportunities for sharing information and receiving feedback regarding the *draft Principal Quality Practice Standard*. Approximately 170 participants representing the various stakeholders were involved in the focus group meetings. Written feedback from the small groups and individual participants was submitted and has subsequently been compiled for the consideration of the Stakeholder Advisory Committee.

Standard Seven: College of Alberta School Superintendents Practice Standard

The *CASS Practice Standard* (CPS) is the second leadership standard used in our analysis. Table 4.8 presents the *standard* and its eight leadership dimensions. The descriptors, which provide detailed expectations related to each leadership dimension, are detailed in the complete document (College of Alberta School Superintendents 2008).

The CPS was designed through a process that mirrored the PQPG development process in a number of ways. A consultant and a stakeholder advisory committee developed a first draft early in the fall of 2007, following a review of research and consideration of standards developed in similar jurisdictions. The draft was then taken to the general membership in November of 2007, with changes coming back to the committee for consideration in early 2008.

The consultant then took this second draft to each of the five CASS zones for further discussion and refinement. Approximately 200 of the 250 CASS members contributed to its development. After a final meeting of the committee in the spring of 2008, the standard underwent a legal review that has led to small wording changes. The CPS was adopted at a Special General Meeting in November 2008.

Education policy content informed by
• Research
• Exemplary practice
• Policy learning

Table 4.9 A research-informed standard – quality education policy content

Standard Eight: Quality Education Policy Content

The basic premise of research-informed policy content is that quality education policy occurs when policymakers – through ongoing analysis of the social, political, and educational context – design and enact policy content based on the prevailing research consensus in each of the policy's major conceptual areas (Brandon 2005).

Is it reasonable to expect all important education policies to meet similar research-based tests in content areas where a scholarly consensus exists? It would be naïve to think that research would ever be the sole determinant of a government's policy agenda. However, it is reasonable, in our judgment, to expect that significant policy choices should, at the very least, be justified on the basis of recognized education research. In cases where policy choices are being made in the advance of an existing research consensus, policy impacts should be carefully studied from the early stages of implementation. To the greatest extent possible, the content of significant education policy should be founded on current research. In policy content areas where no clear research consensus exists, policy impacts should be carefully studied from the early stages to enable research-based refinements along the way (Table 4.9).

Policies based on research have increased chances of succeeding, as do those that are based on evidence of positive results in similar jurisdictions through policy learning or lesson-drawing (Bennett and Howlett 1992; Hall 1993; Howlett and Ramesh 1995; Rose 1993). As Rose (1993) noted, politicians learn from experience, whereas policy analysts more frequently take their lessons from formalized research sources (p. 19). An additional element supported by our research review is that effective policy designs should ensure that policies are well matched to their political context and that key values in the policy align with those prevalent in wider society.

Standard Nine: Quality Education Policy Process

Quality education policy occurs when policymakers – through ongoing analysis of the social, political, and educational context – design and enact research-based proposals through processes characterized by dialogic adoption and implementation as learning (Brandon 2005). Though policy development is a nuanced, iterative, and complex political undertaking, four stages often characterize quality education policy development: (a) informed design, (b) dialogic adoption, (c) implementation

Table 4.10 A research-informed standard – quality education policy process

Education policy development through

- Informed design *that*
  - Pursues modest goals with a real chance to improve student learning
  - Is based on research or evidence of positive results in similar settings
  - Is part of comprehensive and coherent plan
  - Matches proposals to political and social contexts
- Dialogic adoption *that*
  - Provides for public input and open debate through authentic consultation
  - Yields modified and improved proposals through consultation, collaboration, or partnering
- Implementation as learning *that*
  - Provides ongoing support and capacity building in the work setting
  - Is viewed as ongoing policy learning with opportunities for refinement based on experiences in the field
- Meaningful outcomes *that*
  - Are clearly and coherently explained in the design phase
  - Are framed so that the benefits to students are clearly evident

as learning, and (d) meaningful outcomes. These four phases coincide closely with the four stages in Levin's (2001) policy process model. Among others, the following eight studies have significantly influenced the thinking that yielded this policy process standard: Earl et al. (2002), Elmore (2000, 2002, 2004), Fullan (2001a), Hightower (2002), Leithwood et al. (2002), Levin (2001), Levin and Wiens (2003), and Wilson et al. (2001). Each of the phases is now briefly explained.

The informed design research consulted suggests that policy reform is more likely to achieve its intentions when goals are clearly focused on those things that are likely to yield desirable student outcomes. By focusing energy and resources on achievable targets, policymakers demonstrate thoughtful stewardship of available resources. Attention to design clarity enhances opportunities for practitioners to develop understanding and ownership as they translate the policy into action (Leithwood et al. 2002, p. 9).

Dialogic adoption calls for adoption strategies that provide opportunities for public input and open debate through authentic consultation processes. Quality policy processes should actually yield modified and improved proposals through stakeholder consultation and collaboration. Several of the studies consulted noted that governments are becoming more aware of the benefits of public debate and the incorporation of a variety of voices in the policy process. An open, inclusive approach to policy adoption can build legitimacy for the proposal. As Hightower (2002) observed, "building support for the change is crucial, in a politically volatile situation, as is building professional support" (p. 23) (Table 4.10).

The standard's *implementation as learning* notion indicates that an effective implementation plan should provide ongoing support and capacity building for those who are expected to translate policy intentions into practice. A learning orientation to implementation taps into educator motivation and heightens efficacy. Another indicator of effective implementation is that the process of implementation itself is used as a basis for ongoing policy learning. Refinements to practice are made in the field based on the actual implementation experiences of educators.

A substantive research base supports these ideas about implementation. Fullan (2001b) described a "recent remarkable convergence of theories, knowledge bases, ideas, and strategies that help us confront complex problems… a new mind-set – a framework for thinking about and leading complex change more powerfully than ever before" (p. 3). Capacity building implementation strategies are founded on the understanding that policymakers must pay more attention to the perspectives of those in the field. In the end, it is the "street-level" commitment and actions of school-based educators that determine the success or failure of policy initiatives (Lipsky 1980).

The standard's conception of *meaningful outcomes* asserts that in the final analysis, educational policy changes should be judged on the student learning outcomes they generate. It is, however, very difficult to precisely determine effects of any individual policy, whether considering student outcomes, education system outcomes, or social outcomes. What seems to be significant in the outcome phase is the notion that greater clarity and coherence can be developed when meaningful outcomes are spelled out in the design phase. Also worth noting in this short treatment of the construct of meaningful outcomes is this recurring finding: Educators will be more willing to translate policy into practice when they believe that the policy will make a positive difference for students (Earl et al. 2002; Elmore 2000, 2002, 2004; Fullan 2001a; Hightower 2002; Leithwood et al. 2002; Levin 2001; Levin and Wiens 2003).

Assessments for Learning – Improving Teaching, Leading, and Professional Learning

The research-informed assessment standards presented in section "Assessment standards" were designed to create clear pictures of quality student assessment policy or practice. These standards will be used in sections "Assessments for learning – Improving teaching, leading, and professional learning" and "Assessments for learning – Improving provincial education policy" to reflect upon the state of student assessment practice and to analyze selected policies, standards, and professional development structures in the Canadian province of Alberta – our assessments for policy and practice learning.

In each case, elements of the formative assessment method we utilized are explained first. Next, a summary table conveying our assessment is presented. Explanatory remarks related to the assessment are then provided to conclude each subsection. The first four assessments are designed to provide information to enhance efforts to develop research-informed teaching and leadership practice in the case of Representative School Division (RSD). Assessment Five analyzes three

Alberta professional learning structures within the context of RSD. The same subsection assesses two additional professional development institutions from an overall provincial perspective.

Our assessments are not meant to be definitively defensible assessments for policy and practice learning. Rather, they represent attempts to nest our reflections on current policy and practice within a conceptual framework that links to what we know about quality assessment. Our analyses of practice in RSD are qualitative judgments based upon observations and conversations over a 6-month period in 2008. As these data were translated onto assessment tables to communicate descriptions of performance, the initial assessments were reviewed and verified by two separate groups of educational leaders. A group of six school administrators provided initial feedback to adjust our assessments. Additional refinements were then made through conversation with the nine members of the RSD's System Leadership Team. Our views were further influenced by the writing of three members of the System Leadership Team, who recently reported on several aspects of RSD administrator and teacher growth in evidence-based assessment practice.

Representative School Division is a medium-size suburban school system. It serves approximately 7,000 students, with a teaching staff of nearly 400 in 25 schools (including 7 that may be classified as alternative schools). The system does quite well on measurable provincial outcomes, with recently documented strengths in high school achievement, staff learning, provision of a safe and caring environment, and offering students a strong and broad program of studies. A three-pronged approach to capacity building seems to be serving the district well: (a) persistent attention to shared instructional leadership, (b) a learning community emphasis through the Alberta Initiative of School Improvement (AISI), and (c) ongoing implementation of a district-wide learning coaching program. Learning more about research-informed student assessment has been a focus for the district through these means for the past 2 years.

Assessment One: Quality Teaching as Situated, Collective Expertise-in-Action

This subsection's two assessments for learning reflect on current teaching and leadership practice in RSD in relation to our research-informed standard of *quality teaching as situated, collective expertise-in-action.* Our descriptive feedback utilizes the same three-point scale used in teacher and administrator evaluations in the province. Practice is described as exceeding, meeting, or not meeting the descriptor's expectations. Reflections are based to a large extent on our general observations and self-assessing conversations with school and system administrators. Additional insights were provided through reflecting on 24 administrative evaluations and over 100 teacher evaluations written or reviewed over the past 4 years.

We believe that Table 4.11 presents a clear picture of pedagogic and leadership progress in relation to the standard of quality teaching as situated, collective

Table 4.11 Assessment One

Evidence of quality teaching in representative school division	Teaching practice	Leadership support
Quality teaching as situated, collective expertise-in-action that		
• Is contingent on the dynamic interplay of content, teacher, learner, and context	+	+
• Involves professional commitment to collegial practice and reflection over time	=	+
• Accesses scientific and artistic pedagogic tools in a fluent, seamless, holistic, and constantly evolving pattern of practice.	=	=

Scale: + exceeding; = meeting; – not meeting

expertise-in-action. RSD teachers and administrators exceed the expectations expressed through the first indicator: Quality teaching is contingent on the dynamic interplay of content, teacher, learner, and context. Observed teachers demonstrated strengths in adjusting outcome-focused teaching in response to the unique needs of their learners within the distinct contexts of their schools. Evaluations written by administrators and conversations related to classroom visits with school administrators indicate that school leaders understand the descriptor and possess the necessary supervisory skill set.

Teachers and school administrators meet the expectations expressed in the other two descriptors. In the case of *professional commitment to collegial practice and reflection over time*, our analysis suggests that leaders have a strong understanding and appreciation of the impact of working through a learning community approach. Many representative leaders have focused on this area of growth through their professional learning plans over the past few years. Teachers, particularly those who have engaged in AISI shared leadership work or have served as learning coaches, are demonstrating increasing strength and commitment to this approach to collective practice. Both groups of professionals intuitively understand and demonstrate a fluent, seamless, holistic, and constantly evolving pattern of practice. We see evidence of movement toward more fully articulated conceptualization of both scientific and artistic pedagogic tools in both cases.

Assessment Two: Formative Assessment as Generative and Informative Teaching

Our second assessment considers teaching and administrative practice in relation to the image of *formative assessment as generative and informative teaching*. The descriptive feedback summarized in Table 4.12 utilizes a four-point scale common to many assessment rubrics. Practice is described along a continuum: exemplary, skilled,

Table 4.12 Assessment Two

Evidence of research-informed formative assessment in representative school division	Teaching practice	Leadership support
Formative assessment as a key aspect of teaching and learning that provides students with clear pictures of progress and how to improve – during the learning process by		
• Utilizing ongoing descriptive and encouraging feedback to support learning	D	S
• Fostering student involvement in, reflection on, and ownership of the learning process	D	D
• Providing feedback to inform instruction	D	S

Scale: *E* exemplary; *S* skilled; *D* developing; *P* partial

developing, and partial. Judgments in this case are based on our general observations along with conversations with teachers, school, and system administrators.

Evidence indicates that the provision of research-based professional development opportunities to school administrators has increased the understanding and use of formative assessment in RSD schools. In particular, administrators have shown a skilled level in using feedback to encourage learning and providing feedback to inform instructional practice and are providing professional development opportunities to staff in this area. Further support is evident through the work of well-trained learning coaches and the use of external educational consultants. Several principals have taken staff members to national and international conferences to deepen and expand teacher understanding.

The Division should continue to develop administrator and teacher understanding and skill in the area of fostering student involvement in, reflection on, and ownership of the learning process. Continued professional learning about the value of student ownership of learning is advised.

Assessment Three: Summative Assessment, Grading, and Reporting as Consistent and Accurate Outcome – Referenced Descriptions of Learning

The image of *summative assessment, grading, and reporting as consistent, accurate outcome – referenced descriptions of learning* guides this third assessment. The assessments of RSD teaching and administrative practice summarized in Table 4.13 use the same four-point scale used in Assessment Three. Comments on practices in comparison to the standard are again based on general observations along with conversations with teachers, school, and system administrators.

Representative School Division has engaged administrators and teachers in professional learning about how to best inform students and their parents with a clear picture of achievement in relation to the learning outcomes or individual program

Table 4.13 Assessment Three

Evidence of research-informed summative assessment, grading, and reporting in representative school division	Teaching practice	Leadership support
Summative assessment, grading, and reporting that provide students and their parents with clear pictures of achievement in relation to learning outcomes in the Program of Studies or in an Individual Program Plan – at the end of a learning episode		
• Provides consistent, accurate, and outcome-referenced descriptions of learning	D	S
• Based upon informed professional judgment using varied assessment tools to show best available evidence of learning	D	S
• Fosters student involvement in, reflection on, and ownership of the learning process	D	S

Scale: *E* exemplary; *S* skilled; *D* developing; *P* partial

plan at the end of a learning episode. This has helped to improve summative assessment practices. Evidence indicates tighter alignment with the Program of Studies and increasingly clear communication with parents and students about what is being taught and evaluated.

Assessment Four: External Assessment as Complementary Outcome – Referenced Descriptions of Learning

Two different groups are the objects of this subsection's assessments for learning. We reflect on current provincial and system leadership practice in relation to our research-informed standard of *external assessment as complementary outcome – referenced descriptions of learning*. Our descriptive feedback utilizes the same four-point scale used in Assessments Two and Three. Judgments are based primarily on our observations and conversations with system educational leaders and Alberta Education management personnel in a variety of settings over an extended period.

A high degree of skilled knowledge and practice is evident in senior educational leadership ranks across the province. There is widespread appreciation that external assessments, such as the Alberta Diploma Examinations and the Provincial Achievement Tests, provide snapshots of achievement in relation to a significant portion of the outcomes in the Program of Studies (see Table 4.5). Both system education leaders and ministry managers work from strong operational understanding of the image's first indicator. There is agreement that the primary benefit of external exams is to policymakers and curriculum developers. Results over time provide data that are useful for policy development and program review. Another agreed upon value of external assessment is in the provision of data that inform longer-term instructional, school, and system improvement planning when used in

Table 4.14 Assessment Four

Evidence of research-informed external assessment	System leaders	Alberta education
External assessments as complementary outcome – referenced descriptions of learning that provide snapshots of achievement in relation to a significant portion of the outcomes of the Program of Studies		
• Provide data over time to aid policymaking and curriculum development	S	S
• Provide data over time to be used in combination with classroom, school, and jurisdiction data to inform longer-term instructional, school, and system improvement planning	S	S
• One of many assessment tools to inform professional judgment in relation to summative assessment, grading, and reporting	S	S

Scale: *E* exemplary; *S* skilled; *D* developing; *P* partial

combination with classroom, school, and jurisdiction data. While both groups understand this, the government position does seem to emphasize the external exam result in itself as the "gold standard" when determining how well a school or jurisdiction is doing in a particular area (Table 4.14).

On the final descriptor, both groups recognize and are beginning to reap the benefits of using external assessment as one additional tool at the disposal of the teacher to inform professional judgment in relation to summative assessment, grading, and reporting. If we are indeed "on the threshold of an exciting new educational context" (Brandon 2008, p. 9), then the climate may be ripe for more open dialogue about what the provincial examinations can and cannot offer in the way of student assessment insights. Productive results are more likely if all parties steer clear of rigidly entrenched ideological or organizational positions.

Assessment Five: Professional Learning as Coherent, Incremental Capacity Building

Our fifth assessment focuses on the third goal of ASAS: "to identify professional development models to build capacity in assessment (of, for, and as) learning." The evidence indicates that this aim can be achieved by optimizing current structures. Individual professional growth planning, AISI learning community work, and school-based professional development in RSD stand up well in terms of the expectations of the research-informed standard of *teacher growth as coherent, incremental capacity building*. The descriptive feedback summarized in Table 4.15 utilizes another four-point scale common to many assessment rubrics. Practice is described along a frequency continuum: consistently, usually, occasionally, and seldom.

Table 4.15 Assessment Five

Evidence of research-informed professional learning	IPGP	SBPD	AISI	AAC	RPDC
Teacher growth as coherent, incremental capacity building that					
• Expects and nurtures staff learning within a community of professional practice	4	4	4	3	3
• Integrates ongoing opportunities for reflection, professional dialogue, and continuous pedagogic learning in – or directly related to – the school setting	3	4	4	2	2
• Gradually improves student learning, increases teacher efficacy, and builds school capacity	3	3	3	3	3

Note: Scale = consistently (*4*); usually (*3*); occasionally (*2*); and seldom (*1*)
IPGP Individual Professional Growth Plan; *SBPD* school-based professional development; *AISI* Alberta Initiative for School Improvement; *AAC* Alberta Assessment Consortium; *RPDC* Regional Professional Development Consortium

Professional growth blossoms when there is coherent support for educator learning at all levels: individual, school, district, and region/province. In RSD, professional learning opportunities are provided in frequent increments. At least 1 day a month is dedicated to professional development for staff at the school or district level. Staff members also have the opportunity to learn through their Individual Professional Growth Plans, where each staff member is expected to choose a topic, learn from it, and apply it to his or her professional practice. These are expected to align with school or divisional objectives. Success is based on a combination of the willingness of the staff member to engage in this process and administrator skill in engagement through reflective dialogue. School-based professional development generally follows the school's self-identified AISI plan. School-based professional development sessions vary from administrator or teacher leader presentations of research-informed practice to the use of guest speakers or more focused staff work in professional learning communities.

District-wide initiatives on assessment are provided to administrators and teachers on an ongoing basis. Administrators and learning coaches facilitate many additional staff learning opportunities in the area of student assessment. Educators in the district also connect with regional or provincial professional development activities to scaffold individual, school, or division professional learning. Specifically, the district provides support for a team of teachers to work with the Alberta Assessment Consortium to become assessment specialists. A relationship with the Regional Professional Development Consortium is fostered so that teachers may attend Regional Professional Development Consortium–offered courses that align with personal, school, or divisional professional learning.

Each approach to professional development has the potential to engage educators in reflection and ongoing improvement of assessment practice. Research suggests that locally provided professional development has a greater impact on teaching practice.

At the same time, both consortia offer quality experiences from a distance. Hence, the consortia receive a lower assessment on Table 4.15. Distant opportunities do not as easily lend themselves to integrating deep reflection, professional dialogue, and continuous pedagogic learning.

Assessments for Learning – Improving Provincial Education Policy

While Assessments Six and Seven focus on the third ASAS goal (strengthening leadership), our analysis also sheds light on Goal Four (policy recommendations). In this subsection and the next three, our reflections are based upon our observations, document analysis, related literature, and conversations with key provincial leaders. The scales used in these assessments mirror the scales used in Alberta Education's color-coded *Accountability Pillar Report.*

Assessment Six: Policy Content – Leadership Quality Standards

A quick glance at Table 4.16 makes it clear that both the draft *Principal Quality Practice Standard* and the draft *CASS Practice Standard* fare well as research-based policy positions. When each is reviewed for its content in relation to our four teaching-related standards, they do well. The excellence that we awarded to the PQPG and the CPS in relation to our evidence-based image of quality teaching starts from the fact that in each case, the standard statement calls for the leader to be "an accomplished teacher" who focuses leadership efforts on providing all students with optimum learning opportunities. In each case, leaders are guided by leadership dimensions, such as instructional leadership, effective relationships, visionary leadership, leading a learning community, and external influences on education. Within these dimensions are numerous descriptors that underline the importance of understanding and demonstrating quality teaching in the two leadership roles.

Neither leadership standard rates excellence in any of the other four assessment content areas. They both rate *good* for the reflection of research-informed content with respect to our images of formative, summative, and external assessment. Each draft standard acknowledges the importance of assessment. The PQPG requires principals to "ensure that student assessment and evaluation practices throughout the school are fair, appropriate and balanced" (Alberta Education 2008, p. 6). The CPS goes a little further in expecting that:

- CASS members ensure alignment of teaching and student assessment with the provincial curriculum.
- Student learning is assessed, evaluated, and reported using a fair, appropriate, and balanced program of multiple indicators and sources of evidence.
- Student assessment is used to shape and inform instruction (CASS 2008, p. 2).

Table 4.16 Assessment Six

Evidence of quality policy content	Principal quality practice standard	CASS practice standard
Content informed by research on		
• Quality teaching	E	E
• Formative assessment	G	G
• Summative assessment	G	G
• External assessment	G	G

Scale: *E* excellent; *G* good; *A* acceptable; *I* issue; *C* concern

That the PQPG and CPS provide strong conceptual starting points for addressing the ASAS goal of strengthening educational leadership at the system and school levels to enhance classroom assessment practice is already well recognized across Alberta. Provincial and regional educational organizations (e.g., CASS, the Alberta Teachers' Association, the Centre for Leadership in Learning), Alberta universities, and several school jurisdictions are already using the seven PQPG leadership dimensions as the learning outcome framework for their leadership development or graduate programs in educational administration. At the district level, there is a growing number of systems that are employing variations of the PQPG to anchor their administrative growth, supervision, and evaluation programs. CASS plans to use the CPS to build a system of modules as requirements for professional certification.

Assessment Seven: Policy Process – Leadership Quality Standards

As models of quality policy development, the draft PQPG and draft CPS can also provide insights in support of the fourth ASAS goal that focuses on the development of a holistic policy framework for classroom assessment for the province. Both leadership standards were developed through processes described in Assessment Standards Six and Seven (section "Assessment standards"). Table 4.17 communicates our very positive assessment of these policy development processes used to generate each standard. They are good examples of what can happen when policy-makers design and enact evidence-based proposals through processes characterized by dialogic adoption and implementation as learning. Our color-coded assessments reveal excellent processes across the board in both cases.

Assessment Eight: Policy Content – Selected Alberta Education Policies

Attention now turns to the ASAS mandate to develop policy recommendations to shape classroom assessment in the province. Observations, document analysis, related studies, and conversations with key provincial leaders are used to examine

Table 4.17 Assessment Seven

Evidence of quality policy process	Principal quality practice standard	CASS practice standard
Policy development through informed design		
• Modest goals focused on student learning	E	E
• Based on research or results in similar settings	E	E
• Is part of comprehensive and coherent plan	E	E
• Matches political and social contexts	E	E
Dialogic adoption		
• Public input, open debate, and authentic consultation	E	E
• Modified and improved proposals through consultation processes	E	E
Implementation as learning		
• Provides ongoing support and capacity building		
• Viewed as ongoing policy learning with field-based refinements		
Meaningful outcomes		
• Clearly and coherently explained in design phase	E	E
• Framed so that benefits to students are clearly evident	E	E

Scale: *E* excellent; *G* good; *A* acceptable; *I* issue; *C* concern

Table 4.18 Assessment Eight

Evidence of quality policy content	TQS 2006	GLA	CAA	PAT	PDE	Preliminary 6/9 PAT Reporting
Research-informed content						
• Formative assessment	G		A			
• Summative assessment	G	G	A	G	G	C
• External assessment	E		A	G	E	E	C

Scale: *E* excellent; *G* good; *A* acceptable; *I* issue; *C* concern; *CAA* Computer-Adapted Assessment Program; *PDE* Provincial Diploma Examination

six existing provincial policy positions. Our assessments in relation to the research-informed standard for quality policy content are portrayed in Table 4.18 through the government's Accountability Pillar Reporting color scheme. Comments on each of the policies follow.

Our assessments of the content of five of the six policies are quite favorable. The 2006 supplement to the *Teaching Quality Standard* (Alberta Education 1997) titled *Effective Student Assessment and Evaluation in the Classroom* (TQS 2006) is research-based and compares favorably to all three of our assessment standards. Similarly, the idea of *Grade Level of Achievement* (GLA) initiative is well founded on the summative evaluation research. Claims to support the reporting of GLA to the province are not as well supported. Evidence to support the content of two yearly provincial examinations as good summative assessments and excellent examples of external assessments is well founded.

Though we see the promise of the Computer Adaptive Assessment program, its content is strongest in the realm of external and summative assessment at this point in its development. While the potential to support teacher judgments in the area of formative assessment is recognized, we rate it as *acceptable* at this time. We find that Alberta Education's requirement for Preliminary Reporting of multiple choice portions of the grades 6 and 9 Provincial Achievement Test (PRPAT) results directly to parents for the first time at the end of the current year is not supported by the research. In fact, the PRPAT initiative has the potential to further undermine teacher support for the PAT program, in our view.

Assessment Nine: Policy Process – Selected Alberta Education Policies

Analysis of the six selected policies in relation to our quality policy process standard is presented in Table 4.19. A mixed picture of Alberta provincial policymaking emerges. From a positive viewpoint, there is strong evidence of excellent policymaking in each of the four development components: informed design, dialogic adoption, implementation as learning, and meaningful outcomes. On the other hand, the evidence reveals issues and concerns that should spur reflection and policy learning on the part of Alberta Education. Discussion of policy processes is now presented in relation to the four policy development phases.

Three of the selected policies provide examples of excellent policy development through informed design. The 2006 supplement to the *Teaching Quality Standard* (Alberta Education 1997) titled *Effective Student Assessment and Evaluation in the Classroom* (TQS 2006) and two provincial examination programs have modest goals that focus on student learning, are research-based, and are part of a coherent plan that fits the provincial education context to a large measure. These are excellent examples of informed design.

While the GLA is founded on summative assessment research, there is little evidence to support the requirement of schools to report of GLA to the province. The fact that this initiative has been such a political hot-button issue is attributable to the perception that it is part of a larger unwelcome program that could provide one more point of exposure for schools and districts through expanded Accountability Pillar Reporting. Though the GLA remains a highly contested policy, it may be that it was "a little too far ahead of the curve" for the context into which it was introduced. It may yet endure as a heroic first step toward heralding the virtues of teacher judgment as the new "gold standard" in student assessment.

Table 4.19 Assessment Nine

Evidence of quality policy process	TQS	GLA	CAA	PAT	PDE	Preliminary 6/9 PAT reporting
Policy development through:						
Informed design						
• Modest goals focused on student learning	E	G	I	E	E	C
• Based on research or results in similar settings	E	A	A	E	E	C
• Is part of comprehensive and coherent plan	E	A	I	E	E	C
• Matches political and social contexts	E	I	I	E	E	C
Dialogic adoption						
• Public input, open debate, and authentic consultation	A	I	I	E	E	C
• Modified and improved proposals through consultation processes	A	A	I	E	E	C
Implementation as learning						
• Provides ongoing support and capacity building	I	E	A	G	G	C
• Viewed as ongoing policy learning with refinement based on field experiences	I	E	A	G	G	C
Meaningful outcomes						
• Clearly and coherently explained in design phase	E	A	A	A	A	C
• Framed so that benefits to students are clearly evident	E	A	A	A	A	C

Scale: *E* excellent; *G* good; *A* acceptable; *I* issue; *C* concern

Quite good examples of dialogic adoption and implementation as learning can be found in processes historically used to develop and implement provincial examinations. Considerable stakeholder consultation has characterized the development of these examinations over the years. Refinements have been made to their content and administration based on field experiences. TQS 2006 provides a good policy example of developmental processes that clearly and coherently explain the meaningful outcome in the design phase and that are framed so that the benefits to student learning are clearly evident.

The jury is still out on the design of the Computer Adaptive Assessment program. It may well end up having very positive impacts on student learning, but the large amount of government money assigned to the project at a time of resource scarcity and the outsourcing of the project to private corporate interests have undermined stakeholder support for the goals of the project.

The Preliminary Reporting of multiple choice portions of the grades 6 and 9 PATs is a good example of how not to develop provincial policy. This hastily implemented and little discussed initiative has the potential to undermine public confidence in teacher assessment. It is an example of a policy that runs strongly against both the policy content and policy process research. This initiative needs to be withdrawn as soon as possible.

Improving Student Assessment in Alberta – Paradoxes for Progress

The assessments for learning presented in this chapter are intended to generate further reflection, dialogue, and inquiry to spur continuing progress in student assessment policy and practice in Alberta. We now focus on the larger question posed in ASAS Goal Four, "where do we go from here in developing a holistic framework for classroom assessment for the province?" Four paradoxes arise from our analysis. As Deal and Peterson (1994) explained, each paradox represents "a seemingly contradictory situation or statement that runs counter to common sense and yet appears to be true" (p. 41). The four paradoxes are "to be embraced and creatively addressed, not to be seen as an either-or choice" (Deal and Peterson 1994, p. 9). In our view, the way forward is not a simple linear path. Rather, the pathway to further progress is through embracing the nuanced complexity of evidence-informed policy and practice.

Paradox One: While formative assessment has tremendous promise for improving student learning and is enthusiastically embraced by classroom teachers, summative assessment, grading, and reporting must be given equal attention in improving student assessment practice.

Research-informed assessment is not an either-or proposition. We need to ensure that students and their parents receive accurate and consistent descriptions of progress in relation to provincial or individual program plan outcomes. The challenge is how to do this in such a way that student confidence and ownership of learning developed through quality formative assessment are not undermined.

Paradox Two: There is considerable research evidence to inform classroom assessment practice. It is important to use such evidence to help educators to develop informed professional judgment rather than to impose informed prescriptions to govern practice.

There is an underlying misconception whereby professional development should be based on having practical ideas that can be used in the classroom as soon as possible. This notion must be challenged. It is important for teachers to understand the research behind good practice and to strive for deeper understanding. It is only when teachers fully embrace the "why" of good practice that truly professional teaching will become widespread.

Paradox Three: There are legitimate concerns about the misuses of external assessment; nevertheless, external assessments are a necessary mechanism for building confidence in the provincial school system.

Alberta students perform well on provincial, national, and international assessments. And public confidence in the Alberta education system is quite high despite legitimate educator concerns about media-reported competitive ranking of schools by a neoconservative political organization. Alberta Education should continue to participate in and report on large-scale assessments while following the lead of the Ontario government in negotiating media agreements to lessen the public profile given to the misuses of external assessment results.

Paradox Four: Alberta Education and key provincial stakeholders hold sharply divergent views on approaches to student assessment. In order to sustain momentum in improving student assessment in the province, movement toward a greater consensus is necessary.

The ASAS is providing an exemplary public forum through which a new provincial consensus direction for student assessment is possible. Forward progress is contingent upon Alberta Education, the Alberta Teachers Association, and other stakeholder groups striving for common ground through the dispassionate consideration of the best available evidence. All parties must engage in solution-focused dialogue to capitalize on the opportunities presented at this time.

References

Alberta Education. (1997). *Ministerial order (#016/97) teaching quality standard applicable to the provision of basic education in Alberta*. Edmonton, AB: Alberta Government.

Alberta Education. (2007). *Presentation to the Program Standards and Accountability Stakeholder Advisory Committee*. November 2007, Edmonton, AB.

Alberta Education. (2008). *Draft principal quality practice: Successful school leadership in Alberta*. Edmonton, AB: Alberta Government.

Bennett, B., & Rolheiser, C. (2001). *Beyond Monet: The artful science of instructional integration*. Toronto, ON: Bookation.

Bennett, C., & Howlett, M. (1992). The lessons of learning: Reconciling theories of policy learning and policy change. *Policy Sciences, 25*(3), 275–294.

Black, P., & Wiliam, D. (1998). Inside the black box: Raising standards through classroom assessment. *Phi Delta Kappan, 80*, 139–148.

Brandon, J. (2005). *A standards-based assessment of Alberta's teacher growth, supervision and evaluation policy*. Unpublished doctoral dissertation, University of Calgary, Calgary.

Brandon, J. (2008). Assessment for leading in the new Alberta context. *The CASS connection* (Spring, 2008), 9.

Chappuis, C., & Chappuis, J. (2007). The best value in formative assessment. *Educational leadership, 65*(4), 14–18.

Chappuis, C., Stiggins, R., Arter, J., & Chappuis, J. (2005). *Assessment for learning: An action guide for school leaders*. Portland, OR: Assessment Training Institute.

College of Alberta School Superintendents. (2008). *Draft CASS practice standard*. Edmonton, AB: College of Alberta School Superintendents.

Costa, A., & Kallick, B. (2004). Launching self-directed learners. *Educational leadership, 62*(3), 51–55.

Danielson, C. (1996). *Enhancing professional practice: A framework for teaching*. Alexandria, VA: Association for supervision and Curriculum Development.

Darling-Hammond, L. (1994). *Standards for teachers*. New York: American Association of Colleges for Teacher Education.

Darling-Hammond, L. (1999). *Reshaping teaching policy, preparation and practice: Influences of the National Board for Teaching Standards*. New York: American Association of Colleges for Teacher Education.

Darling-Hammond, L. (2001). Standard setting in teaching: Changes in licensing, certification, and assessment. In V. Richardson (Ed.), *Handbook of research on teaching* (pp. 751–776). Washington, DC: American Educational Research Association.

Darling-Hammond, L., & Sclan, E. (1992). Policy and supervision. In C. Glickman (Ed.), *Supervision in transition* (pp. 7–29). Alexandria, VA: Association for Supervision and Curriculum Development.

Davies, A. (2000). *Making classroom assessment work*. Courtenay, BC: Connections Publishing.

Deal, T., & Peterson, K. (1994). *The leadership paradox: Balancing logic and artistry in schools*. New York: Jossey-Bass Publishers.

Earl, L., Watson, N., & Torrance, N. (2002). *Front row seats: What we've learned from the national literacy and numeracy strategies in England*. Paper presented at the Annual Meeting of the American Educational Research Association in New Orleans.

Elmore, R. (2000). *Building a new structure for school leadership. A policy paper prepared*. Washington, DC: The Albert Shanker Institute.

Elmore, R. (2002). *Bridging the gap between standards and achievement: The imperative for professional development in education. A policy paper prepared*. Washington, DC: The Albert Shanker Institute.

Elmore, R. (2004). *School reform from the inside out: Policy, practice and performance*. Cambridge, MA: Harvard Education Press.

Fullan, M. (2001a). *The new meaning of educational change*. New York: Teachers College Press.

Fullan, M. (2001b). *Leading in a culture of change*. San Francisco, CA: Jossey-Bass.

Fullan, M. (2003). *The moral imperative of school leadership*. Thousand Oaks, CA: Corwin Press.

Glickman, C., Gordon, S., & Ross-Gordon, J. (2001). *Supervision and instructional leadership: A developmental approach*. Needham Heights, MA: Allyn and Bacon.

Guskey, T. R. (2000). *Evaluating professional development*. Thousand Oaks, CA: Corwin Press.

Guskey, T. R. (2003). What makes professional development effective? *Phi Delta Kappan, 84*(5), 748–750.

Hall, P. (1993). Policy paradigms, social learning and the state: The case of economic policymaking in Britain. *Policy Studies Review, 25*(3), 128–152.

Hightower, A. (2002). *San Diego City Schools: Comprehensive reform strategies at work* (CTP Policy Brief No. 5). Seattle, WA: Center for the Study of Teaching and Policy, University of Washington.

Howlett, M., & Ramesh, M. (1995). *Studying public policy: Policy cycles and policy subsystems*. Don Mills, ON: Oxford University Press.

Leithwood, K., Jantzi, D., & Mascall, B. (2002). *A framework for research on large-scale reform*. Paper presented at the Annual Meeting of the American Educational Research Association in New Orleans.

Levin, B. (2001). *Reforming education: From origins to outcomes*. New York: RoutledgeFalmer.

Levin, B., & Wiens, J. (2003). There is another way: A different approach to education reform. *Phi Delta Kappan, 84*(9), 658–664.

Lieberman, A., & Miller, L. (1999). *Teachers – Transforming their world and their work*. New York: Teachers College Press.

Lipsky, M. (1980). *Street-level bureaucracy: Dilemmas of the individual in public services*. New York: Russell Sage Foundations.

Marzano, R. (2006). *Classroom assessment and grading that work*. Alexandria, VA: Association for Supervision and Curriculum Development.

Marzano, R., Pickering, D., & Pollock, J. (2001). *Classroom instruction that works: Research-based strategies for increasing student achievement.* Alexandria, VA: Association for Supervision and Curriculum Development.

O'Connor, K. (2002). *How to grade for learning: Linking grades to standards.* Thousand Oaks, CA: Corwin Press.

O'Connor, K. (2007). *A repair kit for grading: 15 fixes for broken grades.* Portland, OR: Educational Testing Service.

Organization for Economic Co-operation and Development. (1994). *Quality in teaching.* Paris: OECD Centre for Educational Research and Innovation.

Reeves, D. (2007). From the bell curve to the mountain: A new vision for achievement, assessment and equity. In D. Reeves (Ed.), *Ahead of the curve* (pp. 1–12). Bloomington, IA: Solution Tree.

Richardson, V. (2003). The dilemmas of professional development. *Phi Delta Kappan, 84*(5), 401–407.

Rose, R. (1993). *Lesson-drawing in public policy.* Chatham, NJ: Chatham House Publishers.

Sanders, J. (1997). Applying the personnel evaluation standards to teacher evaluation. In J. Stronge (Ed.), *Evaluating teaching: A guide to current thinking and best practice* (pp. 91–104). Thousand Oaks, CA: Corwin Press.

Scherer, M. (2001). How and why standards can improve student achievement: A conversation with Robert J Marzano. *Educational Leadership, 59*(1), 1–7.

Schon, D. (1987). *Educating the reflective practitioner.* San Francisco, CA: Jossey-Bass.

Sparks, D. (2002). *Designing powerful professional development for teachers and principals.* Oxford, OH: National Staff Development Council.

Stiggins, R., & Chappuis, J. (2005). *Classroom assessment for student learning: Doing it right—Using it well.* Portland, OR: Educational Testing Service.

Stigler, J., & Hiebert, J. (1999). *The teaching gap: Best ideas from the world's teachers for improving education in the classroom.* New York: The Free Press.

Stronge, J. (2002). *Qualities of effective teachers.* Alexandria, VA: Association for Supervision and Curriculum Development.

Tomlinson, C. (2007). Learning to love assessment. *Educational Leadership, 65*(4), 8–13.

Webber, C.F., Aitken, N., Lupart, J., & Scott, S. (2009, May). *The Alberta student assessment study final report* (Report). Edmonton, AB: Alberta Education.

Wilson, S., Darling-Hammond, L., & Berry, B. (2001). *Connecticut's story: A model state teaching policy* (CTP Policy Brief No.4). Seattle, WA: Center for the Study of Teaching and Policy, University of Washington.

Chapter 5
Fair and Ethical Student Assessment Practices

Jean L. Pettifor and Donald H. Saklofske

Assessment goes hand in hand with all aspects of educational practice. It is impossible to imagine that a "teacher could teach"—no matter what his or her style (teacher- or student-centered), instructional method (inquiry, direct instruction), or subject area (performing arts or physics) is, or whether he or she is in elementary school classrooms or large university lecture theaters or police training programs—without reliable and valid information to inform his or her decisions. The purposes of assessment have certainly been elaborated on in this book and in a lengthy history of extensive writings, including books, articles, and monographs. Teacher training programs include assessment as core coursework for anyone aspiring to become a professional educator. Assessment is as old as educational practice and teaching, but the controversies surrounding assessment in education continue to this day and with even more intensity and division of opinion.

In a nutshell, assessment is the process of obtaining the kind and amount of *good* information needed to make informed decisions that will guide subsequent actions. Where this information comes from will vary from teacher-made classroom tests, observations of student performance, and interviews, to externally produced standardized tests of achievement and intelligence. Decisions include those made at the school and system-wide level (e.g., adding a program for intellectually gifted children, introducing a new science curriculum in secondary school increasing funding for English as a Second Language programs) to the literally hundreds of decisions and actions that a classroom teacher must make on a daily basis. These can range from deciding on the benefits of grouping children with particular learning needs, examining errors on a grade 6 math quiz to determine where some remedial or corrective teaching is required, concluding that there is a need to refer a

J.L. Pettifor • D.H. Saklofske (✉)
University of Calgary, Calgary, AB, Canada
e-mail: don.saklofske@ucalgary.ca

C.F. Webber and J.L. Lupart (eds.), *Leading Student Assessment*,
Studies in Educational Leadership 15, DOI 10.1007/978-94-007-1727-5_5,
© Springer Science+Business Media B.V. 2012

student for a comprehensive learning disability assessment by the school psychologist, determining that a particular student has mastered the prerequisites needed to conduct a science project, or that a university student does not have sufficient grounding in a course to warrant a pass mark. The recipients of such assessment information can range from the student (e.g., I got an A on my health quiz; My teacher says that I need to develop a stronger conclusion in my essays), parents, and other teachers and educators, to the larger education system that may use the results from high-stakes testing and other large-scale assessment programs (e.g., Programme for International Student Assessment) to guide broader and more system-wide educational decisions (e.g., increased emphasis on reading instruction in elementary schools).

A common view in the educational measurement literature is the more information available, and the better it is, the better will be the decisions that are to be made. Thus, assessment essentially involves the collection of relevant information, putting it into some useable framework—whether quantitative (e.g., Jon is a grade 3 student reading at a grade 5 level; Mary obtained 85% on her Psychology 101 midterm) or qualitative (e.g., Gonggu, this is a readable and well-crafted essay that meets all of the standards described in the course rubric)—and then using this framework for the purpose of evaluation and subsequent decision making (e.g., Jon should be given the opportunity to read books at a higher grade level; Gonggu, I believe you are ready to move on to the unit on writing short stories). As a further example, a grade 6 teacher wishes to have students become familiar with the scientific method and then carry out a study and report the findings. But she first conducts an open discussion about research in science followed by a short multiple-choice and sentence completion test to determine how much knowledge her students have of the scientific method. Based on these findings, she notes some key misunderstanding and incomplete knowledge which now informs her of where she can now do some direct teaching to ensure that all students have the fundamental underpinnings to carry out the main objective of this unit, an actual scientific study. Likely one of the most informative publications to focus on assessment is Manitoba Education, Citizenship and Youth's (2006) "Rethinking Classroom Assessment with Purpose in Mind." Here, assessment practices are elaborated on in the context of assessment for learning, as learning, and of learning.

Collecting information, organizing it into some meaningful way whether quantitatively or qualitatively, and then drawing from this to making evaluations and decisions would seem to be fairly straightforward and as much a part of education as are teachers, students, and curriculum. But that is not always the case, and in fact, the issue of assessment and evaluation in education has caused as much controversy and divided opinions as anything else in education, including curriculum issues (e.g., teaching religion or sex education) and behavior management (e.g., use of time out, the strap). A case in point is the use of intelligence tests which were so very successfully introduced at the start of the twentieth century in France but have been challenged regularly in U.S. schools. Accusations that intelligence tests were responsible for discriminatory educational practices and placements led to court cases in the United States in the 1970s and onwards. Some schools have declared moratoriums or abolished the use of standardized intelligence tests, and daily in coffee conversations, we often hear anecdotal reports of a student *harmed* by intelligence tests. But the issue goes even deeper than just a focus on externally produced standardized tests as teachers attempt to use both informal and formal methods to assess student learning and inform their teaching practices. Alfie Kohn and other outspoken critics of assessment argue against many of the current assessment practices that include teacher-made tests using objective formats, such as multiple-choice, matching, true-false items, and completion items. Articles with titles such as "tests hurt more than they help" still fill the newspapers and popular magazines, as well as personal and professional web pages and blogs.

But these issues are more complicated than simply the call for a "ban on tests." First, it is not at all clear whether tests or any other assessment methods are the culprits, if there is one. As indicated above, assessment is a process of collecting relevant information for the purpose of decision making, whether through the use of teacher-made or standardized tests, informal assessment, observations, or interviews. One can argue for or against particular methods of gathering information. In fact, a test is really another name for a means and method of gathering a sample of whatever it is one wants to know more about. So if the purpose of assessment is to see if a child has learned to tell time, then there are multiple ways of assessing this ranging from paper–pencil matching items (e.g., match the clock pictures with the correct times) to completion items (e.g., draw the clock hands showing 9:20) and spontaneous questions where a record of responses is noted (e.g., Rosa, please look at the clock and tell me what time it is? Moshe, how much time do we have left before the lunch bell?). It can also be argued that some item formats may discriminate or penalize a child. For example, a student with a reading disability will likely be at a disadvantage on a long multiple-choice test, but this can be addressed by simply using a more appropriate method to obtain the same sample of behavior, learning, and knowledge (i.e., oral presentation). Rather than condemn all tests or means of assessing learning when we need this information to teach effectively, a more appropriate method should be used. Of course, if assessing the skills needed to be a pilot, there may be little choice in the methods used as they should be directly related to the actual skills required.

The information obtained, in turn, is organized into a quantitative or qualitative framework, and on the basis of either or both external and internal criteria, an evaluation and decision are rendered. The recipient of the decision can be the individual student, other teachers and school staff, the larger educational setting, or the society (e.g., reported results from a high-stakes testing program comparing schools). We sometimes hear that the problem with assessment is that it *quantifies* children. Remember, we are not evaluating the child when we assess reading rate, comprehension, or accuracy; rather, we are determining the child's reading competencies. To do so requires using various assessment tools that either allow us to quantify reading skills and compare it to some standard (i.e., criterion referenced) or to other similar children (i.e., norm-referenced). Qualitative assessment may prefer the use of narratives or student conferences, but the intent is still the same: to determine how much and what a student knows, understands, and can apply or use for higher-order kinds of learning (i.e., analysis, synthesis, evaluation). Again then, whether quantitative or qualitative, both are intended as ways of describing a student's learning needs or learning outcomes.

Probably the biggest area of contention goes beyond the actual ways we assess learning and learners or even the way we organize this information in a quantitative or qualitative format. It is likely the *evaluative* part of assessment that is the major issue, and it is important for us to sort this out from issues, either with the methods of assessment or the "data" description side. Two quotes stand out for us that capture in part the issue at stake here, and also reflect the misplaced view that all assessment is *bad* and should be abandoned. First is a comment that teachers often make: "People just don't like to be assessed and evaluated ... who wants to be told they failed a test or didn't make the team or that they scored in the bottom half of the class on their science project ...." This seems very much to be the crux of the issue. It may be argued that the methods of assessment were biased or flawed leading to calls to abolish all kinds of assessment. But if the use of the information gleaned from a final exam is accurate and reflects the objectives of the class, then it is the evaluation itself that is either inaccurate or not what the recipient wanted to hear. If that is the case, it is unreasonable to blame the tests or the use of norm-referenced comparisons. The second quote captures part of this view: "tests don't make decisions, we do ....Tests are neutral; it is what we do with them that makes them useful or useless, the problem or the answer...." Recall the often heard argument in the assessment literature that essentially says that we are all of equal value as human beings, but that differ in a number of ways that could include height and weight or math ability or athletic skills.

At first glance from the above comments, there would seem to be a dichotomy mainly between the technical capacity to measure the educational objectives set for the classroom or larger educational context on the one hand and the evaluative decision making component on the other. But the situation is not quite that simple. In fact, decisions are made at all stages of assessment from deciding what our instructional objectives are to how will we measure this; this is akin to the 'W5' of assessment (i.e., what is being assessed, who is being assessed, when and where will assessment occur, and why are we assessing). While there is considerable psychometric and technical sophistication that can be used to create the measures we use in educational settings, this does not always mean that we have considered the full extent of the 'W5's of assessment. That introduces questions such as fairness and bias in assessment. It raises questions of whether assessment is serving the best interests of the individual child, the school, and wider society. If these factors have not also been fully considered, then any decisions and actions resulting from assessment of any and all kinds will be called into question.

There are many books and publications on how to build technically sound assessment techniques ranging from the rules for writing multiple-choice items to scoring essay tests. The point of this chapter is to look beyond the mechanics of test building and measurement to these other issues that are best captured in the literature addressing fair and ethical assessment practices.

More Than Just Testing: Fair and Ethical Educational Assessment Practices

With all of these points in mind, we wish to revisit the issues raised above through the lens of both *fair* and *ethical* assessment practices. Collaborations between major professional organizations, such as the American Educational Research Association, American Psychological Association, and National Council on Measurement in Education, have resulted in the publication of *The Standards for Educational and Psychological Testing* (1999) that details *best practices* related to test construction, evaluation, documentation together with fairness in testing, and testing applications. The *Principles for Fair Student Assessment Practices for Education in Canada* (Joint Advisory Committee 1993) was developed as a practical guide for all those engaged in the assessment of students in Canadian schools and postsecondary learning centers. The intent of the document is to provide guideposts from which educators can build a fair and meaningful assessment program that would include day-to-day in-class teacher-made assessment to standardized tests produced external to the classroom and school. Both authors are proud to have served on the Joint Advisory Committee that oversaw the development of these "Principles."

Another perspective that is somewhat less prescriptive in a direct way but that can shed some much needed light on assessment issues comes from codes of ethics. These are not *rule-governed* views, but rather perspectives to aspire to that provide a foundation for positive relationships. While teachers in schools are governed also by codes of ethics, the ethical principles followed by such major professional groups as the American and Canadian Psychological Associations provide some very insightful perspectives on assessment practices. Similarly, the theme of fair assessment practices shares some considerable overlap with codes of ethics. All fair assessment documents and ethical guidelines address technical competence, choice of appropriate instruments, consideration of ethnicity, culture, language, gender, disabilities, and the enhancement of the quality of services for the benefit of people (i.e., students).

Principles for Fair Student Assessment Practices in Canada

Assessment is broadly defined as the process of collecting, interpreting, and reporting information for the purposes of (1) providing feedback to students, and where applicable, to their parents/guardians, about their progress toward attaining the knowledge, skills, and attitudes to be learned; and (2) informing educational decisions (i.e., instruction, promotion, graduation, diagnosis admissions, placement) to be made with reference to students. Adding to this is the notion that assessment must also be viewed in the context of what is fair. As mentioned above, *The Principles for Fair Student Assessment Practices for Education in Canada* (Joint Advisory Committee 1993) was developed to inform and guide educational practice, particularly in Canadian schools and postsecondary learning institutions. The term *fair* is not defined in practice documents and seems to be taken for granted. However, Webster's Collegiate Thesaurus uses synonyms such as honest, just, and freedom from improper influence that might be translated into objective, impartial, unbiased, and nondiscriminatory practice. It might also include open-minded and equitable, all of which may require professional judgment. However, as we shall see, fair is best defined not by a few words but by the very depth and breadth of practices outlined by the Joint Advisory Committee (1993).

The *Principles for Fair Student Assessment Practices for Education in Canada* has "stood the test of time" and continues to be the most practical guide for best practices in student assessment in the Canadian education context. Assessment depends on professional judgment, and the principles and guidelines identify the issues to consider in exercising this professional judgment and in striving for the fair and equitable assessment of all students. The document is divided into two sections:

1. Classroom Assessments: This section is directed toward the development and selection of assessment methods and their use in the classroom by teachers and is based on the *Standards for Teacher Competence in Educational Assessment of Students* (American Federation of Teachers, National Council on Measurement in Education, and National Educational Association 1990). There are seven broad areas that are described along with more specific guidelines to guide educational personnel in test development and use.
2. Assessments Produced External to the Classroom: Here, the focus is on both the development and use of standardized assessment methods with recommendations for both test developers and educators who elect to use externally produced measures.

Because of page limitations, we have elected to comment mainly on the section addressing Classroom Assessments. While many of the issues surrounding educational assessment are directed at standardized testing, whether part of a high-stakes program or the individually administered intelligence test, it is the everyday classroom practices that are likely the most significant in assessing "*for* learning, *as* learning, and *of* learning." We direct readers to consult the B section of the "Principles" (Joint Advisory Committee 1993) for an elaboration on Assessments Produced External to the Classroom.

The section of the "Principles" focusing on Classroom Assessments is divided into five parts. Each section has essentially identified an area of assessment practice that has the potential to raise issues around fairness, and thus by being proactive, guidelines have been introduced and elaborated that should prove of direct benefit and relevance to the classroom teacher.

Developing and Choosing Methods for Assessment

This theme addresses the issue that assessment methods should be appropriate for and compatible with the purpose and context of the assessment. Specific attention is drawn to the following seven points:

1. Assessment methods should be developed or chosen so that inferences drawn about the knowledge, skills, attitudes, and behaviors possessed by each student are valid and not open to misinterpretation.
2. Assessment methods should be clearly related to the goals and objectives of instruction and be compatible with the instructional approaches used.
3. When developing or choosing assessment methods, consideration should be given to the consequences of the decisions to be made in light of the obtained information.
4. More than one assessment method should be used to ensure comprehensive and consistent indications of student performance.
5. Assessment methods should be suited to the backgrounds and prior experiences of students.
6. Content and language that would generally be viewed as (in)sensitive, sexist, or offensive should be avoided.
7. Assessment instruments translated into a second language or transferred from another context or location should be accompanied by evidence that inferences based on these instruments are valid for the intended purpose (Joint Advisory Committee 1993, pp. 5–7).

This is a foundational theme; if the very methods and techniques we use for assessment are biased or inappropriate to the task or for the student, then all that follows is flawed. The issue here is not whether we use performance tests, multiple-choice quizzes, essays, portfolios, performance tasks, or projects, but whether they result in valid, reliable, and meaningful information that will be relevant and useful to all who would be guided by such assessment information. Something as simple as "if you want to know if a child can read, ask them to read" is sometimes lost in how we overcomplicate assessment. Furthermore, no matter how we assess learning and learners, the purpose should be to reflect the goals and intent of instruction— that is, learning objectives and outcomes.

It is one thing to gather continuous information about a student's progress in language arts or science. Any bit of information that appears anomalous (e.g., due to "a bad day," misread instructions) can be examined in the context of the larger picture and either averaged in or replaced if invalid. But single assessments (e.g., final exams accounting for the full course grade) do not have that flexibility. Again though, it may depend on what is being assessed. It is very much more important that a pilot trainee scores 100% on "take offs and landings" than might be the case in an accounting exam where the student scores 95% with a passing grade cutoff set at 80%. Another key issue here is the need to not rely unthinkingly on only one kind of assessment. While that may be the case in more advanced job training (e.g., air traffic controller) or even in very specific school programs (e.g., playing guard on the school basketball team), it is less likely so in the usual curriculum where a multimethod and continuous approach to assessment is more likely to provide meaningful and robust information to inform decision making.

Bias in assessment is never to be tolerated. Knowing that a child has a significant visual problem suggests that lengthy paper–pencil/question–answer exams will likely not be the ideal format for assessing the student's knowledge in language arts. That does not always mean that we are initially aware of such biases, but when we are, then it must be addressed immediately and effectively. The potential for bias in assessment that is grounded in culture, sex, gender, ethnicity, religion, exceptionalities, and so forth must be continuously monitored. For example, the question of bias in *imported* standardized tests is, in part, an empirical question and can be determined through careful empirical examination.

Collecting Assessment Information

The major point associated with collecting assessment information is that students should be provided with sufficient opportunity to demonstrate the knowledge, skills, attitudes, or behaviors being assessed and includes the following key recommendations:

1. Students should be told why assessment information is being collected and how this information will be used.
2. An assessment procedure should be used under conditions suitable to its purpose and form.
3. In assessments involving observations, checklists, or rating scales, the number of characteristics to be assessed at one time should be small enough and concretely described so that the observations can be made accurately.
4. The directions provided to students should be clear, complete, and appropriate for the ability, age, and grade level of the students.
5. In assessments involving selection items (e.g., true-false, multiple-choice), the directions should encourage students to answer all items without threat of penalty.
6. When collecting assessment information, interactions with students should be appropriate and consistent.
7. Unanticipated circumstances that interfere with the collection of assessment information should be noted and recorded.
8. A written policy should guide decisions about the use of alternate procedures for collecting assessment information from students with special needs and students whose proficiency in the language of instruction is inadequate for them to respond in the anticipated manner (Joint Advisory Committee 1993, pp. 7–8).

It is often interesting to listen to students as they leave a classroom test or quiz. Comments such as the following are very telltale of the differing views of students and teachers, not only about the course content and objectives but also the focus of assessment: "I studied all of the major plays and authors we covered in class but the test only focused on Shakespeare's Romeo and Juliette" or "I didn't know we were expected to know such detail; the teacher indicated this course was to help us develop creative writing skills but the test focused on grammar, punctuation, and essay structure." Clearly here the aims and content of instruction as perceived by the students, in contrast to what was asked on the tests, are at odds. We sometimes hear that teachers should not be teaching to the test. While there is partial truth to that, the instructional objectives should guide both the test maker and taker. If an objective states that the student will correctly solve 20 written addition problems in 10 min without the aid of a calculator, it should come as no surprise if the way of measuring this is to have a test with 20 written addition problems, a 10 min time limit, and a preset criterion of 100%.

Tests can produce performance anxiety in some students, and all students want to do their best to showcase their achievement. So the tests should not introduce unknown levels of anxiety (e.g., "I just don't know what this question is asking … should I answer with a general overview or take one issue and explore it in depth?"). Students should understand not only the question but also how it will be scored and evaluated.

There are times when the unexpected happens and it can impact students' demonstration of their knowledge. To use the idea of reliability, an obtained test score is comprised of "true" score variance and error; the more error or noise not tapping what should be measured by the test, the less accurate measure and ensuring evaluation of the student's learning. Where and when needed, there are multiple ways of assessing many kinds of student learning and they should be used as required. For example, a child may have quite an extensive vocabulary, but because of an expressive language problem, the child may not be able to orally show this. Using a writing format or having the child point to pictures to demonstrate word meaning will give quite a different view of this child's vocabulary knowledge.

Judging and Scoring Student Performance

Procedures for judging or scoring student performance should be appropriate for the assessment method used and be consistently applied and monitored. Fair assessment practices would encourage the following:

1. Before an assessment method is used, a procedure for scoring should be prepared to guide the process of judging the quality of a performance or product, the appropriateness of an attitude or behavior, or the correctness of an answer.
2. Before an assessment method is used, students should be told how their responses or the information they provide will be judged or scored.
3. Care should be taken to ensure that results are not influenced by factors that are not relevant to the purpose of the assessment.

4. Comments formed as part of scoring should be based on the responses made by the students and presented in a way that students can understand and use them.
5. Any changes made during scoring should be based upon a demonstrated problem with the initial scoring procedure. The modified procedure should then be used to rescore all previously scored responses.
6. An appeal process should be described to students at the beginning of each school year or course of instruction that they may use to appeal a result (Joint Advisory Committee 1993, pp. 9–10).

This section moves evaluation from the stage of data collection, no matter how that might be done, to the point of judging the competency or adequacy of a student's knowledge and skills and summarizing the results. Again we often hear the classic disagreement between teacher and student: "I have no idea why I got such a low mark on this essay, I did everything expected...." It is only fair that students know how the teacher will score a test or arrive at a mark or grade (e.g., right minus wrong, 10 extra points for including both tables and figures to show your results; in order to earn an A on this project, you must do the following ...). As a teacher, you should decide in advance how you will assess more subjective assignments such as essays (e.g., global vs. analytic scoring) and ensure that this is communicated to your students. This will also assist the teacher in minimizing biases that might creep into the assessment process (e.g., halo effects, emphasizing trivial or unimportant areas for deducting marks).

Number or letter grades, unless at the extremes (i.e., A or F), do not communicate much useful information to students especially on process-type assessments, essays exams, performance tests, etc. Here, narrative and other more detailed feedback is needed for students to both understand the mark but also to be empowered to know what to do to improve their grade and most especially the learned skills. And if students wish to discuss or even challenge your assessment of their work, view this as a learning opportunity. Students are more likely to be motivated when they feel they know the content to be tested and will do well on a test, rather than if they view it as another "unknown or the black hole of assessment."

Summarizing and Interpreting Results

Procedures for summarizing and interpreting assessment results should yield accurate and informative representations of a student's performance in relation to the goals and objectives of instruction for the reporting period. Here, we are referring to:

1. Procedures for summarizing and interpreting results for a reporting period should be guided by a written policy.
2. The way in which summary comments and grades are formulated and interpreted should be explained to students and their parents/guardians.

3. The individual results used and the process followed in deriving summary comments and grades should be described in sufficient detail so that the meaning of a summary comment or grade is clear.
4. Combining disparate kinds of results into a single summary should be done cautiously. To the extent possible, achievement, effort, participation, and other behaviors should be graded separately.
5. Summary comments and grades should be based on more than one assessment result so as to ensure adequate sampling of broadly defined learning outcomes.
6. The results used to produce summary comments and grades should be combined in a way that ensures that each result receives its intended emphasis or weight.
7. The basis for interpretation should be carefully described and justified.
8. Interpretations of assessment results should take account of the backgrounds and learning experiences of the students.
9. Assessment results that will be combined into summary comments and grades should be stored in a way that ensures their accuracy at the time they are summarized and interpreted.
10. Interpretations of assessment results should be made with due regard for limitations in the assessment methods used, problems encountered in collecting the information and judging or scoring it, and limitations in the basis used for interpretation (Joint Advisory Committee 1993, pp. 10–12).

The key points here are quite basic but most important. Remember that the results of assessment should inform the teacher, other teachers and school personnel, the student, the student's parents, and other agencies and organizations such as university registrars when students apply for postsecondary education. More to the point, reports of student achievements should be understood by all who need to know about a student's learning. Without an understanding of how the evaluation was made or what results were used on a report, this does nothing to inform others. Ongoing feedback to all concerned parties usually comes from what is called *formative* evaluations, while it is the summary grades or *summative* evaluation that appears on report cards and transcripts. Again, all parties need to know how these final assessments were arrived at. Here is where teacher discretion and ingenuity comes into play. Imagine a student who missed several classes because of illness but came back and was faced with a unit test on which he did quite poorly (30%). On an essay handed in a week later, he achieved 90%, and on another end of term quiz (that included content from the first quiz), he earned 80%. If the teacher equally weights these three measures and does not allow for the fact that the student had missed the bulk of material at the time of the first quiz, his summative mark for that course will be 67%. Does this "truly" reflect or summarize this student's achievement?

Of course, if the metric for reporting student achievement is not known, again this will only create confusion. Does a final mark of 80 indicate that the student achieved 80% on average on various measures (i.e., of varying reliability and validity), that he or she scored higher than 80% of the students in the class, that 80 is actually a low mark since the majority of students earned marks of 90 and higher? And as a final word here, test scores and grades should be clear in what they reflect. To say that while a student did only an average report but will be given a higher grade because of effort and a positive attitude in class will simply cloud the meaning of the mark for all, especially the student. At the same time, low achievement in a class should not be confused with other factors. A recent immigrant child who is barely familiar with English and not at all familiar with the current curriculum will not nor should be expected to "do well" in the regular school curriculum upon first arrival. Here, the issue is adapting the curriculum to the child and addressing the child's learning needs.

Finally, it is important to remember that measurement and evaluation are imperfect. As we said before, the more information you have and the better it is, the better the decisions you will make as a teacher.

Reporting Assessment Findings

Assessment reports should be clear, accurate, and of practical value to the audiences for whom they are intended. We have addressed some of these points above but more specifically:

1. The reporting system for a school or jurisdiction should be guided by a written policy.
   Elements to consider include such aspects as audiences, medium, format, content, level of detail, frequency, timing, and confidentiality.
2. Written and oral reports should contain a description of the goals and objectives of instruction to which the assessments are referenced.
3. Reports should be complete in their descriptions of strengths and weaknesses of students so that strengths can be built upon and problem areas addressed.
4. The reporting system should provide for conferences between teachers and parents/guardians. Whenever it is appropriate, students should participate in these conferences.
5. An appeal process should be described to students and their parents/guardians at the beginning of each school year or course of instruction that they may use to appeal a report.
6. Access to assessment information should be governed by a written policy that is consistent with applicable laws and with basic principles of fairness and human rights.
7. Transfer of assessment information from one school to another should be guided by a written policy with stringent provisions to ensure the maintenance of confidentiality (Joint Advisory Committee 1993, pp. 12–13).

The major point to be made here is the importance of providing accurate and also meaningful information to all who need to know. For this reason, report cards or any reporting format should contain the needed detail so that the information can be understood and is relevant and useful to all parties. Supplementing written reports with conferences and ongoing communication will do much to ensure a partnership between home and school and add resources to the teaching–learning environments of the student.

The need for appeal processes and agreements for information transfer, including issues of confidentiality, are most likely part of each school jurisdiction's administrative makeup and should be understood and adhered to by all school personnel.

Assessments Produced External to the Classroom

Assessments produced external to the classroom in *Principles for Fair Student Assessment Practices for Education in Canada* (Joint Advisory Committee 1993) applies to the development and use of standardized assessment methods used in student admissions, placement, certification, and educational diagnosis, and in curriculum and program evaluation. These methods are primarily developed by commercial test publishers, ministries and departments of education, and local school systems. We will not address this section in this chapter but merely outline it and encourage readers who use externally produced tests to consult the "Principles."

The principles and accompanying guidelines are organized in terms of four areas:

I.   Developing and selecting methods for assessment
II. Collecting and interpreting assessment information
III. Informing students being assessed
IV. Implementing mandated assessment programs

The first three areas of Part B are adapted from the *Code of Fair Testing Practices for Education* (1988) developed in the United States. The principles and guidelines as modified in these three sections are also intended to be consistent with the *Guidelines for Educational and Psychological Testing* (Canadian Psychological Association 1986) developed in Canada. The fourth area has been added to contain guidelines particularly pertinent for mandated educational assessment and testing programs developed and conducted at the national, provincial, and local levels.

Merging Concepts of Ethics and Fair Assessment Practices

We wish to advocate the merging of ethical language and concepts with good practice as a means of enhancing the effectiveness of fair educational assessments in serving the learning needs of students. While we would encourage readers to consult other ethics codes created by such organizations as the American Psychological

Association and the *Universal Declaration of Ethical Principles for Psychologists* (2008), recently adopted by both the International Union of Psychological Science and International Association of Applied Psychology, we will base our discussion of ethical principles in the language used in the code of ethics of the Canadian Psychological Association, also adopted by the Canadian Association of School Psychologists. The *Canadian Code of Ethics for Psychologists* (Canadian Psychological Association 2000) describes four broad principles: Respect for the Dignity of Persons, Responsible Caring, Integrity in Relationships, and Responsibility to Society. Priority will be placed on the well-being of the student (i.e., "How does this help the grade 3 child, the grade 11 student in Math 20, the university student majoring in fine arts?").

We maintain that ethical relationships need to be recognized and honored in addition to the assessor's technical knowledge and skills in developing, administering, reporting, and interpreting the results of assessments. Examples of real-life vignettes relative to the application of good practice standards and ethical principles will be presented. Finally, key questions will be raised about those aspects of western societies that sometimes erode the individual professional's ability to provide the highest standards in quality assessment practices. The solutions to these problems go well beyond the classroom even though they have major consequences for local students, teachers, and others.

Standards for educational assessments, or for good practice, or for fair assessment practices, focus on competency as defined in knowledge, skills, and attitudes of fairness. The "assessor" is the expert applying his or her knowledge to enhance the learning of the recipient or student. On the other hand, ethical principles provide a moral framework to guide professionals in their relationships with those with whom they interact in a professional capacity. To be ethical requires competent practice because incompetent practice results in harm to others. To be ethical, in addition to technical competence, requires relationships that are respectful, caring, and honest and that are demonstrated when one considers issues of informed consent and choice, appropriate confidentiality, respect for professional boundaries, conflict of interest, and relationships with third parties. Ethical concepts are clearly associated with *competencies* and *fairness*, thus overlapping with *good/best practices* in the assessment process and also adding another dimension that is necessary in ensuring the best outcome for the student. Good practice guidelines and codes of ethics both place full responsibility on individual professionals for their actions (e.g., teachers, social workers, nurses, psychologists) without recognizing the reality that a professional's choices may be influenced or even determined by external forces (e.g., administrative and funding policies, lack of resources, restrictive agency policies). All may result in compromising the quality of services offered in education, health, social services, and assessment practices, thus presenting ethical dilemmas for the teacher or other helping professionals. A modification of the ethical decision-making steps of the two codes of ethics referenced above is offered to help in making decisions when there are conflicting loyalties on how to address such dilemmas.

Let us present a short description of each of the overarching ethical principles that are included in the codes of ethics of the Canadian Psychological Association. Each will be followed by a short vignette in which the problem arises from a lack of attention to the ethical relationships rather than to any deficiency in knowledge or skills in conducting an educational assessment. We shall also challenge the reader with questions and themes to be considered.

Respect for the Dignity of Persons

Respect is at the core of all other ethical principles. In valuing the inherent worth of all persons, the professional attends to free informed choices and consent, confidentiality of personal information, privacy, protection of vulnerable persons, and avoidance of discrimination and unfair treatment. Practice guidelines also require fair treatment and providing information on the reason and the use that will be made of the assessment information.

Vignette

Liz was assessed by the school psychologist because she was 2 years behind in all grade expectations. The mother signed a standard consent form for a psychoeducational assessment that Liz brought home from school. Upon completion, the assessment results were shared immediately with the teacher. When the mother was seen by the psychologist and teacher the following week, she was shocked that her daughter's intellectual ability was in question, that information was shared with the teacher before the mother, and that the teacher would not give the mother any information. She threatened to remove Liz from this school.

What went wrong here? This assessment may have been *competent* (i.e., administered by a trained psychologist using a psychometrically good test), but it does not appear to be helping Liz. The principal had told the teacher and psychologist before their meeting that this family was not always cooperative. The mother said that her child was nervous but not a slow learner, and besides, the teacher had never asked how Liz managed at home or in other nonschool contexts. The school psychologist said that it was not in her job description to interview the parents; that was the task of the teacher.

The psychologist seemed bound to the test/instruments and perhaps missed consideration of other factors that could contribute to problems in learning. Ethically, the mother was not treated with respect relative to consent and confidentiality and seemed to feel that she and Liz were devalued. Where in the school system was there a breakdown in adequate communication with the mother? Had she been treated with more respect, would the outcome have been much more positive for Liz?

Responsible Caring

Caring that is responsible involves applying one's knowledge and skills for the benefit of others and taking extra care to protect the most vulnerable. This principle is similar to good practice because of the common emphasis on competence. The difference is that ethics focuses on the benefit to the client, while practice standards focus on the knowledge of the professional.

Vignette

You have given your grade 12 class the final examination, which following from your practice serves as a major component in determining final grades. You are disappointed to see that Maya, whose second language is English, has earned only a B minus. She lacks confidence in expressing herself in English, but is bright, creative, and generally outgoing, and she wants to attend university to become a teacher. She will need higher grades, and a B minus seems very unfair relative to her ability. In other words, the teacher does not think that this test gave Maya the opportunity to indicate the extent of her learning. Maya's English will improve over time. Would it be fair to raise her grade to an A minus?

What went wrong here? Both alternatives (leaving the mark as is or changing it) seem unfair and both could have negative results for the student. How might this situation have been prevented? The exam was well constructed and seemed quite appropriate for the remainder of the class. What is the ethical and fair response right now? Are there lessons to be learned that can guide the teacher in ensuring fair and reasonable assessment practices not only for Maya but for all students?

Integrity in Relationships

Integrity in relationships involves honesty, accuracy, objectivity, and avoidance of bias, conflict of interest, and exploitation. Fair practice standards indicate that methods should be suited to the backgrounds and prior experiences of students especially relative to ethnicity and culture.

Vignette

One of your best friends is a neighbor woman, raising three children on her own. She has shared with you many of the traumatic events in her life to date. You try to be supportive and understanding. This year, one of her children is in two of the classes that you teach. The student's work is sometimes borderline, sometimes excellent, and at other times, it is just not completed. Because you understand how disturbed this child's life has been, you make allowances and up her grades somewhat, which you see as helpful to both the student and her mother. The mother is very appreciative of your support. Is this fair or not to this child, other children in the class, others who will use these results? What should you do?

Ethically, you likely are too personally involved with the family to be objective or you need to find other ways to enhance the student's learning than simply give unearned credits. Your supportive role as a friend has been established for some time. Perhaps someone else should be responsible for assessing her learning and helping to develop remedial measures. However, you are still faced with what to do now; what factors must you consider in guiding your actions and decisions?

Responsibility to Society

Responsibility to society involves maintaining high standards of practice, supporting positive aspects of society, and advocating for change where aspects of society violate ethical standards. Fair assessment practice standards to enhance and evaluate the learning of students are supported by some aspects of society and not by others. We have an ethical responsibility to contribute to changing those aspects of society that are detrimental to learning for students.

Vignette

Your main job is assessing the learning needs of children. Your supervisor suggests that you provide more diagnoses that correspond to the special funding criteria in order to increase the grants received by the school. You are reluctant to do so; inasmuch as these labels may be detrimental to the children in the long term, it is dishonest, and there is a financial incentive to misdiagnose. You disagree with the policies on funding criteria. What are the issues of fairness for the students? What responsibility do you have, if any, to advocate for change in the criteria for special funding?

Where is the problem? You know that providing the funded diagnoses will result in actual funding for special services for some students whose learning difficulties are not sufficiently severe yet to meet the criteria, but without early attention they are likely to become more severe. Ethically, what can you do in the short term and in the long term? What options are available to you that will benefit the student?

Ethical Decision Making

The previous discussion and illustrations with vignettes suggest that a combination of ethical principles and practice standards may serve you well in resolving dilemmas. Some ethical decisions are made automatically by applying clearly defined principles and standards. Sometimes, a decision requires a careful consideration of existing rules and good practices. The more difficult dilemmas occur when there is conflict between existing principles or between the interests of different parties. Dilemmas that involve cultural diversity are often among the more difficult to resolve in ways that respect all parties.

The following steps may be useful in considering the various responses to a dilemma on what is the right thing to do based on both good practice standards and ethical principles—the one focusing on competencies and the other on respectful caring relationships.

A Model for Ethical Decision Making

1. Identify the individuals and groups potentially affected by the decision.
2. What ethically relevant and good practice issues are involved in the situation?
3. What are the particular interests of persons affected in this situation?
4. How might your personal biases, stresses, self-interests influence your choice of action?
5. Develop alternative courses of action along with the potential benefits or harms associated with each? Whom would you consult?
6. Choose a course of action, act and evaluate the results, and if necessary, reengage in further decision making.
7. Consider if any actions on your part might prevent this kind of problem from occurring in the future.

Implications of Politics, Policies, and Funding on Fair and Ethical Practice

Obviously, there are some clear guidelines and prescriptions that can be directly drawn from these complementary perspectives on assessment. On the other hand, fair and ethical guideposts are just that; they do not always provide precise and direct rules to follow that will always lead to best practices. Rather, they stimulate us to think outside of the box and to be sensitive to other human issues that are not addressed in the mechanics of assessment.

Here are some questions that we hope will stimulate dialogue with your colleagues about conditions that may present barriers for students benefiting from student assessments. Each one merits discussion beyond what can be addressed here, and it is the heuristic value leading to further discussion around issues of fair and ethical assessment practices that will be the greatest benefit gleaned from reading this chapter.

1. Are differences in ethnicity, culture, language of students a deterrent to "fair" assessment practice in a society that is ever increasing in diversity and

globalization? Are our standards adequate to address the range of diversity in our schools?

2. Do pressures for quantitative test scores in a context of limited resources limit teachers and other educational personnel from doing comprehensive educational assessments? What do test scores alone mean in helping and empowering students?

3. Does school funding for individual special education depend on labeling or coding a child and the severity of the code to match funding formulas? What are the implications for those doing the assessments and for the students meeting or not meeting the criteria?

4. Does school funding ever depend on the overall performance of the students in the school? Do schools benefit financially from good student performance and are they penalized for poor performance, or if there are students with special needs or learning difficulties? Would the above practice promote higher standards in the school performance of the students or might it have any negative consequences for individual students?

5. Does the philosophy that every child deserves the same academic recognition that is accorded age-peers regardless of level of performance benefit students, or is it a disservice to them? How would this help children? How would it affect fair assessments?

6. What is the nature of training and competencies for those who make the funding policies and decisions? Is there a disconnect between the values of running a business and ethical values of respect, caring, and integrity in providing human services? How do funding policies and decisions help students?

We have raised the issue of merging guidelines for fair student assessments with explicit ethical guidelines as a means of increasing the benefits derived from the assessments for the students. We have not developed any detail on exactly how this might be done in the belief that more dialogue must occur on whether this proposal is viable and likely to benefit students, teachers, assessors, families, and most of all, the students.

References

American Educational Research Association, American Psychological Association, National Council on Measurement in Education. (1999). *The standards for educational and psychological testing*. Washington, DC. AERA, APA, NCME.

American Federation of Teachers, National Council on Measurement in Education, and National Educational Association. (1990). *Standards for teacher competence in educational assessment of students*. Washington, DC: AFT, NCME, NEA.

American Psychological Association. Joint Committee on Testing Practices. (1988). *Code of fair testing practices in education*. Washington, DC: APA/JCTP.

Canadian Psychological Association. (1986). *Guidelines for educational and psychological testing*. Ottawa, ON: CPA.

Canadian Psychological Association. (2000). *Canadian code of ethics for psychologists* (3rd ed.). Ottawa, ON: CPA. http://www.education.ualberta.ca/educ/psych/crame/files/eng_prin.pdf

Joint Advisory Committee. (1993). *Principles for fair student assessment practices for education in Canada*. Edmonton, AB: JAC. http://www.education.ualberta.ca/educ/psych/crame/files/eng_prin.pdf

Manitoba Education, Citizenship and Youth. (2006). *Rethinking classroom assessment with purpose in mind*. Winnipeg, MB: Government of Manitoba. http://www.edu.gov.mb.ca/k12/assess/wncp/index.html

Universal Declaration of Ethical Principles for Psychologists. Adopted by the General Assembly of the International Union of Psychological Science in Berlin on July 22nd, 2008 and Board of Directors of the International Association of Applied Psychology in Berlin on July 26, 2008.

Chapter 6
How Can Psychological Assessment Inform Classroom Practice? The Role of the School Psychologist in Canadian Schools

Joan Jeary and Vicki L. Schwean

Psychological Assessment Practices in Support of Classroom Teaching and Learning

School psychologists are experts in assessment. This is not to say that teachers do not hold professional expertise in the assessment of their students but rather, that by working together, teachers and psychologists can engage in assessment practices that lead to a better understanding of students' learning and behavior. Information is gathered from a variety of sources and in a variety of ways that lead to effective interventions both at home and at school.

Teachers have the responsibility of assessing and reporting upon student learning in schools; however, sometimes students have challenges in their learning, behavior, or social development, and teachers require the assistance of others in the assessment process. The challenges that students experience may be related to academic difficulties in grasping and applying concepts, meeting behavioral and social expectations, or possibly, as in the case of gifted learners, requiring enrichment additional to the regular curricula. Whatever the referral reason, teachers want instructionally relevant information and practical strategies for teaching the student. Psychologists are in a unique position to work with teachers to both assess students as well as to translate assessment results into programming strategies. Psychologists have a foundational understanding of the underlying psychological processes and considerations that influence learning and behavior and can address the "why" questions for learning and behavioral challenges through the use of standardized measures, as

J. Jeary (✉)
University of Calgary, Calgary, AB, Canada
e-mail: jeary@wynndel.ca

V.L. Schwean
University of Western Ontario, London, ON, Canada

C.F. Webber and J.L. Lupart (eds.), *Leading Student Assessment*,
Studies in Educational Leadership 15, DOI 10.1007/978-94-007-1727-5_6,
© Springer Science+Business Media B.V. 2012

well as through the application of a scientist–practitioner model. In the scientist–practitioner model, the role of the "local clinical scientist" is best described by Trierweiler and Stricker (1998) as

> a critical investigator who uses scientific research and methods, general scholarship, and personal and professional experience to develop plausible and communicable formulations of local phenomena. This investigator draws on scientific theory and research, general world knowledge, acute observational skills, and an open, skeptical stance toward the problem to conduct this inquiry (p. 24–25).

The assessment practices used by psychologists and the intervention strategies recommended are based on evidence and best practice. State-of-the-art research and training programs are at the center of preparation for school psychologists.

Psychological assessment is a multifaceted process designed to evaluate individuals in their current life settings. The assessment process is grounded in the scientist–practitioner model and involves a systematic problem-solving approach that yields either an in-depth evaluation of a specific area of functioning or a comprehensive description of an individual's strengths and weaknesses in several areas. Areas of development that are typically assessed may consist of intellectual ability, memory, attention, language abilities, social skills and peer relationships, motivation and learning strategies, and self-concept and self-esteem. Relationships within the family and factors within the instructional environment are also areas of inquiry. Sattler (2001) described assessment as a way of gaining understanding of the child to make informed decisions. He outlined several purposes of assessment including (a) screening, which is designed to identify children eligible for a certain program, who have a disability in need of remediation, or who may require a more comprehensive assessment; (b) problem-solving, which gives a detailed evaluation of a specific area of functioning to address a diagnostic question or skill question; (c) diagnostic, which gives a detailed evaluation of a child's strengths and weaknesses in several areas designed to address diagnosis; (d) counseling or rehabilitative, which emphasizes the child's abilities to adjust to and successfully fulfill daily responsibilities; and (e) progress evaluation, which focuses on the day-to-day, week-to-week, month-to-month, or year-to-year progress of the child. Within each of these areas of assessment, psychologists are committed to a holistic examination of an individual that incorporates a multimodal, multi-source approach and employs such clinical tools as observation, interviews, rating scales, informal procedures, and norm-referenced tests. Of paramount importance is that the assessment process not only gathers information but also uses theoretical and research knowledge to interpret the findings and synthesize the results. The results then lead to recommendations for educational and treatment interventions that are based on best practice research. Theoretical conceptualizations of various conditions guide decision-making regarding assessment techniques. For example, in the assessment of a client referred for significant attentional issues, the decision-making process would involve the inclusion or exclusion of various causal explanatory hypotheses (i.e., ADHD, depression, auditory processing deficit, cognitive disability, etc.) toward the outcome of differential diagnoses. A variety of tests designed to assess constructs underlying these conditions would be used (i.e., intelligence, memory, and executive functioning), as well as measures such as rating scales completed by parents/caregivers and teachers.

A resiliency framework is at the heart of school psychology particularly as it relates to the formulation of educational and treatment interventions. It is critically important to identify strengths in the individual's development and personal interests. These strengths may be relative in nature but can still provide an entry point at which intervention may occur. For those students who are experiencing difficulty in school and may be discouraged and confused, it is essential to engage in proactive and positive intervention. Through appropriate intervention, an individual can come to understand his or her disability/disorder/difficulty, participate in setting appropriate expectations and goals, and engage in a successful educational program or treatment regime.

Promoting Psychologically Healthy Environments for All Children

To respond to the question of how psychological assessment can inform teaching and learning, it is helpful to understand the mission of school psychologists. The National Association of School Psychologists (NASP 2000) has the following mission statement: "To promote educationally and psychologically healthy environments for all children and youth by implementing research-based, effective programs that prevent problems, enhance independence, and promote optimal learning" (p. 12). The mission of school psychologists is realized in many different ways and at many different levels of school and community practice. The Canadian Psychological Association (2007) identified four levels of intervention for school psychologists: (a) student-focused indirect interventions (consultation, program planning, parent collaboration, goal-setting, teacher assistance, interagency networking, referrals), (b) student-focused direct interventions (individual psychological assessment, individual therapy, group behavior skills development), (c) district/system-wide interventions (in-service education, screening, evaluation, best practices, intervention programs, outreach, networking, advocacy), and (d) research. Psychologists promote healthy environments for children and youth through working with individual students and families; within classrooms through supporting teachers; and at the school, system, and community levels, through policy-making and consultation.

In the Family

Characteristics of the family can either promote or act as a detriment to a student's development, learning, and behavior. The school psychologist works with families on two levels. The first is the family of an identified student and the second is through general parent education. In the first instance, parents are helped to gain an understanding of their child's development as compared to other children of the same age. For some parents, the assessment findings are confirmation of an existing disability or disorder, but for other parents, it is often the first time a diagnostic descriptor has been used in relation to their child. Having a specific disability or disorder confirmed can be a relief to many parents who have been seeking answers to questions about their child's learning and/or behavioral challenges in school. The conference with the school psychologist is often the beginning step in establishing appropriate expectations and developing an action plan to address the child's needs. School psychologists are committed to the meaningful participation of families in the identification of students with special educational needs. Parents should be involved in decision-making processes in assessment, intervention, and program planning. At times, psychologists also provide direct services to families regarding strategies that promote academic, behavioral, and social success in both home and school environments.

Direct services provided by psychologists may occur with individual families or may be offered as part of a parent education program. Parenting children in today's world is complex and often confusing, particularly for parents who have a child with special needs. Children with ADHD, oppositional behavior, or who are highly anxious present parenting challenges in terms of planning daily events and in setting and consistently maintaining appropriate expectations for learning and behavior. Parent education programs that focus on helping parents understand their child's characteristics and respond appropriately and consistently are invaluable in developing strong and positive parent–child relationships.

In the Classroom

Teachers are frequently stymied about particular students and seek comprehensive understanding to design an effective instructional program. Through working collaboratively with school psychologists, teachers can gain the understanding and information required to set appropriate expectations and develop individual program plans to address the needs of students with exceptionalities. Later in the chapter, we will give case studies of children assessed through the University of Calgary Applied Psychological and Educational Services. The case studies are excellent examples of teachers, parents, physicians, and psychologists working together to assess cognitive strengths and weaknesses, as well as learning profiles of school-aged children and youth. The assessments are then linked to interventions.

School psychologists contribute to creating educationally and psychologically healthy classroom environments by consulting with classroom teachers on a wide variety of topics. Topics such as classroom management, creating safe learning environments, learning and teaching strategies specific to curricula such as reading and mathematics, student motivation, preventative mental health programs, and working effectively with parents are examples of topics in which school psychologists influence the thinking and practice of classroom teachers and subsequently the learning environment of children and youth.

Psychologists can also provide valuable feedback to teachers by conducting a systematic observation in the classroom. Ysseldyke and colleagues (Ysseldyke and Christensen 1987; Ysseldyke et al. 1994) advocated for an assessment of the instructional environment to determine whether specific instructional factors correlating with academic achievement were present or absent in the student's classroom environment. According to the authors, the rationale for assessing the learning environment reflects a belief that student performance in school is a function of an interaction between the student and the learning or instructional environment. It has increasingly become recognized by school psychologists that in order to make recommendations concerning the instructional needs of students, it is necessary to assess students in the context of the surroundings in which learning occurs.

In the School

At the school level, the knowledge and expertise of psychologists about cognitive and social development can be very useful in decision-making and policy development. Psychologists are frequently involved in assisting school administrators in developing school-wide policies such as discipline policies, homework policies, and bully-proofing programs.

There is a role for psychologists to play in assisting schools to establish strong home–school collaboration by facilitating the development of relationships between families and schools. In a position statement of NASP (2000), recognition is given to the fact that families and educators may differ in their expectations, goals, and communication patterns, sometimes leading to frustration and misunderstanding among students, families, and educators. The position statement speaks to the role of the school psychologist in using a problem-solving approach to overcome barriers and building mutual trust. NASP encourages its members to advocate for increased home–school collaboration and identify strategies to encourage family participation.

A third way in which psychologists fulfill their mission of creating educationally and psychologically healthy environments for children is through providing in-service training to teachers and school administrators. Psychologists have much to contribute to the professional growth of teachers. Common topics for workshops and presentations include, but are not limited to, the following: suicide prevention and intervention, classroom management, tests and testing, information about a wide variety of exceptionalities, teaching and learning strategies, home–school collaboration, gifted education, and mental health prevention.

The last way in which psychologists are typically involved in the life of the school is through their involvement as members of school-wide teams (Student Assistance Teams or Student Services Teams). The purpose of the team is to assist and support teachers with the identification and intervention of students who have learning, behavioral, and/or emotional needs. Through this model of interprofessional collaboration, psychologists can both contribute to the knowledge and skills of teachers as well as learn about the other professional perspectives on the team. It is a collaborative approach to the assessment process that incorporates multiple sources of information and multiple procedures, and occurs across multiple settings and contexts. Teachers, school administrators, parents, resource teachers, speech therapists, and other professionals, as required, are members of the team. Students ultimately benefit from having a comprehensive and coordinated assessment and intervention plan.

In the System/District

School psychologists have been instrumental in influencing policies and decisions regarding topics such as student promotion and retention, early literacy programs, suicide prevention and intervention, and special education policies, as well as serving on standing committees to advise on a wide variety of educational issues. Since psychologists have knowledge of research, statistics, and evaluation methods, they are often requested to assist in translating research into practice and also to design and conduct investigations and program evaluations for school districts. For example, when deciding to implement a program to ensure optimal development for children presenting with various conditions, school psychologists will often be charged with the responsibility of identifying evidence-based interventions and practices and supporting teachers in developing the expertise to implement these interventions with fidelity. In other instances, school psychologists may be asked to evaluate program efficacy by assessing exit outcomes of children receiving specialized services.

In the Community

Collaborative partnerships are at the center of community initiatives focused upon student health, multicultural programs and services, preventative mental health programs, and other programs responsive to the needs and issues within specific neighborhoods, for example, vandalism, early school dropouts, poverty, homelessness, lack of parental supervision, lack of recreational opportunities, and school attendance. Psychologists work with other professionals and community and government agencies to develop programs and services to ensure that families receive the support they require, and children and youth have equitable opportunities to participate in psychologically healthy and evidence-based educational and community programs. Community partnerships involve families, educators, and community members working together to support students' educational and mental health needs. By way of example, school psychologists are integral to the functioning of community-based school models (e.g., Stroul and Blau 2008). They work in collaboration with others to implement community-based models; develop policies and procedures, including referral and servicing mechanisms; monitor and enhance learning and service experiences; oversee research initiatives; and assist in the training and ongoing functioning of interprofessional teams.

Standards for Training and Practice of School Psychologists

Psychologists working in schools are guided in their practice by two professional organizations: the Canadian Psychological Association and NASP. In 2007, the Canadian Psychological Association published a document titled *Professional Practice Guidelines for School Psychologists in Canada*, which guides the practice of psychology in schools and also informs other educational and health professionals about the role of the school psychologist. NASP (2000) published a document titled *Standards for Training and Field Placement Programs in School Psychology and Standards for the Credentialing of School Psychologists*. The NASP and the Canadian Psychological Association documents clearly outline the professional and ethical principles which serve to promote excellence in the services provided by school psychologists.

The NASP document identifies 11 domains of professional practice in school psychology. It is the responsibility of training programs in school psychology to ensure that graduates demonstrate the professional skills in each domain. Graduates of school psychology programs bring a sound foundation in their knowledge of both psychology and education. In some areas of the country, there continues to be a false notion that school psychologists are "testers" and that assessment is a matter of giving "tests." Nothing could be further than the truth! To assist in understanding and appreciating the breadth and depth of training and the extensive knowledge and skills school psychologists contribute to schools, and in particular to special education, a brief discussion of the 11 domains follows.

Data-Based Decision-Making and Accountability

School psychologists understand systematic and effective data-based decision-making and problem-solving processes. They use these processes when undertaking assessments with individual students. Assessment is a process of collecting data in order to make decisions. Psychologists working in schools are well versed in a variety of methods to collect information such as formal and informal test administration, behavioral assessment, curriculum-based measurement, interviews, and environmental assessment. Information or "data" is collected about instructional environments as well as home and school environments; information is also gathered about cognitive, emotional, social, and behavioral factors that have a significant impact on school achievement. The data collected is evaluated within the context of current theories, models, and empirical research findings, and a subsequent diagnosis or identification of causal environmental and child characteristics is made that explains why the child is having learning or behavioral difficulties. Assessment results are linked to intervention by choosing evidence-based treatments and/or educational programs and strategies that best match the child's competencies and areas of need.

School psychologists also use data-based decision-making to assist school administrators in demonstrating accountability. As previously mentioned, there is a role for psychologists in the development of school-based programs and policies. Through collecting systematic data, school-specific issues can be identified which influence learning and behavior, and programs can be developed to respond to these issues. The initiatives can then be evaluated in terms of improved student outcomes.

Consultation and Collaboration

Establishing collaborative working relationships is critical to the work of school psychologists whether it be with parents, teachers, or other education and health care professionals. Knowledge of consultation and collaboration is applied in multiple contexts. Teachers appreciate the opportunity to discuss questions and concerns with the school psychologist. Their concerns may involve an individual student or be more general such as questions about classroom management or discipline strategies. Psychologists have the interpersonal skills and communication skills to assist teachers in gaining a different perspective.

As a member of a team, psychologists are instrumental in facilitating positive communication among team members and working toward consensus in decision-making. In the case where schools and parents disagree about student needs and/or programming, psychologists can assist in resolving the conflict in a way that keeps the student's needs at the center of the discussion.

Effective Instruction and Development of Cognitive/Academic Skills

Psychologists understand human diversity and the cognitive and academic skills of students with different abilities, disabilities, strengths, and needs. They are sensitive to the nuances of specific assessment and intervention strategies with students with diverse backgrounds and experiences. They have current knowledge of "best practice" instruction and alternative instructional approaches for students with special education needs or students with diverse strengths and needs. Psychologists working in schools link assessment information to the development of instructional responses that respect both the learner and the teacher. They recognize the importance of assisting students to gain independence and autonomy through the development of such skills as study skills, self-monitoring, planning/organization, and time management, and they work with teachers to ensure this outcome for students.

Socialization and Development of Life Skills

"School psychologists have knowledge of human developmental processes, techniques to assess these processes, and direct and indirect services applicable to the development of behavioral, affective, adaptive, and social skills" (National Association of School Psychologists 2000, p. 26). Given the importance for all students to acquire prosocial behaviors, it is imperative that respectful and safe classroom environments be created. School psychologists collaborate with parents and teachers to teach children responsible behavior. Examples of whole classroom strategies are (a) well-established classroom routines and rules, (b) fair and consistent expectations, (c) expectations which are firmly maintained through the use of consequences, (d) conflict resolution, and (e) social problem-solving approaches. In those instances where individual students have difficulty expressing appropriate social behaviors, school psychologists can become involved by assessing the student using appropriate behavioral assessment strategies (i.e., standardized and/or functional and/or ecological) which then result in the development and implementation of interventions which cross settings (i.e., school, home, community). Behavioral interventions are monitored and evaluated for effectiveness with regard to desired student outcome.

Student Diversity in Development and Learning

As stated earlier, school psychologists recognize that students come to school from very different backgrounds and with very different experiences. They understand the individual differences that students bring in all areas of their development and also the influences of social, cultural, socioeconomic, ethnic, language, and gender in child development and learning. The knowledge and appreciation of diversity are reflected in the assessment processes used by school psychologists as well as in the design and implementation of interventions. The academic and social/behavioral interventions that are recommended reflect children and families' cultures, backgrounds, and individual learning characteristics. Further, school psychologists recognize that they too may bring subtle racial, class, gender, and cultural biases that may influence decision-making (National Association of School Psychologists 2000).

School and Systems Organization, Policy Development, and Climate

Earlier in the chapter, we discussed the ways in which school psychologists promote educationally and psychologically healthy environments for children in schools. It is through their knowledge of general education and special education that psychologists achieve an understanding of schools as systems. NASP (2000) made the following statement in referring to school psychologists:

> They use their knowledge to assist schools and other agencies in designing, implementing, and evaluating policies and practices in areas such as discipline, problem-solving, instructional support, staff training, school and other agency improvement plans, program evaluation, transition plans, grading, retention, and home-school partnerships. School psychologists

have knowledge of and apply effective principles of organizational development and systems theory to assist in promoting learning, preventing problems, creating climates that result in mutual respect and caring for all individuals in the system, facilitating decision-making and collaboration, and fostering a commitment to quality, effective services for all children, youth, and families (p. 29).

Prevention, Crisis Intervention, and Mental Health

Psychologists know that some children, by virtue of biological, familial, and social stresses, are more vulnerable and may not develop the resiliency to bounce back from adverse circumstances. These children are "at risk" of developing mental health problems. By recognizing the precursors to academic, behavioral, and serious personal difficulties, it is possible to prevent some mental health problems. It is also possible, through early identification, to engage in programs and services to support the health and adjustment of children. Psychologists practicing in schools are in an optimal position to both promote mental health and also to collaborate with other education and health care professionals to intervene effectively when students have been identified with severe learning and behavior problems.

Weisz et al. (2005) described a conceptual model which links the prevention and treatment of mental health issues in youth. Their unifying framework has a research component. Research is an important part of the model to ensure that interventions are evidence-based and effectiveness has been empirically supported. The authors advocated bringing intervention science and practice closer together. There have been numerous meta-analyses which have evaluated studies of school-based prevention and intervention programs with the conclusion that the programs were generally effective. Since children and youth spend large portions of their day in school, it makes sense to offer both prevention and intervention programs and services in schools, and psychologists working in schools are in an ideal position to facilitate such programs, services, and research. Efforts to promote psychological well-being, prevent disorders, and intervene to treat problems and disorders should be part of a comprehensive school mental health program in which the school psychologist plays a leadership role.

Home/School/Community Collaboration

We have discussed the role of the psychologist in assisting schools to establish strong relationships and connections with families. Psychologists recognize the influence of family systems on students' cognitive, motivation, and social functioning and therefore, the importance of involving families in their child's education in positive and proactive ways. School psychologists, through collaborating with others, develop the educational and support programs that assist parents/caregivers to support their children's learning and behavior at school.

Advocating for home/school/community collaboration is expected of school psychologists and is particularly important when working with parents who have children with special education needs. Parents often require support when participating in the individual program planning process and advocating for programs and services for their children. School psychologists can also assist parents in accessing community resources and other professional supports and services.

Research and Program Evaluation

Psychologists' knowledge of research design and statistics enables them to plan and conduct their own research as well as critique and evaluate published research. They have knowledge of measurement and psychometric standards which provides the foundation for selecting and using assessment techniques and standardized tests.

It is an expectation of NASP (2000) that psychologists maintain a professional knowledge base of research findings, professional literature, and other information relevant to their work and apply the knowledge base to all components of their work. They base their practice on sound research and translate new research findings into service delivery improvements (p. 33).

Psychologists practicing in schools have the opportunity to provide leadership in assisting schools in understanding research and evaluation data and in interpreting the use of school and/or district data.

School Psychology Practice and Development

School psychologists possess knowledge related to the foundations of their profession, and they are aware of and comply with professional, legal, and ethical guidelines and standards. They use this knowledge to advocate for the rights and well-being of children, youth, and families and to promote new policies and practices in schools.

It is expected that psychologists recognize their own limitations and biases, as well as those areas in which they have training and expertise. They will evaluate their own knowledge, professional competencies, and the outcomes of their services and plan continued professional development accordingly. School psychologists maintain training, certification, or licensure and engage in ongoing professional development.

Information Technology

School psychologists recognize the impact of technology on their professional practice. It is important to use the technology in ways that enhance the quality of services to children (e.g., accessing information sources, test-scoring software, and assistive technology for children and youth with disabilities). Current knowledge of technology resources is important when designing, implementing, and evaluating instructional programs or interventions for children and youth in schools.

Summary

Cameron (2006), writing in the United Kingdom, described the distinctive contribution of "educational" psychologists. The following five distinctive factors were identified:

(a) Adopting a *psychological perspective* of the nature of human problems
(b) Drawing on the knowledge base of psychology to uncover *mediating variables* which may provide an explanation of why certain events may be related
(c) Unraveling *problem dimensions* using sophisticated models which can be used to navigate through a sea of complex human data and to provide a simple but useful map of the interaction between people factors and aspects of their living/ learning environments
(d) Using information from the research and theoretical database in psychology to recommend *evidence-based* strategies for change
(e) Promoting innovative concepts or *big ideas* which are underpinned by psychological research evidence and theory and which can enable clients to spot potential opportunities for positive change (p. 293)

The Changing Face of School Psychology Services in Canada

Schools exert powerful influences on children's learning, health, and psychological and emotional well-being. Indeed, schools can provide children with one of the best opportunities they have to improve their satisfaction with life and ability to enjoy a healthy lifestyle. Unfortunately, schools traditionally have placed primary emphasis on children's cognitive and academic development. Yet, growing research suggests that a child's ability to be ready for, stay in school, and succeed in school depends on the integrity of developmental processes in multiple, interconnected domains (see Fig. 6.1). Consider, for example, the bioecological model of development proposed by Bronfenbrenner (2004). Within this framework, Bronfenbrenner conceptualized child development within various domains as occurring within the context of a complex system of relationships in his or her immediate, as well as more distant, environments. Of critical importance is the acknowledgement that a child does not develop these domain capacities in isolation, but rather is powerfully shaped by the bidirectional interactions between his or her own biology, family, school, community, and larger society. According to this model, the development of various capacities

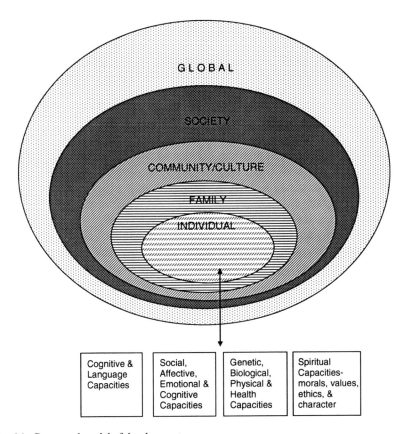

Fig. 6.1 Contextual model of development

> ... takes place through proximal processes – increasingly complex reciprocal interactions between the child and the people, objects, and symbols in his or her immediate environment. Proximal processes are seen as the primary engines of development. Developmental outcomes are the result of the interaction of proximal processes and characteristics of the child. Context can shape the occurrence of these processes as well as moderate their impacts. The length, frequency, and regularity of exposure to proximal processes are also important to consider (Evans et al. 2007).

Numerous factors can interrupt children's emerging developmental processes and deny or minimize their opportunities for optimal development. While Canada's children are generally doing well, a number of indicators show that a significant percentage of children face adversity. Strong links between prevailing neo-liberalist policies in Canada and inequitable economic, social, and political trends have contributed to the proliferation of conditions that threaten the well-being and health of children and families and pose significant challenges to schools. Classrooms in today's schools are populated by a diverse complement of children, many of whom live with challenges that impede their ability to learn. With an estimated 20% of all Canadian children living in poverty (Child and Family Canada 1997; Rothman 2007;

Willms 2002a, b), we are facing a growing population of children failing to achieve their potential. Children in families that face systemic discrimination run a much higher risk of growing up in poverty: children of recent immigrants, children living in racialized communities, children of single mothers, and children and families with disabilities and/or mental health problems. Aboriginal children and those youngsters residing in inner cities are among those at greatest risk of experiencing the negative effects associated with poverty. Although socioeconomic status is, in and of itself, a poor indicator of early adversity, it is a powerful correlate of multiple risk factors that act in concert to thwart positive adaptation. In particular, children's health, learning, and well-being are strongly related to socioeconomic factors. Poverty has been associated with higher incidences of learning disability, developmental delays, cognitive challenges, and emotional and behavioral problems. There is strong evidence of a socioeconomic gradient whereby children at the lower end of the social hierarchy tend to have poorer physical, psychological, social, and long-term educational outcomes than those further up the social hierarchy. Specifically, children and youth growing up in families of lower socioeconomic status tend to do less well in academic pursuits, are less likely to complete secondary school, and tend to be less successful in entering the labor market than those from more advantaged backgrounds (Sloat and Willms 2002).

Further, Canadian inquiries into children's mental health have concluded that despite the development of efficacious prevention and treatment interventions, the burden of suffering remains unacceptably high (Bijl et al. 2003; McEwan et al. 2007; Mental Health Evaluation and Community Consultation Unit 2002; Waddell et al. 2002). Recent surveys indicate that anywhere from 14% to 20% of children aged 4–17 years have clinically important mental disorders at any given time. This translates to over 800,000 Canadian children who experience mental disorders that cause significant distress and impairment at home, school, and in the community. Of significant concern is that reports from across Canada indicate that the burden of suffering imposed by children's mental health problems and disorders is increasing. When present, mental health problems permeate every aspect of development and functioning, including family relationships, school performance, and peer relationships (British Columbia Ministry of Child and Family Development 2003). Moreover, various disabilities affect more than half million children aged 5–14 years in Canada, with chronic health conditions, learning disabilities, and speech and language difficulties being most prevalent. Approximately 32% of these children have also been identified by their parent as having emotional, psychological, or behavioral conditions that limit their activities (Government of Canada, Public Health Agency of Canada 2002; Hanvey 2002; Statistics Canada 2001).

It is also important that we acknowledge that the families of today are very different than those of the past (see Juby et al. 2004; Federal/Provincial/Territorial Early Childhood Development Agreement [Canada] 2002; Government of Canada 2002). For example, by the age of 15 years, almost 30% of children born within a couple will have experienced their parents' separation. Most of these children will reside with their mothers. Births to single mothers have increased dramatically. Research has shown that children growing up in lone-parent families have a greater likelihood of being disadvantaged throughout their lives – largely as a result of greater economic and emotional stresses – compared to children in two-parent families. In terms of their health, behavior, academic achievements, and relationships, children in lone-parent families have a greater likelihood of negative outcomes than do children in the general population. Moreover, a growing number of Canadian children are subjected to child maltreatment including physical abuse, sexual abuse, neglect, and emotional maltreatment (Canadian Incidence Study of Reported Child Abuse and Neglect 2001). For example, one study showed that about 4% of boys and 10% of girls experienced severe sexual abuse before the age of 17 (MacMillan et al. 1997), while another reported that 61% of all victims of sexual assault reported to the police were children and youth under 18 years (Alberta Association of Sexual Assault Centres 2005). Children with disabilities are at high risk for sexual assault and abuse: 40–70% of girls and 15–30% of boys with developmental disabilities have experienced sexual abuse (Alberta Association of Sexual Assault Centres 2005).

Constant high immigration to Canada since 1946, and expanding diversity of origins of immigrants since the 1970s, has resulted in quickly growing numbers of immigrant children and youth. Indeed, immigrant children and children of immigrants represent a growing component of the Canadian population and will make up an increasing proportion of Canada's population in the future (Citizenship and Immigration Canada 2005). The 1996 Census of Canada found that children under 15 comprise 19.8% of the total population (Human Resources and Development Canada 2005). They tend to be concentrated in a few major cities across Canada (including Calgary), and many reside in neighborhoods of high immigrant density within those cities (Hou and Bourne 2004). Many live in poverty (Lee 2000; Pendakur and Pendakur 1998). Measures of school success, especially dropout rates, indicate that immigrant children and youth are falling behind their peers in education. Studies comparing the academic performance of children of immigrants in Canada (Statistics Canada 2001) to that of Canadian-born children report that despite the economic disadvantage that some immigrants face, the former generally achieve levels commensurate with the latter, although initially these children are weaker in reading. Interestingly, those children of immigrants who speak English or French as their first language outperform their Canadian counterparts. Moreover, more youth of immigrants attain more university than their Canadian-born peers. The reciprocal influence of poverty, racism, and second-language status, however, significantly alters the trajectory for these children. The Canadian Coalition for Immigrant Children and Youth argued (e.g., Cortese 2008) that the social, economic, and political consequences of ignoring the needs of immigrant children and youth create risks of foregoing their potential contribution in this country and allowing the growth of a sizeable group of distressed and disaffected students. They point out that current low levels of quality of service are significantly disadvantaging immigrant children and youth relative to their non-immigrant counterparts.

For the majority of children facing various vulnerabilities and adversities, the school is the sole provider of primary support and services. While schools can play a strong equalizing role in delivering a wide range of assessment and intervention services, profiles of school psychology services throughout Canada show a severe shortage of school psychologists, particularly in Northern and rural communities (see Special Issue of the Canadian Journal of School Psychology 2001; Saklofske et al. 2000, 2007; Lupart et al. 2001). A cross-Canada assessment undertaken for Health Canada found extremely long waiting periods for at-risk students to be assessed within schools, with waiting times for services ranging from 6 to 24 months. Hann (2001) stated that because of the paucity of school psychologists, case loads in most Nova Scotia school districts are excessive, and it is not uncommon for one school psychologist to serve three to four thousand students distributed over approximately 12 schools. Similarly, Carney (2001), in describing the Ontario scene, revealed that the ratio of psychology staff to students in large school boards typically ranges from 1:100 to 1:12,000. Further, Janzen and Carter (2001) reported that large urban school systems in Alberta will have full-time psychologists on a ratio of 1:10,000 students, while Saklofske and Grainger (2001) demonstrated that the public school system in Saskatoon, Saskatchewan, has a ratio of about 1:4,400 while the Catholic system, which employs just one school psychologist, has a ratio of 1:14,000. Given the high student to low psychologist ratio within schools, only children with the most severe and apparent vulnerabilities are likely to receive appropriate psychological services. The vast majority of children at risk are much less likely to be identified at an early and critical point. In turn, the likelihood of children receiving early intervention services is minimal. Our lack of investment at a critical stage in the development of these children will be reflected in long-term disadvantage and economic and social dependency.

Within the broader context of North America, there is also a shortage of school psychologists, and it is projected that a major, more profound shortage is likely to occur in the near future (Fagan and Wise 2007). Some of the latest estimates reveal that only one fourth of school psychology positions in the United States meet the 1:1,000 school-psychologist-to-student ratio recommended by the National Association of School Psychologists (Charvat 2005; Charvat and Charvat 2003). Further, approximately 10–20% of school psychologists reported that they were planning to retire within the next 3 years. The shortage of school psychologists across North America is reflected in recent statistics showing school psychology is among those areas of psychology that show the greatest expansion of career opportunities for master and doctoral psychologists over the last decade (American Psychological Association 2009).

Services to Canadian children facing vulnerabilities are further compromised by significant fragmentation of child services among various federal and provincial jurisdictions, sectors, and disciplines. Several ministries and agencies – including education, social services, justice, and health – typically deliver services to children and families with little coordination among them. Contributing further to the fragmentation, many institutions, agencies, and professionals function within disciplinary "silos" which further impairs our ability to effectively and efficiently use our existing services, including those available in schools. In concert, the shortage of school psychologists, the prevailing service delivery model that focuses primarily on the delivery of specialist services within a deficit-oriented model, and fragmentation of services suggest that systemic changes are needed to adequately meet the needs of a diverse child population in Canada.

Given this context, contemporary models of school psychology and health services call for a "universal" paradigm shift toward a comprehensive service delivery system that emphasizes the promotion of healthy development for all children, the prevention of disorders in children at risk, and the provision of treatment for children with disorders (Huang et al. 2005; Tolan and Dodge 2005; Waddell et al. 2005). Many child advocates have argued that the logical place to situate this system is within schools as they are accessible community settings that are comfortable and non-stigmatizing for most children and their families and house well-trained personnel, access to supportive services, and mandated service delivery mechanisms (Kirby and Keon 2004; Kirby and LeBreton 2002).

> The value of providing. . .services within the school setting is intuitively apparent. Schools offer familiar environments to intervene with children and adolescents. . .and in many jurisdictions are recognized as key players in the provision of. . .services and supports. . ..The Committee was advised that when appropriate, services should be delivered in places where children, adolescents, and their families spend most of their time (schools and homes) and at appropriately flexible times of the day (Kirby and Keon 2004).

Realization of comprehensive servicing within schools can best be implemented through adopting a *Systems of Care* approach (see, for example, Pumariega and Winters 2003). Systems of Care essentially involve all agencies working together to ensure that children with needs and their families have access within their home, school, and community to the services and supports they need to succeed. Generally, Systems of Care are developed around the principles of being child-centered, family-driven, strength-based, culturally competent, community-based, cost-effective, interdisciplinary, collaborative, and multimodal/integrative. They are driven by objective, clinical research and program evaluation data while also being responsive to the unique needs and perspectives of the child and family. Of critical importance is the creation of a separate, single funding envelope that combines various funding streams for delivery of services. Many Systems of Care adopt *Wraparound* as an implementation vehicle. In essence, Wraparound is a definable planning process involving the child and family that results in a unique set of community services and natural supports individualized for that child and family to achieve a positive set of outcomes. While many argue that achievement of this vision within Canadian schools and communities is a "pipe dream," there are already numerous examples of Systems of Care that have been successfully implemented within school divisions throughout Canada.

Several practices are integral to the success of Systems of Care in schools, including the need of psychologists to take on expanding roles. In contrast to the current situation in Canada where most school psychologists in Canada spend a disproportionate amount of their work day involved in student-focused direct and indirect assessment and intervention (i.e., delivery of specialized services), the school psychologist within a Systems of Care would broaden his/her role to include roles such as:

- Front-line provider of educational and mental health services
- Advocate for the child, family, and system
- Interprofessional team participant or leader

- Consultant to other professionals
- Administrative leader in delivery organization/system
- Quality assurance/improvement consultant
- Outcome evaluator/research in Systems of Care
- Provider of in-service training
- Case manager
- Developer of educational and mental health services policy and planning within communities, regions, and provinces

Strength-based assessment, promotion, and prevention strategies based within resiliency models are of critical importance to the success of such systemic changes. Resilience is defined as the capability of individuals and systems (i.e., families, groups, and communities) to cope successfully in the face of significant adversity or risk (Luthar et al. 2000; Masten 2001; Werner 2000). This capability develops and changes over time, is enhanced by protective factors within the individual/system and the environment, and contributes to the maintenance or enhancement of overall psychosocial well-being. Research has identified several categories of protective factors: individual attributes, family qualities, and supportive systems outside the family. Individual attributes that contribute to positive outcomes include biological factors such as general health, predisposition, temperament, and gender. Cognitive (e.g., intelligence, cognitive style, coping ability), intrapersonal (e.g., self-esteem, self-awareness, internal locus of control, optimism, motivation, curiosity), and interpersonal (e.g., social responsiveness, cooperative, socially skilled, positive out-look toward authority) competencies also show a positive relationship to resiliency. Various family (e.g., parental rules, consistent expectations, establishing acceptable behavioral standards, opportunity to establish a close bond with a family member who provides stable care and appropriate adequate attention) and community factors (e.g., community resources, peers as sounding boards and confidants) also contribute to the heightened likelihood of success. Within this framework, school psychologists will place considerable emphasis on contextualized assessment that builds an understanding of the various individual, family, and community strengths that a child brings to his or her learning environment. The key underlying premise is that resilience can be fostered through interventions that enhance children's out-comes, further develop their talents and competencies, and protect or buffer them against environmental adversities.

The construct of resiliency must be understood within the context of non-independent (i.e., person-related) and independent risks, that is, current or past hazards that have the potential to derail normative development. The importance of identifying and evaluating risks is to activate moderating and mitigating resources that have the potential to counterbalance the adversity they pose. For example, a child demonstrating significant attention deficithyperactivity disorder may present with family strengths that help moderate his or her behavior; however, without addressing the risks that are posed by an underlying neurobehavioral condition, optimal learning performance will not be achieved. Thus, assessment becomes a complex task of assessing not only the strengths and risks within the individual child but also those within the family, community, and larger society.

An emerging body of literature has also explored school-based resiliency and risk factors that influence learning (see Wang and Gordon 1994; Waxman et al. 2003, 2004). Knowledge of this research can inform the assessment process by alerting the school psychologist to protective mechanisms that mitigate against adversity and support educational success. Individual protective factors include higher self-concepts and educational aspirations, internal locus of control, proactive participation and higher level of academic and social interaction with teachers and peers, social maturity, and task orientation, among others. Within the family context, academic success has been positively related to the quality of the parent–child relationship, family cohesion and warmth, secure attachments, the expression of high expectations for academic success, and active engagement of family members in school-related activities. The teacher can also serve as a protective factor for children facing various adversities by articulating concern and high expectations; fostering sustained, close relationships; maximizing learning time; maintaining a high degree of classroom engagement; providing differentiated instruction; and so on. The curriculum itself is of importance in promoting positive developmental outcomes. Studies have found that the provision of challenging curriculum content and instruction tailored to individual strengths and learning needs, materials that promote high-order thought processes, and the enhancement of student motivation by ensuring that curriculum is connected to their experiences are all instrumental in the well-being of students. Lastly, the school-wide culture plays a significant role in mediating adversity through reinforcing students' accomplishments; emphasizing student involvement and belonging; strengthening attachment to teachers, classmates, and the school; engaging in shared decision-making; nurturing a pleasant and friendly school climate; sustaining attractive and well-maintained physical facilities; promoting social and cultural norms that express high expectations for good citizenship and educational success; and offering programs that engage children/youth in activities designed to promote social and moral reasoning, among other initiatives. In acknowledging this growing literature, the school psychologist will take careful note of child attributes, teacher and classroom practices, curriculum, and the broader school culture when assessing a child's learning strengths and challenges.

Within the framework we have presented, one of the most important roles of the school psychologist will be to engage in assessment practices that allow for the prevention and early identification of risks so as to maximize positive outcomes. School psychologists will undoubtedly encounter numerous barriers in their efforts to engage in these tasks: the fragmentation of service delivery systems limits accessibility to information that is outside the mandate of the school but may contribute to understanding a child's learning performance (e.g., family dynamics or socioeconomic status); lack of psychometrically reliable, valid, and culturally sensitive screening measures; and limited financial resources and supports for prevention and early identification, among others. Another critical role of the school psychologist will be to engage in intervention and program evaluation so as to ensure that in seeking to "grow" strengths in children, we are engaging in practices that are firmly grounded in evidence while also being responsive to the unique needs and perspectives of the child and family.

Case Studies

To illustrate the complex, dynamic, and contributive role that school psychologists play in understanding those factors that enhance and impede children's learning within a school context, we have chosen to present two case studies. The case studies are examples of children referred to the University of Calgary Applied Psychological and Educational Services (UCAPES) for psychological assessment. UCAPES is a multidimensional service delivery system and encompasses clinical services, professional development, and research/program evaluation. These three facets work in a dynamic and synergistic way to offer graduate students in the Division of Applied Psychology at the University of Calgary experiential learning opportunities. Clinical services include individual counseling and psychological interventions, group counseling and interventions, psychological and educational assessments, educational interventions, and clinical consultation with schools and other community agencies. The clinical services are provided by graduate students, and supervision is provided by registered psychologists who are members of the division's faculty. Supervision guidelines are in accordance with the standards and requirements of the Canadian Psychological Association and the College of Alberta Psychologists. UCAPES is founded upon a community of practice model, and all initiatives reflect scientist–practitioner, evidence-based practice. Interprofessional collaboration is a cornerstone of the work as evidenced by the many partnerships UCAPES has with community agencies and organizations. The two case studies presented provide clear examples of how the psychological educational assessment process informed classroom practice.

Case Study #1: Clyde

Clyde was an 11-year-old boy in Grade six at a rural school. The referral indicated that Clyde was making very poor progress in school, and the parents and school staff questioned the presence of attention deficit hyperactivity disorder (ADHD), non-verbal learning disability, and/or possibly autism spectrum disorder. Clyde had previously been diagnosed with ADHD but was not on medication. There had been past emotional issues as a result of a prolonged custody dispute when he was in early elementary school. His mother, who has since remarried, felt that the issues related to the custody dispute impacted Clyde's learning, and he "fell behind in the first 3 years of school and then never caught up." She also indicated that she did not agree with the previous diagnosis of ADHD. Clyde interacted positively with his step-father, who was in the process of legally adopting Clyde. He was the only child in the family. Clyde was described by his teacher as "a good-natured, busy, social boy who is often unfocused, lacks confidence in his ability, but loves to have fun." His teacher indicated that Clyde was only minimally disruptive in class, almost always inattentive, and demonstrated poor social skills.

Clyde was seen individually on three occasions, and interviews were held with his parents and teachers. Parents and teachers also completed rating scales. Clyde was administered the Wechsler Intelligence Scale for Children – Fourth Edition, Woodcock-Johnson Cognitive Abilities Test, Children's Memory Scale, Wechsler Individual Achievement Test – Second Edition, selected subtests from a neuropsychological test battery, and the Continuous Performance Test. Parents and teachers provided feedback on the Behavior Assessment System for Children – Second Edition, Adaptive Behavior Assessment System – Second Edition, and the Gilliam Autism Rating Scale – Second Edition.

The results of the assessment indicated that Clyde was functioning within the borderline intellectual range, and all attention and executive functioning areas measured (i.e., language, memory, and sensorimotor) were below average. His visuospatial abilities were in the average range. Clyde had average decoding skills in reading and was below average in all other academic areas. There was some symptomatology of autism, but it was restricted to communication and a few stereotypical behaviors. The stereotypical behaviors were first apparent during the time of the custody dispute, and Clyde's mother felt that they were a way that Clyde comforted and calmed himself (e.g., lining up his toys in a particular order) and was able to gain some control of his environment. She described the behaviors more as habits now rather than stereotypical behaviors. There was no evidence of a true attention deficit but rather a tendency for Clyde to become disengaged and off-task when the work was too difficult or he was unable to grasp new concepts.

At the conference with the parents, school staff, and family physician, assessment findings were shared, and strategies were discussed to assist Clyde in being more successful in school. School staff (i.e., principal, classroom teachers, and resource teacher) was surprised to learn that Clyde was limited in his intellectual functioning and recognized that expectations for academic performance would need to be adjusted. His teachers indicated that they would engage him in learning activities that were at his level of ability and that by making modifications and adaptations to instructional content and processes, they would be able to accommodate him in the classroom more effectively. The pace of instruction would be adjusted to allow Clyde more time to process information as well as complete his work. Expectations for finished products would also be modified. It was agreed that Clyde would benefit from individualized programs in math and reading comprehension so he would be put on an individual program plan. It was also agreed that Clyde could benefit from social skills "coaching" in order to improve peer relationships and interaction, so he was referred to the school district counselor who will work with Clyde and his teachers in offering him support. There was discussion about Clyde's strengths and the need to provide leadership opportunities for him in the classroom and in the school.

Case Study #2: Bonnie

Bonnie was a 6-year-old girl who was referred with questions about obsessive-compulsive disorder (OCD), ADHD, and/or autism spectrum disorder. She was the only child residing at home in a rural community; however, there were two siblings from her mother's previous marriage. Her father was not married previously.

Although Bonnie was only 6 years old, she had attended four different educational programs in rural communities and at the time of the assessment was in Grade two. She was accelerated at her mother's request as she felt that her daughter's learning needs were not being met. Her current teacher reported that there are no behavioral concerns; however, it was noted that Bonnie sometimes becomes preoccupied with specific topics (e.g., horses) and cannot, or will not, move off the topic. She reads about horses, writes about horses, and talks about horses. The teacher has been encouraging her to research and write about other topics. He reported that she is strong academically and has no difficulty keeping up with her classmates despite the fact that she is a year or two younger than most of them. Mother sought help because of extreme behaviors in the home. She reported that Bonnie constantly demands attention and can be aggressive. She reported that Bonnie had frequently hit her when she was frustrated or if her mother denied a request. She described Bonnie as having a high activity level and intense emotionality. Mother questioned whether Bonnie is in the best educational program and also stated that she requires support in dealing with Bonnie at home.

Bonnie was seen four times individually, and her teacher and mother were also interviewed. Her mother and teacher completed rating forms. Bonnie was administered the Wechsler Intelligence Scale for Children – Fourth Edition, Children's Memory Scale, Wechsler Individual Achievement Test – Second Edition, selected subtests from a neuropsychological test battery, Multidimensional Anxiety Scale for Children, and the Continuous Performance Test. Parents and teachers provided feedback on the Behavior Assessment System for Children – Second Edition, Gilliam Autism Rating Scale – Second Edition, Clinical Autism Diagnostic Interview, Family Assessment Measure – Third Edition, and in a clinical interview with Bonnie's mother. Bonnie's behavior was observed in the classroom as part of the data collection process.

The assessment results indicated that Bonnie was functioning in the very superior range of intelligence. In regard to her behavior, there were inconsistencies between home and school. In school, expectations for behavior, learning, and social interaction were clear, and Bonnie was able to regulate her attention and behavior. She had a very positive relationship with her teacher, and the inquiry-based program allowed her to extend and expand her learning in many different ways. She had many gifted peers in the classroom with whom she could interact and work on projects. She was observed to interact appropriately with peers both in the classroom and on the playground. At home, her parents reported clinically high ratings of hyperactivity and atypicality. Her attention as measured in the testing situation, and as observed in the classroom, was in the nonclinical range. She did not meet the criteria for further investigation on the autism screening instruments. She demonstrated a relative weakness in visual memory. Family relationships were reported to be below average for task accomplishment, communication, and involvement.

In a conference with parents, school staff, and medical practitioners (i.e., psychiatrist, occupational therapist, mental health nurse, family therapist), it was agreed that Bonnie was experiencing success in school. Her teacher indicated that they would designate her as a gifted student. This designation requires an individual program plan, and although he was not opposed to developing an individual program plan for Bonnie, he felt that his program currently met the need for challenge and enrichment. He also indicated that there were other gifted students in the classroom, so she had peers with whom to interact and learn. He felt that the school could accommodate Bonnie's needs and that an alternative program was not necessary. OCD was ruled out with the recognition that Bonnie has a tendency to engage in behaviors which are typical of children with OCD, but that these behaviors are not sufficient to constitute diagnosis of a syndrome. Bonnie's mother reported that some of Bonnie's behaviors may have been learned. It was agreed that these behaviors would be closely monitored at home and school. The psychiatrist Bonnie has been seeing on a regular basis will continue to provide individual therapy.

Summary

The overarching goal of this chapter is to enhance and elaborate understandings of how school psychologists support classroom teachers in enhancing positive outcomes for all children. Schools exert powerful influences on children's health and well-being. Indeed, they can provide children with one of the best opportunities they have to improve their satisfaction with life and enjoy a healthy lifestyle. But, can they do it alone? Numerous factors can interrupt children's emerging development processes and deny or minimize their opportunities for optimal academic, social, emotional, and adaptive development. While Canada's children are generally doing well, a number of indicators show that a significant number of children face adversity. Classrooms in today's schools are populated by a diverse complement of children, many of whom live with challenges and vulnerabilities that impede their ability to learn. No one profession has the skills, knowledge, or energy to adequately meet the needs of these students. Indeed, there is growing consensus that if our children are to thrive and succeed, we must engage multidisciplinary professionals to support school personnel. School psychologists are integral and necessary members of these teams.

References

Alberta Association of Sexual Assault Centres. (2005). *Children and sexual assault/abuse*. Report available at 222.aasac.ca/txt-fact-children-sexual-assault-abuse.htm

American Psychological Association. (2009). *Careers for the twenty-first century*. Washington, DC: Author.

Bijl, R. V., deGraaf, R., Hiripi, E., Kessler, R. C., Kohn, R., Offord, D. R., et al. (2003). The prevalence of treated and untreated mental disorders in five countries. *Health Affairs, 22*, 122–133.

British Columbia Ministry of Child and Family Development. (2003). *Child and youth mental health plan*. Victoria, BC: Government of British Columbia.

Bronfenbrenner, U. (2004). *Making human beings human: Bioecological perspectives on human development*. Thousand Oaks, CA: Sage Publications.

Cameron, R. J. (2006). Educational psychology: The distinctive contribution. *Educational Psychology in Practice, 22*(4), 289–304.

Canadian Incidence Study of Reported Child Abuse and Neglect. (2001). Report available through the National Clearinghouse on Family Violence, Ottawa, ON: www.hc.sc.gc.ca/nc-cn

Canadian Psychological Association. (2007). *Professional practice guidelines for school psychologists in Canada.* Available at http://www.cpa.ca/cpasite/userfiles/Documents/publications/CPA%20Guideline%20Practice.pdf

Carney, P. (2001). The practice of psychology in Ontario schools. *Canadian Journal of School Psychology, 16*(2), 47–57.

Charvat, J. (2005). NASP study: How many school psychologists are there? *Communiqué, 32*(6), 12–13.

Charvat, J., & Charvat, T. (2003). The school psychologist shortage: Evidence for effective advocacy. *Communiqué, 32*(2), 1. 4–5.

Child & Family Canada. (1997). *Children and poverty.* Report available at http://www.cfc-efc.ca/does/cccf/00000764.htm

Citizenship and Immigration Canada (CIC). (2005). *Facts and figures 2004. Immigration overview. Permanents and temporary residents* (Cat. No. Cil-8/2004E-PDF). Ottawa, ON: Minister of Public Works and Government Services Canada.

Cortese, A. (2008). *The role Alberta's boom plays in the lives of immigrant/refugee children and youth.* Available online: http://canada.metropolis.net/events/10th_national_halifax08/presentations/D2-Cortese%5EAntonella.pdf

Evans, G. W., Eckenrode, J., & Marcynyszyn, L. (2007). *Poverty and chaos.* First Urie Bronfenbrenner Conference, Cornell University, Ithaca, NY.

Fagan, T., & Wise, P. (Eds.). (2007). *School psychology: Past, present, and future perspectives* (3rd ed.). Bethesda, MD: National Association of School Psychologists.

Federal/Provincial/Territorial Early Childhood Development Agreement (Canada). (2002). *The well-being of Canada's young children: Government of Canada report, 2002.* Ottawa, ON: Human Resources Development.

Government of Canada, Public Health Agency of Canada. (2002). *The well-being of Canada's young children: Government of Canada report.* Report available through the National Clearinghouse on Family violence, Ottawa, ON. (http://www.socialunion.gc.ca/ecd/2002/ecd-report-2002-toc-e.html)

Hann, G. S. (2001). School psychology in Nova Scotia. *Canadian Journal of School Psychology, 16*(2), 19–24.

Hanvey, L. (2002). *Children with disabilities and their families in Canada: A discussion paper* (Report commissioned by the National Children's Alliance for the First National Roundtable on Children with Disabilities). Ottawa, ON: Government of Canada.

Hou, F., & Bourne, L. S. (2004). *Population movement into and out of Canada's immigrant gateway cities: A comparative study of Toronto, Montreal and Vancouver* (Analytical Studies Branch Research Paper Series, Statistics Canada, Business and Labour Market Analysis, Cat. No. 11 F0019, no 229)

Huang, L., Stroul, B., Friedman, R., Mrazek, P., Friesen, B., Pires, S., et al. (2005). Transforming mental health care for children and their families. *Journal of the American Psychological Association, 60*(6), 615–627.

Human Resources and Skills Development Canada. (2005). *Health immigrant children: A demographic and geographic analysis – October 1998.* Report available through Human Resources and Skills Development website (http://www.hrsdc.gc.ca/eng/cs/sp/sdc/pkrf/publications/research/1998-000133/page04.shtml)

Janzen, H. L., & Carter, S. (2001). State of the art of school psychology in Alberta. *Canadian Journal of School Psychology, 16*(2), 9–13.

Juby, H., Marcil-Gratton, N., & Le Bourdais, C. (2004). *Research report: When parents separate: Further findings from the National Longitudinal survey of children and youth.* Ottawa, ON: Minister of Justice and Attorney General of Canada.

Kirby, M. J. L., & Keon, W. J. (2004). *The Standing Senate Committee on Social Affairs, Science and Technology: Report 3: Mental health, mental illness and addiction: Issues and options for Canada.* Available on the Parliamentary Internet: 222.parl.gc.ca

Kirby, M. J. L., & LeBreton, M. (2002). *The health of Canadians. The federal role: Recommendations for reform.* Ottawa, ON: The Standing Senate Committee on Social Affairs, Science and Technology. Report available online: http://www.parl.gc.ca/37/2/parlbus/commbus/senate/com-e/soci-e/rep-e/repoct02vol6-e.htm

Lee, K. K. (2000). *Urban poverty in Canada: A statistical profile* (Report available from the Canadian Council on Social Development). http://www.ccsd.ca/pubs/2000/up/.

Lupart, J. L., Goddard, T., Hebert, Y., Jacobsen, M., & Timmons, V. (2001). *Students at risk in Canadian schools and communities.* Hull, QC: HRDC Publications Centre.

Luthar, S. S., Cicchetti, D., & Becker, B. (2000). The construct of resilience: A critical evaluation and guidelines for future work. *Child Development, 71*(3), 543–562.

MacMillan, H., Fleming, J., & Trocme, N. (1997). Prevalence of child physical and sexual abuse in the community: Results from the Ontario health supplement. *Journal of the American Medical Association, 278*(2), 131–134.

Masten, A. S. (2001). Ordinary magic: Resilience processes in development. *American Psychologist, 56*(3), 227–238.

McEwan, K., Waddell, C., & Barker, J. (2007). Bringing children's mental health "out of the shadows". *Canadian Mental Health Association Journal, 176*(4), 423.

Mental Health Evaluation and Community Consultation Unit. (2002). *Prevalence of mental disorders in children and youth.* Vancouver, BC: University of British Columbia.

National Association of School Psychologists. (2000). *Standards for training and field placement programs: School psychology standards for the credentialing of school psychologists.* Report available at http://www.nasponline.org/standards/FinalStandards.pdf

Pendakur, K., & Pendakur, R. (1998). The colour of money: Earnings differentials among ethnic groups in Canada. *Canadian Journal of Economics, 31*(3), 518–548.

Pumariega, A. J., & Winters, N. C. (Eds.). (2003). *The handbook of child and adolescent systems of care.* San Francisco, CA: Jossey-Bass.

Rothman, L. (2007). Oh Canada! Too many children in poverty for too long. *Education Canada, 47*(4), 49–53.

Saklofske, D. H., Bartell, R., Derevensky, J., Hahn, G., Holmes, B., & Janzen, H. (2000). School psychology in Canada: Past present and future perspectives. In T. Fagan & P. Wise (Eds.), *School psychology* (2nd ed., pp. 313–354). Bethesda, MD: NASP.

Saklofske, D. H., & Grainger, J. (2001). School psychology in Saskatchewan: The end of a decade, the start of a century. *Canadian Journal of School Psychology, 17*(1), 67.

Saklofske, D. H., Schwean, V. L., & Bartell, R. (2007). School psychology in Canada: Past, present, and future perspectives. In T. Fagan & P. Wise (Eds.), *School psychology: Past, present, and future perspectives* (3rd ed.). Bethesda, MD: National Association of School Psychologists.

Sattler, J. M. (2001). *Assessment of children: Cognitive applications.* San Diego, CA: Jerome M. Sattler.

Sloat, E., & Willms, J. D. (2002). A gradient approach to the study of childhood vulnerability. In J. D. Willms (Ed.), *Vulnerable children* (pp. 23–44). Edmonton, AB: University of Alberta Press.

Statistics Canada. (2001). *A profile of disability in Canada, 2001.* Report available at http://www.statcan.ca/english/freepub/89-577-XIE/index.htm

Stroul, B. A., & Blau, G. M. (Eds.). (2008). *The system of care handbook: Transforming mental health services for children, youth and families.* Baltimore, MD: Paul H. Brookes.

Tolan, P. H., & Dodge, K. A. (2005). Children's mental health as a primary case and concern: A system for comprehensive support and service. *Journal of the American Psychological Association, 60*(6), 601–614.

Trierweiler, S. J., & Stricker, G. (1998). The local clinical scientist. In S. J. Trierweiler & G. Stricker (Eds.), *The scientific practice of professional psychology.* New York: Plenum.

Waddell, C., McEwan, K., Shepherd, C. A., Offord, D. R., & Hua, J. M. (2005). A public health strategy to improve the mental health of Canadian children. *Canadian Journal of Psychiatry, 50*(4), 226–233.

Waddell, C., Offord, D. R., Shepard, C. A., Hua, J. M., & McEwan, K. (2002). Child psychiatric epidemiology and Canadian public policy-making: The state of the science and the art of the possible. *Canadian Journal of Psychiatry, 45*, 825–832.

Wang, M. C., & Gordon, E. W. (1994). *Educational resilience in inner-city America: Challenges and prospects.* Hillsdale, NJ: Lawrence Erlbaum Associates.

Waxman, H. C., Gray, J. P., & Padron, Y. N. (2003). *Review of research on educational resilience.* Center for Research on Education, Diversity & Excellence. Berkeley: University of California.

Waxman, H. C., Padrón, Y. N., & Gray, J. (Eds.). (2004). *Educational resiliency: Student, teacher, and school perspectives.* Charlotte, NC: Information Age Publishing.

Weisz, J. R., Sandler, I. N., Durlak, J. A., & Anton, B. S. (2005). Promoting and protecting youth mental health through evidence-based prevention and treatment. *American Psychologist, 60*(6), 628–648.

Werner, E. F. (2000). Protective factors and individual resilience. In J. P. Shonkoff & S. J. Meisels (Eds.), *Handbook of early childhood intervention* (2nd ed., pp. 115–132). Cambridge, UK: Cambridge University Press.

Willms, J. (2002a). The prevalence of vulnerable children. In J. D. Willms (Ed.), *Vulnerable children* (pp. 45–70). Edmonton, AB: University of Alberta Press.

Willms, J. (2002b). Socioeconomic gradients for childhood vulnerability. In J. D. Willms (Ed.), *Vulnerable children* (pp. 71–104). Edmonton, AB: University of Alberta Press.

Ysseldyke, J. E., & Christensen, S. L. (1987). Evaluating students' instructional environments. *RASE, 8*(3), 17–24.

Ysseldyke, J. E., Christensen, S. L., & Kovaleski, J. F. (1994). Identifying students' instructional needs in the context of classroom and home environments. *Teaching Exceptional Children, 26*(Spring, 3), 37–41.

Chapter 7
Current Issues in Assessing Students with Special Needs

John Venn

This chapter investigates critical issues associated with the processes and procedures for assessing students with special needs. The chapter covers issues associated with formal standardized testing, informal classroom assessment, and accommodations in testing. The chapter begins by defining key issues and presenting a conceptual framework. A detailed investigation of the issues follows the conceptual framework.

Defining the Issues

Many issues surround the processes and procedures for conducting formal testing, carrying out informal assessment, and providing accommodations to students with special needs (Allbritten et al. 2004; Bowen and Rude 2006; DeLuca 2008; Koretz and Barton 2004; McLaughlin and Thurlow 2003). Some issues, like fairness in testing, apply to all of these topics while others are unique to specific types of assessment (Gilbertson and Ferre 2008; Perner 2007) such as testing deaf students. Many of the most critical current issues surround formal, standardized testing.

Formal, standardized testing most often refers to giving a test in a structured manner for the purpose of obtaining a score. Some formal tests have norms, which serve as the basis for interpreting student performance. Other formal tests interpret performance using predetermined criteria, competencies, or standards. Some of the most controversial formal tests are the high-stakes tests that schools use as accountability measures. Lee (2008) described many of the limitations, uncertainties, and

J. Venn (✉)
College of Education and Human Services, University of North Florida,
Jacksonville, FL, USA
e-mail: j.venn@unf.edu

C.F. Webber and J.L. Lupart (eds.), *Leading Student Assessment,*
Studies in Educational Leadership 15, DOI 10.1007/978-94-007-1727-5_7,
© Springer Science+Business Media B.V. 2012

inconsistencies associated with high-stakes testing. Lee called for more use of scientific research evidence in developing test-driven external accountability policies. While holding schools accountable for student learning is vital, using high-stakes testing to accomplish this presents a number of problems for students with special needs. In addition to accountability, other issues in formal testing with students who have special needs include questions about fairness, issues related to computer-based testing, and challenges in implementing new assessment procedures. Formal testing is generally highly structured, static, standardized, episodic, and product-based. With many formal tests, the focus is on a single test score or set of scores. In contrast, informal assessment tends to be more flexible, dynamic, individualized, continuous, ongoing, and process-based. With most informal assessments, the focus is broader than a single test score result.

Informal assessment refers to the many different types of evaluation procedures that teachers use in the classroom and in other instructional settings with students who have special needs. These assessment procedures include teacher-made tests, checklists of skills, behavior rating scales, rubrics, observations, and grading. Informal assessments focus more on content and performance rather than test score results (Weaver 2007). For example, running records are informal assessments that indicate how well students read the content of specific books. Scores such as 8 out of 10 correct, the percent of words read correctly, and checklist scores are also informal in nature. Issues in informal assessment include the low quality of many classroom assessments, validity concerns, and questions about reliability.

Many of the newest issues in assessing students with special needs are associated with accommodations in testing. Accommodations are alterations in presentation or response mode that do not change the content, grade level, or performance requirements of the test (Case 2005). Accommodations provide students who have disabilities with the opportunity to demonstrate their knowledge of the content being tested. Issues associated with accommodations include how to select appropriate accommodations and concerns about the effectiveness of accommodations.

A Conceptual Framework

Organizing assessment into steps or stages provides a helpful framework for understanding current issues and explaining the process of assessing students with special needs. Experts (McLoughlin and Lewis 2008; Oosterhof 2009) have identified distinct steps or stages in the process including screening, identifying, intervening, and measuring progress. These steps are like a map for the assessment process. Although overlap occurs among these steps, each has a distinct purpose and relies on specific assessments. These steps also explain how and when students are assessed and provide a way to connect assessment in a logical sequence. A chart illustrating the stages appears in Fig. 7.1. An explanation of each step follows, beginning with screening.

Fig. 7.1 The steps in the assessment process: a conceptual framework for assessing students with special needs

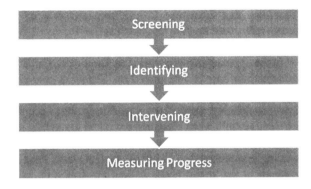

Screening

The first step in assessment, usually referred to as screening, is the initial stage in the process. Screening occurs when a parent, educator, or other professional suspects that a child may have a learning or behavior problem. This sets into motion a series of screening procedures. The specific procedures vary depending on the age of the child and the type of suspected disability. Most screening relies on brief and informal tests and evaluations. For this reason, the validity of screening data and information is an ongoing issue. To insure assessment with the highest possible fidelity, screening decisions should be based on multiple data and information sources. The screening process is almost always guided by a team, often called the child study team, consisting of professionals and the parents. When the screening results indicate the child may have a disability, the team makes a formal referral for more in-depth testing and evaluation to determine if a student qualifies and could benefit from special education and related services.

One of the pressing issues in screening is the need to develop more effective school-wide screening programs to identify students with special needs. Many experts (Deno et al. 2009; Fuchs and Fuchs 2005; Fuchs et al. 2007) recommend using universal progress-monitoring systems. For example, the approach recommended by Deno et al. (2009) involves screening all students at the elementary level in reading at the beginning of each school year using a response to intervention (RTI) model. RTI is an assessment and intervention process that relies on ongoing progress monitoring. A variety of RTI procedures are available to screen students who are at risk for failure, to help identify students with disabilities, and to monitor student progress. There are a number of universal screening systems which have been created using the RTI model. These employ a variety of assessments including curriculum-based measurement (CBM; Fuchs and Fuchs 2005; Salvia et al. 2007), curriculum-based assessment (CBA; Deno et al. 2009), the *Dynamic Indicators of Basic Early Literacy Skills* (Good et al. 2001; University of Oregon Center on

Teaching and Learning 2003), and subtests of individually administered, norm-referenced reading tests such as the *Woodcock Reading Mastery Test–Revised/ Normative Update* (Woodcock 1998).

In the approach recommended by Deno et al. (2009), students are identified using a curriculum-based maze procedure. The maze procedure is a multiple-choice silent reading cloze process for assessing reading comprehension. The cloze process involves deleting words from a reading passage according to specific criteria such as every seventh word. Students are asked to read the passage and insert the missing words as they read. This procedure is an excellent diagnostic technique for assessing reading comprehension. After all students have been screened, the progress of the students at the lowest levels is then monitored on an ongoing basis. The students who continue to experience failure in reading are referred for comprehensive evaluation to determine if they have a reading disability. Universal screening systems like this one hold much promise for improving the process of accurately screening students. Accurate screening leads directly to more effective formal assessment, which occurs during the process of identifying students with special needs.

Identifying

Identifying students with disabilities is a more comprehensive assessment process than screening, and it relies primarily on formal, norm-referenced testing (Lerner et al. 2003). Formal testing is episodic and product-based in that it focuses on interpreting the results of a score or group of scores from one-time testing. However, more ongoing, process-based identification procedures based on RTI are being used with increasing frequency, especially with students who may have learning disabilities (Fuchs and Fuchs 2007). RTI approaches are also being used to help identify children who are gifted (Rollins et al. 2009). Regardless of the type of assessment, formal or informal, the identification of students with disabilities should be based on multiple measures of student achievement, ability, and performance, and all measures should produce reliable and valid results. The goal of identification is to pinpoint the specific nature of the disability based on the child's present levels of performance, strengths, weaknesses, and educational needs. A team of professionals works together in this process to arrive at an appropriate diagnosis and disability label. For example, if the screening identifies a possible reading disability, the members of the assessment team may include a reading specialist to determine the exact nature of the reading problem and a psychologist to measure the child's overall aptitude.

Parent involvement in identification is a key element. Parents must be fully apprised throughout the process, and they must give informed permission for testing. Further, parents are important team members because they provide essential information to the other members of the assessment team. For this reason, parents should be encouraged to actively participate in the meetings in which decisions are made about the identification, assessment, and educational placement of their child (Taylor 2009).

The process of identifying young children and older students with disabilities includes some special considerations (Cohen and Spenciner 2007). With young children, for example, reliable assessment is difficult due to the inadequacies of assessment instruments and the rapid changes that characterize the development and growth of infants, toddlers, and preschoolers. Further, many of the disability categories designed for older children may not be appropriate as labels for young children. One of the unique aspects in the process of identifying teenagers and young adults is that it usually includes significant participation by the student in the process. Student participation can be highly beneficial, especially in developing educational goals and in deciding which programs and services would best meet those goals.

While the process of identifying children with various special needs is different for each type of disability, reliance on assessment is a common element of all identification processes and procedures. It is the assessment results in the form of test scores along with other data and information which provide the foundation for deciding which students are eligible and can benefit from special education and related services. The test scores are also necessary in the process of developing an initial intervention plan. This plan is first developed as part of the identification process, and it is based on the student's present levels of educational performance. After being implemented, the plan is periodically revised during intervention.

Intervening

The third step in the process is providing appropriate educational and related services for the student. The exact nature and extent of the intervention program provided depends on the nature of the student's disability, age, learning style, and related factors. For example, a young student with a severe disability may benefit from a home intervention program with a curriculum focusing on developmental skills. In contrast, a school-age student with a mild disability may be best served in an inclusive classroom with special education support services and a general education curriculum focus with appropriate accommodations in assessment and instruction. A teenager with a severe disability may benefit from a community-based supported employment program in which special education services are provided by an employment specialist and the curriculum focus is on employment and work skills. Regardless of the type of disability, assessment should be an integral element in providing the best possible intervention program for each student based on appropriate learning goals and outcomes. A wide range and variety of assessment processes and procedures are available for use as part of the intervention. These include CBA, CBM, portfolio assessment, and observation.

CBA involves evaluating student performance and the effects of instructional interventions within the curriculum in a given classroom or school program. According to Payne et al. (2007), the CBA process involves identifying key skills in the curriculum and developing brief measures or probes to track changes in those skills as instruction is provided. When the results of the measures or probes are graphed or charted, teachers may analyze data and information to make decisions about the effectiveness of the instructional interventions. CBA is useful for assessing academic performance at all grade levels, and as such, it is a general term for a number of different techniques, procedures, and strategies. These include checklists of skills, error pattern analysis, informal reading inventories, cloze procedures, rubrics, and work samples. CBA is a valuable tool for effectively and efficiently identifying student knowledge and skill levels within specific curricula used for instructional intervention (Burns 2002).

CBM is another widely used direct assessment procedure that is helpful in the intervention process, especially in the academic learning areas of reading, mathematics, spelling, and written expression. With CBM, teachers obtain weekly data and information about student performance with brief, timed samples, or "probes" using material from classroom lessons. The weekly probes normally take from between 1 and 5 min to give and to score. Data from these probes informs teachers about how well students are learning and helps gauge the success of the instructional intervention program. The results of each probe are recorded on a graph, which allows comparison of the student's performance with expected performance levels (Wright 2007).

Use of CBM procedures to gauge the effectiveness of intervention is continuing to increase in schools, and efforts are ongoing to improve and expand best practices. Improvement efforts are focusing on how to implement CBM with high fidelity, to support teachers, and to best use CBM data. Extensive research has been conducted on implementation of CBM tasks and procedures, especially in literacy and math (Brown-Chidsey et al. 2005). Most of this research has investigated specific questions about narrow aspects of CBM. Research indicates that teachers benefit from ongoing support to develop and make instructional intervention changes that result in positive improvement gains for students (Stecker et al. 2005). Without sufficient supports, teachers and other practitioners may not effectively use CBM as an integral part of intervention. Using CBM accurately can be difficult. Therefore, as more practitioners use this approach, training and other support should be provided, especially in the appropriate use and interpretation of data (Codding et al. 2005). CBM data yields extensive information about students' current capabilities and rates of progress, but using these data is complex and requires high-level data gathering, management, and interpretation skills. CBM helps practitioners to accurately identify intervention priorities, to plan more effective individual programs, and to establish appropriate learning goals and objectives.

Portfolio assessment is also widely used in classrooms, schools, and school systems (Miller et al. 2009). Teachers use portfolios in their classrooms for ongoing assessment of student progress. When used in this way, the assessment results are excellent for helping to determine grades and for reporting to parents. When schools use portfolio assessment, it enables evaluation of student progress in the curriculum across teachers, programs, and grade levels. Entire school systems may use portfolio assessment as an accountability measure.

Observation continues to be one of the best ways to assess certain elements of learning and behavior (Miller et al. 2009). For example, when teachers keep informal written records over time, these anecdotal documents can be a valuable source of information about student learning. Even more useful is formal, systematic observation data and information. Observational data from functional behavior analysis, for example, may help determine how well students are responding to a variety of educational interventions, especially those designed to reduce problems in social and emotional behaviors.

These different assessment strategies and procedures are illustrative of what is available for use in intervention programs for students with special needs. These same types of approaches are also useful in measuring progress to insure the program and services are meeting the child's needs. Measuring progress involves assessing both student progress and program effectiveness.

Measuring Progress

A key principle in all facets of assessment, including measuring progress, is using multiple measures to monitor and track student growth, achievement, and performance (Lerner et al. 2003). Logsdon (n.d.) identified several appropriate progress measures including observing student achievement, performance, and behavior; using rating scales; reviewing school records and related information; interpreting results from informal, criterion-referenced and formal, norm-referenced tests; and gathering data and information from authentic assessments such as portfolios. Other useful evaluation procedures include CBM, CBA, adaptive testing, and large-scale assessments. Multiple measurements help determine overall gains and progress in meeting the learning goals and objectives established for the student. The best progress data is collected continuously over time, and it is linked with curriculum standards and learning outcomes. The learning gains of the students in a class or program provide one of the best measures of program effectiveness. Other program effectiveness measures include student mastery of standards and outcomes as well as student performance on large-scale assessments.

Another key consideration is incorporating progress measurement into the educational program rather than leaving it as a separate, disconnected component. Quenemoen et al. (2003) cited several challenges in developing integrated standards-based progress-monitoring and accountability systems. These challenges include limited access to the general education curriculum and to general education assessment for students with disabilities, limited use of assessment data and information in evaluating instructional interventions and program services, and questions about the most appropriate measurement standards. Another challenge is including multiple measures of progress. Responding to these challenges requires additional resources, especially training for practitioners. Training should include in-service, coaching, and collaborative problem solving on how to use assessment data. Training coupled with ongoing support will help educators respond to the multiple challenges of implementing and maintaining integrated progress-monitoring systems.

The steps in the assessment process include screening, identifying, intervening, and measuring progress. These steps provide a conceptual framework for considering the issues in assessment and for understanding how and when to assess students with special needs. The four steps also provide a foundation for considering specific issues beginning with formal testing.

Issues in Formal Testing

Several critical issues are associated with formal, standardized testing and students who have special needs. The most pressing issues are associated with fairness in testing and educational accountability. Fairness in testing is a longstanding issue, but much progress has been made in reducing bias in recent years.

Fairness in Testing

Fairness in testing is concerned with the equity of test results for all students including students with specific disabilities. Fairness has long been a concern because in the past, students with special needs were routinely tested in ways that resulted in biased results. For example, giving an intelligence test that relies heavily on oral language questions to deaf students produces biased results. A better procedure is to give only the performance or nonverbal subtests of an intelligence test to deaf students. This produces a better estimate of the true cognitive ability of deaf students, and this has become standard procedure in recent years. This example illustrates the progress that has been made in eliminating bias by changing the way in which tests are administered. Progress has been made in other areas as well. Test norms have been drastically improved, and many specialized tests have been developed for children with specific disabilities. Further, best practices now call for the use of multiple measures rather than just one test. Multiple measures provide a better picture of a child's performance than the results from just a single test score.

While significant improvements have been made in the way tests are developed, not as much progress has occurred in the way test results are interpreted. Thus, interpreting test results in ways that are fair for students with special needs is an ongoing issue. For example, students with disabilities may score lower on formal tests due to their disabilities. Taking differences in scores due to disabilities into account in interpreting scores is difficult, but it is necessary to insure fairness.

Educational Accountability

Educational accountability is another critical issue associated with formal testing.

The specific meaning of accountability in education is confusing given the current situation with multiple reforms and restructuring initiatives (Heim n.d.), and accountability has different meanings for practitioners, policy makers, and researchers.

In the United States, the accountability focus is on student outcomes as measured by performance on high-stakes achievement tests. These tests are used to measure student progress and to gauge the effectiveness of schools and programs. In recent years, emphasis on educational accountability using high-stakes tests has lead to several problems. For teachers, one effect has been pressure to teach to the high-stakes test; therefore, student learning is often focused around acquiring the factual knowledge necessary to pass a multiple-choice, high-stakes accountability test.

Many of the problems associated with high-stakes tests were summarized in a paper by Stiggins (2007). Stiggins contended that a major problem has to do with the lack of evidence to support a connection between school improvement and the use of high-stakes tests as accountability measures. Stiggins suggested that one reason for this is that school and community leaders do not have the necessary knowledge and skills to use assessment in ways that result in improved schools. Likewise, Stiggins indicated that most teachers are inadequately prepared to conduct assessments and to interpret test results in ways that lead to higher student achievement. This problem with test interpretation is especially severe with students who have special needs and score the lowest on standardized tests. In a related paper, Popham (2008) indicated that most educators fail to realize how useful formal testing data can be in making instructional decisions. Further, Popham explained that educators need to develop additional knowledge and skills in order to successfully use test data in educational decision making. Popham identified the ability to identify the most useful test score data as a key competency for all educators. Finally, Stiggins indicated that grades and test scores do not motivate students to become reflective learners. These problems are especially relevant to students who score the lowest on standardized tests including students with special needs.

This discussion of high-stakes testing highlights some of the many issues associated with accountability and formal testing. It also illustrates the many different dimensions surrounding questions of how best to account for student learning in the schools. The accountability movement will certainly continue to be an area of emphasis in education. Given this, issues associated with accountability including high stakes will remain at the forefront.

Issues in Informal Assessment

One major issue in informal assessment has to do with the barriers practitioners face in insuring quality assessment. Other key issues are related to questions about the reliability and validity of informal assessment processes and procedures.

Barriers to High-Quality Informal Assessment

High-quality classroom assessment is essential, but teachers face a number of significant barriers to achieving this in their classrooms. The roadblocks are especially significant with students who have disabilities due to their individual and often unique needs. In a discussion of barriers to quality classroom assessment, Stiggins (2001) cited negative feelings about assessment as a key obstacle. The problem is that many practitioners have had negative personal experiences with assessment, and this impacts their view of assessment in the classroom. Further, students with disabilities themselves may have extremely negative attitudes about assessment. This may include an expectancy to fail tests based on poor performance over time on numerous assessments. These negative experiences make developing and implementing high-quality assessments difficult. A second barrier identified by Stiggins is lack of support for teachers who strive to conduct high-quality assessments. This problem may be particularly severe with students who have special needs because they often present the most difficult assessment challenges. Lack of support is often coupled with the many demands on teachers. As a result, classroom assessment may be left undone or incomplete simply due to insufficient time to plan and carry out comprehensive testing and measurement of student performance. Finally, teachers often lack the necessary knowledge and skills for developing comprehensive assessment plans for students with special needs who may perform below grade levels in academic achievement and may exhibit behavior problems in the classroom. Best practices call for teachers to identify present levels of performance, strengths, weaknesses, and priorities for intervention with students who have difficulties. These assessment and intervention tasks require sufficient time and appropriate support.

Reliability and Validity of Informal Assessment

Reliability is concerned with the consistency of assessment results. Validity is really a question of effectiveness. Classroom assessment involves collecting and giving meaning to data and information related to student learning. When this is done in a consistent, effective manner, it produces results that teachers may use with confidence to make accurate interpretations about student progress and sound instructional decisions about student learning. When this is done haphazardly, the results may fail to help teachers make appropriate decisions and may even lead to inaccurate interpretations of student performance.

Because most classroom assessment is informal and directly related to student performance on class lessons and assignments, the reliability and validity issues differ from those associated with formal tests. Teachers gather assessment data and information from a variety of sources such as teacher-made tests, class assignments, homework, and observations. Assessment sources like these use a criterion frame of reference for measuring the focused and specific behaviors being taught in a lesson or instructional unit. This is much different than formal testing, which uses a normative frame of reference (Thorndike 2005).

The issues associated with the reliability and validity of informal classroom assessment have to do with the informal way in which most classroom tests and assessment are given and scored. Although flexibility is a distinct advantage of informal assessment, it can lead to potential reliability and validity problems.

When teachers give, score, and interpret informal assessments in ways that are not consistent, the results fail to effectively measure what they were designed to measure.

Experts (Brookhart and Nitko 2008; Nitko and Brookhart 2007) indicate informal classroom assessment should meet several reliability and validity standards. First, informal assessments should include content reflecting the lesson or instructional unit and should be connected with the standards and objectives for the lesson. The best assessments also include a range of thinking levels and skills. Effective classroom assessments should also be efficient to give and score while maintaining accuracy. The most reliable classroom assessments use multiple measures of student performance and provide students with more than one way to demonstrate that they have met a particular standard or competency. Fairness is also a key consideration, especially with students who have disabilities. One of the ways to insure fairness with informal assessments and formal tests is to provide accommodations for students with disabilities.

Issues in Providing Accommodations

Accommodations in testing include changes in setting, timing, scheduling, administration, or response method (Case 2005). Accommodations are often described as a way to level the playing field by giving students with disabilities the opportunity to demonstrate their knowledge of the content being tested. Sireci (2006) described accommodations as a way to remove the barriers in testing that prevent appropriate measurement of a student's present levels of performance. Current issues include how to select appropriate accommodations, concerns regarding the effectiveness of accommodations, questions about how to create more flexible tests that avoid the need for accommodations, and confusion about differences between accommodations and modifications.

Selecting Accommodations

Selecting accommodations is an issue because practitioners and policy makers are often unsure about which accommodations are effective and appropriate. One reason is that no one set of accommodations exists for all students with disabilities. Instead, accommodations must be individualized to meet the needs of the student (McKevitt and Elliot 2003). Two of the most frequently used accommodations are extended time to take a test and reduced distractions while testing, such as a separate room (Pitoniak and Royer 2001). Available evidence (Sireci 2006) indicates that these two accommodations can be both helpful and appropriate for many students with disabilities. For example, some students with attention deficit hyperactivity disorder cannot concentrate on a test in a group setting. Testing in a separate room accommodates for this disability. Many other accommodations are provided to students, depending on the nature and extent of their disability. These include, but are not limited to, sign language interpreters for deaf students, computers for word processing on essay tests, scribes who write for a student, and readers.

Effectiveness and New Procedures

Other accommodation issues have to do with effectiveness and developing new assessment procedures. Effectiveness is an issue because more research is needed to establish the validity of most accommodations. As a result, many policies guiding how we provide accommodations are not based on sound research evidence (Sireci et al. 2005). Although court decisions have provided some guidance, developing policy that specifies reasonable accommodations is an ongoing need. Current debate includes questions about policies for providing calculators, reading questions aloud, sign language interpretation of questions, and using spell checkers as accommodations in various testing situations (Lazarus et al. 2009). One answer to these current issues is to develop new, more flexible tests that avoid the need for accommodations (Sireci et al. 2003). New innovations in creating flexible tests include promoting test accessibility through the use of universal design strategies and techniques. For example, some computer-based tests now offer customizable options such as read-aloud test content. This is an example of how to reduce access barriers for students with disabilities (Dolan et al. 2005). In the future, it is possible that a new generation of assessments using universal design for assessment (UDA) techniques will reduce the need for accommodations. According to Ketterlin-Geller (2005), UDA holds promise for the development of individually designed tests for students with disabilities and for students from diverse cultural and linguistic backgrounds. UDA may make it easier for students with disabilities to participate in general education assessments. In a longitudinal study of accommodations policies since 1993, Lazarus et al. (2009) indicated that the focus on developing universally designed assessments may reduce the need for accommodations. This would minimize the ongoing issues about which accommodations should be available in different testing situations.

Modifications and Alternative Assessments

Another issue has to do with modifications including alternative assessments. Modifications are changes to a test or an assessment procedure that fundamentally alter the content, the level, or the administration procedure. Modifications are generally provided only for students with more severe disabilities who require such extensive changes in assessment that they cannot take regular assessments even with accommodations. Alternative assessments include portfolios, skills checklists, and performance assessments that directly measure skills and are based on modified achievement standards (Cohen and Spenciner 2007; Towles-Reeves et al. 2009).

In the United States, federal legislation caps at 2% the number of students who can take alternate assessments. Federal legislation and state and district procedures also require extensive documentation for students who receive alternative assessments. Policies and procedures for modifications and alternative assessments are relatively new, and this has resulted in a considerable amount of confusion including misunderstanding about the difference between modifications and accommodations. As policy makers and practitioners develop expertise in this aspect of assessing students with special needs, the current questions will hopefully be resolved. Appropriate accommodations should be provided in both formal testing situations and in informal classroom assessment such as when students with disabilities take teacher-made tests. In the classroom, teachers may exercise a great deal of flexibility in how they provide accommodations.

Emerging Themes

Several themes emerge from the issues discussed in this chapter. One theme has to do with progress, and clearly progress has been made in developing new and innovative solutions to difficult assessment issues. For example, many of the accommodations in testing are relatively new, and most of the alternative assessments are even newer. These solutions are helping to make the testing process fair for students with special needs. One of the implications for educators is the need to become more familiar with how to best select and provide accommodations in both formal and informal situations.

A second emerging theme concerns the ongoing development of new assessment procedures. RTI is an example of a new, process-based approach that is faster and more accurate than older, more traditional product-based techniques. RTI is both an assessment and intervention system that provides increasingly intensive services for struggling students. Fletcher et al. (2004) pointed out that RTI represents a major change in how we identify and serve struggling students. Although there is no single RTI approach, a basic framework has emerged using a three-tiered model. The first tier, referred to as primary intervention, includes high-quality, research-based instruction in the general education class, screening to identify failing students, and progress measuring of students who are not responding to instruction. Progress is measured weekly using brief assessments, and data are charted on a graph to visually illustrate student performance. Students identified as failing to respond to intervention in the first tier are provided with second-tier interventions for approximately 8 weeks. These second-tier interventions are more intensive, the student groups are smaller, and the intervention specialist has special skill training. Progress continues to be monitored weekly using brief measurements. After 8 weeks, students who are still failing to respond are referred for streamlined testing to determine if they qualify for special education services. Special education services are part of the intensive third-tier interventions provided by a special education teacher (Bradley et al. 2007).

Dynamic assessment is another assessment procedure that, like RTI, is experiencing ongoing development. Dynamic assessment is similar to RTI in that it consists of a collection of informal evaluation approaches with a set of common features. These features (Dynamic Assessment n.d.) include active interaction between the learner and the evaluator, a focus on identifying the problem-solving skills and the learning styles of the learner, and use of an instructional scaffolding measurement strategy. The scaffolding strategy involves providing increasingly detailed prompts to determine how well the learner acquires skills with help and support from the teacher. Because of these characteristics, dynamic assessment is often referred to as a type of mediated assessment in which learning and testing are merged (Garb 1997). In a comprehensive review of 24 research studies on dynamic assessment, Caffrey et al. (2008) found that it was useful when used in concert with traditional testing to provide information about a student's readiness to learn, especially with students who had special needs.

A third emerging theme is how the educational accountability movement is changing the way educators and others think about and define assessment. Much more emphasis is being placed on student outcomes than ever before, and formal standardized tests are the tool for deciding if students are meeting the outcomes. In other words, scores from large-scale, high-stakes tests have become a key tool in educational accountability. This presents an array of problems for students with disabilities.

Conclusions

In addition to these emerging themes, several general conclusions can be drawn from this discussion of issues in assessing students with special needs. First, it is encouraging that assessment practices and procedures continue to change and improve. Changes include new and revised tests, improved assessment strategies, and procedures for providing accommodations to students with special needs when they take formal standardized tests and informal classroom assessments. Second, assessment is an essential element in educating students with special needs. Assessment assists in identifying students with disabilities. It helps practitioners gauge present levels of performance, recognize strengths and weaknesses, and develop effective intervention programs. Assessment is also the key component in the process of monitoring student progress. Third, assessment is complex and complicated, especially with students who have special needs. This complexity occurs because there are several stages of assessment and numerous tests and measurement tools and because assessment is influenced by numerous disciplines and is guided by an array of legislative and legal mandates.

The responsibilities and challenges for practitioners, policy makers, and researchers in responding to issues in assessing students with special needs are significant. Each group also has specific responsibilities and faces unique challenges.

Responsibilities and Challenges for Practitioners

Practitioners need to continue to build their knowledge and skills in a number of assessment areas. Given the increasing demands to account for student learning, practitioners should become better informed about how to use assessment data and information from educational accountability measures so that they can help students meet learning goals and demonstrate acquisition of standards. Providing accommodations to students with disabilities during assessment and instruction is another area in which practitioners should continue to build their knowledge and skills. This is especially important as schools include more and more students in general education programs with appropriate supports and special education services. In order for practitioners to improve in their use of assessment in the teaching and learning process, policy makers need to provide more support and researchers should conduct practice-centered investigations that produce findings that teachers can use to improve classroom assessment. Additional support will encourage teachers to look beyond their classrooms and schools for answers to the difficult assessment problems.

Responsibilities and Challenges for Policy Makers

Policy makers are faced with a wide variety of assessment challenges. One of the key challenges is giving practitioners additional support so that they may overcome the barriers to high-quality assessment in the classroom. Like practitioners, policy makers need to develop their knowledge and skills in how to best use assessment data and information in educational decision making. Decision making is the key step in the assessment process. The decisions made from test results help students with disabilities when used appropriately or hurt students with disabilities when used in an unfair or inaccurate manner. Finally, given the significant problems with high-stakes testing, policy makers should consider alternative ways, such as portfolio assessment, to account for student progress in meeting educational outcomes.

Responsibilities and Challenges for Researchers

The responsibilities and challenges faced by researchers include the need to gather evidence to support the connection between school improvement and the use of high-stakes tests as accountability measures. This need is key for students who fail to perform well on the high-stakes tests, including students with disabilities. In the area of informal assessment, investigators need to assist teachers in improving the reliability and validity of classroom-based measurement strategies and procedures.

The need for research on accommodations is particularly critical since most accommodations are relatively new and the potential for accommodations to assist students with special needs is so great. Researchers can help by conducting applied studies with direct implications for practitioners. Researchers should strive to make their investigations accessible to policy makers, and policy makers should find new ways to incorporate research findings into new policies and procedures.

Summary

This chapter has considered a variety of issues associated with assessing students who have special needs, with a focus on concerns related to formal testing, informal assessment, and accommodations. These issues were investigated within the conceptual framework of the steps in the assessment process. Although progress is being made in solving the dilemmas of current practice, practitioners, policy makers, and researchers still face significant challenges. Finding answers to these challenges will enable assessment to achieve its potential to truly become an essential element in the teaching and learning process. The goal is to use assessment as a tool in ways that assist and guide us in helping students with special needs learn, grow, achieve, and progress to the maximum extent possible.

References

Allbritten, D., Mainzer, R., & Ziegler, D. (2004). Will students with disabilities be scapegoats for school failures. *Educational Horizons, 82*(2), 153–160.

Bowen, S. K., & Rude, H. A. (2006). Assessment and students with disabilities: Issues and challenges with educational reform. *Rural Special Education Quarterly, 25*(3), 24–30.

Bradley, B., Danielson, L., & Doolittle, J. (2007). Responsiveness to intervention: 1997 to 2007. *Teaching Exceptional Children, 35*, 8–13.

Brookhart, S. M., & Nitko, A. J. (2008). *Assessment and grading in classrooms.* Upper Saddle River, NJ: Pearson Education.

Brown-Chidsey, R., Johnson, P., & Fernstrom, R. (2005). Comparison of grade-level controlled and literature-based maze CBM reading passages. *School Psychology Review, 34*, 387–394.

Burns, M. K. (2002). Comprehensive system of assessment to intervention using curriculum-based assessments. *Intervention in School and Clinic, 38*, 8–13.

Caffrey, E., Fuchs, D., & Fuchs, L. S. (2008). The predictive validity of dynamic assessment: A review. *The Journal of Special Education, 41*(4), 254–271.

Case, B. J. (2005). *Accommodations to improve instruction and assessment of students who are deaf or hard of hearing.* Retrieved from http://pearsonassess.com/NR/rdonlyres/318B76DB-853A-449F-A02E-CC53C8CFD1DB /0/Deaf.pdf

Codding, R. S., Skowron, J., & Pace, G. M. (2005). Back to basics: Training teachers to interpret curriculum-based measurement data and create observable and measurable objectives. *Behavioral Interventions, 20*, 165–176.

Cohen, L., & Spenciner, L. (2007). *Assessment of children and youth with special needs* (3rd ed.). Upper Saddle River, NJ: Pearson Education.

DeLuca, C. (2008). Issues in including students with disabilities in large-scale assessment programs. *Exceptionality Education International, 18*(2), 38–50.

Deno, S. L., Reschly, A. L., Lembke, E. S., Magnusson, D., Callender, S. A., Windram, H., et al. (2009). Developing a school-wide progress-monitoring system. *Psychology in the Schools, 46*, 44–55.

Dolan, R., Hall, T. E., Banerjee, M., Chun, E., & Strangman, N. (2005). Applying principles of universal design to test delivery: The effect of computer-based read-aloud on test performance of high school students with learning disabilities. *Journal of Technology, Learning, and Assessment, 3*(7), 3–32. Retrieved from http://www.jtla.org.

Dynamic Assessment. (n.d.). *What is dynamic assessment.* Retrieved from http://www.dynamicassessment.com/_wsn/page2.html

Fletcher, J., Coulter, A., Reschly, D., & Vaughn, S. (2004). Alternative approaches to the definition and identification of learning disabilities: Some questions and answers. *Annals of Dyslexia, 54*(2), 304–331. Retrieved from http://www.springerlink.com/content/k37lw7q32357tuq7/?p=19e6669769f64f4e98299b2 3633dbe71&pi = 7

Fuchs, D., & Fuchs, L. S. (2005). Responsiveness-to-intervention: A blueprint for practitioners, policymakers, and parents. *Teaching Exceptional Children, 38*, 57–61.

Fuchs, L. S., & Fuchs, D. (2007). A model for implementing responsiveness to intervention. *Teaching Exceptional Children, 39*, 14–21.

Fuchs, L. S., Fuchs, D., Compton, D. L., Bryant, J. D., Hamlett, C. L., & Seethaler, P. M. (2007). Mathematics screening and progress monitoring at first grade: Implications for responsiveness to intervention. *Exceptional Children, 73*, 311–330.

Garb, E. (1997). *Dynamic assessment as a teaching tool: Assessment for learning and learning from assessment.* Retrieved from http://www.etni.org.il/etnirag/issue2/erica_garb.htm#it_work

Gilbertson, D., & Ferre, S. (2008). Considerations in the identification, assessment, and intervention process for deaf and hard of hearing students with reading difficulties. *Psychology in the Schools, 45*(2), 104–120.

Good, R. H., Simmons, D. C., & Kameenui, E. J. (2001). The importance and decision-making utility of a continuum of fluency-based indicators of foundational reading skills for third-grade high-stakes outcomes. *Scientific Studies of Reading, 5*, 257–288.

Heim, M. (n.d.). *Accountability in education: A primer for school leaders.* Retrieved February 10, 2009, from http://www.prel.org/products/Products/Accountability.htm

Ketterlin-Geller, L. R. (2005). Knowing what all students know: Procedures for developing universal design for assessment. *Journal of Technology, Learning, and Assessment, 4*(2), 3–23. Retrieved from http://www.jtla.org.

Koretz, D., & Barton, K. (2004). Assessing students with disabilities: Issues and evidence. *Educational Assessment, 9*(1/2), 29–60.

Lazarus, S. S., Thurlow, M. L., Lail, K. E., & Christensen, L. (2009). A longitudinal analysis of state accommodations policies: Twelve years of change, 1993–2005. *The Journal of Special Education, 43*, 67–80.

Lee, J. (2008). Is test-driven external accountability effective? Synthesizing the evidence from cross-state causal-comparative and correlational studies. *Review of Educational Research, 78*, 608–645.

Lerner, J., Lowenthal, B., & Egan, R. (2003). *Preschool children with special needs: Children at risk, children with disabilities* (2nd ed.). Upper Saddle River, NJ: Pearson Education.

Logsdon, A. (n.d.) *Top 6 ways student progress is measured in special education: Assessing achievement and progress.* Retrieved from http://learningdisabilities.about.com/od/publicschoolprograms/tp/measureprogress.htm

McKevitt, B. C., & Elliot, S. N. (2003). Effects and perceived consequences of using read-aloud and teacher-recommended test accommodations on a reading achievement test. *School Psychology Review, 32*, 583–600.

McLaughlin, M. J., & Thurlow, M. (2003). Educational accountability and students with disabilities: Issues and challenges. *Educational Policy, 17*, 431–451.

McLoughlin, J. A., & Lewis, R. B. (2008). *Assessing students with special needs* (7th ed.). Upper Saddle River, NJ: Pearson Education.

Miller, M. D., Lynn, R. L., & Gronlund, N. E. (2009). *Measurement and assessment in teaching* (10th ed.). Upper Saddle River, NJ: Pearson Education.

Nitko, A. J., & Brookhart, S. M. (2007). *Educational assessment of students* (5th ed.). Upper Saddle River, NJ: Pearson Education.

Oosterhof, A. (2009). *Developing and using classroom assessments* (4th ed.). Upper Saddle River, NJ: Pearson Education.

Payne, L. D., Marks, L. J., & Bogan, B. L. (2007). Using curriculum-based assessment to address the academic and behavioral deficits of students with emotional and behavioral disorders. *Beyond Behavior, 16*(3), 3–6.

Perner, D. E. (2007). No child left behind: Issues of assessing students with the most significant cognitive disabilities. *Education and Training in Developmental Disabilities, 42*, 243–251.

Pitoniak, M. J., & Royer, J. M. (2001). Testing accommodations for examinees with disabilities: A review of psychometric, legal, and social policy issues. *Review of Educational Research, 71*(1), 53–104.

Popham, J. W. (2008). All about assessment: Anchoring down the data. *Educational Leadership, 66*(4), 85–86.

Quenemoen, R., Thurlow, M., Moen, R., Thompson, S., & Morse, A. B. (2003). *Progress monitoring in an inclusive standards-based assessment and accountability system* (Synthesis Report 53). Minneapolis, MN: University of Minnesota, National Center on Educational Outcomes. Retrieved from http://education.umn.edu/NCEO/OnlinePubs/Synthesis53.html

Rollins, K., Mursky, C. V., Shah-Coltrane, S., & Johnsen, S. K. (2009). RTI models for gifted children. *Gifted Child Today, 32*(3), 20–31.

Salvia, J., Ysseldyke, J. E., & Bolt, S. B. (2007). *Assessment in special and inclusive education* (10th ed.). Boston: Houghlin Mifflin.

Sireci, S. G. (2006). *Test accommodations and test validity: Issues, research findings, and unanswered questions*. Amherst: University of Massachusetts [PowerPoint Slides]. Retrieved from cehd.umn.edu/NCEO/Teleconferences/tele12/TestAccommTestValidity.ppt

Sireci, S. G., Li, S., & Scarpati, S. (2003). *The effects of test accommodations on test performance: A review of the literature*. Retrieved from www.education.umn.edu/NCEO/OnlinePubs/TestAccommLitReview.pdf

Sireci, S. G., Scarpati, S., & Li, S. (2005). Test accommodations for students with disabilities: An analysis of the interaction hypothesis. *Review of Educational Research, 75*, 457–490.

Stecker, P. M., Fuchs, L. S., & Fuchs, D. (2005). Using curriculum-based measurement to improve student achievement: Review of research. *Psychology in the Schools, 42*, 795–819.

Stiggins, R. J. (2001). *Student-involved classroom assessment* (3rd ed.). Upper Saddle River, NJ: Merrill/Prentice Hall.

Stiggins, R. J. (2007, October 17). Five assessment myths and their consequences. *Education Week, 27*(8), 28–29. Retrieved from www.childrensprogress.com/documents/2007_10_07_EducationWeek.pdf

Taylor, R. (2009). *Assessment of exceptional students: Educational and psychological procedures* (8th ed.). Upper Saddle River, NJ: Pearson Education.

Thorndike, R. M. (2005). *Measurement and evaluation in psychology and education* (7th ed.). Upper Saddle River, NJ: Pearson Education.

Towles-Reeves, E., Kleinert, H., & Muhomba, M. (2009). Alternate assessment: Have we learned anything new? *Exceptional Children, 75*, 233–252.

University of Oregon Center on Teaching and Learning. (2003). *The school-wide model*. Retrieved from https:\\dibels.uoregon.edu\swm

Weaver, B. (2007). *Formal versus informal assessments*. Retrieved from http://content.scholastic.com/browse/article.jsp?id=4452

Woodcock, R. W. (1998). *Woodcock reading mastery test – Revised/normative update*. Bloomington, MN: Pearson Assessments.

Wright, J. (2007). *The RTI toolkit: A practical guide for schools*. Port Chester, NY: National Professional Resources.

Chapter 8
Student and School Characteristics Related to Student Achievement: A Methodological Approach

John O. Anderson

Introduction

Student achievement of valued learning outcomes is an important index of educational performance. For individual students, the achievement of learning outcomes has significant long-term consequence for life success. A clear example comes from the results of the International Assessment of Adult Literacy (IALS; Organisation for Economic Co-operation and Development, and the Ministry of Industry, Canada 2000) that show consistently strong positive relationships between levels of literacy[1] to employment status and to earnings. For all 20 countries participating in the IALS, employment is directly related to literacy—with higher literacy levels associated with higher levels of employment (Fig. 8.1 illustrates the relationship for four countries: Canada, Germany, Ireland, and United States). In Canada, for those individuals in the top three levels of adult literacy, the employment rate is over 80%, whereas for the lowest two levels of literacy, the employment rate is less than 70%. In terms of salary, there is a clear positive relationship between level of literacy achievement and salary in Canada (Fig. 8.2). The proportion of individuals in the top 60% of earners increases steadily as one moves from lower levels of literacy to higher levels— this is consistent for the three forms of literacy measured by the IALS: prose, document, and quantitative. A study analyzing achievement data over the past four decades for 50 countries (Hanushek et al. 2008) demonstrated the strong relationship,

---

[1] The IALS results are reported on a five-point scale: *Level 1* indicates persons with very poor skills; *Level 2* respondents can deal only with material that is simple, clearly laid out, and in which the tasks involved are not too complex; *Level 3* is considered a suitable minimum for coping with the demands of everyday life and work in a complex, advanced society; and *Levels 4 and 5* describe respondents who demonstrate command of higher-order information processing skills.

J.O. Anderson (✉)
University of Victoria, Educational Psychology
and Leadership Studies, Victoria, BC, Canada
e-mail: anderson@uvic.ca

C.F. Webber and J.L. Lupart (eds.), *Leading Student Assessment,*
Studies in Educational Leadership 15, DOI 10.1007/978-94-007-1727-5_8,
© Springer Science+Business Media B.V. 2012

Fig. 8.1 Employment rates
(%) at low and high levels of
IALS literacy (Organisation
for Economic Co-operation
and Development
and Ministry of Industry
Canada 2000)

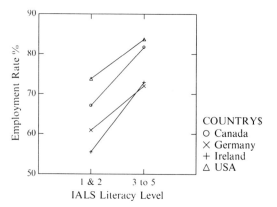

LITERACY

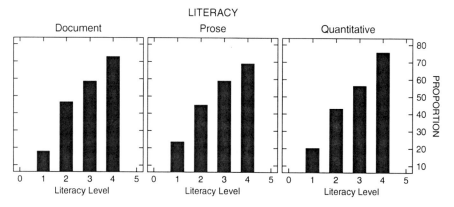

Fig. 8.2 Proportion of adult Canadians in top 60% of earners in Canada for the three IALS literacy measures (Organisation for Economic Co-operation and Development and Ministry of Industry Canada 2000)

at the national level, of student achievement to economic indicators such as growth in gross domestic product per capita: a difference of 0.5 standard deviation in average achievement is related to an annual 1% difference in growth. Over a 40-year period, this difference is substantial.

Public education through curriculum and instruction strives to engender and enhance the literacy levels of students. But the relationship of schooling to student achievement is complex. Factors in addition to curriculum and instruction—student characteristics on entry, teacher and school traits, and home and community characteristics—have been shown to have significant relationships to student achievement, and these relationships vary from one grade to another, one school to another, and one subject area to another (Anderson et al. 2006; Fitz-Gibbon 1998; Ma 2001; Mandeville and Anderson 1987; Rumberger 1995). Better understandings of student, home, and school traits and their relationships to student achievement should contribute to enhanced learning.

In some ways, we know quite a lot about learning outcomes in terms of degree of student success in formal education as indicated by student scores on tests of academic achievement by graduation rates and by employment statistics. This information is often reported in the form of school and country rankings in terms of mean performance on achievement tests. The results typically show that some schools perform better than others in the different skill areas and at different grades. In some public reports (e.g., Cowley and Easton 2008) schools are ranked in terms of student results on these tests (often by aggregating results across subject areas) in an attempt to monitor system quality. Typically, some schools show consistently above, below, or at-average performance across all areas and grades, whereas other schools have varied performance in comparison with their provincial or national counterparts. The publication of these rankings implies that variation in student performance is solely due to school effects. Willms and Kerckhoff (1995) suggested that at a minimum, the results of large-scale assessments have to be considered at three levels: the gross level of test score averages; the level of net productivity in which scores are modified to better reflect the variation in the conditions of schooling; and the level of inequality of student characteristics on entry are accounted for before results are interpreted. Given that most information related to human endeavors is complex, in order to understand educational performance at the school level, not only the simple ranking of schools on the basis of test results should be taken into account, but also the underlying context of factors and situations that influence these results. These factors include home and community characteristics such as number of parents in the home, income levels of the home, employment rates in the community, educational backgrounds of parents, or number of children in the home.

Our understanding of empirical relationships between student, home, and school correlates of learning outcomes is not well developed. There is a dearth of meaning and understanding that can be attributed to the scores and statistics in relation to educational policy and practice. To attain this, we need better understandings of the relationships between achievement measures and student, home, and school characteristics, identifying those characteristics that are consistently and strongly related to student achievement and are accessible to policy. For example, if we can establish that student motivation is positively related to achievement and we can influence levels of student motivation by instructional intervention, then modification to education policy and practice to enhance student motivation would be reasonable. For instance, it is generally shown that there is a persistent positive relationship between the socioeconomic status (SES) of students and achievement in many important learning outcomes (Nonoyama-Tarumi 2008; Willms 2004). However, direct intervention in modifying student SES is not feasible, and so direct policy intervention is unavailable. But there may be ways in which the effects of student-level SES can be modulated through educational interventions, and it has been shown that in some schools, there is a near-zero relationship between SES and achievement. By identifying those characteristics of schools with high levels of achievement and equity in terms of SES and contrasting them to schools with relatively low equity (a strong relationship between SES and achievement), we could identify pathways to school improvement by modulating the effects of SES.

The relationships between school system traits and the outcomes of schooling are of basic interest and significance to the educational policy community. The logic to this interest lies in what may be termed the *path of policy influence* (Kennedy 1999a): those elements of public schooling that are accessible to policy makers (e.g., funding, certification qualifications of professional staff, curriculum, the nature and extent of instructional support and supervision, the provision of opportunities for professional development, and school organizational structure) should show some influence over the key consequences of schooling such as student learning, graduation rates, and ease of entry into the labor market. The empirical investigations associated with this field often take the form of studies of the correlation between educational indicators such as expenditures (school resource inputs) and test scores (student learning achievement outcomes). The field has a history of equivocal findings. Even the interpretation of this history is not without controversy. Some claim there are clear patterns of association among various educational indicators whereas others claim the opposite (e.g., Greenwald et al. 1996a, b; Hanushek 1996). Even from the analytic perspective there is equivocation. For example, there is evidence that the level at which the system traits are aggregated influence the predictivity of results. Yair (1997) pointed out that within-school variation in student achievement is generally greater than between-school variation—the consequence being that system traits should be aggregated at the classroom level rather than the school or district level in studies of system input/outcome relationships. Work of this nature falls into the domain of educational indicators research that is conducted within the academic research milieu.

Educational indicator systems have several potential uses that range from a simple description of the educational system to the development of cause–effect models to inform policy decisions (Camilli and Firestone 1999). Much of the work done with educational indicators has adopted a production function model of description (Bryk and Hermanson 1993) in which system inputs, such as funding and human resources, interact with schooling processes to result in outcomes, in particular, student achievement. This modeling has been premised on the expectation of instrumental utility of results in the monitoring of schools, evaluation of programs, formulation of policy, and implementation of school change. But as Lindblom (1968, 1990) has pointed out time and again, the desire for models of complex social systems, such as public education, to have an instrumental use remains an elusive dream. Models of complex social systems are likely to be, at best, enlightening, allowing incrementally expanding understandings of complex and dynamic systems such as public schools (Kennedy 1999b). In order for these indicator models to have an enlightenment function and to expand understandings of educational systems, the analyses and models must be of a school-relevant and long-term nature, and have to be clearly communicated to a broad and varied audience, and informed discussion initiated and sustained over a period of time. It seems unlikely that one model will suffice. Variation is to be anticipated: one school to another, one province to another, one grade to another, and one achievement database to another.

Secondary Data Analysis

So the question arises: Where can we find empirical evidence to base investigations on which to identify and describe policy-relevant relationships of student, home, and school characteristics to achievement of valued learning outcomes? Large-scale assessment programs can provide such information. Educational jurisdictions in Canada have a long history of collecting information about student achievement of learning outcomes, funding inputs, and, to a lesser extent, student, school, and home characteristics. At the provincial level, most provinces assess student achievement at selected grades in selected subject areas annually. At the national level, Canada has recently developed the *Pan-Canadian Assessment Program* (PCAP; formerly the *School Achievement Indicators Program*) that assesses 13-year-old students in reading, writing, mathematics, and science (Council of Ministers of Education Canada 2008). Canada is also an active participant in international studies of student achievement such as the Trends in Mathematics and Science Study (National Center for Educational Statistics n.d.), the aforementioned IALS, and the Programme of International Student Assessment (PISA) (Organisation for Economic Co-operation and Development n.d.). These data are a rich source of information directly related to the performance and quality of schools in Canada. The challenge is to access, analyze, and interpret the information in meaningful ways that will inform our understandings of schools and educational outcomes.

Basing research on the analysis and modeling of data that has been collected by others is termed *secondary data analysis* (SDA). It is a form of research generally encouraged by the originators of large-scale assessment programs and has a number of distinct advantages. The data generated are generally of high quality in that the test and survey instruments have been carefully designed and developed to yield reliable information on clearly described variables. The sampling procedures used for test and survey administration are well designed to yield representative sampling of populations of interest. And of course since the data have already been collected and organized into datasets available to researcher, the costs associated with data collection have been met by the originating agency. However, there are a number of limitations associated with SDA. A fundamental limitation is the definition and operationalization of variables. The originating agency (the Organisation for Economic Co-operation and Development in the case of PISA or the Council of Ministers of Education Canada in the case of the PCAP) has predefined the variables (e.g., the nature of achievement being measured or the way in which student self-concept or school climate is defined), and this definition cannot be changed by the SDA researcher even if it is not an exact match to what variable is desired in the analysis to be conducted. Likewise, the sample of respondents is predetermined—in the case of PCAP, 13-year-old students in Canadian schools and their teachers and principals are sampled—and cannot be changed by the SDA researcher. Although not confined to SDA, but characteristic of large-scale multivariate studies, missing data is generally an issue that has to be addressed and tends to reduce the power of analyses conducted (Rogers et al. 2006). Another limitation of large-scale studies is that the results are in the form of general patterns and relationships that apply to a large group of individuals, with substantial variation at the individual student level.

The analyses of these data often involve the development of statistical models to identify and describe relationships among important variables. A contemporary approach widely used in education is multilevel modeling or hierarchical linear modeling (HLM).

Hierarchical Linear Modeling

HLM (Raudenbush and Bryk 2002) is a regression-based analysis that explicitly incorporates into the analysis the hierarchical structure common to many educational datasets—in the case of PCAP, students are nested within schools within provinces, and with PISA, students are nested within schools within countries. The data required for these analyses consist of both achievement (performance) and personal measures of students (level 1) and measures of school traits for each school (level 2) attended by the students (Anderson et al. 2007).

At the first level, HLM allows us to describe the linear relationships of achievement to student characteristics such as gender, SES, student motivations, and attitudes toward self or toward school. This can be represented as the familiar regression equation, for example, modeling mathematics achievement (Math for student i in school j) with student gender, SES, and motivation:

$$\text{Math}_{ij} = \beta_{0j} + \beta_{1j}\text{Gender}_i + \beta_{2j}\text{SES}_i + \beta_{3j}\text{Motivation}_i + \text{error}_{1j} \qquad (8.1)$$

where each student's mathematics score is modeled as the intercept (β_{0j}—roughly similar to the mean mathematics score—in this case for each of j schools) plus the weight (β_{1j}) associated with gender plus the weighted (β_{2j}) SES level for that student plus the weighted (β_{3j}) motivation score plus individual error. However, unlike multiple regression, it must be noted that the weights are subscripted by j, signifying that a weight (e.g., the β_{1j} for gender) is calculated for each of the j schools in the dataset. So if the weight for gender is 1.3 for a particular school and males are coded as 0 and females as 1, then on average females score 1.3 points more than males in that school. Also, HLM explicitly models variation in the gender relationships across schools and evaluates whether the variation is 0 or not. This can be done for every coefficient (the β's) in Eq. 8.1—a second set of regression equations is developed. These are termed the level-2 models. For example, in modeling the intercept (β_{0j}, which can be thought of as the conditioned school mean mathematics scores) not only is school variation in the intercept modeled (the error term—error$_{0j}$), but school-level traits, such as school size and an index of teacher morale, can be incorporated into the equation:

$$\beta_{0j} = \gamma_{00} + \gamma_{01}\text{school size}_j + \gamma_{02}\text{teacher morale}_j + \text{error}_{0j} \qquad (8.2)$$

Here, the school intercept is modeled with a level-2 intercept (γ_{00}, which is constant for all schools in the dataset) plus in this example, a weighted (γ_{01}) measure of school size plus a weighted (γ_{02}) measure of teacher morale plus a school-level error term. This models the average school mathematics score as a function of the overall average mathematics score, school size, and teacher morale. HLM then tests the significance of the residual error variation in school mean mathematics scores (the intercepts—β_{0j}'s) once mathematics achievement has been conditioned (in this equation) on school size and teacher morale. If the error variance is significant, it can be interpreted to mean that there is still significant variation in the average school scores after conditioning on school size and teacher morale, whereas a non-significant error variance term suggests that once school size and teacher morale are accounted for, there is no significant variation in mean scores from one school to another.

Likewise, the gender, SES, and student motivation slopes or gradients in the student-level Eq. 8.1 can be modeled with school-level variables. This modeling of slopes is something that is unique to multilevel modeling—modeling of relationships. For example, it may be that at the student level (level 1), SES is significantly and positively related to mathematics achievement (in our example, this would mean that γ_{20} in Eq. 8.3 is significant and positive). But it may be the case that there are substantial differences between schools for this relationship (the β_{2j} slopes in Eq. 8.1). One school may have a steep positive slope suggesting that student home background has a strong relationship to achievement whereas another school may have a near-zero SES slope suggesting that the school is more equitable in relation to student SES (it may also mean that there is little variation in student SES within that school). HLM analysis explicitly estimates and evaluates these relationships for each school and in doing so provides the researcher with the opportunity to model the school slope variation with school traits. For example, if the SES slopes (β_{2j} in Eq. 8.1) vary significantly across schools, they can be modeled with school traits such as measures of school academic focus or teacher morale:

$$\beta_{2j} = \gamma_{20} + \gamma_{21}\text{academic focus}_j + \gamma_{22}\text{teacher morale}_j + \text{error}_{2j} \qquad (8.3)$$

If student SES is highly related to mathematics achievement (a significant level-2 intercept: γ_{20}) and teacher morale has a negative relationship (γ_{22}) to this slope, this suggests that schools with higher levels of teacher morale (according to the perceptions of the school principal) will tend to be more equitable (lower SES slopes—the β_{2j} for that school) in terms of student SES. This finding would suggest that teacher morale moderates the relationship of student SES to achievement, meaning that in schools with high teacher morale, student SES is not as strongly related to student achievement as in schools with lower teacher morale. A policy implication could be that if steps are taken to enhance teacher morale, SES equity could be positively influenced. Further, by explicitly modeling school-level error (the error$_{2j}$ term in Eq. 8.3), we can evaluate if there is any significant variation in the SES slopes remaining after we account for teacher morale and academic focus. If so, what other school traits could be influential in this relationship?

Table 8.1 Intraclass
correlation coefficients
(ICC)—PISA 2003

Country	ICC	Country	ICC
ISL	0.042	THA	0.374
FIN	0.048	MEX	0.388
NOR	0.070	KOR	0.415
SWE	0.108	LIE	0.418
POL	0.127	TUN	0.426
DNK	0.132	URY	0.433
CAN	0.168	SVK	0.435
IRL	0.171	BRA	0.445
NZL	0.180	IDN	0.454
MAC	0.185	FRA	0.459
ESP	0.196	HKG	0.471
AUS	0.212	CZE	0.523
LVA	0.223	ITA	0.527
GBR	0.223	JPN	0.537
USA	0.263	AUT	0.553
RUS	0.307	TUR	0.560
LUX	0.317	BEL	0.562
CHE	0.334	DEU	0.581
PRT	0.341	HUN	0.586
GRC	0.363	NLD	0.626
YUG	0.364	**Mean**	**0.345**

Another fundamental outcome of HLM analyses is the intraclass correlation coefficient generated by running an unconditioned model (the so-called null model; Raudenbush and Bryk 2002, p. 24). This statistic is an index of the proportion of variance in the outcome measure that can be accounted for by level-2 units. The results from PISA 2003 (Table 8.1) show that on average 35% of the variance in mathematics achievement can be attributed to schools. However, there is a broad range of values across countries, from 4% for schools in Iceland to over 60% for schools in the Netherlands. Canadian schools typically account for less than 20% of the variance in student achievement measures and in PISA 2003 accounted for 17% of variance in student mathematics achievement. The variation in intraclass correlations suggests structural differences in the ways school characteristics are related to student performance. Although both Iceland and the Netherlands are relatively high performing countries (in the top 10% in terms of national mean mathematics achievement), in Iceland—and Finland, the top performing country in PISA 2003—school differences account for almost no variation in student mathematics achievement. This is not the case in the Netherlands, where the nature of the schools, which by design are structurally distinct with academic and vocational tracks, is more strongly related to student achievement. This example demonstrates how the measurement and modeling of school traits can lead to better understanding of educational performance as indexed by mathematics achievement.

School Characteristics and Student Traits Related to Achievement

In this internationally comparative study, an HLM approach was used to investigate the relationship of student SES to mathematics achievement from an international perspective using data from the PISA 2003 program that assessed mathematics achievement in 41 countries (Organisation for Economic Co-operation and Development 2003). In addition, the effects of selected school characteristics were explored using the multilevel modeling analyses to evaluate the extent to which they modulate what could be termed the inequity of SES effects on student achievement.

The SES variable developed in PISA is labeled Economic Social and Cultural Status and is derived from student responses to questionnaire items asking the highest occupational status of the father or mother, the highest level of education of the father or mother, and the number of books in the home as well as access to educational and cultural resources (Organisation for Economic Co-operation and Development 2003). The SES index is positively related to mathematics achievement in each of the 41 participating countries. The average correlation is 0.39 (Table 8.2), and it ranges from a low of 0.14 for Macedonia to a high of 0.52 for Hungary. The correlation for Canada is 0.32 indicating that SES accounts for about 10% of the variation in mathematics achievement for 15-year-old Canadian students.

Table 8.2 Correlation of economic social and cultural status to mathematics achievement for PISA 2003

Country	Correlation	Country	Correlation
AUS	0.370	KOR	0.377
AUT	0.400	LIE	0.454
BEL	0.491	LUX	0.413
BRA	0.391	LVA	0.323
CAN	0.324	MAC	0.137
CHE	0.410	MEX	0.414
CZE	0.441	NLD	0.431
DEU	0.478	NOR	0.375
DNK	0.420	NZL	0.410
ESP	0.375	POL	0.408
FIN	0.329	PRT	0.419
FRA	0.443	RUS	0.316
GBR	0.444	SVK	0.472
GRC	0.399	SWE	0.391
HKG	0.255	THA	0.337
HUN	0.520	TUN	0.361
IDN	0.264	TUR	0.472
IRL	0.403	URY	0.399
ISL	0.255	USA	0.436
ITA	0.369	YUG	0.375
JPN	0.340		
Mean = 0.386			

To investigate school effects on the SES gradients, two models will be developed. Model 1 (the baseline model) will consist of student SES (Economic Social and Cultural Status in the PISA dataset) in level 1, and the level-2 model will have no school-level predictors, but both the intercept and the SES gradient equation will include random school-level variation—this will allow for an estimation of the association of student-level SES on mathematics achievement. Model 2 will add a school-level predictor to both the intercept term and the SES slope equation:

Level 1

$$\text{Math}_{ij} = \beta_{0j} + \beta_{1j}\text{SES}_i + \text{error}_{1j}$$

Level 2

$$\beta_{0j} = \gamma_{00} + \gamma_{01}\text{School trait }1_j + \text{error}_{0j}$$

$$\beta_{1j} = \gamma_{10} + \gamma_{11}\text{School trait }1_j + \text{error}_{1j}$$

School traits will be modeled one at a time so a total of six analyses will be conducted and reported. A significant coefficient on the predictor in the intercept equation (γ_{01}) will indicate an association with school mean mathematics scores. A significant positive coefficient on the school-level predictor in the SES gradient equation (γ_{11}) will indicate an association of the school trait with the relationship of student-level SES to mathematics achievement. Given that for all countries SES is positively related to mathematics achievement, a significant coefficient (γ_{11}) on the school trait would mean that the relationship between SES and achievement is increased (and therefore equity decreases), whereas a negative coefficient would mean that the SES–achievement relationship is flattened (equity is enhanced). The analyses were conducted using the computer analysis program SAS (Statistical Analysis Software n.d.) and the subroutines Proc Mixed (available from the PISA website) with normalized student final weighting (Organisation for Economic Co-operation and Development 2007, Annex A8).

To evaluate the effect of the school trait on the SES gradient, the coefficient for the school trait (γ_{11} in the model 2 equations) is reported for each country. To evaluate the effect of the school trait on the mean mathematics scores for schools in each country, the coefficient on the intercept term (γ_{01} in the model 2 equations) will be reported for each country. In regard to coefficients, if the coefficient is nonsignificant ($\alpha = 0.05$), it will be reported as 0, and this value will be used in calculating overall means. To evaluate the overall effect of the school trait for each country, the between-school variance reduction of the SES gradient of model 2 compared to model 1 will be calculated (Raudenbush and Bryk 2002). This index will quantify the proportional reduction in school-to-school variance of the SES relationship.

For these analyses, six school traits will be modeled: (a) school size; (b) ratio of teachers to students; (c) quality of educational resources; (d) student morale; (e) number of assessments per year in the school; and (f) ability grouping of students. These variables were viewed as commonly accessible school traits both in

Table 8.3 Country sample means for school variables

Country	School size	S/T ratio	Education resource	Student morale	Freq assess	Ability group
AUS	875.15	13.42	0.48	0.45	1.96	2.44
AUT	563.10	12.07	0.40	0.18	2.03	1.59
BEL	647.65	9.28	0.19	−0.29	2.05	1.93
BRA	1202.23	32.93	−0.82	0.09	2.58	2.28
CAN	641.99	16.02	−0.07	0.35	2.11	2.37
CHE	389.39	11.95	0.60	−0.12	1.92	2.26
CZE	486.09	14.95	−0.06	−0.37	2.03	1.51
DEU	668.69	17.37	0.20	−0.48	2.12	1.75
DNK	422.78	11.15	0.07	0.19	1.67	1.90
ESP	693.22	13.08	−0.03	−0.47	2.40	2.27
FIN	344.73	10.35	−0.04	0.03	1.74	1.73
GBR	964.55	14.65	0.16	0.43	1.80	2.71
GRC	259.23	9.45	−0.39	−0.08	1.42	1.32
HKG	1047.43	18.13	0.36	−0.15	1.48	2.08
HUN	470.27	11.12	−0.02	−0.45	2.12	1.86
IDN	664.72	–	−0.67	1.33	1.83	2.22
IRL	579.65	14.23	−0.05	0.30	1.78	2.58
ISL	262.62	9.63	0.18	0.09	2.05	2.14
ITA	600.79	9.12	0.28	−0.07	2.24	1.86
JPN	840.31	13.86	−0.03	0.23	1.52	1.58
KOR	1152.30	16.66	0.56	−0.08	1.56	1.82
LIE	174.92	7.22	1.03	−0.64	2.08	2.25
LUX	1209.97	9.60	0.08	−0.62	1.86	1.86
LVA	608.64	12.40	−0.46	−0.25	2.31	2.27
MAC	1591.22	22.88	−0.16	−0.07	1.90	1.74
MEX	821.86	–	−0.47	0.40	1.82	2.04
NLD	964.92	15.41	0.52	−0.14	1.87	2.53
NOR	298.22	10.12	−0.28	−0.12	1.82	2.71
NZL	996.43	16.13	0.22	0.31	1.96	2.42
POL	432.39	13.19	−0.65	−0.01	1.59	2.22
PRT	925.79	10.89	−0.08	−0.09	2.05	2.10
RUS	678.01	14.34	−1.13	−0.09	1.83	2.36
SVK	511.77	14.86	−0.79	−0.47	1.99	2.24
SWE	515.27	12.38	0.08	0.28	2.15	2.44
THA	1560.28	22.20	−0.60	1.11	1.68	2.22
TUN	1047.62	19.46	−0.46	0.32	1.68	2.00
TUR	1081.08	21.70	−1.33	−0.25	1.35	2.19
URY	441.30	16.19	−0.72	−0.03	1.95	2.00
USA	1303.92	15.41	0.48	0.32	2.32	2.37
YUG	906.88	–	−0.80	−0.92	1.21	2.10
Mean	**746.18**	**14.43**	**−0.11**	**0.00**	**1.90**	**2.11**

terms of collecting the data and in terms of access to policy intervention. Data were available for 40 countries participating in PISA 2003 (school-level data for France was not available), and the country averages for each of the six variables are provided in Table 8.3.

In reporting the results, two relationships will be described and tabulated for each country: first, the relationship of the school trait to the school mean math score (the intercept equation); and second, the relationship to the SES gradient. As noted, the effect size reported is that for the variance reduction on the SES gradient.

School Size

School size is the total school enrollment provided by the school principal. The international average school size is 746, but it ranges from a low of schools in Iceland (ISL) averaging 263 students to Macedonia (MAC) averaging 1,591 students (Table 8.3).

For 31 countries, school size showed a positive association with average school math scores (Table 8.4), indicating that larger schools tended to attain higher math scores than smaller schools. Eight countries had no significant relationship. One country (Iceland: −2.54) showed a negative relationship, indicating that in Iceland, larger schools tended to have lower average math scores than smaller schools. For all but two countries (Slovakia: 1.19 and Thailand: 0.38), school size had no significant association with the SES gradient.

Student–Teacher Ratio

The student–teacher ratio was measured in PISA by dividing the total number of students in the school by the number of teachers (both full- and part-time teachers differentially weighted). This means that as the number of teachers per student increases, the ratio decreases. The international average is 14 students per teacher with a range from 7 in Liechtenstein (LIE) to 33 in Brazil (BRA).

In modeling the ratio of teachers to students, there was a general trend of school mean math scores to increase with an increase in the ratio (mean coefficient = 1.82), but there was variation across the 37 countries with sufficient data to analyze (Table 8.5) with 14 countries showing no association, 9 countries showing a negative association, and 14 countries with positive coefficients. For example, Tunisia (TUN) shows a negative relationship (−9.13), indicating that as the ratio increases (fewer teachers per student) across schools, the average school math scores tend to decline. Whereas for both Liechtenstein (LIE: 26.17) and Hong Kong (HKG: 16.70), the reverse pattern is observed—fewer teachers per student (a higher ratio) are related to higher mean math scores for schools. The relationship between student–teacher ratio and average school math scores then is certainly different across these 37 countries.

In regard to the SES gradient, there is not a strong relationship for most countries with 32 countries showing a nonsignificant relationship of student–teacher ratio to the SES gradient. However, for Australia (AUS: −1.50) and Tunisia (TUN: −1.22), an increasing ratio across schools within these countries is associated with a reduction

Table 8.4 Model 2
coefficients: school size

| Country | School size coefficients | | |
	School mean	SES slope	Effect size
AUS	3.36	0.00	0.00
AUT	4.72	0.00	0.00
BEL	6.49	0.00	0.00
BRA	1.08	0.00	0.00
CAN	1.83	0.00	0.00
CHE	1.87	0.00	0.00
CZE	0.00	0.00	0.00
DEU	3.58	0.00	0.00
DNK	4.11	0.00	0.00
ESP	1.71	0.00	0.00
FIN	2.02	0.00	0.00
GBR	1.77	0.00	0.00
GRC	0.00	0.00	0.00
HKG	22.43	0.00	0.00
HUN	6.70	0.00	0.00
IDN	2.11	0.00	0.00
IRL	2.01	0.00	0.00
ISL	−2.54	0.00	0.00
ITA	2.49	0.00	0.00
JPN	4.33	0.00	0.00
KOR	4.85	0.00	0.00
LIE	16.83	0.00	0.00
LUX	0.00	0.00	0.00
LVA	4.18	0.00	0.00
MAC	1.33	0.00	0.00
MEX	1.96	0.00	0.00
NLD	4.78	0.00	0.00
NOR	0.00	0.00	0.00
NZL	1.94	0.00	0.00
POL	0.00	0.00	0.00
PRT	4.27	0.00	0.00
RUS	2.65	0.00	0.00
SVK	3.24	1.19	0.03
SWE	1.80	0.00	0.00
THA	2.57	0.38	0.11
TUN	3.01	0.00	0.00
TUR	0.00	0.00	0.00
URY	6.72	0.00	0.00
USA	0.00	0.00	0.00
YUG	0.00	0.00	0.00

in the SES gradient suggesting a more equitable (in terms of SES effect) situation in schools with fewer teachers. Whereas for Czechoslovakia (CZE: 0.94), Greece (GRC: 1.25), and Slovakia (SVK: 1.02), the reverse pattern is found. So for most countries, the effects of SES on mathematics achievement do not appear to be influenced by the school trait: student–teacher ratio.

Table 8.5 Model 2
coefficients: student:teacher
ratio

Country	Student:teacher ratio coefficients		
	School mean	SES slope	Effect size
AUS	3.47	−1.50	0.07
AUT	0.00	0.00	0.00
BEL	7.94	0.00	0.00
BRA	−0.99	0.00	0.00
CAN	1.59	0.00	0.00
CHE	0.00	0.00	0.00
CZE	−6.44	0.94	0.11
DEU	0.00	0.00	0.00
DNK	3.72	0.00	0.00
ESP	1.37	0.00	0.00
FIN	0.00	0.00	0.00
GBR	−2.62	0.00	0.00
GRC	0.00	1.25	0.14
HKG	16.70	0.00	0.00
HUN	0.00	0.00	0.00
IDN	–	–	–
IRL	0.00	0.00	0.00
ISL	0.00	0.00	0.00
ITA	1.56	0.00	0.00
JPN	8.06	0.00	0.00
KOR	7.06	0.00	0.00
LIE	26.17	0.00	0.00
LUX	0.00	0.00	0.00
LVA	4.92	0.00	0.00
MAC	0.00	0.00	0.00
MEX	–	–	–
NLD	9.55	0.00	0.00
NOR	−2.94	0.00	0.00
NZL	3.57	0.00	0.00
POL	0.00	0.00	0.00
PRT	0.00	0.00	0.00
RUS	−1.30	0.00	0.00
SVK	−2.56	1.02	0.05
SWE	1.45	0.00	0.00
THA	−1.54	0.00	0.00
TUN	−9.13	−1.22	0.57
TUR	−2.21	0.00	0.00
URY	0.00	0.00	0.00
USA	0.00	0.00	0.00
YUG	–	–	–

Educational Resources

The quality of a school's educational resources was measured by principal responses
to items asking about the extent to which instruction was impacted by the availability
of resources such as textbooks, computers, software, library materials, audio-visual

Table 8.6 Model 2 coefficients: educational resources

Country	Educational resources coefficients		
	School mean	SES slope	Effect size
AUS	8.85	0.00	0.00
AUT	0.00	0.00	0.00
BEL	10.74	0.00	0.00
BRA	21.14	0.00	0.00
CAN	6.55	−1.61	−0.00
CHE	0.00	0.00	0.00
CZE	0.00	0.00	0.00
DEU	0.00	0.00	0.00
DNK	5.79	0.00	0.00
ESP	6.55	0.00	0.00
FIN	0.00	0.00	0.00
GBR	11.69	0.00	0.00
GRC	0.00	0.00	0.00
HKG	0.00	0.00	0.00
HUN	13.09	0.00	0.00
IDN	0.00	0.00	0.00
IRL	0.00	0.00	0.00
ISL	0.00	0.00	0.00
ITA	18.86	−1.90	0.00
JPN	0.00	4.46	0.18
KOR	0.00	0.00	0.00
LIE	0.00	0.00	0.00
LUX	0.00	7.45	0.14
LVA	0.00	0.00	0.00
MAC	0.00	0.00	0.00
MEX	7.71	0.00	0.00
NLD	0.00	0.00	0.00
NOR	7.68	0.00	0.00
NZL	8.05	0.00	0.00
POL	0.00	0.00	0.00
PRT	0.00	0.00	0.00
RUS	15.70	0.00	0.00
SVK	11.81	0.00	0.00
SWE	0.00	0.00	0.00
THA	21.28	3.36	0.13
TUN	10.31	0.00	0.00
TUR	18.91	0.00	0.00
URY	15.07	0.00	0.00
USA	8.71	0.00	0.00
YUG	0.00	0.00	0.00

resources, and science lab equipment. A higher score is interpreted as higher levels of instructional resources. The average level of resource quality was −0.11 and ranged from a low of −1.33 in Turkey (TUR) to a high of 1.03 in Liechtenstein (LIE).

For 19 countries, there was a positive relationship between educational resources and mean school math scores (Table 8.6). That is, higher levels of educational resources were related to higher levels of educational performance. However, for 21 countries, there was no significant relationship to school math performance.

Most countries (35) showed no relationship between educational resources and the SES gradient. Two countries—Canada (CAN: −1.61) and Italy (ITA: −1.90)—showed a negative coefficient indicating that as the level of school's educational resources increased, there was a flattening of the SES gradient suggesting greater equity in terms of student-level SES. Three countries—Japan (JPN: 4.46), Luxembourg (LUX: 7.45), and Thailand (THA: 3.36)—showed a positive coefficient suggesting that the schools with higher levels of educational resources had higher levels of association between student-level SES and math achievement.

Student Morale

Student morale is a composite index developed in PISA that is based on the responses of school principals to seven questionnaire items such as *Students enjoy being in school, Students value academic achievement, and Students do their best to learn as much as possible.* Higher scores would be associated with higher student morale and commitment within the school. Student morale was reported on a scale with an international mean of 0.0 with a range from a low of −0.92 in Yugoslavia (YUG) to 1.33 in Indonesia (IND).

Student morale was generally (30 countries) associated with higher school math achievement, but for nine countries there was no significant relationship, and for Liechtenstein (LIE: −49.58) there was a negative association (Table 8.7).

Student morale generally had no association with the SES gradient—37 countries showed no significant relationship of student morale to the SES gradient. Two countries (Czechoslovakia: −4.98 and Great Britain: −2.50) showed a negative association, indicating that as the level of student morale within a school increased, the SES gradient flattened suggesting a more equitable situation for students of varying SES levels. However, New Zealand (NZL: 3.60) had a positive association suggesting that as student morale in schools increases there is a tendency for the SES gradient to increase, thereby leading to a stronger association of student-level SES to mathematics achievement.

Frequency of Assessments

The frequency of assessment variable was derived from summarizing the number of assessments students are administered throughout a school year: standardized tests, teacher-developed tests, portfolios, teacher ratings, and assignments and projects. The reported frequencies were categorized into one of three values: 1 = less than 20/year; 2 = 20–39/year; and 3 = more than 40/year. The international average (1.9) suggests that between 20 and 39 assessments per year are common for students in schools, and this ranges from 1.1 (close to less than 20/year) to 2.6 (near 40 or more than 40/year).

Table 8.7 Model 2
coefficients: student morale

Country	Student morale coefficients		
	School mean	SES slope	Effect size
AUS	16.42	0.00	0.00
AUT	14.20	0.00	0.00
BEL	41.36	0.00	0.00
BRA	· 14.52	0.00	0.00
CAN	8.37	0.00	0.00
CHE	11.39	0.00	0.00
CZE	18.65	−4.98	0.04
DEU	17.21	0.00	0.00
DNK	9.85	0.00	0.00
ESP	13.94	0.00	0.00
FIN	4.79	0.00	0.00
GBR	16.98	−2.50	0.26
GRC	0.00	0.00	0.00
HKG	40.20	0.00	0.00
HUN	18.48	0.00	0.00
IDN	0.00	0.00	0.00
IRL	11.33	0.00	0.00
ISL	0.00	0.00	0.00
ITA	14.94	0.00	0.00
JPN	31.39	0.00	0.00
KOR	24.57	0.00	0.00
LIE	−49.58	0.00	0.00
LUX	25.87	0.00	0.00
LVA	11.50	0.00	0.00
MAC	0.00	0.00	0.00
MEX	4.66	0.00	0.00
NLD	27.91	0.00	0.00
NOR	0.00	0.00	0.00
NZL	6.33	3.60	0.31
POL	0.00	0.00	0.00
PRT	12.59	0.00	0.00
RUS	16.36	0.00	0.00
SVK	13.06	0.00	0.00
SWE	9.14	0.00	0.00
THA	0.00	0.00	0.00
TUN	0.00	0.00	0.00
TUR	17.68	0.00	0.00
URY	0.00	0.00	0.00
USA	12.98	0.00	0.00
YUG	11.97	0.00	0.00

The relationship of frequency of assessment to mean school math scores varied widely across countries (Table 8.8). Thirty countries showed no significant relationship, six countries had a negative association, and four countries had a positive association. For example, in Italy (ITA: −15.85), as the number of assessments

Table 8.8 Model 2
coefficients: frequency of
assessments

Country	Assessment frequency coefficients		
	School mean	SES slope	Effect size
AUS	0.00	0.00	0.00
AUT	0.00	0.00	0.00
BEL	0.00	0.00	0.00
BRA	0.00	0.00	0.00
CAN	−4.37	1.59	0.02
CHE	0.00	0.00	0.00
CZE	0.00	0.00	0.00
DEU	−4.66	0.00	0.00
DNK	0.00	0.00	0.00
ESP	0.00	0.00	0.00
FIN	0.00	0.00	0.00
GBR	0.00	0.00	0.00
GRC	0.00	0.00	0.00
HKG	0.00	0.00	0.00
HUN	0.00	0.00	0.00
IDN	0.00	0.00	0.00
IRL	0.00	0.00	0.00
ISL	0.00	0.00	0.00
ITA	−15.85	0.00	0.00
JPN	0.00	0.00	0.00
KOR	0.00	0.00	0.00
LIE	0.00	0.00	0.00
LUX	0.00	0.00	0.00
LVA	0.00	0.00	0.00
MAC	28.42	0.00	0.00
MEX	0.00	0.00	0.00
NLD	0.00	0.00	0.00
NOR	0.00	0.00	0.00
NZL	−3.87	0.00	0.00
POL	8.41	0.00	0.00
PRT	0.00	0.00	0.00
RUS	0.00	0.00	0.00
SVK	0.00	0.00	0.00
SWE	4.82	0.00	0.00
THA	0.00	0.00	0.00
TUN	11.47	0.00	0.00
TUR	0.00	0.00	0.00
URY	−14.60	0.00	0.00
USA	−1.98	0.00	0.00
YUG	0.00	7.86	0.11

increases in schools, there is a tendency for a decrease to mean school scores, whereas in Macedonia (MAC: 28.42), an increase in assessments within schools is associated with increased levels of school mean achievement.

Only two countries show a relationship of frequency of assessments to the SES gradient. In both Canada (CAN: 1.59) and Yugoslavia (YUG: 7.86), as the number of assessments per year increases from one school to another, there is an associated increase in the SES gradient suggesting greater inequity in terms of SES. For all other countries, there is no significant relationship between assessment frequency and the association of student-level SES and math achievement (the SES gradient).

Ability Grouping of Students

The PISA ability grouping variables were derived from principal responses to four questionnaire items asking the extent to which students were grouped for mathematics instruction on the basis of ability. The variable had three values: with no ability grouping (1), with ability grouping for some classes (2), and ability grouping for all classes (3). The international average of 2.1 suggests that some ability grouping generally occurs in schools. Greece (GRC: 1.32) reports the lowest levels of ability grouping of students within schools, whereas Great Britain (GBR: 2.7) reports most frequent use within schools.

For most countries (28), ability grouping had no significant association with mean school mathematics scores (Table 8.9). Eleven countries showed a negative relationship between ability grouping and school mean math scores, meaning that the more ability grouping was used within schools of that country, the more there tended to be a lower average math score. Sweden (SWE: 6.33) was the only country in which the increased use of ability grouping within a school was associated with higher school mean math scores.

Only two countries showed a relationship between ability grouping and the SES gradient. Liechtenstein (LIE: −21.43) and Sweden (SWE: −5.40) suggested that higher levels of use of ability grouping tended to have a reduced association of student-level SES to math achievement.

In Closing

The purpose of this study was to explore the relationships of student and school characteristics to mathematics achievement in order to better understand educational performance. More specifically, using data from PISA 2003, two main analyses were conducted for 40 of the participating countries: the relationship of 13-year-old students' SES on mathematics achievement and the relationship of a selection of six school traits to the SES–mathematics relationship. In regard to the first, and in accord with much previous research, there was a positive relationship of SES to math achievement for all countries, but the magnitude of the relationship varied considerably across countries. As part of the multilevel approach to these analyses, the proportion of mathematics achievement that can be attributed to school was calculated and indicated that schools do count in that there was a significant intraclass correlation for all countries. But again, countries varied substantially in terms of magnitude.

Table 8.9 Model 2
coefficients: ability grouping

Country	Ability grouping coefficients		
	School mean	SES slope	Effect size
AUS	0.00	0.00	0.00
AUT	−32.17	0.00	0.00
BEL	0.00	0.00	0.00
BRA	−9.95	0.00	0.00
CAN	0.00	0.00	0.00
CHE	−5.10	0.00	0.00
CZE	0.00	0.00	0.00
DEU	−4.56	0.00	0.00
DNK	0.00	0.00	0.00
ESP	0.00	0.00	0.00
FIN	0.00	0.00	0.00
GBR	−2.78	0.00	0.00
GRC	0.00	0.00	0.00
HKG	−40.00	0.00	0.00
HUN	0.00	0.00	0.00
IDN	0.00	0.00	0.00
IRL	0.00	0.00	0.00
ISL	0.00	0.00	0.00
ITA	−6.93	0.00	0.00
JPN	−19.14	0.00	0.00
KOR	0.00	0.00	0.00
LIE	0.00	−21.43	0.40
LUX	0.00	0.00	0.00
LVA	0.00	0.00	0.00
MAC	0.00	0.00	0.00
MEX	0.00	0.00	0.00
NLD	0.00	0.00	0.00
NOR	0.00	0.00	0.00
NZL	−5.97	0.00	0.00
POL	0.00	0.00	0.00
PRT	−11.35	0.00	0.00
RUS	0.00	0.00	0.00
SVK	−8.44	0.00	0.00
SWE	6.33	−5.40	1.00
THA	0.00	0.00	0.00
TUN	0.00	0.00	0.00
TUR	0.00	0.00	0.00
URY	0.00	0.00	0.00
USA	0.00	0.00	0.00
YUG	0.00	0.00	0.00

In the second set of analyses in which six school traits were separately modeled on the school mean mathematics scores and on the SES gradient, the predominant characteristic was fluctuation across countries. The relationships of school trait to the mean math score (the intercept) were more often significant than were the coefficients for the SES gradient. School size generally had a positive relationship to mean math score, but one country showed a negative relationship and eight countries showed no relationship. Student–teacher ratio had similar results in general but with greater mixture in direction of relationship. Educational resources showed more consistency in that all significant relationships were positive. Student morale was similar with the exception of one country with a negative relationship of student morale to school mean achievement. Frequency of assessment showed no relationship to school mean math scores for most countries and a mix of positive (4) and negative (6) significant relationships. The use of ability grouping, although nonsignificant for most countries, was negative for all (11) but one country with a significant relationship.

The effects of school traits on SES gradients were generally nonsignificant with the usual variant exceptions. School size was related to increases in the SES gradient in two countries and for one of these (Thailand), the effect size was 0.11 suggesting that over 10% of school-to-school variation in SES gradient could be attributed to school size. Student–teacher ratio generally had no effect on the SES gradient with the exception of five countries—one of which (Tunisia) the effect size was a substantial 0.57. Educational resources showed significant relationship to the SES gradient in only five countries, and these had varied direction of relationship. Student morale had substantial effect in Great Britain (effect size = 0.26) and New Zealand (effect size = 0.31), but the direction of the relationship was negative in Great Britain and positive in New Zealand; for all other countries except Czechoslovakia, there was no significant relationship. Frequency of assessments had relationship to the SES slope only in Canada and Yugoslavia. Grouping students by ability had relationship to the SES gradient only in Liechtenstein and Sweden but with great effect. The effect sizes for ability grouping were 0.40 and 1.0, respectively. This suggests that for Sweden, grouping students by ability eliminates between-school variation in the SES slopes. Although there was still a positive relationship between SES and mathematics achievements, it was consistent across schools.

The main message arising from these results is that the relationships of student and school characteristics to educational performance as measured by mathematics achievement are complex, and they do not lend themselves to universal generalization. Certainly, schools are important in their effect on student performance, but the magnitude of effect varies from one country to another, as does the magnitude, but not direction of relationship of student SES to achievement. Further, in some countries increased school size is related to an increase in the SES gradient, whereas in other countries an increase in the quality of educational resources is related to a decrease in the SES gradient. To understand educational performance, a single model describing how it all works is unlikely to suffice. In fact, it is unlikely to reflect reality. These results strongly suggest that careful prolonged investigation is needed to build understandings of specific educational situations. This will require data collection designed to garner reliable information about significant student, home, and school traits. One route to attain this end is the careful design of large-scale assessment programs to serve this purpose. The reconceptualization of student assessment programs into long-term research initiatives could better serve the purposes of not only monitoring school performance in more informed ways but also providing evidence-based understanding and evaluation for policy development and implementation. This reformation of large-scale student assessment programs should lead to programs that would not only monitor student achievement in important curricular areas, but also provide an evidentiary basis for meaningful analysis and better understanding of educational performance.

References

Anderson, J. O., Lin, H.-S., Treagust, D. F., Ross, S. P., & Yore, L. D. (2007). Using large-scale assessment datasets for research in science and mathematics education: Programme for International Student Assessment (PISA). *International Journal of Science and Mathematics Education, 5*, 591–614.

Anderson, J. O., Rogers, W. T., Klinger, D. A., Ungerleider, C., Glickman, V., & Anderson, B. (2006). Student and school correlates of mathematics achievement: Models of school performance based on pan-Canadian student assessment. *Canadian Journal of Education, 29*(3), 706–730.

Bryk, A. S., & Hermanson, K. L. (1993). Educational indicator systems: Observations on their structure, interpretation and use. In L. Darling-Hammond (Ed.), *Review of research in education* (Vol. 19). Washington, DC: American Educational Research Association.

Camilli, G., & Firestone, W. A. (1999). Values and state ratings: An examination of the state-by-state education indicators in quality counts. *Education Measurement: Issues and Policies, 18*(4), 17–25.

Council of Ministers of Education Canada. (2008). *Pan Canadian assessment program.* Retrieved August 27, 2009, from http://cmec.ca/Programs/assessment/pancan/Pages/default.aspx

Cowley, P., & Easton, S. (2008). The *report card on British Columbia's elementary schools: 2008 edition.* Vancouver, BC: Fraser Institute. Retrieved August 27, 2009, from http://www.fraserinstitute.org/researchandpublications/publications/5527.aspx

Fitz-Gibbon, C. (1998). Indicator systems for schools: Fire fighting it is! In D. Shorrocks-Taylor (Ed.), *Directions in educational psychology.* London: Whurr Publications Ltd.

Greenwald, R., Hedges, L. V., & Laine, R. D. (1996a). The effect of school resources on student achievement. *Review of Educational Research, 66*(3), 361–396.

Greenwald, R., Hedges, L. V., & Laine, R. D. (1996b). Interpreting research on school resources on student achievement: A rejoinder to Hanushek. *Review of Educational Research, 66*(3), 411–415.

Hanushek, E. A. (1996). A more complete picture of school resource policies. *Review of Educational Research, 66*(3), 397–410.

Hanushek, E. A., Jamison, D. T., Jamison, E. A., & Woessmann, L. (2008). Education and economic growth: It's not just going to school, but learning something while there that matters. *Education Next, 8*(2), 62–70.

Kennedy, M. M. (1999a). Approximations to indicators of student outcomes. *Educational Evaluation and Policy Analysis, 21*(4), 345–363.

Kennedy, M. M. (1999b). Infusing educational decision making with research. In G. J. Cizek (Ed.), *Handbook of educational policy.* New York: Academic.

Lindblom, C. E. (1968). *The policy-making process.* Englewood Cliffs, NJ: Prentice-Hall.

Lindblom, C. E. (1990). *Inquiry and change: The troubled attempt to understand and shape society.* New Haven, CT: Yale University Press.

Ma, X. (2001). Stability of school academic performance across subject areas. *Journal of Educational Measurement, 38*(1), 1–18.

Mandeville, G. K., & Anderson, L. W. (1987). The stability of school effectiveness indices across grade levels and subject areas. *Journal of Educational Measurement, 24*(3), 203–216.

National Center for Educational Statistics. (n.d.). *Trends in mathematics and science study.* Retrieved from http://nces.ed.gov/timss/

Nonoyama-Tarumi, Y. (2008). Cross-national estimates of the effects of family background on student achievement: A sensitivity analysis. *International Review of Education, 54*, 57–82.

Organisation for Economic Co-operation and Development. (2003). *The PISA 2003 assessment framework – Mathematics, reading, science and problem solving: Knowledge and skills.* Paris: Author.

Organisation for Economic Co-operation and Development. (2007). *PISA 2006: Science competencies for tomorrow's world.* Paris: Author.

Organisation for Economic Co-operation and Development & Ministry of Industry, Canada. (2000). *Literacy in the information ion age: Final report of the international adult literacy survey.* Paris:author.

Organisation for Economic Co-operation and Development. (n.d.). *Programme for International Student Assessment – PISA.* Retrieved from http://www.pisa.oecd.org

Raudenbush, S. W., & Bryk, A. S. (2002). *Hierarchical linear models: Applications and data analysis methods* (2nd ed.). Newbury Park, CA: Sage Publications.

Rogers, W. T., Anderson, J. O., Klinger, D. A., & Dawber, T. (2006). Pitfalls and potential pitfalls of secondary data analysis of the Council of Ministers of Education, Canada national assessments. *Canadian Journal of Education, 29*(3), 757–770.

Rumberger, R. W. (1995). Dropping out of middle school: A multilevel analysis of students and schools. *American Educational Research Journal, 32*(4), 583–625.

Statistical Analysis Software. (n.d.). *SAS statistical analysis.* Retrieved from http://www.sas.com/technologies/analytics/statistics/stat/index.html

Willms, J. D. (2004). *Reading achievement in Canada and the United States: Findings from the OECD programme for international student assessment: Final report.* Ottawa: Human Resources and Skills Development Canada. Retrieved May 13, 2008, from www.hrsdc.gc.ca/en/cs/sp/lp/publications/2004-002611/page01.shtml

Willms, J. D., & Kerckhoff, A. C. (1995). The challenge of developing new educational indicators. *Educational Evaluation and Policy Analysis, 17*(1), 113–131.

Yair, G. (1997). When classrooms matter: Implications of between classroom variability for educational policy in Israel. *Assessment in Education, 4*(2), 225–249.

Chapter 9
Student Voice in Fair Assessment Practice

Nola Aitken

Introduction

Fullan (1991) wondered, "What would happen if we treated the student as someone whose opinion mattered?" (p. 170). Possibly this thought-provoking question would be even more intriguing if we were to add, "to not only hear students' voices but to listen with pedagogical tact[1] and take appropriate action." Grennon Brooks and Brooks (1993) agreed: "Valuing students' points of view means not only recognizing them but also addressing them" (p. 61). The *Alberta Student Assessment Study Final Report* (ASASFR; Alberta Education 2009) concurred with Grennon Brooks and Brooks and is clear that student voice should be explicit in assessment design and that teachers should incorporate student voice into all assessment practices. Fullan found that as students progress through schooling, the proportion of them who report that teachers listen to them decreases, from 41%, 33%, and 25% in elementary, junior high, and high school, respectively. The perception of teachers not listening or honoring students' voices could indicate a breakdown of the pedagogical relationship that further weakens the potential for student learning.

A pedagogical relationship implies a teacher having a personal relation with the student, where the intent of the teacher is to understand and care for the student as he or she is, and for what that student may become (van Manen 1992). Both teacher assessment knowledge and pedagogical relationality are evident in teachers who

---

[1] Pedagogic thoughtfulness and tact, or action-sensitive knowledge, are essential elements of pedagogic competence (van Manen 1984, 1991).

N. Aitken (✉)
University of Lethbridge, Lethbridge, AB, Canada
e-mail: nola.aitken@uleth.ca

C.F. Webber and J.L. Lupart (eds.), *Leading Student Assessment*,
Studies in Educational Leadership 15, DOI 10.1007/978-94-007-1727-5_9,
© Springer Science+Business Media B.V. 2012

embody such virtues as dedication, patience, belief in children, tactfulness, and subject matter expertise. Few would disagree that these are the qualities that are significant and are at the heart of teaching.

Subject matter expertise means knowing or embodying what you teach. When you identify with your subject matter in this way, students feel you *are* what you teach (van Manen 1992). Confidence is apparent when teachers first have a deep understanding of their subject matter, and second, know how to assess it. When teachers know how to carry out fair assessment practice and teach in purposeful and meaningful ways, they do not engage in secrecy, trickery, or test-question ambiguity. Knowledgeable teachers construct tests and assignments that are fair and meaningful to encourage students to demonstrate their knowledge and understanding. Students respect teachers with these qualities and those who encourage student voice into teaching and learning.

Questions and issues such as those of Fullan's (1991) and students will be addressed through the student-voice literature to illustrate how students can be involved in their learning and assessment, and subsequently, guide teachers' instruction and fair assessment practice. The chapter will begin with a brief literature review followed by student anecdotes and suggestions for and implications of student-involved assessment strategies. Conclusions and recommendations will close the chapter.

A Brief Review of the Literature

It would have been preposterous 50 years ago to ask seriously students' opinions about their learning, instruction, and assessment. Education at that time for the most part was teacher centered, mirroring the behaviorist tradition (Hetherington et al. 2005; Skinner 1989). Teacher-centered learners were expected to be passive learners, rather than active learners, becoming active only when reacting to stimuli in the environment. The teacher's task was to create an environment that stimulated the students to exhibit the desired behavior and discourage those behaviors held to be undesirable (Burke 2005; Grennon Brooks and Brooks 1993; Liu et al. n.d.). Environments such as these did not encourage authentic voice or students' opinions about how they learned or how they would like to learn and be assessed. In recent years, there has been a move away from behaviorism, which means that now students must be involved in their metacognition and take responsibility for their own learning "not only as a contributor to the learning process, but also as the critical connector between them….This is the regulatory process in cognition" (Earl 2003, p. 25).

The students' voice is honored through conversations and interviews in assessment. These are vital ways to evoke students' thoughts and feelings about their learning (Lambert 2003). Lambert holds that tactful pedagogical conversation has "an almost magical effect on what we say: issues and problems are held at arms length and examined from all sides instead of being subjected to quick opinions and ready solutions" (p. 34). Gadamer (1990) concurred with the notion of careful and deliberate examination in conversation and remarked that the first condition of the art of conversation is ensuring that the other person is *with* us, rather than *against* us, genuinely examining the issue from all sides:

> To conduct a conversation means to allow oneself to be conducted by the subject matter to which the partners in the dialogue are oriented. It requires that one does not try to argue the other person down but that he really considers the weight of the other's opinion. Hence it is an art of testing. But the art of testing is the art of questioning. For we have seen that to question means to lay open, to place in the open....Dialectic consists not in trying to discover the weakness of what is said, but in bringing out its real strength. (p. 367)

Repositioning this concept to student assessment then, the teacher or examiner does not appear as one against us, but instead, a critical friend, offering students the opportunity to celebrate and acknowledge their strengths and weaknesses. The important part of this idea is to focus not only on the weakness, but to balance the assessment by including acknowledgment and celebration of the strength:

> We test the strength of a rope, the power of will, the firmness of a conviction, the validity of a view, etc......we do *not* test the weakness of the rope, the lack of willpower, the softness of a conviction, the wrongness of a view. Why then do so many students feel that school tests do test their failing, shortcomings, weakness? Or do they? How do tests bring out the real strength in each child, rather than sort the strong ones from the weak ones? (M. van Manen, personal communication, December 1991).

Sitting down in conversation is related to the etymological practice of assessment. *Assess* is defined as "'to sit by'; asseoir: an appraisal or evaluation as of merit as in a critical assessment of the composer's work" (Oxford English Dictionary of Etymology 1933). Research indicates that assessment is not always practiced as pedagogical conversation and yet it is preferable for many students such as Tannys, a secondary-school student: "Sometimes I wish that the teacher would just sit down and talk with me to see what I have learned. An oral test gives you more control to demonstrate what you know" (Aitken 1994, p. 44). Like Tannys, students in the past have been rarely consulted about their role or choice in their assessment. Their voices have not been seriously acknowledged; consequently, students are less able to reveal what they know and can do to reach their potential. Barzun (as cited in Hoffmann 1964) believed that students do not really know what they have learned until they have actually explained it to someone else. Without the opportunity to have this assessment alternative, the teacher might not have a valid inference of what the student knows and can do. Effective teachers know multiple and varied assessment strategies are required to draw out the unique student strengths and weaknesses. When such alternatives are not offered to them, such as the oral test that Tannys described, the "real me" is not revealed. Aoki et al. (1977) noted:

> Whenever we see a picture of ourselves taken by someone else, we are anxious that justice be done to the "real me." If there is disappointment, it is because we know that there is so much more to the "real me" than has been momentarily captured by the photographer's click. So, too, with assessment: there are deeper and wider dimensions to the total subject that can be justly dealt with from such a hasty glance. Any ensuing dissatisfaction should not be taken as a measure of the assessment's failing but as a testimony to that crucial vitality of the subject that eludes captivity on paper. (p. 49)

Aoki et al. (1977) reaffirm the importance of the need for addressing the "wider dimensions" via varied assessments, and this is further supported by *Principles for Fair Student Assessment Practices for Education in Canada* (1993) that stated: "Students should be provided with a sufficient opportunity to demonstrate the knowledge, skills, attitudes, or behaviours being assessed. Assessment information can be collected in a variety of ways (observations, oral questioning, interviews, oral and written reports, paper-and-pencil tests)" (p. 5).

There are few studies that focus *exclusively* on what students themselves think about their learning and assessment; however, there are some exceptions. S. G. Paris (personal communication, October 28, 1992) and Witte and Blakey (1991) surveyed grade-school students about their views, and Albas and Albas (1984) observed and interviewed university students. More recently, McInerney et al. (2009) investigated students' perspectives on assessment for learning; however, very few other researchers really *listened* to students' perspectives on testing and documented its effects on learning. Grennon Brooks and Brooks (1993) argued:

> Seeking to understand students' points of view is essential to constructivist education.... Students' points of view are windows into their reasoning. Awareness of students' points of view helps teachers challenge students, making school experiences both contextual and meaningful. Each student's point of view is an instructional entry point that sits at the gateway of personalized education. Teachers who operate without awareness of their students' points of view often doom students to dull, irrelevant experiences, and even failure. (p. 60)

Many of these "dull and irrelevant experiences" occur in assessment. By not providing a variety of assessments, some students who cannot cope with performance tests, such as oral exams or demonstrations, likely fail. Alternatively, those who cannot express themselves with a selected-response test, such as a multiple-choice test, are also candidates for failure.

Some teachers are diligent but ineffective because they do not listen or relate to their students and are not aware of their students' points of view. They miss the opportunity to hear and understand how students learn effectively and what it takes to create engaged, active learners. Lack of relationality encourages students to be passive learners. Passive learning means taking in information and returning it more or less verbatim, or "parroting" (O'Brien 1999). Parroting results in shallow learning at best. Without the presence or opportunity for metacognition and language in either verbal or written form that is inextricably linked to thinking, it is not deep learning or learning for understanding (Grennon Brooks 2002; Grennon Brooks and Brooks 1993; Vygotsky 1978). For these reasons, it is imperative that student voice be heard in both learning and assessment to guide teachers in their teaching, and learners in their learning.

Because of my interest in student voice in learning and assessment, I conducted research studies in 1994 and 2007 using protocol writing and interviews about students' lived experience in assessment. From the data, I rooted out the emerging themes using hermeneutic phenomenological methodology. This approach requires a hermeneutic facility to make interpretative sense of the students' accounts of their lifeworlds to see the pedagogic significance of situations in which students are involved (Merleau-Ponty 1962; Osborne 1990; Polkinghorne 1983; Valle and King 1978; van Manen 1990). The emerging themes ranged from issues of teacher power and secrecy to student punishment and oppression. These themes linked to the practical nature of assessment, such as unclear assignment targets, test question ambiguity, timed tests, and unfair grading. In the following, I will address these issues of power and secrecy and other themes to provide a background to some of the teacher classroom practices that result in poor assessment practice. While some of these poor practices could be due to teachers' lack of assessment knowledge, some are associated with lack of teacher confidence, and others with lack of student trust. Although educational research informs us that philosophical underpinnings in teaching, learning, and assessment have changed dramatically during the past 50 years, it is important to note that in practice, there is disappointing evidence of this. Much of the old attitudes about grading and using assessment as weapons to coerce, reward, and punish prevail. While these practices are not rampant, some unfair assessment practice is still evident today impacting the lives of far too many students (Guskey 2004; Popham 2002, 2004; Stiggins 2002).

Student Voice: Anecdotes About Test-Taking and Other Assessment Experiences

In the 1994 and 2007 studies, I gathered anecdotes about students' assessment experiences from over 250 students. In this chapter, I have arranged them to correspond with those topics from the *Principles* (1993) document: planning and developing, collecting assessment information, judging and scoring student performance, summarizing and interpreting results, and reporting assessment findings. These same topics will serve as a framework to illustrate student voice and fair assessment practice.

Planning and Developing Student Assessment

Mindful student assessment planning and developing is paramount when designing courses of study (Chappuis et al. 2009; Fisher and Frey 2009; Wiggins and McTighe 2005). When teachers' course planning does not include student assessment upfront, a host of student assessment issues arise, such as content misalignment with assessment, ambiguous instructions for assessment assignments and tests, and unclear scoring guides (rubrics). These issues can result in unreliable test results, invalid assessment inferences, and invariably, student stress. Students take exception to thoughtless assessment planning, and they made valid comments about their experiences in the 1994/2007 studies.

Alignment with Instruction

Pedagogically oriented teachers carefully plan assessment as they plan the course using a "backward design" approach. By using this approach, the assessment is aligned with important learning outcomes (Wiggins and McTighe 1998). Subsequently, students are clear about what they need to know and how they need to demonstrate what they know and can do. The assessment is oriented to content "big ideas" and not sidetracked by trivia. It is centered on curricular outcomes rather than "flavor of the month" topics—and it works. There are no unfair surprises here for students—what is taught is assessed. Student frustration results when the assessment is not related to coursework. For example, Tina felt she was prepared for the test, but she was in for a surprise. Tina wrote:

> I was just about to write a stats final exam. I was feeling really confident about the whole situation. I knew my material well and my grade going in was excellent…. I read the first question. I didn't know how to do it, so I read the second question. Again I didn't know how to do it…. I read the third and fourth questions. I couldn't believe it, *I didn't know where these questions were coming from!* I had no clue how to start them…. I scanned the rest of the exam for a question I could answer. Yes! I found one. It was a start—but by now there was only half an hour left….I had worked so hard in this class and was saying goodbye to the good mark I had, all because of this exam. (Aitken 1994, pp. 61–62)

Tests not clearly aligned to the program and instruction yield invalid inferences about student achievement in relation to the mandated curriculum (Popham 2002, 2004). Not only do they provide invalid inferences about what students know and can do, but also unreliable information for program or instructional improvement. The ASASFR recommended that assessment tools and strategies be aligned overtly to the Program of Studies (Alberta Education 2009). Further, *Principles* (1993) stated:

> Assessment methods should be clearly related to the goals and objectives of instruction, and be compatible with the instructional approaches used.
> To enhance validity, assessment methods should be in harmony with the instructional objectives to which they are referenced. Planning an assessment design at the same time as planning instruction will help integrate the two in meaningful ways. Such joint planning provides an overall perspective on the knowledge, skills, attitudes, and behaviors to be learned and assessed, and the contexts in which they will be learned and assessed. (p. 4)

Students in the 1994 and 2007 studies indicated that one of their concerns was the test and course misalignment, resulting in unanticipated test questions. Students found these tests most unfair and frustrating. A fair test has no surprises. Pedagogically oriented teachers are clear about what will be tested and make certain that the test is aligned to the curriculum and instruction. With fair assessment firmly in place, it guides teachers in future instruction. In this way, assessment then becomes integral with instructional process.

Variety of Assessments

Fair assessment practice requires that students have a variety of assessment opportunities to demonstrate knowledge, skill, and understanding (Alberta Education 2006a).

This principle is supported by the ASASFR (Alberta Education 2009) and *Principles* (1993). *Principles* stated: "More than one assessment method should be used to ensure comprehensive and consistent indications of student performance" (p. 4). However, students in the studies railed about the lack of assessment variety. In frustration, one student reported, "It was all multiple-choice! Good grief, hadn't he ever heard of an *essay*??" (Aitken 2007, n. p.). Other students in the 2007 study complained about the same problem, for example, "Profs, PLEASE…avoid sticking to only one style of assessment and avoid so many multiple-choice exams—short answer or long answer questions allow us to *apply* our knowledge" (Aitken 2007, n. p). Another student suggested that teachers "break the test down to give a variety of question types within the test and within the major plan" (Aitken 2007, n. p.). Other students agreed and suggested to "mix it up—multiple-choice, short answer, true or false.…"

Students in both studies were adamant about test format variation, and for compelling reasons. For example, different students demonstrate strengths in different ways—some demonstrate strengths via multiple-choice tests, and some demonstrate what they know and do more effectively in performance-based assessments such as oral presentations, as Tannys described earlier. The various assessment formats have strengths and weaknesses as well: multiple-choice tests primarily are appropriate for students to demonstrate breadth of knowledge, and performance-based tests and assignments (research projects) primarily are appropriate for assessment of depth of knowledge. *Principles* (1993) agreed: "Assessment methods should be developed or chosen so that inferences drawn about the knowledge, skills, attitudes, and behaviors by each student are valid and not open to misinterpretation" (p. 3). For example, if teachers want to assess students' writing skills, teachers would give students a performance-based assessment such as an essay test, not a multiple-choice test, so that students have a relevant context in which to exhibit strengths and weaknesses.

Multiple Assessments

Whatever assessments teachers choose, the question remains: How many assessments should teachers use to find out what students know and can do? For reliability purposes, there should be multiple assessments that are carefully selected. A midterm and a final exam do not suffice. A student having an "off day" and doing poorly on an equally weighted midterm with the final exam will have to do well on the final to pass the course. Fair assessment requires at least three well-constructed summative tests to be carried out to obtain a reliable indicator of student knowledge and understanding (Brookhart 2009; Stiggins 2001). Unfortunately, some university students do not have three assessment opportunities in a semester, such as this student describes: "A single comprehensive exam for an entire semester—how can this happen??" (Aitken 2007, n. p.). Students felt it most unfair to have so much weight on only two or three exams, particularly when the test was of one type only, such as a lab exam or paper-and-pencil test. The university students admitted that the heavily weighted finals encouraged cramming instead of long-term learning: "What's totally unfair is a low number of assignments and exams that are weighted highly, not enough variety of assessment tools" (Aitken 2007, n. p.). In elementary and secondary schools, however, teachers reported that they provided a multiple and variety of assessments for students (Alberta Education 2009). Because of the impact of these approaches, the ASASFR recommended: "Educators will provide multiple, ongoing opportunities for students to demonstrate learning outcomes in a variety of ways" (p. 135). *Principles* (1993) is clear about providing multiple assessment opportunities:

> Summary comments and grades should be based on more than one assessment result so as to ensure adequate sampling of broadly defined learning outcomes. More than one or two assessments are needed to adequately assess performance in multifacet areas such as Reading. Under-representation of such broadly defined constructs can be avoided by ensuring that the comments and grades used to summarize performance are based on multiple assessments, each referenced to a particular facet of the construct. (p. 10)

Stiggins (2001, 2002) believed there is no one best assessment tool for students, and assessment tools should be multiple and varied as they suit the purpose. Stiggins' conviction is echoed by other researchers who recommend that multiple and varied approaches are necessary for effective evaluation (e.g., Alberta Assessment Consortium 2007; Alberta Education 2006b; Black et al. 2003, 2004; Burger and Krueger 2003; Davies 2000; Johnson and Johnson 2002; Wiggins 1993).

Assessment purpose and clear targets prepared and communicated to students upfront. Students typically ask, "What's going to be on the test?"

Teachers typically reply: "Everything."

This is unhelpful for students, and it promotes cramming "everything" instead of encouraging them to think deeply about essential understandings. Pedagogically thoughtful teachers share test blueprints to inform students about the test content, types of test questions, and test-question weighting. By providing the blueprint, students have the desired outcomes to study and likely will be more focused and less stressed; however, many teachers do not prepare students this way because they are concerned with "spilling the beans"; hence, students cram as much content as they can as a result. Long-term retention is at the mercy of such an approach. Unmistakably, secrecy in this context does not enhance learning (Reeves 2002). Tests are not for the purpose to catch students out, like "gotcha tests" as Maeroff (1991) terms them. Tactful teachers, on the other hand, spill the beans and share the test marking criteria and purpose, formative or summative. Only then are students able to respond in an appropriate manner to provide relevant information. If students know that the purpose is formative, to diagnose strengths and weaknesses and provide meaningful feedback instead of assigning a grade, they can take risks to reveal weaknesses. If students know that the purpose is summative for a grade, they know that they need to respond in a way that will maximize their strengths. When teachers share the assessment purpose, whether it is diagnostic or for grading, students can demonstrate what they know and can do accordingly.

Clear criteria and purpose are critical for student success in learning and achievement. Concealing the test targets and learning expectations does little for lifelong learning; all it does is assist the adept student to ferret out teachers' test questions. Here is one such example freely offered from Deana:

> Tests? Oh I love tests. I always do well on a test. I learned how to do that in elementary school. I love the challenge of second-guessing the teacher and seeing how close I've come to guessing what's on the test. That's the challenge for me. *After awhile, I became more interested in how good I was at second guessing and studying the right material rather than studying to learn.* It was just a game to me, and one I got to be pretty good at. [emphasis added] (Aitken 1994, p. 45)

Charlie, a university student, is another matter; he is not test-wise like Deana. He wrote:

> Of equal importance in writing a test is not only knowing content material, but also my peace of mind. I take time to calm myself, relax, possibly to meditate. I reinforce the concept of self by reminding myself that I have done well to this point and why would I blow this test? The answer of course is the *wild card* (professor). The question remains, will the professor include in the exam any material which was vaguely or obscurely raised in class? (Aitken 1994, p. 62)

Virgil, too, has difficulty in second-guessing what the professor really wants. He wrote:

> After receiving the test, panic and anxiety enter. What if he gave us stuff he didn't tell us would be on the test? I came to an area on the test which asked to choose three out of ten statements and explain them. Another dilemma. I need to choose three that I can write a lot on, but I also have to make absolutely sure that it is what they mean. Maybe I should choose another one? Would the professor be impressed if I chose this explanation over the other one? Did I write enough about this statement?
>
> Next set of questions. Define and explain. For this one word there are two answers to the explanation part. I'm sure of one of the explanations and kind of sure about the second one. But I'm still not sure about the second one. But if I write both down I will get more marks. I'm still not sure about the second answer. Now there is a second word that I think has the same meaning as another one. Is this a trick question to throw us off or did I study the wrong definition? (Aitken 1994, pp. 62–63)

On this matter, students in the 2007 study had several suggestions for teachers and professors, such as "Share the [test] blueprint if you want students to learn the content" (Aitken 2007, n. p.). They were disappointed with teachers who did not provide clear performance-based assessment expectations and rubrics. They suggested that teachers take the time to determine the rubrics so students know "what a 100% project looks like" (Aitken 2007, n. p.). However, as some students noted, the rubrics when they were provided, were unclear, and second, students were not involved with the rubric construction to enable them to more easily "hit the target" (Stiggins 2001). Research strongly supports the use of student-constructed rubrics to not only help students demonstrate what they know and can do, but to also promote a valid inference of student achievement and learning (Alberta Education 2009; Danielson as cited in Willis 1996).

At exam time, students reported that they were not prepped for the type of exam presented; for example, the students studied for a multiple-choice test, but were presented with an essay test. Further, they said that some instructors had test questions that were not covered in class or in the textbook, and some instructors did not even cover material that was on the test because they had run out of time during the semester. Another student shared this test frustration: "I studied every concept, every detail of this—such as characteristics of a gothic novel—to find the test composed of quotes from novels where we had to identify the characters, the situation, and the significance" (Aitken 2007, n. p.). Not apprising students of the test format, content, and criteria is a clear example of unfair assessment practice. In support of fair assessment practice, the ASASFR recommended that "Students know assessment purposes, criteria, and performances prior to being assessed" (Alberta Education 2009, p. 135). *Principles* (1993) concurred:

> Before an assessment method is used, students should be told how their responses or the information they provide will be judged or scored. Informing students prior to the use of an assessment method about the scoring procedures to be followed should help ensure that similar expectations are held by both students and their teachers. (p. 8)

Further,

> The directions provided to students should be clear, complete, and appropriate for the ability, age and grade level of the students.
> Lack of understanding of the assessment task may prevent maximum performance or display of the behavior called for…. sample material and practice should be provided to further increase the likelihood that instructions will be understood. (p. 6)

Inappropriate Test Time Allowance

Pedagogically thoughtful teachers use timed tests appropriately. Timed test formats that do not relate to the curricular outcomes are inappropriate (Alberta Education 2009); they do not enhance learning or allow students to demonstrate their knowledge and understanding properly. These inappropriate timed tests are stressful, reducing students' capacity to think clearly (Levine 1995; Sylwester 1998; Tobias 1993; Wolfe 2001). Berlak et al. (1992) agreed:

> The significant achievements of disciplined inquiry often cannot be produced within rigidly specified time periods. Adults working to solve complicated problems, to compose effective discourse, or to design products rarely are forced to work within the rigid time constraints imposed on students such as the 50-minute class, or the two-hour examination. (p. 79)

In some cases, however, timed tests, or "speed tests" are appropriate for specific purposes, such as mental arithmetic, if they are aligned to the program outcomes (Reynolds et al. 2009). In the real world, too, timed tests are justifiable: a chef is timed in meal preparation, a mechanic for oil changes, a dentist in applying an amalgam, and a journalist for meeting magazine deadlines.

The 1994 study data revealed that well-prepared students, such as Minda, were frustrated when time was unnecessarily restricted: "I could have done all the questions if I had been given enough time!" (p. 92). Phil, echoing Minda, wrote: "[M]y full potential [was not realized] due to lack of time….all thoughts crossing my mind was to get down as much as I possibly could on paper within the time allowed" (p. 92). Melinda's mind "blanked" when under time pressure. She said:

> Often time is a problem. I like to take my time on tests but often the time forces me to go as quickly as possible. Suddenly I'm one of the last people writing the test and I'm concentrating so hard on finishing the test, my mind goes blank. (Aitken 1994, p. 99)

Another student, Ann, suggested a commonsense approach toward time limits and wondered why teachers and professors don't adapt time allotment according to complexity and length of tests or assignments (Aitken 1994). One student in the 2007 study suggested that teachers allow point form if there was a time limit.

Young children are also flustered by time restrictions such as when the teacher says the next spelling word before students finish the one they are writing, and it "makes it hard to remember what came before" (Witte and Blakey 1991, p. 75). Other researchers such as Popham (2008) claimed that timed tests are "educationally indefensible" (p. 87) and do not serve any purpose other than frustrate and turn students off taking tests. Pedagogically oriented teachers plan test timing with care and assign time limits only when relevant as recommended by the ASASFR (Alberta Education 2009). *Principles* (1993) stated that adequate time limits appropriate to the purpose and form of the assessment are necessary. Burke (2005) suggested that teachers allow approximately twice as much time for students to do the test, as it would take the teacher.

Assignments and tests are less effective if teachers are not thoughtful about appropriate time limits. Disappointingly, student complaints about being given insufficient time to complete assigned work and tests rang as true in 2007 as they did in 1994.

Providing Students Choice in the Assessment

The students in both studies indicated that assignment choice motivated them to be engaged. Motivated and engaged students in assessment more likely will provide valid inferences about student knowledge and understanding (Wiggins 1993). When provided such choice, students work toward the same outcome but in their choice of mode or topic. For example, when allowed to choose an area to demonstrate their knowledge and understanding of descriptive statistics, they can gather relevant real-world data about traffic or hockey statistics. Mindful teachers, who balance student choice with teacher choice, provide another avenue for student engagement in assessment. *Principles* (1993) agreed that there is a place for student choice in evaluation assignments: "Students should be told why assessment information is being collected and how this information will be used….This is especially true for assessment methods that allow students to make choices, such as in optional writing assignments or research projects" (p. 5).

Assignment and Test Weighting

One of the most common errors teachers make is inappropriate assignment and test weighting (Popham 2004). Weighting should be appropriate for the content importance and done during the initial course planning. Often teachers discover at the end of the term a mystifying array of marks and grades that are difficult to prioritize or select for the final grading process. Weighting lesser important outcomes the same as important outcomes is erroneous and misleads the student, parent, and receiving teacher about the students' learning and achievement (Guskey 1996; Marzano 2000, 2006; O'Connor 2002; Reeves 2002; Stiggins et al. 2004; Wiggins 1993). *Principles* (1993) advised:

> When the results of a series of assessments are combined into a summary comment, care should be taken to ensure that the actual emphasis [weight] placed on the various results matches the intended emphasis for each student. (p. 10)

Students in the studies had several concerns about inappropriate test weightings, especially when tests consisted of rote learning and trivia instead of critical thinking and depth of understanding. Harried teachers fall into the trap of testing trivia, because it is easier to construct trivial test questions and assignments than multistep complex problem situations. This is disappointing for diligent students who prepared for meaningful tests and assignments to demonstrate their skills and depth of understanding. It is preferable to construct fewer worthwhile tests that reveal depth of understanding than many of "trivial pursuit" (Etobicoke Board of Education 1987; Perkins 1992; Popham 2002). Hastily assembled and trivia-based tests frustrate conscientious students like Marg who wrote:

> …. A particular test that sticks out in my mind is one that caused me a tremendous amount of stress….not because I was not well prepared, but because the subject matter was much too large….[and] the professor…was not interested in concepts and ideas of understanding, but rather with the regurgitation of specific details with no real relevance to the grand scheme of things. There was also too much riding on this exam—60% of my final mark….I know a lot about this subject area and really enjoyed it….what ticked me off was that I knew I would not be able to express it. Rather I would have to index through all the mindless, temporary sets of facts to think of some irrelevant word from page 63 and what it means. (Aitken 1994, p. 74)

Students in the 2007 study also reported having tests riddled with trivia worth 50% or more of the total grade. The students reported that tests should involve more than memory work, that the tests should have application questions, and include psychomotor, affective, and cognitive domains. In response to tests of memorization, one very frustrated student declared, "Regurgitation sucks!" (Aitken 2007, n. p.)

Trivia incorporated into test questions borders on test trickery. A trick test question, as described by Nitko and Brookhart (2007), is "an item in which an option's correctness depends on a trivial fact, an idiosyncratic standard, or an easily overlooked word or phrase" (p. 169). As well as being unfair, trick questions do not help teachers or students with instruction and learning. One student suggested, "With only a few opportunities to check for understanding, don't waste your questions on trivia. Students find it insulting as well" (Aitken 2007, n. p.). One irritated student suggested that teachers should simply "lose the tricks."

Thoughtful Test Question Construction

Ambiguous test questions are equally tricky and occur when teachers leave test planning until the last minute. Hastily written test questions cause students grief.

Students in the 2007 study said they resented ambiguous questions and found them stressful when trying to guess what the teacher wanted. One of the students referred to the ambiguity as "Guess what I am thinking....?" They also commented on the plethora of "double negatives" in test questions and it was the "test-wise" who succeeded. Students who have tactful teachers have no need to develop test-wiseness skills to outwit the test. Tactful teachers construct tests without surprises, tricks, or ambiguity. Tactful teachers provide students every opportunity for them to demonstrate their understanding. Students with tactful teachers respond not with teacher mistrust or suspicion, but instead, respect. By 2007, the guessing game should have been over, but according to one thoughtful student, it clearly was not: "A test is not an exercise in mind games; it's an exercise to find out what students know, understand, and can do" (Aitken 2007, n. p).

Clear Test Directions

Clear instructions are paramount in assisting students to demonstrate their knowledge and skills during test administration. Proctors not conversant with test directions add further frustration for students because often proctors do not know what the instructor means either. Students are left baffled about how they should craft their response to gain optimal marks. Students need to know the test-question weighting and the distinction between terms such as "discuss" and "explain" (Etobicoke Board of Education 1987). For example, Sue had this experience: ".... I lost most of the points on one question. The question ended with the phrase, 'Be specific.' I had only outlined the answer" (Aitken 1994, p. 61). By misreading a question, Sue lost the marks that she possibly deserved. A simple way to alleviate this problem would be for the teacher to be available and take the time before starting the test administration to clarify the instructions and expectations.

Test instruction misinterpretations such as Sue's do not provide valid inferences about knowledge and skills. *Principles* (1993) agreed that students should have opportunity for clarification *before* as well as *during* tests to ensure that every opportunity is available for students to display their knowledge:

> When collecting assessment information, interactions with students should be appropriate and consistent. Care must be taken when collecting assessment information to treat all students fairly....When writing a paper-and-pencil test, a student may ask to have an ambiguous item clarified, and, if warranted, the item should be explained to the entire class. (pp. 6–7)

Thoughtful and caring teachers take the time to ensure that students are clear about test expectations. If clarification is necessary for one student, the teacher will clarify and share the clarification with the rest of the class for uniform fairness.

Test and Assignment Schedules

Busy administrators and teachers often neglect the needs of the student when constructing examination schedules, and students duly noted this in the 1994 study.

Some students reported that exams were scheduled on special days, such as Graduation Day, while others said that they did several exams over the course of the day. Students wondered why more teachers did not collaborate and spread tests out over several days. Such inappropriate scheduling could result with invalid inferences of the students' knowledge and understanding. When teachers do not collaborate, tests are sometimes inappropriately scheduled as Laura reported:

> I wish that a whole bunch of tests was not always scheduled at once. It seems like that in every subject the teachers always seem to schedule their tests on the same day. Tomorrow I have my Social Studies 10 final as well as my Science 10 final. (Aitken 1994, p. 68)

James agreed:

> It's difficult to tell if teachers plan the date of tests together, for if not, they should. Tests seem to come in small bunches and a student may be burdened with up to five tests to study for on one day.... I just wish teachers would start to realize or even *care* that students have other classes. A little consideration is all that is needed. (Aitken 1994, p. 69)

Setting too many tests in a short period of time is unfair as this elementary student explained, "too many tests in one week, for example, nine tests" (Alberta Education 2009, p. 49). The ASASFR acknowledges students' concerns and recommends that the frequency of assessments is not overwhelming for students.

Thoughtful scheduling is not only a matter of obtaining a valid inference of student work, but being sensitive about students' needs. Tactful teachers plan carefully and ensure as much as possible that test schedules are humane and that they do not schedule tests on special days because of administrative convenience.

Collecting Assessment Information

Poor Test Administration: Uncomfortable Test Room and Distractions

Test administration procedure can influence the outcome of the students' test results. For example, infractions, such as uncomfortable room temperature, stuffiness, and disturbances in and outside the examination room, distract students as Kevin described: "The room was stuffy and it felt like a gaol that I couldn't get out of if I tried." Severyn added, "The room was silent and cold and it smelled like sweaty gym suits" (Aitken 1994, pp. 85–86). Rob reported that some teachers contributed to distractions by demonstrating lack of sensitivity and tact during the test:

> Writing any final exam for any class sucks. Right when you get comfortable in doing the test it seems to be the teacher's duty to come and watch over your shoulder. Yeh! Like that makes you comfortable. You start to sweat and your hands get clammy. And everybody in the gym seems to be staring at you. Your mind then goes blank for a while until they [teachers] leave. But in becoming comfortable again it takes a little time because the teacher has rudely interrupted you. (Aitken 1994, p. 68)

Jim agreed: "The sound of the teacher's pacing the rows and interfering with my thought processes are still very real" (Aitken 1994, p. 68). Suzette also complained about the incessant interruptions:

> As I was writing the exam, it was hard to concentrate because there were so many interruptions. The teachers were walking around the gym with their shoes clanging against the floor, the recess bell ringing every fifty-five minutes, and people kept getting up to go to the bathroom, or get more paper. (Aitken 1994, p. 68)

Usually, teachers try to be unobtrusive but often students do not interpret it as such. Julie felt her teacher was irritating: "I'm finding the test harder than I thought.... I can't get focused. I am having trouble concentrating. And my dumb teacher is walking around the room asking people if they want more candies! I really don't like candy" (Aitken 1994, p. 68).

The 2007 study participants noted new distractions, such as technological innovations as WebCT, and one student was adamant about its problems in test-taking situations: "I hate WebCT … it's noisy and distracting." One student described his experience this way:

> Imagine going to WebCT to complete a multiple-choice exam. The room is full, everyone is typing. You open the test. The questions are obscure, unclear and full of grammatical errors. I choose an answer then remember to save—paranoid I will somehow lose it all.... And no prof. to be seen to clarify questions! P.S. Proctors—don't bring in your smelly micro-waved food, either. (Aitken 2007, n. p.)

Students unfamiliar with WebCT found it problematic, particularly with their cognitive and psychomotor processing. One student said: "Going from high school we wrote tests by hand, we were studying by paper. Then university we had to do everything by computer or WebCT. Threw off how we thought and wrote tests" (Aitken 2007, n. p.).

Students noted the many annoying distractions during test-taking times. *Principles* (1993) in support, advised:

> Optimum conditions should be provided for obtaining data from and information about students so as to maximize the validity and consistency of the data and information collected. Common conditions include such things as proper light and ventilation, comfortable room temperature, and freedom from distraction (e.g., movement in and out of the room, noise). Adequate workspace, sufficient materials, and adequate time limits appropriate to the purpose and form of the assessment are also necessary.... (pp. 6–7)

Students with Special Needs

Although regular-stream students have many concerns about the test-taking conditions, students with special needs, such as English as an additional language student, Mei-Lei, sometimes are doubly penalized:

> .... I made mistake on answer paper. I needed one more answer paper. I asked teacher to give me one more answer paper, but he rejected. I didn't feel to keep taking the exam. However I had to continue it.... [T]he examiner said, "time is over." I was really mad,

because I could not finish the test and not because I am not able to answer, but because I was slow in answering. It is natural because English is not my mother tongue. (Aitken 1994, p. 99)

Mei-Lei and others with special needs require special test arrangements. Mei-Lei was frustrated because she was penalized for not being able to demonstrate her understanding in a second language. On this issue, the ASASFR (Alberta Education 2009) recommended that students with special needs should have differentiated assessment and accommodations. *Principles* (1993) agreed:

> It may be necessary to develop alternative assessment procedures to ensure a consistent and valid assessment of those students who, because of special needs or inadequate language, are not able to respond to an assessment method (for example, oral instead of written format, individual instead of group administered, translation into first language providing additional time). (p. 7)

Although it takes more time and effort to accommodate students with special needs, pedagogically oriented teachers intuitively take care of them and provide every opportunity for students to demonstrate their knowledge and understanding.

Judging and Scoring Student Performance

Grading Criteria

Students in both studies reported that they should know the blueprint and scoring guide ahead of the test or assignment, for example, "Please—no surprises at the 11th hour!" (Aitken 2007, n. p.). The ASASFR supports the students on this issue recommending that students should know scoring criteria prior to being assessed (Alberta Education 2009). *Principles* (1993) concurred:

> Before an assessment method is used, a procedure for scoring should be prepared to guide the process of judging the quality of a performance or product, the appropriateness of an attitude or behavior, or the correctness of an answer. To increase consistency and validity, properly developed scoring procedures should be used. (p. 7)

The marking and scoring rubric is critical in allowing students to do their best work. Too often teachers do not share the rubric with the students often because rubrics are not constructed until after the assignment or test is done. Pedagogically oriented teachers provide rubrics to assist students as much as possible in allowing them to reveal their strengths (and weaknesses) so that these can be reflected upon by both teacher and students and dealt with in subsequent instruction.

Assessment is integral to instruction and all assessment should anticipate action to improve learning (Clarke 1992). It is critical then that clear scoring procedures are in place for students to provide responses that generate valid inferences so that teachers can use the information to judge the students' performances and to help improve instruction and student learning. The students' anecdotes illustrate that students appreciate disclosure of the rubrics so they can respond accordingly and be judged fairly.

Tactful teachers who take the time to provide clear rubrics allow greater likelihood that the assessments will provide valid inferences about student learning and achievement and accurate judgment of student performance.

Summarizing and Interpreting Results

Teacher Perceptions of Students: Winners and Losers

In the 1994 study, it was evident to some students that the test results, no matter how valid, were powerful enough to label winners and losers. Students knew they were not losers or "dumb," yet if the test, fairly constructed or not, indicated this, the test result was legitimate and trumped student opinion. Apple (1979) argued that when a teacher perceives a student as dumb the child becomes dumb. In other words, the results of the test, valid or otherwise, become a self-fulfilling prophecy.

It is not only in the academic sense where winners and losers are identified; behavior and favoritism play key parts. In the Alberta Student Assessment Study (Alberta Education 2009), students reported that teachers favored some students over others; for example, some boys felt that girls received higher grades than them because of boys' misbehavior. "Boys shouldn't be marked down if they misbehave or are being rude" and "Boys talk more and their behaviour is their mark" (p. 126). A senior high student reported, "If they don't like you, they mark you more harshly" (p. 127). Another secondary student said, "Teacher bias is a real problem. Students who are favored get better marks" (p. 48). Other secondary students reported, "grades are reduced for misbehavior" and "if a student is disruptive then grades go down" (Alberta Education 2009, p. 48).

Surveys from the Alberta Education (2009) study indicated that approximately 70% of elementary students agreed or strongly agreed that "Report card marks change because of good/naughty behaviour" (p. 119) and approximately 81% of secondary students agreed or strongly agreed that "Students' behaviour in class affects the grades they get" (p. 122). Some secondary teachers noted that there should be a separation of behavior from academic and actual learning; thus, the ASASFR recommends that assessment of achievement should not be aggregated with assessment of behavior. *Principles* (1993) concurred:

> Combining disparate kinds of results into a single summary should be done cautiously. To the extent possible, achievement, effort, participation, and other behaviors should be graded separately....For example, letter grades used to summarize achievement are most meaningful when they represent only achievement. When they include other aspects of student performance, such as effort, amount (as opposed to quality) of work completed, neatness, class participation, personal conduct, or punctuality, not only do they lose their meaningfulness as a measure of achievement, but they also suppress information concerning other important aspects of learning and invite inequities.... (p. 10)

Pedagogically oriented teachers do not favor students. Students are treated with equity, not equality. Pedagogically oriented teachers are respected for not playing favorites and do not use assessment as a weapon to reward or punish.

Reporting Assessment Findings

Returning the Grade

What is it like for students to await test grades? Ronnie, a Grade 4 student, dramatized the event: "I went to school the next day and she handed out the test and every time she handed out the test the whole class goes [to the tune of a suspense thriller], 'dah de da dah, dah de da dah!'" (Aitken 1994, p. 97).

Students cringed upon hearing their grade announcement in class. High-school student, Rookie, experienced humiliation when her grade was returned publicly: "Why can't teachers just help a student when they don't do too good instead of making them look like a class clown? I just wish that teachers would respect students' privacy more often" (Aitken 1994, p. 70). Grade 3 students reported having grades returned to them publicly as well. They were comfortable if the marks were high but not if the marks were low because, "it's embarrassing" (pp. 70–71).

Perhaps it doesn't occur to teachers that students feel uncomfortable about teachers calling out grades in class. Teachers themselves may not have had these experiences when they were students and so they would not think of this as being a traumatic event. Nevertheless, tactful teachers with students in mind return grades privately and with constructive feedback.

Feedback for Learning

Black et al.'s (2004) research indicated the importance of focusing on teacher feedback, not the grade. Their research showed that "while student learning can be advanced by feedback through comments, the giving of numerical scores or grades has a negative effect, in that students ignore comments when marks are also given" (p. 13). When providing constructive feedback, it should be clear and timely so that students can reflect on their success and where they can improve their work. The ASASFR concurred: "Teacher feedback to students must be clear, honest, frequent, timely, sensitive, constructive, and motivating" (Alberta Education 2009, 135). *Principles* (1993) recommended regular conferences and follow-up action when providing feedback:

> Conferences scheduled at regular intervals and, if necessary, upon request provide parents/ guardians and, when appropriate, students with an opportunity to discuss assessment procedures, clarify and elaborate their understanding of the assessment results, summary comments and grades, and reports, and, where warranted, to work with teachers to develop relevant follow-up activities or action plans.

When assessment is used in a constructive way via conversation with written communication, learning and pedagogical relationships are enhanced. Clearly, teachers who are on the students' side are teachers who use assessment for learning.

Summary

I intertwined the students' voice with the research throughout the studies. It is evident that students accept the necessity of assessment and evaluation, but only if done fairly. The document *Principles for Fair Student Assessment Practices for Education in Canada* (1993) supports and underscores the students' voices about the need for fair assessment practice. The students' anecdotes resonated with research that proposes the following:

1. When collecting assessment information for the purposes of obtaining valid inferences about what students know and can do, provision must be made for optimal test administration such as ensuring adequate test room environment conducive to testing and eliminating distractions. Also, students with special needs must be fairly accommodated by providing a specially modified test or added time to complete the tests.
2. When judging and scoring student performance, clear scoring procedures must be in place for students so teachers can generate valid inferences. Students need clear directions so that they can respond to the assignment and test questions in a way that allows them to show what they know and can do.
3. In summarizing and interpreting results, teachers need to be cautioned about forgone perceptions of students that might warrant favoritism due to prior class-room conduct or "halo" effects due to high performances or past history of performance.
4. When reporting assessment findings, teachers should return graded papers, or grades privately. Further, publicly sharing the grades with the class contravenes the *Freedom of Information and Protection of Privacy Act* (Government of Alberta 2006).

The most important part of assessment occurs as the learning cycle is repeated, when evaluation results are used as a secondary purpose as feedback for learning. A significant opportunity for increasing student learning and achievement is possible when these results are used for instructional improvement as well (Black and Wiliam 1998).

Implications for Incorporating Student Voice into Student Learning and Assessment

Power, mistrust, and secrecy are obstacles to pedagogical relationships. van Manen (1991) holds that "Mistrust or suspicion makes real pedagogy quite impossible" (p. 167). Tests can be tools to wield power, by keeping students unaware about test content and scoring guides. The teacher holds the keys to these secrets. Sometimes tests are used to discipline and punish; to sort winners from losers, and humiliate when grades are announced. For some teachers, however, power is not the deep issue, but instead, lack of confidence that propels teachers to use power to conceal their insecurity. The teacher is afraid to "let go" and trust the students to empower themselves to take responsibility for their own learning. Lack of confidence encourages teachers to resort to tactics that do little to support students in fair assessment practice. Some teachers suspect that the students will take advantage of them if they share information about the assessments. However, students respect pedagogically oriented teachers who authentically involve them in their learning and assessment.

To implement student voice successfully into assessment, teachers not only have to have the knowledge and skills, but more importantly, an attitude of care and tact in student learning. They have to trust the students, become mentors and coaches, and work with students to help them be part of the conversation. Teachers have to let go of total control and invite students into their own assessment. Aoki (1990) referred to this as "letting learn" or "pedagogical leave-taking":

> Often a pedagogical tact in teaching is to say to a student, "I leave it to you," suggesting a letting go of decision-making to the student. Such an understanding reflects teaching understood as delegating or allocating power assumed to reside in the teacher. (p. 39)

Pedagogical leave-taking takes time to understand and achieve and like most significant understandings, it takes time to develop. Once students see that teachers are on "their side," then teachers share in the rewarding experience of shared power. Pedagogical thoughtfulness and tact are essential elements of pedagogic competence. Teachers embodying tact no longer hold the hierarchical position of the keepers of the keys, but instead, are the empowering partners in student learning. Student assessment knowledge and pedagogical relationality are the powerful partners in fair student assessment practice. The student voice is the glue that holds them together to set the students up for success and lifelong learning (Fig. 9.1).

Student Voice: Directions for Teaching and Learning

A pedagogically tactful teacher is sensitive to students' needs and through trust invites students to be part of the assessment process. Some ways to do this are by using student-constructed tests, student-constructed rubrics, and peer and self-assessment. Other ways are by reviewing tests, assignments, and listening to and taking action upon students' suggestions to clarify and improve the assessment strategy or tool.

Student-Constructed Tests

Student-constructed tests are based on sound research (Clarke 1992; Smith 2009). Perkins (1992) noted that a testing culture promotes the notion of a teacher-centered classroom while an assessment culture requires a student-centered classroom.

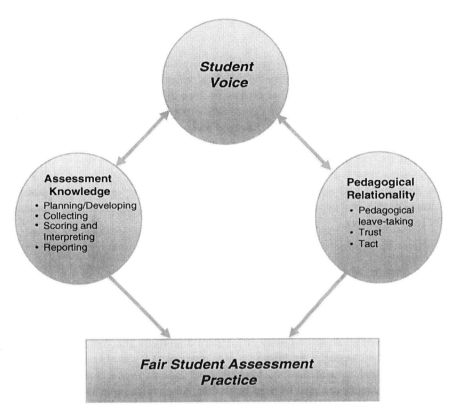

Fig. 9.1 A model connecting student voice, assessment knowledge, and pedagogical relationality to engender fair student assessment practice

In student-centered classrooms, teachers share power as they do knowledge. They believe that teachers need to step back and trust the students to take responsibility for their own assessment and learning. Student-constructed tests can be an important component of student-centered classrooms because here, students are involved in test-question construction. Clarke (1992) concurred and believes that "student-constructed tests offer both an effective assessment tool and a powerful review strategy to assist students in organizing their knowledge of the topic" (p. 27).

To introduce the student-constructed test, the teacher involves students first in writing story problems in mathematics, for example. Students write their problems in real contexts, contexts that have meaning for them, such as those embedded in their school, home, or family, instead of irrelevant contexts described in commercial workbooks. Students as young as Grade 1 can write these problems for peers as a class activity (Silverman et al. 1992). Finally, the teacher can use selected and revised student-constructed problems to use in formative or summative assessment. Demonstrating trust and confidence in the students like this strengthens the pedagogical relationship as well as student engagement in learning.

Student-Constructed Rubrics

Student-constructed rubrics are key ways to incorporate student voice into learning. Danielson (as cited in Willis 1996) believes that students involved in creating rubrics have a better understanding of what must be done to reach learning outcomes. As well, by using rubrics as guides, students learn to monitor their own progress through self-assessment to improve their learning and achievement. Although student-constructed rubrics take time and effort initially to develop, once students learn how to design and use them, they save time later on.

Students sense the trust that teachers have when teachers allow them to be part of the assessment and rubric development. Power and secrecy are inconsequential because targets and expectations are clear, and a comfortable, secure environment for learning ensues.

Peer Assessment

Peer assessment can be done informally throughout the course by providing descriptive feedback to improve peers' work (Reynolds 2009). Black et al. (2004) hold that peer assessment is valuable because students are more likely to accept criticism from peers than from teachers. Additionally, peer assessment is also beneficial because students use their natural discourse to explain and learn through examiners' roles.

Peer assessment can also be used in grading, albeit with some caution (Knight et al. 2000). The rationale is that the "behind the scenes" work is difficult for teachers to ascertain and to assess fairly in cooperative learning. A way to include student voice into assessment is to invite students to construct their peer-assessment rubric. By being involved this way, students focus on the criteria and understand what it means to be an effective contributing group member, for example. When used formatively, peer assessments are used constructively by sharing each other's feedback so that they know how to improve their group contribution. Research shows that when students know the criteria, they assess fairly and their summative assessments are consistent with their teachers' assessment (Weaver and Cotrell 1986).

When developing cooperative learning peer assessment rubrics, students are given the responsibility to construct fair and clear rubrics so that there are no misunderstandings in group work. Students take this responsibility seriously and appreciate trusting teachers giving them this opportunity to have their say in what they expect of one another in working toward common goals.

Self-assessment (Self-regulation)

The most important of these assessment strategies is self-assessment. Self-assessment empowers students as learners as they take responsibility for their own learning.

This is the notion of pedagogical leave-taking—taking leave, trusting students—to learn and assess their learning to make informed decisions for further lifelong learning. Metacognition and reflection are critical in lifelong learning. Costa and Kallick (1992) agreed: "We must constantly remind ourselves that the ultimate purpose of evaluation is to have students become self-evaluating" (p. 275). Tactful teachers encourage students to expose their weaknesses and strengths to improve learning though sensitive dialogue. Once this trusting relationship is built, it becomes second nature for students to think and dialogue critically with others about their learning.

Student Voice Conclusion

Student voice in assessment is crucial for fair assessment practice. By listening to students and reflecting on what they say, teachers will have important information to improve student learning and teacher praxis. Pedagogically oriented teachers not only listen to the students' voice respectfully, but also step back and trust students for taking much of the responsibility for their own assessment and learning. Perkins (1992) concurred and explained this stepping-back approach this way:

> It is this act of stepping back that enables teachers to practice and infuse the habit of reflection into their own pedagogical approach. In this light, teachers become researchers in the classroom, posing central questions to better inform their sense of student learning, their approach to teaching strategies, and the development of their own reflective habits. (p. 65)

Removing oneself from the center of student learning and genuinely listening to and acting upon student voice allow students to be an important part of their lifelong learning. Valuing student voice and authentically addressing it indicate teachers with pedagogical tact, those who embody assessment with sensitivity. Pedagogic thoughtfulness and tact are essential elements of pedagogic competence and fair assessment practice, the foundation and heart of teaching and learning.

In these studies, the students' prime concern was opportunity for fair assessment practice that embodied the pedagogical relationship and teacher expertise. Teachers who are supported by colleagues and professional development will have the courage and confidence to entertain the notion of pedagogical leave-taking, to step back, and invite students to be partners in their learning. Only when partnerships such as these come to fruition will we fully realize the students' possibilities and potential that await them this new century.

References

Aitken, E. N. (1994). *A hermeneutic phenomenological investigation of students' experience of test taking.* Unpublished doctoral dissertation, University of Alberta, Edmonton, AB.

Aitken, E. N. (2007, October). *Student-constructed tests: An assessment tool for learning.* Paper presented at the Mathematics Council of the Alberta Teachers' Association Annual Conference Edmonton, AB, Canada.

Albas, D. C., & Albas, C. M. (1984). *Student life and exams: Stresses and coping strategies.* Winnipeg, MB: Kendall/Hunt.

Alberta Assessment Consortium. (2007). *AAC…Everyday assessment tools for teachers.* Retrieved from http://www.aac.ab.ca/

Alberta Education. (2006a). *Accountability pillar.* Retrieved from http://education.alberta.ca/media/526352/apbrochurefinalnov2006.pdf

Alberta Education. (2006b). *Effective student assessment and evaluation in the classroom: Knowledge, skills, and attributes.* Edmonton, AB: Author.

Alberta Education, A. (2009). *The Alberta student assessment study final report.* Edmonton, AB: Author.

Aoki, T. T. (1990). *Inspiriting curriculum and pedagogy: Talks to teachers.* Edmonton, AB: Curriculum Praxis/University of Alberta.

Aoki, T. T., Langford, D., Williams, D. M., & Wilson, D. C. (Eds.). (1977). *The British Columbia social studies assessment summary report: A report to the Ministry of Education.* Victoria, BC: Ministry of Education.

Apple, M. (1979). *Ideology and curriculum.* London: Routledge/Kegan Paul.

Berlak, H., Newmann, F. M., Adams, E., Archbald, D. A., Burgess, T., Raven, J., et al. (1992). *Toward a new science of educational testing and assessment.* New York: SUNY.

Black, P., Harrison, C., Lee, C., Marshall, B., & Wiliam, D. (2003). *Assessment for learning.* New York: Open University Press.

Black, P., Harrison, C., Lee, C., Marshall, B., & Wiliam, D. (2004). Working inside the black box: Assessment for learning in the classroom. *Phi Delta Kappan, 86*(1), 8–21.

Black, P., & Wiliam, D. (1998). *Inside the black box: Raising standards through classroom assessment.* Retrieved from http://www.pdkintl.org/kappan/kbla9810.htm

Brookhart, S. M. (2009). The many meanings of "multiple measures". *Educational Leadership, 67*(3), 7–12.

Burger, J. M., & Krueger, M. (2003). A balanced approach to high-stakes achievement testing: An analysis of the literature with policy implications. *International Electronic Journal for Leadership in Learning, 7*(4). Retrieved from http://www.ucalgary.ca/~iejll/

Burke, K. (2005). *How to assess authentic learning* (4th ed.). Thousand Oaks, CA: Corwin Press.

Chappuis, S., Chappuis, J., & Stiggins, R. (2009). The quest for quality. *Educational Leadership, 67*(3), 14–19.

Clarke, D. J. (1992). Activating assessment alternatives in mathematics. *Arithmetic Teacher, 39*(6), 24–29.

Costa, A. L., & Kallick, B. (1992). Reassessing assessment. In A. L. Costa, J. A. Bellanca, & R. Fogerty (Eds.), *If minds matter: A forward to the future* (Vol. II, pp. 275–280). Palatine, IL: IR/Skylight.

Davies, A. (2000). *Making classroom assessment work.* Merville, BC: Connections.

Earl, L. M. (2003). *Assessment as learning: Using classroom assessment to maximize student learning.* Thousand Oaks, CA: Corwin Press.

Etobicoke Board of Education. (1987). *Making the grade.* Scarborough, ON: Prentice-Hall.

Fisher, D., & Frey, N. (2009). Feed up, back, forward. *Educational Leadership, 67*(3), 20–25.

Fullan, M. G. (1991). *The new meaning of educational change.* New York: Teachers College Press.

Gadamer, H. E. (1990). *Truth and method.* (2nd Rev. ed.). New York: Crossroad.

Government of Alberta. (2006). *Freedom of information and protection of privacy act.* Retrieved from http://foip.alberta.ca/

Grennon Brooks, J. (2002). *Schooling for life: Reclaiming the essence of learning.* Alexandria, VA: Association for Supervision and Curriculum Development.

Grennon Brooks, J., & Brooks, M. (1993). *In search of understanding: The case for constructivist classrooms.* Alexandria, VA: Association for Supervision and Curriculum Development.

Guskey, T. (Ed.). (1996). *Communicating student learning.* Alexandria, VA: Association of Supervision and Curriculum Development.

Guskey, T. (2004). Zero alternatives. *Principal leadership (Middle Level Edition), 5*(2), 49–53.

Hetherington, M. E., Parke, R., & Schmuckler, M. (2005). *Child psychology: A contemporary viewpoint* (2nd ed.). Toronto, ON: McGraw-Hill Ryerson.

Hoffmann, B. (1964). *The tyranny of testing*. New York: Collier Books.

Johnson, D. W., & Johnson, R. T. (2002). *Meaningful assessment: A manageable and cooperative process*. Boston: Allyn & Bacon.

Knight, P., Aitken, E. N., & Rogerson, R. J. (2000). *Forever better: Continuous quality improvement in higher education*. Stillwater, OK: New Forums Press.

Lambert, L. (2003). *Leadership capacity for lasting school improvement*. Alexandria, VA: Association for Supervision and Curriculum Development.

Levine, G. (1995). Closing the gender gap: Focus on mathematics anxiety. *Contemporary Education, LXVII*, 42–45.

Liu, R., Qiao, X., & Liu, Y. (n.d.). A paradigm shift of learner-centered teaching style: Reality or illusion? *Arizona Working Papers in SLAT, 13*, 77–79. Retrieved from http://w3.coh.arizona.edu/awp/AWP13/AWP13%5BLiu%5D.pdf

Maeroff, G. I. (1991). Assessing alternative assessment. *Phi Delta Kappan, 73*(4), 273–281.

Marzano, R. J. (2000). *Transforming classroom grading*. Alexandria, VA: Association for Supervision and Curriculum Development.

Marzano, R. J. (2006). *Classroom assessment and grading that work*. Alexandria, VA: Association for Supervision and Curriculum Development.

McInerney, D. M., Brown, G. T. L., & Liem, G. A. D. (2009). *Student perspectives on assessment: What students can tell us about assessment for learning*. Charlotte, NC: Information Age.

Merleau-Ponty, M. (1962). *Phenomenology of perception*. New York: The Humanities Press.

Nitko, A. J., & Brookhart, S. M. (2007). *Educational assessment of students* (5th ed.). Upper Saddle River, NJ: Pearson Education.

O'Brien, T. C. (1999). Parrot math. *Kappan, 80*(6), 434–438.

O'Connor, K. (2002). *How to grade for learning* (2nd ed.). Thousand Oaks, CA: Corwin Press.

Osborne, J. W. (1990). Some basic existential-phenomenological research methodology for counsellors. *Canadian Journal of Counselling, 24*(2), 79–91.

Oxford English Dictionary of Etymology. (1933). London: Oxford University Press: Author.

Perkins, D. (1992). *Smart schools*. New York: The Free Press.

Polkinghorne, D. (1983). *Methodology for the human sciences*. Albany, NY: State University of New York Press.

Popham, W. J. (2002). *The truth about testing: An educator's call to action*. Alexandria, VA: Association of Supervision and Curriculum Development.

Popham, W. J. (2004). *Classroom assessment: What teachers need to know* (4th ed.). Boston: Allyn & Bacon.

Popham, W. J. (2008). Timed tests for tykes? *Educational Leadership, 65*(8), 86–87.

Principles for Fair Student Assessment Practices for Education in Canada. (1993). Edmonton, AB: Centre for Research in Applied Measurement and Evaluation, University of Alberta. Retrieved from http://www.education.ualberta.ca/educ/psych/crame/files/eng_prin.pdf

Reeves, D. (2002). *The daily disciplines of leadership: How to improve student achievement, staff motivation, and personal organization*. San Francisco: Jossey Bass.

Reynolds, A. (2009). Why every student needs critical friends. *Educational Leadership, 67*(3), 54–57.

Reynolds, C. R., Livingstone, R. B., & Wilson, V. (2009). *Measurement and assessment in education* (2nd ed.). Upper Saddle River, NJ: Pearson.

Silverman, F. L., Winograd, K., & Strohauer, D. (1992). Student-generated story problems. *Arithmetic Teacher, 39*(8), 6–12.

Skinner, B. F. (1989). The origins of cognitive thought. *American Psychologist, 44*(1), 13–18.

Smith, K. (2009). From test takers to test makers. *Educational Leadership, 67*(3), 26–30.

Stiggins, R. (2001). *Student-centered classroom assessment* (3rd ed.). Upper Saddle River, NJ: Merrill.

Stiggins, R. J. (2002). Assessment crisis: The absence of assessment *FOR* learning. *Phi Delta Kappan, 83*(10), 758–765.

Stiggins, R., Arter, J., Chappuis, J., & Chappuis, S. (2004). *Classroom assessment for student learning: Doing it right-using it well*. Portland, OR: Assessment Training Institute.

Sylwester, R. (Ed.). (1998). *Student brains school issues*. Arlington Heights, IL: Skylight.

Tobias, S. (1993). *Overcoming math anxiety*. New York: W. W. Norton.

Valle, R. S., & King, M. (Eds.). (1978). *Existential-phenomenological alternatives for psychology*. New York: Oxford University Press.

van Manen, M. (1984). Practicing phenomenological writing. *Phenomenology and Pedagogy, 2*(1), 36–69.

van Manen, M. (1990). *Researching lived experience: Human science for an action sensitive pedagogy*. Toronto, ON: The Althouse Press.

van Manen, M. (1991). *The tact of teaching: The meaning of pedagogical thoughtfulness*. Albany, NY: The Althouse Press.

van Manen, M. (1992, March). *On pedagogy as virtue and the question of the education of teacher educators*. Text of a Lecture/Discussion on the occasion of the Faculty of Education 50th anniversary Lecture Series, University of Alberta, Edmonton, AB.

Vygotsky, L. S. (1978). *Mind in society*. London: Harvard University Press.

Weaver, W., & Cotrell, H. W. (1986). Peer evaluation: A case study. *Innovative Higher Education, 11*, 25–39.

Wiggins, G. P. (1993). *Assessing student performance: Exploring the purpose and limits of testing*. San Francisco: Jossey-Bass.

Wiggins, G., & McTighe, J. (1998). *Understanding by design*. Alexandria, VA: Association for Supervision and Curriculum Development.

Wiggins, G., & McTighe, J. (2005). *Understanding by design*. (Expanded 2nd ed.). Upper Saddle River, NJ: Merrill/ASCD.

Willis, S. (1996). Transforming the test. *ASCD Update, Association for Supervision and Curriculum Development, 38*(4), 1 & 4.

Witte, D. L., & Blakey, J. M. (1991). The child's view of evaluation: Voice as pattern through time. *The Journal of Learning About Learning, 1*(1), 72–79.

Wolfe, P. (2001). *Brain matters: Translating research into classroom practice*. Alexandria, VA: Association for Supervision and Curriculum Development.

Chapter 10
Grade Level of Achievement Data: Key Indicators for School-Based Decision-Makers*

John Burger and Anna Nadirova

Introduction

This chapter highlights the results of the recent pilot of the province-wide (Alberta, Canada) implementation of the classroom-based assessment data collection system (Grade Level of Achievement data or GLA) in addition to the external standardized student achievement tests.

Large-scale, standardized provincial achievement tests (PATs) in Grades 3, 6, and 9 provide valid achievement data. PATs are criterion-referenced, external achievement tests administered in Language Arts and Mathematics in Grade 3 and in Language Arts, Mathematics, Social Studies, and Science in Grades 6 and 9. However, based on the successful collaboration with seven school jurisdictions representing approximately half of the provincial student population, the Alberta Department of Education (Alberta Education) identified the potential for more comprehensive achievement data to inform program evaluation and decision-making in schools, jurisdictions, and the Ministry (Alberta Learning 2002). GLA data reported to Alberta Education is a teacher's judgment of academic progress for students in Grades 1–9. High school (Grades 10–12) course marks are also reported to the

*The views expressed in this chapter are those of the authors and not necessarily Alberta Education.

With permission of the original publisher, this chapter draws upon components of the following document: Dr. Burger, John and Dr. Nadirova, Anna. *Grade Level Achievement Data: Key Indicators for School-Based Decision-Makers*. Edmonton, AB: Government of Alberta, Alberta Education, 2006–2007.

J. Burger (✉)
Director of Schools, Rocky View Schools, Airurie, AB, Canada
e-mail: jburger@rockyview.ab.ca

A. Nadirova
Senior Research Officer, People and Research Division, Alberta Education,
Edmonton, AB, Canada
e-mail: Anna.Nadirova@gov.ab.ca

Ministry of Education, primarily for transcript purposes. GLA is based on the learner outcomes in a subject area after a course for a specific grade level has been completed and reflects the results from the full range of teacher-developed classroom assessments over the entire school year. Triangulation of large-scale external assessment data with teacher-generated classroom-based assessment grounded in clear curriculum standards provides opportunities to create more complete and informative models of student achievement.

The chapter examines PAT and GLA data at the provincial level as a means to explore what we can discover when we consider achievement data in a more holistic and balanced context, and reflects on the implications for parallel analysis at the jurisdiction, school, and classroom levels. Given the comprehensiveness of classroom-based assessment, analysis of GLA data in relationship to PAT results can provide unique insights into factors that influence student achievement. Both PAT and GLA data provide teachers, principals, central office staff, and Alberta Education personnel with additional tools to help inform and engage students and parents in the learning process, and to analyze and evaluate the achievement of different populations of students to ensure that their learning needs are better understood and met. When both PAT and GLA data are reported to parents and teachers, this information benefits students through accurate, comprehensive, continuous, and timely communication of achievement information as they move from one grade to the next or between schools.

The objective of this chapter is to consider GLA data collected during the last GLA pilot in 2006–2007 in relationship to PAT data for the same school year and demonstrate how this combined information can be interpreted to provide insight into factors that affect student achievement. Further, the relationships between GLA and PAT data will be explored as one way of unpacking meaning from data and dispelling myths about the relationships between classroom-based and external assessment data.

Background

From the provincial perspective, the need to evaluate programs and their effectiveness for all students and particular subsets of students, at provincial, jurisdictional, and school levels, represents a key mechanism to lever systemic improvement in student achievement. This is especially true in light of provincial priorities such as improving the high school completion rate and learning in Mathematics and Science. The GLA Reporting initiative grew out of these needs. It was also seen as an opportunity to support and further develop teacher capacity to do good classroom assessment work, to improve pedagogy by more fundamentally linking assessment with instructional decision-making, and as an approach to better engage teachers, administrators, students, and parents in formative assessments in ways that complement summative assessments.

GLA pilots, designed to demonstrate and build GLA reporting capacity, were run in 2003–2004 and again with a larger set of schools in 2005–2006 and 2006–2007.

Detailed analyses of the outcomes of these three stages of implementation supported the reliability and validity of the initial GLA data collection initiatives (Alberta Education 2005, 2007, 2008a) and provided support for continuing with the implementation of the GLA initiative for all public system schools (i.e., public, separate [Catholic], Francophone, and charter).

This chapter describes some of the outcomes associated with the 2006–2007 GLA pilot data analysis to explicate how classroom-based assessment when considered in light of external test results can more fully inform education decision-makers.

The provincial GLA report (Alberta Education 2008a) demonstrated support for the following four purposes for reporting GLA as defined in the *GLA Handbook* (Alberta Education 2006, p. 4):

- To provide richer information at the system level (both jurisdictional and provincial) to inform effective practices to determine the impact of specific programs on student learning (e.g., English as a Second Language and special education) and to determine processes to further refine these programs
- As a catalyst within the school's professional learning community to focus on individual student learning needs and interests
- To determine effective practices and strategies to foster higher levels of student achievement and confidence
- To contribute to the data or evidence used to report student achievement to parents/ guardians, fulfilling the school's responsibility as outlined in the *Guide to Education: ECS to Grade 12* in the section entitled *Assessment as the Basis for Communicating Individual Student Achievement* (Alberta Education 2008b)

Theoretical Underpinnings

Educational accountability has become entrenched firmly in learning systems across North America and Europe. Policy makers and educators alike can appreciate the benefit of stimulating student improvement around the concept of making education goals known and using a broad range of measures of the progress toward those goals.[1] Effective accountability is premised upon creating open education systems that clearly state the goals educators wish to accomplish, complemented by the right to ask appropriate questions at the appropriate levels about what went wrong if the goals are not achieved. For the most part, setting standards, ensuring some commonality in measures, and reporting and reserving the right to hold people accountable for their actions if the results are not as expected is not unreasonable for a publicly funded education system. However, if the public need for information on student, school, and system performance is not compatible with internal school-based assessment and improvement approaches, then these dysfunctional disconnections can undermine the utility of available data.

---

[1] See, for example, the National Centre for Educational Accountability in the United States. Their mission states firmly that they aim to promote student achievement by improving state data collection to improve decision-making. http://www.nc4ea.org/index.cfm?pg=about_us

A key challenge in making accountability meaningful for school-based educators lies in providing opportunities for teachers to see benefit and acquire ownership for the accountability processes including generating data and making sense of that data (Louis et al. 2005). The disconnect occurs when the primary participants in classroom assessment, the teachers, see a gap or even a conflict between their assessment efforts and the external assessment initiatives of governments. One solution to this dilemma may lie in creating school improvement scenarios where the amount of accountability effort in education measured using formative, well-rounded classroom assessment methods (assessment for learning) is balanced with summative assessments (standardized, classroom, and otherwise assessment of learning) so that comprehensive and compatible information is available to more fully inform decisions around what is working for students (Earl and Katz 2002; Stiggins 2001).

Educators such as Bloom (1980), Stiggins (2001), and Reeves (2004) are quick to point out that students do not improve most when only assessment of learning or summative assessment techniques are employed, but when assessment for learning or formative assessment techniques are used in an appropriate balance with the summative forms. Yet, media around the world have a tendency to place an exclusive emphasis on summative assessments in their coverage of school results.

Standardized tests and other forms of summative assessment undoubtedly have a place in education accountability owing to the high quality of these instruments and the valid and reliable nature of the data they provide. However, standardized testing is only one piece of the accountability puzzle.[2] Hence, the Grade Level of Achievement Reporting initiative is partly premised on the notion that summative assessment of learning models should not be viewed as the only data sources available to policy makers. However, the collection of GLA data is not intended for use in Alberta Education's Accountability Pillar.[3] It is intended to be used in monitoring program impacts at the provincial level, but can also add considerable depth and meaning to data compiled at the school and jurisdiction levels, especially when considered in relationship to appropriate data from provincial achievement tests and other data resident in the Ministry's student information system such as students' gender, birth month, mobility, socioeconomic status, and other variables.

The other value the Grade Level of Achievement Reporting initiative is premised upon is the view that engaging educators at the classroom level in ongoing assessment for and of learning as a basis for informing GLA reporting is absolutely vital to sound

---

[2] See Burger and Krueger (2003).

[3] The major purpose of the Accountability Pillar is to combine student achievement information with other data to demonstrate on an annual basis how well each school jurisdiction is doing in realizing expected outcomes and which areas require additional work (improvement). It also allows jurisdictions to juxtapose their achievement with provincial standards and to see how they have improved compared to their previous performance. The Accountability Pillar collects data on student achievement from provincial achievement tests (PATs) and diploma exams and additional student outcomes data such as dropout rates and high school completion rates. It also uses information on perceived quality of education from annual student, teacher, and parent surveys (Alberta Education 2009).

pedagogy and teacher professionalism. Accordingly, there is expectedly a willingness among education professionals to embrace the opportunity to relate classroom GLA data to broad-based assessment methods recognizing that, as Reeves (2004) stated,

> …the judgment of the classroom teacher is an integral part of constructive accountability…. Only when accountability, standards, and assessment are fully integrated at the classroom level will we achieve the potential for fairness, equity of opportunity, and improved academic achievement that *teaching professionals crave* and society demands. (p. 107)

Researchers in the United Kingdom have been developing an approach to accountability that recognizes the limitations of overreliance on external assessments attained at the expense of ignoring a key source of information on student achievement (i.e., classroom-based assessment information). This work emanates from the *Assessment Systems for the Future* project based at the Faculty of Education, University of Cambridge. The project was set up by the Assessment Reform Group in September 2003 to consider evidence from research and practice about the summative assessment of students. The role that assessment by teachers can take in summative assessment was the project's particular focus. Their report, *The Role of Teachers in the Assessment of Learning*, (Assessment Reform Group 2006) details a set of prerequisites that are required to make a balanced approach possible, and many if not most of these prerequisites are present to varying degrees in the Alberta context. The research team commented:

This pamphlet considers how to arrive at a comprehensive summative assessment system capable of providing information, based on sound evidence, about a wide range of pupil competencies. Available research evidence leads to the conclusion that systems relying heavily on tests results are found wanting in several respects, particularly in their ability to give a dependable, that is, both valid and reliable, account of pupils' learning. It is argued that the negative consequences of summative assessment for learning and teaching can be minimized by more appropriate use of teachers' judgments. At the same time it is acknowledged that a number of issues need to be addressed in implementing a system making use of teachers' assessment. Some key requirements are for:

- Robust and permanent procedures for quality assurance and quality control of teachers' judgments
- The provision of developmental criteria, which indicate a progression in learning related to particular goals
- Teachers to have access to well-designed tasks assessing skills and understanding, which can help them to make judgments across the full range of learning goals
- Preservice and in-service professional development that extends teachers' understanding and skills of assessment for different purposes.

It is also important that summative assessment procedures are in harmony with the procedures of formative assessment and that they are transparent, with judgments supported by evidence so that all involved can have trust in the results.

An integrated student achievement database, such as envisaged by the UK report, would amplify and balance the data generated by the external provincial achievement testing program with teacher-based classroom assessment of student achievement and provide a much more dynamic, complete, and enriched picture of student curricular-based learning while enhancing the professional role of teachers in this process. Furthermore, the creation and maintenance of such a database does not represent a big leap over existing work that teachers do, but by creating a system to systematically collect and aggregate student GLA data, some significant gaps in our knowledge about what is and what is not working for students' learning can be illuminated.

The remainder of this chapter will describe the results of a quantitative examination of the 2006–2007 GLA data that were collected for students from 60% of the provincial schools and will discuss the implications of this project for teachers and administrators.

Description of 2006–2007 GLA Data

Nine hundred and twenty-three schools from 71 public, Catholic, Francophone, and charter school authorities submitted useable GLA data for 220,682 students, 3,380 of whom were not on a graded curriculum. Jurisdictions were required to report GLA in Language Arts and Mathematics for a minimum of one-third of their schools in Grades 1–9. Many jurisdictions reported more than one-third of schools in the 2006–2007 school year. The data fields collected were as follows:

All Students:

- Student name (surname and given name)
- Alberta Student Number
- Enrolled grade (defined as the grade to which the student was assigned)

GLA data were collected for students on a graded curriculum as defined in the Alberta program of studies, in the following fields, where applicable:

- GLA in English Language Arts
- GLA in French Language Arts (French as the language of instruction or immersion students)
- GLA in Mathematics
- Grade English Language Arts Introduced (for French Language Arts students only)

GLA in 2006–2007 was defined as the grade level expressed as a whole number in relationship to the learning outcomes defined in the program of studies that teachers judged the student to have achieved at the end of the school year. A GLA Handbook (Alberta Education 2006) was developed and distributed in the 2005–2006 school year to facilitate pilot school participation in GLA reporting.

The GLA Handbook encourages teachers to consider GLA assessment in relationship to the full range of formative and summative assessment information available to them over the course of the school year in making a professional judgment of the student's grade level of achievement.

Students not on a graded curriculum also had data submitted. "Not on a graded curriculum" was meant to indicate that the student's program was restricted to

Table 10.1 Enrolled grade distribution in 2007–2008 GLA database and province-wide

Enrolled grade	Number of students in 2006–2007 GLA sample	Percent of total number in GLA sample	Number of students province-wide	Percent of total number in grades 1–9 province-wide
Grade 1	23,692	10.9	42,176	10.6
Grade 2	23,929	11.0	42,493	10.7
Grade 3	23,896	11.0	42,656	10.7
Grade 4	23,954	11.0	42,597	10.7
Grade 5	23,839	11.0	43,858	11.0
Grade 6	24,582	11.3	45,050	11.3
Grade 7	24,240	11.2	45,544	11.5
Grade 8	24,267	11.2	45,790	11.5
Grade 9	24,903	11.5	47,014	11.8
Total	217,302	100	397,178	100

learning outcomes that were significantly different from the provincial curriculum defined in the program of studies and were specifically selected to meet the student's special needs as defined in the *Standards for Special Education* (Alberta Learning 2004). The information collected was teachers' ratings of students' learning outcomes in three areas: communication skills, functional skills, and academic readiness skills. Communication skills refer to the development of expressive and/or receptive communication. This could be verbal communication and/or alternative modes of communication. Functional skills refer to skills that would assist the student in developing independence in the home, school, and community. Academic readiness skills refer to skills that would prepare the student for learning outcomes in the program of studies.

Alberta Education staff used the Alberta Student Number to append data fields such as PAT results (both raw scores and achievement levels—Excellence, Acceptable, and Below Acceptable), student age, gender, number of school registrations, English as a Second Language and any special needs codes associated with the student, and school starting date. Individual student identifiers were replaced with a discrete GLA data ID, leaving no personal identifiers in the dataset used in producing this paper.

There were 217,302 students on a graded curriculum included in this sample for the 2006–2007 school year. The students are roughly evenly distributed by enrolled grade with approximately 11% of the students in each grade cohort. Table 10.1 shows the distribution of the GLA sample data by enrolled grade (Grades 1–9) compared to the grade distribution for the province as a whole. In Table 10.1, the "Province-wide" column refers to the data for the entire province. In the remainder of the report, provincial comparisons refer to the provincial sample of GLA data.

The distribution of students in each of the GLA outcomes categories by subject is shown in Table 10.2.

Table 10.2 Provincial GLA outcomes categories

	Mathematics		English Language Arts		French Language Arts	
	Number of students	Percent of total enrolled	Number of students	Percent of total enrolled	Number of students	Percent of total enrolled
GLA below enrolled grade	21,348	9.8	24,116	11.1	741	5.8
GLA equal to enrolled grade	190,426	87.6	185,148	85.2	10,758	84.8
GLA above enrolled grade	1,027	0.5	540	0.2	45	0.4
GLA NA[a]	4,501	2.1	7,498	3.5	1,142	9.0
Total	217,302	100	217,302	100	12,686	100

[a]GLA NA refers to missing data, i.e., not available

Table 10.3 Correlation between PAT and GLA data

2005–2006		2006–2007	
PAT by GLA–grade and subject	Tau-b	PAT by GLA–grade and subject	Tau-b
Grade 3 English Language Arts	0.378	Grade 3 English Language Arts	0.324
Grade 6 English Language Arts	0.406	Grade 6 English Language Arts	0.337
Grade 9 English Language Arts	0.338	Grade 9 English Language Arts	0.323
Grade 3 Mathematics	0.388	Grade 3 Mathematics	0.342
Grade 6 Mathematics	0.403	Grade 6 Mathematics	0.366
Grade 9 Mathematics	0.399	Grade 9 Mathematics	0.409

Note. All of the above observed relationships are statistically significant at $p < 0.01$ level

Comparison of GLA and PAT Data

The GLA-by-PAT analysis demonstrates that GLA data indeed can supplement PAT data with reasonable reliability and validity (Table 10.3). Kendall's tau-b was used to measure the association between PAT and GLA. This particular test was chosen as it uses ordinal-level data based on pair-by-pair comparisons. The chart above details the correlations for 2005–2006 and 2006–2007.

The PAT and GLA variables were re-coded into the dichotomous categories: either Below Acceptable or At or Above Acceptable for PATs, and either Below Grade Level or At or Above Grade Level for GLA; then the two dichotomous variables were compared. All relationships tested were statistically significant at the $p < .01$ level. The p-value indicates that the observed relationships are not due to chance, and, based on tau-b values, we conclude that the relationships are moderate in strength. A perfect correlation of 1.0 between GLA and PAT is neither an expected nor a desirable condition given the inherent differences in the evaluation designs, which would underlie potentially different learning outcomes being measured with different assessment methods.

The strength of the relationships was lower in more recent 2006–2007 data compared to 2005–2006 data, except for Grade 9 Mathematics. This lower strength may be attributed to the larger GLA sample size in 2006–2007 and, therefore, may represent a truer picture than the correlations of the previous year.

Table 10.4 Comparison of English Language Arts PAT and GLA data

		GLA—English Language Arts		
		At or above grade level	Below grade level or GLA NA	Total
PAT—Grade 3 English Language Arts	Acceptable or excellence	**77.6%** (17,304)	5.7% (1,276)	83.4% (18,580)
	Below acceptable, excused or absent	8.1% (1,801)	**8.5%** (1,905)	16.6% (3,706)
	Total	85.7% (19,105)	14.3% (3,181)	100.0% (22,286)
PAT—Grade 6 English Language Arts	Acceptable or excellence	**77.9%** (18,173)	5.4% (1,266)	83.3% (19,439)
	Below acceptable, excused or absent	8.1% (1,887)	**8.6%** (2,014)	16.7% (3,901)
	Total	85.9% (20,060)	14.1% (3,280)	100.0% (23,340)
PAT—Grade 9 English Language Arts	Acceptable or excellence	**76.2%** (17,489)	4.3% (982)	80.5% (18,471)
	Below acceptable, excused or absent	10.8% (2,483)	**8.7%** (1,999)	19.5% (4,482)
	Total	87.0% (19,972)	13.0% (2,981)	100.0% (22,953)

Note. All of the above observed relationships are statistically significant when measured by Chi-square (significance level at $p < 0.05$ or lower) (Chi-square is defined as "A nonparametric procedure for testing whether the observed frequencies of scores in different categories of a variable differ from the theoretically predicted frequencies" (Harris 1998))
Numbers in bold font represent consistent relationships between GLA and PAT data

Comparison of GLA and PAT Outcomes Using Achievement Levels

In order to further examine the relationship between the GLA data and PATs and to provide an additional perspective on these relationships, both PAT and GLA data were again re-coded into the categories of Below Grade Level and GLA NA (i.e., data not available) and At or Above Grade Level for GLA; and Acceptable or Excellence and Below Acceptable and Excused or Absent for PATs (Tables 10.4 and 10.5). These groupings were chosen based on the current Alberta Education standard for cohort reporting. The groups were then cross-tabulated with the hypothesis being that students who score at or above the acceptable level on PATs tend to be at or above grade level, and likewise those that score below acceptable tend to be below grade level. The following tables show some support for this hypothesis, as 84.9–86.5% of the students in Language Arts and 79.0–86.9% in Mathematics demonstrating congruent results between the PATs and GLA. The data in Tables 10.4 and 10.5 include all students from schools which submitted GLA data for 2006–2007 in Grades 3, 6, or 9.

Table 10.5 Comparison of mathematics PAT and GLA data

		GLA—Mathematics		
		At or above grade level	Below grade level or GLA NA	Total
PAT—Grade 3 mathematics	Acceptable or excellence	**79.6%** (17,753)	3.5% (788)	83.2% (18,541)
	Below acceptable, excused or absent	9.5% (2,120)	**7.3%** (1,632)	16.8% (3,752)
	Total	89.1% (19,873)	10.9% (2,420)	100.0% (22,293)
PAT—Grade 6 mathematics	Acceptable or excellence	**74.0%** (17,279)	3.0% (701)	77.0% (17,980)
	Below acceptable, excused or absent	13.4% (3,134)	**9.5%** (2,226)	23.0% (5,360)
	Total	87.5% (20,413)	12.5% (2,927)	100.0% (23,340)
PAT—Grade 9 mathematics	Acceptable or excellence	**65.8%** (15,056)	3.0% (679)	68.7% (15,735)
	Below acceptable, excused or absent	18.0% (4,129)	**13.2%** (3,022)	31.2% (7,151)
	Total	83.8% (19,185)	16.2% (3,701)	100.0% (22,886)

Note. All of the above observed relationships are statistically significant when measured by Chi-square (significance level at $p<0.05$ or lower). Numbers in bold font represent consistent relationships between GLA and PAT data

It should be noted, in reviewing Tables 10.4 and 10.5, that more students are categorized as Below Grade Level in the PAT results than in GLA ratings. The question of interest in this regard is: does this present a problem for teachers and administrators or is it an opportunity to gain better understanding of student achievement by unpacking what such data discrepancies mean?

The anomalous relationships that are represented by the noncongruent data in Tables 10.4 and 10.5 may indicate several potential issues related to evaluating academic progress, that is:

- The PAT is a more difficult standard to attain than is the GLA.
- The PAT is inherently a more difficult assessment method.
- The differential coverage of the curriculum between PATs and classroom assessment favor enhanced achievement via the classroom assessment coverage of the curriculum objectives.
- It may be more difficult for teachers to assign a Below Grade Level evaluation to one of their students than is the case for the more objective markers of the PAT assessments.
- Student performance on PATs may be attenuated by test anxiety.

- Students may perform better on many assessments over time than on a single paper and pencil test.
- There is a complex combination of these and potentially other unnamed factors fundamentally linked to the teaching and learning context.

The key point to be made here is that, while it is desirable for classroom and external assessment data to be in agreement in terms of results, there are various reasons why the data might vary and by exploring and explicating these reasons, the students, parents, teachers, and administrators are better served.

Variations in GLA Data by Gender

Students' GLA was analyzed by gender in order to observe any patterns that may emerge. In this sample of students, there were a larger number of males than females, except in French Language Arts. Tables 10.6–10.8 show the frequency of female and male students in each of the GLA categories in Mathematics, English Language Arts, and French Language Arts. When testing for independence between genders,

Table 10.6 Variations in provincial mathematics GLA data by gender

	Females		Males	
	Number of students	Percent of total enrolled	Number of students	Percent of total enrolled
GLA below enrolled grade	9,504	9.0	11,844	10.6
GLA equal to enrolled grade	93,918	88.7	96,508	86.7
GLA above enrolled grade	464	0.4	563	0.5
GLA NA (not available)	2,044	1.9	2,457	2.2
Total	105,930	100	111,372	100

Note. All of the above observed relationships are statistically significant when measured by Chi-square (significance level at $p < 0.05$ or lower)

Table 10.7 Variations in provincial English Language Arts GLA data by gender

	Females		Males	
	Number of students	Percent of total enrolled	Number of students	Percent of total enrolled
GLA below enrolled grade	9,335	8.8	14,781	13.3
GLA equal to enrolled grade	92,749	87.6	92,399	83.0
GLA above enrolled grade	308	0.3	232	0.2
GLA NA (not available)	3,538	3.3	3,960	3.6
Total	105,930	100	111,372	100

Note. All of the above observed relationships are statistically significant when measured by Chi-square (significance level at $p < 0.05$ or lower)

Table 10.8 Variations in provincial French Language Arts GLA data by gender

	Females		Males	
	Number of students	Percent of total enrolled	Number of students	Percent of total enrolled
GLA below enrolled grade	360	5.1	381	6.7
GLA equal to enrolled grade	5,980	85.2	4,778	84.4
GLA above enrolled grade	31	0.4	14	0.3
GLA NA (not available)	651	9.3	491	8.7
Total	7,022	100	5,664	100

Note. All of the above observed relationships are statistically significant when measured by Chi-square (significance level at $p < 0.05$ or lower)

Chi-square was used. A statistically significant difference was observed between the genders in both Mathematics and English Language Arts.

Pope et al. (2003) conducted a study that showed larger gender differences in school-awarded marks than in the diploma exam marks in favor of females in almost all diploma courses. Mathematics courses (both Mathematics 30 Pure and Applied) were among those subjects where boys, while being outperformed by girls in school-awarded marks, did better than girls in diploma exam marks. Therefore, the question of gender differences between GLA and PAT results are of interest.

Tables 10.9 and 10.10 illustrate the differences in GLA and PATs across the enrolled grades for each gender. It is quite interesting to note that, similar to the 2003 study, on GLA females outperform males to a statistically significant degree in both subjects in nearly all enrolled grades. The reverse is seen on the Mathematics PAT results with males outperforming females to a statistically significant degree. However, in English Language Arts, females are outperforming males on the PATs. These findings point to a potential area for future research to investigate gender differentials and the causal factors associated with these differences. One hypothesis that would merit study should consider whether boys' greater potential to act out in negative ways in school is a source of bias in classroom assessment. By uncovering these relationships in the GLA data, the opportunity is presented for teachers and administrators to consider whether these relationships are present within their own contexts.

Lack of gender differences in mean GLA Mathematics scores in Grades 1 through 6 in the 2005–2006 GLA sample can be explained by the fact that this data set is less representative of the Alberta student population compared to the fuller 2006–2007 sample. Alternatively, the possibility of lack of gender differences in Mathematics achievement in elementary grades is confirmed by other studies. Lauzon (2001), for example, cites a number of studies indicating that gender differences favoring boys in Mathematics tend not to appear until high school. In this respect it is worth mentioning that a more extensive 2006–2007 GLA sample also reveals lack of gender-based variations in Mathematics for Grades 2 and 3.

Table 10.9 Comparisons of gender-based differences in GLA and PAT outcomes in English Language Arts

English Language Arts GLA						English Language Arts PAT					
Enrolled grade	Gender	05–06 N	05–06 mean GLA	06–07 N	06–07 mean GLA	Enrolled grade	Gender	05–06 N	05–06 mean PAT score	06–07 N	06–07 mean PAT score
1	F	3,562	1.01	11,525	0.93*						
	M	3,518	1.01	12,167	0.88*						
2	F	4,161	1.93*	11,704	1.90*						
	M	4,356	1.89*	12,225	1.85*						
3	F	4,236	2.89*	11,641	2.88*	3	F	4,088	71.03*	10,790	69.72*
	M	4,511	2.84*	12,255	2.83*		M	4,244	68.50*	11,537	66.72*
4	F	4,281	3.86*	11,608	3.87*						
	M	4,633	3.79*	12,346	3.79*						
5	F	4,535	4.81*	11,440	4.84*						
	M	4,664	4.75*	12,399	4.76*						
6	F	4,280	5.80*	12,114	5.82*	6	F	4,039	68.36*	11,451	69.79*
	M	4,689	5.71*	12,468	5.74*		M	4,304	64.90*	11,923	65.40*
7	F	4,127	6.87*	11,790	6.88*						
	M	4,350	6.75*	12,450	6.78*						
8	F	4,444	7.88*	11,849	7.88*						
	M	4,489	7.77*	12,418	7.77*						
9	F	4,466	8.87*	12,259	8.87*	9	F	4,154	71.42*	11,337	68.36*
	M	4,571	8.77*	12,644	8.76*		M	4,139	66.77*	11,742	63.25*

The independent sample t test evaluates the difference between the means of two independent groups (e.g., males and females; Green and Salkind 2003)

*Statistically significant difference between males and females (significance level at $p < 0.05$ or lower) as indicated by independent samples t test

Table 10.10 Comparisons of gender-based differences in GLA and PAT outcomes in mathematics

Mathematics GLA						Mathematics PAT					
Enrolled grade	Gender	05–06 N	05–06 Mean GLA	06–07 N	06–07 Mean GLA	Enrolled grade	Gender	05–06 N	05–06 Mean PAT score	06–07 N	06–07 Mean PAT score
1	F	4,024	1.01	11,525	0.95*						
	M	4,080	1.01	12,167	0.93*						
2	F	4,293	1.95	11,704	1.93						
	M	4,495	1.96	12,225	1.92						
3	F	4,250	2.92	11,641	2.90	3	F	4,083	33.12[a]	10,790	30.60[a]
	M	4,530	2.91	12,255	2.89		M	4,240	34.07[a]	11,537	31.54[a]
4	F	4,274	3.88	11,608	3.89*						
	M	4,640	3.87	12,346	3.86*						
5	F	4,521	4.84	11,440	4.85*						
	M	4,660	4.83	12,399	4.82*						
6	F	4,266	5.83	12,114	5.82*	6	F	4,054	36.64*	11,451	34.47*
	M	4,670	5.80	12,468	5.80*		M	4,335	37.60*	11,923	36.03*
7	F	3,941	6.88*	11,790	6.87*						
	M	4,212	6.83*	12,450	6.82*						
8	F	4,197	7.89*	11,849	7.86*						
	M	4,254	7.80*	12,418	7.81*						
9	F	4,217	8.85*	12,259	8.82*	9	F	4,166	32.44	11,337	30.80*
	M	4,346	8.78*	12,644	8.76*		M	4,162	32.35	11,742	31.36*

*Statistically significant difference between males and females (significance level at $p < 0.05$ or lower) as indicated by independent samples t test

Student Mobility

When students change schools, they must learn to deal with a new physical, social, and learning environment—new teachers, new classmates, possibly different sets of rules, different learning expectations—and may start at a different point in the curriculum than they left behind. It also takes some time for teachers to determine these students' learning level, learning style, interaction skills, etc., and thus define the optimal program for ongoing learning.

Research literature (e.g., Wasserman 2001) pointed to a negative relationship between the number of times students change schools and their academic growth. Wasserman's Alberta study suggests that additional research would be useful to not only enrich the understanding of the relationship, but to highlight any situations in which the negative impacts may have been mitigated by helpful strategies to support better transitions for students and schools. The GLA data provide such an opportunity for additional research. They permit an ongoing analysis of the relationship between the number of school changes students have made and their current grade level of achievement, thus allowing for an assessment of the cumulative impact of mobility.

Student mobility is captured by Alberta Education, once at the end of September and again in March, and compiled in the Student Information System. The Student Mobility Indicator (SMI) provides an indication of the number of times students have changed schools since their entry into the Alberta school system. The SMI is calculated by counting the number of different school registrations each student had accumulated until the most recent calendar year. Students could be changing schools more frequently than is captured; thus, the SMI is a conservative estimate of student mobility. All students start with an SMI of 1 as they have all been registered in at least one school. When a student registers in a different school, the SMI will increase by 1. Student mobility is then broken down into two categories, high and low. In Grades 1–3, high mobility students are those having a mobility indicator of 2 or more. Students having a mobility indicator of 1 are considered low mobility. In Grades 4–6, high mobility students are those having a mobility indicator of 3 or more. Students having a mobility indicator of 2 or less are considered low mobility. In Grades 7–9, high mobility students are those having a mobility indicator of 4 or more. Low mobility students have a mobility indicator of 3 or less.

The majority of students can be described as having low mobility (73.2% of all students with 2006–2007 GLA data). One of the most salient observations from the data is that a notably greater proportion of high mobility students have a GLA below their enrolled grade level compared to low mobility students. As illustrated in Figs. 10.1 and 10.2, consistently, across all nine grades, about twice as many highly mobile students achieved below grade level in English Language Arts and Mathematics compared to low mobility students. This observation supports the hypothesis that mobility negatively affects student achievement.

Based on Chi-square tests, all shown GLA differences in English Language Arts and Mathematics between high and low mobile students are statistically

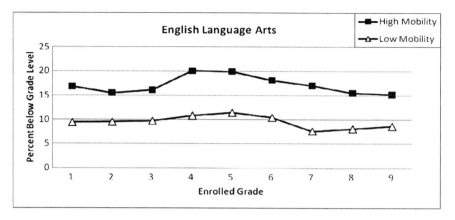

Fig. 10.1 Percent of students below grade level in English Language Arts by mobility category for each grade

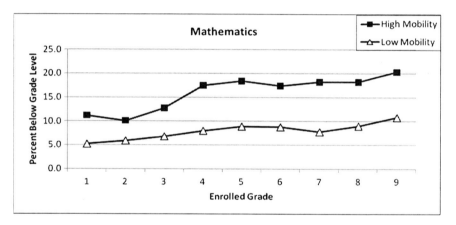

Fig. 10.2 Percent of students below grade level in Mathematics by Mobility category for each grade

significant (p <0.001). The graphs demonstrate that the achievement gap between high and low mobility students broadens as the enrolled grade increases (especially in Mathematics). This may indicate that mobility may have a more pronounced effect as students' age, and may have a more profound impact on Mathematics perhaps due to a more linear curricular structure. The relationship between mobility and GLA are very likely tied to other socioeconomic variables such as whether families rent or own their home, economic volatility, etc. When teachers and administrators can acquire additional insights about the student mobility factor and what kind of interventions and supports might be provided to students to help offset the negative impact of high student mobility within the community context, then the benefits may indeed translate into improved student learning.

GLA and PAT by Age Within Grade Cohorts

Previous Alberta Education studies have indicated that there is a relative age effect between average PAT scores and birth month within grade cohorts, where the older students tend to have higher average test scores than the younger students when measured by the z-score of average PAT results for each birth month group (Alberta Learning 2001).

A comparative analysis was undertaken using GLA data. The percentages of students At or Above their grade level in English Language Arts were converted to z-scores[4] and plotted on graphs (see Figs. 10.3–10.5). There is a noticeable age effect[5] in Grades 1 through 3, which is most pronounced in Grade 1.

The graph in Fig. 10.6 demonstrates that when PAT scores are re-coded into "percent at or above acceptable" to mimic the GLA data, the relative age effect remains and closely mirrors the GLA data.

The age effect, which illustrates that younger students achieve at a lower level than their older counterparts, was apparent in 2006–2007 GLA data in English Language Arts in Grades 1 through 5. After Grade 5, the age effect tapered off and was no longer apparent. In this sample, the age effect persisted longer than in previous analyses of GLA data where the effect dissipated by Grade 3. While many teachers will be very aware of the age effect within their classroom and its effect on student achievement, there is some value in considering what the age effect looks like for a class and a school in relationship to provincial data. Schools that have more pronounced age effects will want to take this into account in interpreting Grade 3 PAT results and may well want to consider strategies that can mitigate the age effect. This data also holds implications for policy makers at the jurisdiction and

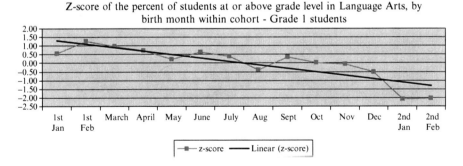

Fig. 10.3 Relationship between English Language Arts GLA and birth month for grade 1 students

---

[4]Z-scores or standard scores convert a distribution of a set of scores to a normal distribution that allows a more consistent analysis of the data. A z-score of +1.0 represents a score equal to one standard deviation above the mean.

[5]Age effect is defined as older students in a grade tending to have higher academic achievement than the younger students in that same grade (Alberta Learning 2001).

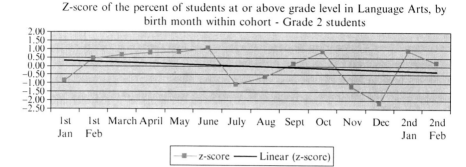

Fig. 10.4 Relationship between English Language Arts GLA and birth month for grade 2 students

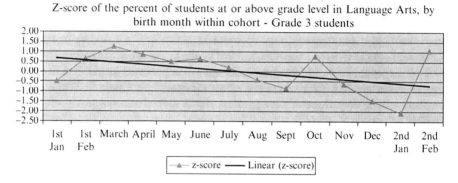

Fig. 10.5 Relationship between English Language Arts GLA and birth month for grade 3 students

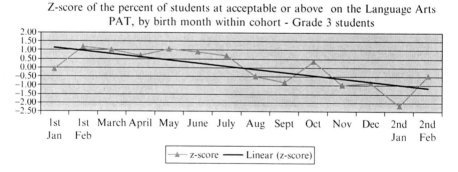

Fig. 10.6 Relationship between English Language Arts PAT and birth month for grade 3 students

provincial levels. Given the potency of the age effect, the case can well be made for multiple entry points into the Early Childhood Services and Grade 1 programs and for careful consideration of the extent to which the age effect might influence student achievement within a specific classroom or school context.

Discussion and Conclusions

Findings and Opportunities for Enhanced Dialogue on Student Achievement

Given that GLA data are fundamentally grounded in the day-to-day assessment work of teachers, it is possible to systematically obtain information on student achievement, which otherwise would not be available. External standardized PATs in Grades 3, 6, and 9 generate high quality data, but GLA provides more continuous data on student achievement and academic progress. GLA provides important consistent information that would not otherwise be available for students in grades not tested by PATs as well as for students absent from these tests. GLA data can be applied as a useful supplement to consideration of PAT outcomes and can be used on its own in grades not tested with large-scale assessments to interpret patterns and trends in student achievement, depending on context and decision-making needs.

Analysis of GLA data in relation to PAT data can provide important information to teachers and administrators. GLA helps overcome limitations of PATs by providing additional, more comprehensive information regarding students' achievement. For example:

• Test bias can influence any assessment instrument; therefore, the more measures available for analysis and interpretation, the greater is the likelihood that the "true" performance levels of students will be known.
• Combined analysis of PAT and GLA data would permit identification and examination of issues that would otherwise be concealed if only PAT data were taken into consideration.

Furthermore, systematic collection of full sets of GLA data makes it possible to conduct trend analysis of achievement for different groups of students at the provincial, jurisdiction, and school levels. The trend data will also support critical reflection and encourage active engagement of students and parents in the learning and assessment process.

This chapter describes some of the outcomes associated with the 2006–2007 GLA pilot data and discusses some of the implications that GLA data may hold for teachers and administrators. The key observations addressed by this paper are (1) relationships exist between factors that may influence student learning and GLA and (2) data from multiple achievement measures can provide a better picture of student performance. The data analysis reveals the following interesting relationships, most of which have practical implications for focused policy development and interventions at a school, district, and system level. For example:

• The larger difference between Mathematics 9 PAT and GLA data continues to be evident. While normally there was close to 80% alignment between students assessed at or above GLA and earning acceptable or excellence grade on PATs, Mathematics 9 PAT and GLA outcomes showed only 66% congruence.

This phenomenon warrants further trend observations and explanations of why such large gaps between Grade 9 Mathematics GLA and PAT assessment results occur. For example, the discrepancies in GLA and PAT results could point to issues such as inflated classroom grading or sources of internal and/or external bias in the PATs. However, it would be useful to try to gain a more detailed understanding of why some students who passed GLA fall below the acceptable standard on PATs or vice-versa. There could be various underlying issues that explain non-congruence between GLA and PAT results. Given that lower than expected student achievement in Mathematics have been a persistent issue in junior and senior high grades in Alberta, it is imperative to uncover the reason for a large inconsistency between GLA and PAT results for Grade 9 Mathematics, including answering the question regarding the predictive validity of both GLA and PAT assessment in Grade 9.

- When comparing GLA and PAT data, females outperform males in GLA in both English Language Arts and Mathematics in nearly all enrolled grades. The reverse is seen on the Mathematics PAT results with males outperforming females. In English Language Arts, females are outperforming males on the PATs. While different learning needs and styles might explain these differences, social and emotional factors that can impact student performance (e.g., Collaborative for Academic, Social and Emotional Learning 2003) also should be taken into account in addressing achievement gaps. The Student Orientation to School Questionnaire recently developed by Alberta Education is designed to address these assessment needs, including identifying specific gender-based as well as other nuances in students' school affect and associated supports (Nadirova et al. 2008).

- A greater proportion of high mobility students (i.e., those who have changed schools more frequently than other students) have a GLA below their enrolled grade level. About twice as many highly mobile students achieved below grade level in English Language Arts and Mathematics compared to students characterized by low mobility. This finding confirms the critical role of stability in students' lives—an issue that transcends school boundaries. Creating safe and supporting school environments would provide necessary stable relationships for transient students and students lacking stability at home. The collaborative effort on the part of the schools, districts, social agencies, government, and communities to provide wraparound, one-stop services at schools for students and their families, including early/family literacy and various student and family counseling, may strengthen family links with both schools and communities. Even a simple intervention, such as providing transportation to students whose families changed their residence to their "old" schools, could help these students avoid transitions and social and academic readjustments and achieve at grade level.

- The age effect is apparent in English Language Arts, mostly in early grades. Schools that have more pronounced age effects will want to take this into account

in interpreting Grade 3 PAT results and may well want to consider strategies that
can mitigate the age effect.
- There are moderate correlations between PATs and GLA (Grades 3, 6, and 9).
  This demonstrates a reasonable degree of concurrent validity of the GLA data.

The vision of accountability and program planning and evaluation in the future
conveyed in this paper is one of a rich environment where assessment of learning and
assessment for learning, informed by both classroom-based assessment and external
tests, are complementary approaches in a comprehensive assessment model. Rich data
will assist professional learning communities to be connected across organizational
boundaries, and educational leadership will be reflected in a complex, interrelated network of professionals informed with timely and comprehensive information and data
that result in programming decisions which improve the quality of education available
to students. Grade Level of Achievement Reporting is one step in this direction.

Finally, collection and analysis of GLA data raise general questions about assessment theory and practices, including standards and comparability of GLA data.
Since teaching approaches may vary in terms of methods and practices depending
on individual groups of students, it would be difficult and undesirable to "uniformly
standardize" GLA assessment techniques. At the same time, it would be useful to
support excellent assessment approaches and methodologies that would improve
comparability and consistency of GLA data coming from different sources. This
requires clear curricular outcomes, supported by performance rubrics and consistent
professional development training and preparation in assessment for already practicing and future teachers. The Alberta Student Assessment Study (Webber et al.
2009) provides insight to these issues.

Future Data Collection and Analysis

Additional analysis of GLA data in relationship to 2006 census data will be available in future GLA reports to provide an indication of the extent to which variables
external to schools influence student achievement. To create the most accurate comparison of the census data and the GLA data, the census data will be broken down
by enrolled students' postal code. Examples of socioeconomic status variables
include Parents' Level of Education, Average Family Income, Home Rental/
Ownership, Percent of Lone Parent Families, etc.

In addition, it would be useful to examine GLA data in conjunction with data on
students' affective orientation to school in order to diagnose at-risk students and
develop effective programs and interventions to help them achieve at an acceptable
or higher level and motivate them to stay in school. The Student Orientation to
School Questionnaire (Nadirova et al. 2008) developed and piloted by Alberta
Education will be available through the Education Testing Service in 2009 for
schools and jurisdictions in Alberta, Canada, and eventually, internationally.

References

Alberta Education. (2005). *Beyond MIRS data technical report*. Edmonton, AB: Author.
Alberta Education. (2006). *Grade level of achievement reporting: Teacher and administrator handbook*. Edmonton, AB: Author. Available at http://education.alberta.ca/media/346277/teachadminhandbook.pdf
Alberta Education. (2007). *Grade level of achievement 2005–06 pilot data – Technical report*. Edmonton, AB: Author. Available at http://education.alberta.ca/media/505076/glatechnicalreport.pdf
Alberta Education. (2008a). *Grade level of achievement 2006–07 pilot data*. Edmonton, Canada: Author. Available at http://education.alberta.ca/media/770300/gla_2006_07_pilot_data%20report.pdf
Alberta Education. (2008b). *Guide to education: ESC to grade 12*. Edmonton, AB: Author. Available at http://education.alberta.ca/admin/resources/guidetoed.aspx
Alberta Education. (2009). *How the accountability pillar works*. Available at http://education.alberta.ca/admin/funding/accountability/works.aspx
Alberta Learning. (2001). *Entry age, age within cohort, and achievement*. Edmonton, AB: Author.
Alberta Learning. (2002). *Beyond MIRS: New directions for program evaluation*. Edmonton, AB: Author.
Alberta Learning. (2004). *Standards for special education*. Edmonton, AB: Author.
Assessment Reform Group. (2006). *The role of teachers in the assessment of learning*. London: Author. Available at http://www.assessment-reform-group.org/ASF%20booklet%20English.pdf
Bloom, B. S. (1980). The new direction in education research: Alterable variables. *Phi Delta Kappan, 61*(6), 382–385.
Burger, J., & Krueger, M. (2003). A balanced approach to high-stakes achievement testing: An analysis of the literature with policy implications. *International Electronic Journal for Leadership in Learning, 7*(4). Available at http://www.ucalgary.ca/iejll/burger_krueger
Collaborative for Academic, Social, and Emotional Learning (CASEL). (2003, March). *Safe and sound: An educational leader's guide to evidence-based social and emotional learning (SEL) programs*. Chicago: Author. Available: http://www.casel.org/downloads/Safe%20and%20Sound/1A_Safe_&_Sound.pdf
Earl, L., & Katz, S. (2002). Leading schools in a data-rich world. In K. Leithwood & P. Hallinger (Eds.), *Second international handbook of educational leadership and administration* (pp. 1003–1022). Dordrecht, the Netherlands: Kluwer Academic Publishers.
Green, S. B., & Salkind, N. J. (2003). *Using SPSS for windows and macintosh: Analysing and understanding data* (3rd ed.). Upper Saddle River, NJ: Prentice Hall.
Harris, M. B. (1998). *Basic statistics for behavioral science research* (2nd ed.). Boston: Allyn & Bacon.
Lauzon, D. (2001, November). *Gender differences in large-scale, quantitative assessments in mathematics and science achievement*. Paper presented at the Statistics Canada – John Deutsch Institute – Western Research Network on Education and Training (WRNET) Conference on Empirical Issues in Canadian Education, Ottawa, ON.
Louis, K. S., Febey, K., & Schroeder, R. (2005). State-mandated accountability in high schools: Teachers' interpretations of a new era. *Educational Evaluation and Policy Analysis, 27*(4), 177–204.
Nadirova, A., Burger, J., Clarke, R., & Mykula, C. (2008). Measuring students' orientation to school to improve high school completion. *CASS Connection: The Official Magazine for the College of Alberta School Superintendents, Spring 2008*, 30–33.
Pope, G. A., Wentzel, C., & Cammaert, R. (2003). Relationships between gender and Alberta diploma scores. *Alberta Journal of Educational Research, 48*(4), 275–286.

Reeves, D. B. (2004). *Accountability for learning: How teachers and school leaders can take charge*. Alexandria, VA: Association for Supervision and Curriculum Development.

Stiggins, R. J. (2001). *Student involved classroom assessment* (3rd ed.). Columbus, OH: Merrill Prentice Hall.

Wasserman, D. (2001). *Moving targets: Student mobility and school and student achievement*. Edmonton, AB: Alberta Learning.

Webber, C., Aitkin, N., Lupart, J., & Scott, S. (2009). *The Alberta student assessment study: Final report*. Edmonton, AB: Alberta Education.

Chapter 11
Teacher Feedback in Formative Classroom Assessment

Susan M. Brookhart

Introduction

Classroom assessment is, arguably, the most important kind of assessment. Although large-scale assessment is more visible to the public, it is the day-to-day, in-class assessments that support students' learning and inform teachers' teaching.

Among classroom assessments, formative assessment (assessment for learning) is arguably more important than summative assessment (assessment for grading). The literature suggests that the use of classroom formative assessment practices increases student achievement in the neighborhood of 0.40–0.70 standard deviations (Black and Wiliam 1998), the equivalent of moving from the 50th percentile to the 65th or 75th percentile, respectively, on a standardized test. [Beware of vendors of large-scale "formative assessments" that "borrow" these effect sizes and claim they apply to their products!] The literature also suggests that over-reliance on summative (graded) assessments contributes to a classroom goal structure where intelligence is viewed as fixed and where learning, therefore, is not entirely under a student's control (Ames and Archer 1988).

Although all parts of the process are important, teacher feedback has a special place within formative assessment (Hattie and Timperley 2007). It is through teacher feedback that students get important information about what they already know and can do and about what they need to do next. Students who perceive they do have the information they need to improve their performances and continue to learn experience feelings of control over their learning. Thus, good feedback can be the key for both enhanced cognition and enhanced motivation.

S.M. Brookhart (✉)
Center for Advancing the Study of Teaching and Learning, School of Education
at Duquesne University, Pittsburgh, PA, USA
e-mail: susanbrookhart@bresnan.net

C.F. Webber and J.L. Lupart (eds.), *Leading Student Assessment*,
Studies in Educational Leadership 15, DOI 10.1007/978-94-007-1727-5_11,
© Springer Science+Business Media B.V. 2012

I write this chapter about teacher feedback in formative classroom assessment from the perspective of both study and experience. I have studied the classroom assessment literature (Brookhart 2004) and also have done my own research in the area of classroom assessment, in the course of which I have interviewed many students and teachers and collected many measures of both motivation and achievement. I also have been a classroom teacher in both elementary and middle schools in the USA.

Issues and Conceptual Framework

This chapter addresses the main question: What kinds of teacher feedback are most effective? The body of the chapter is organized according to the kinds of decisions teachers can make about feedback and presents recommendations for each, along with the rationale from research. In order to do this, it will be helpful for readers to consider two prior questions: What is formative assessment? What is the role of teacher feedback in formative classroom assessment?

What Is Formative Assessment?

The definition of formative assessment most often used is a conceptualization by Sadler (1989) in a now-classic treatise. Formative assessment has three steps. In order to "form" learning, students must understand the learning goal, they must compare their current work against the goal, and they must take action for improvement. Unpacking that definition has become the work in the field of formative assessment. For example, from a teacher's perspective, in order for students to understand the learning goal, the teacher must have a learning target (and understand it himself or herself), must clearly communicate it to students, must check to see if students understand it, and so on.

From the student's perspective, students must actually aspire to the learning target (otherwise it is not a "goal"), must pay attention and work toward it, and so on. Sadler (1989) talked about the place of criteria in instructional systems and what turns a teacher's learning goal into a student's learning target: "In its simplest form, a standard or reference level is a designated degree of performance or excellence. It becomes a *goal* when it is desired, aimed for, or aspired to" (p. 129).

What Is the Role of Teacher Feedback in Formative Classroom Assessment?

Figure 11.1 presents a heuristic for thinking about the role of teacher feedback in formative assessment. The visual organizer in Fig. 11.1 is based on various theories of self-regulation (see Butler and Winne 1995; Greene and Azevedo 2007). It is not

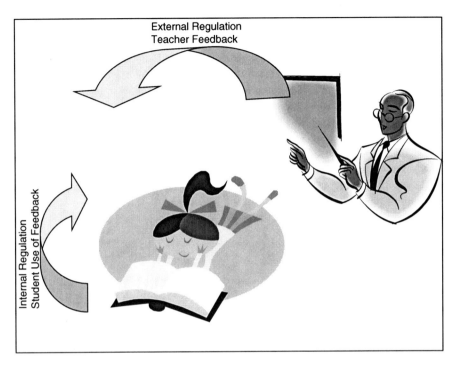

External Regulation
Teacher Feedback

Internal Regulation
Student Use of Feedback

Fig. 11.1 A heuristic for understanding the role of teacher feedback in formative assessment and student learning

a theoretical model in itself, but rather a simplification that will allow readers to organize their thinking as they read the recommendations from literature about what kinds of feedback decisions are effective.

In particular, the visual in Fig. 11.1 reminds us that teacher feedback does not "make" the student learn. Feedback is *what the teacher does*, but in the end what matters is *what the student does*. Teacher feedback is part of the external regulation of learning. Teacher feedback is *not* a guarantee of learning. Feedback helps increase the chances that the student will learn and that the student will want to learn. Once perceiving that useful information is available, most students will feel more in control of learning.

The message that teachers give students about how their work compares with learning goals and what might help them improve is information that comes from outside of a student. Learning happens when students direct their attention to learning goals and, as the saying goes, "wrap their minds around" some concept or increase in some skill. Students do not learn in the absence of this internal regulation of learning. The role of teacher feedback is to present students with the means, motive, and opportunity for internal regulation of learning.

Thus, this chapter discusses teacher feedback, mindful that it is the "teacher contribution" or the external regulation that enhances student self-regulation. The role of teacher feedback in formative classroom assessment is to provide information relevant to the learning task in such a way that the student perceives it as information and uses it for internal regulation of learning. Internal regulation should contribute to student learning in two ways: cognitively, as students take the next steps for improvement, and motivationally, as students grow to understanding their control over the learning.

A methodological note is in order here for readers who may not be familiar with the term *effect size*. All of the effect sizes referenced in the literature review that follows are in the form of standardized differences between treatment and control groups. For example, the difference between a treatment group mean achievement and control group achievement, divided by the standard deviation of the control group, provides a measure of the effect of the treatment in terms of differences on the achievement outcome variable of interest. Such an effect size is interpreted as a measure of the strength of the effect of the treatment.

Effective Teacher Feedback

What kinds of feedback best facilitate students' regulation of learning? In the following sections, I make recommendations for teacher decisions about various aspects of feedback. This chapter differs from other reviews of the feedback literature (e.g., Hattie and Timperley 2007; Kluger and DeNisi 1996) in that this chapter is organized around teacher decisions. My task in the literature review was to connect research about feedback with classroom practices so that what is known about feedback (from research) can be practiced intentionally.

Decisions about feedback *strategies* are decisions about how to give feedback. They include decisions about timing and amount of feedback, about the mode of expression (oral, written, demonstration), and about the audience (individual student or group). Decisions about feedback *content* are decisions about what feedback to give. They include decisions about what the feedback message should focus on; whether the feedback should describe or evaluate the work; the reference against which to locate the feedback (absolute criteria, other students, student's own past work); the valence of the communication (positive or negative); and the clarity, specificity, and tone of the message. The following sections take up each of these decisions in turn.

Timing

Decisions about timing include when to give feedback and how often to give feedback. The literature includes more information about the latter (how often). Recommendations include:

- Give immediate feedback for knowledge of facts (right/wrong).
- Take a bit more time to allow for more comprehensive reviews of student thinking and processing.

- Never delay feedback beyond when it would make a difference to students.
- Give feedback as often as is practical, and definitely for all major assignments.

Most readers know the principle of "immediate feedback." It is also important to take the time to see patterns and get perspective. Feedback about student work patterns is extremely useful, as we will see when we talk about feedback content.

Bangert-Drowns et al. (1991) did a meta-analysis of 35 studies investigating frequent classroom testing on criterion examination performance. Out of 35, 29 effects were positive, and 6 were negative. The average effect size was 0.23. More frequent testing in the same amount of course time, of course, means feedback occurs more often, too. Other reviews (Crooks 1988; Hattie and Timperley 2007; Kluger and DeNisi 1996) have found that feedback that comes soon after the task is the most effective.

Why should this be? Learning theory suggests chunking big bites of information into smaller bites; frequent testing would provide better feedback about smaller bits of course knowledge than less frequent, bigger tests. Also, feedback theories usually posit that feedback "works" by drawing attention to where it is needed (Kluger and DeNisi 1996). For immediate feedback, attention would have a shorter distance to travel because attention had just been focused on whatever the task was.

Amount

Decisions about amount of feedback include how many points to make and how much to say about each point. Recommendations include:

- Prioritize feedback: comment on the most important point(s).
- Choose points that relate to major learning goals.
- Consider the student's developmental level.

Kluger and DeNisi's (1996) review surveyed feedback literature from many disciplines. They did a meta-analysis of 131 studies, with 607 different effect sizes. The average effect size was 0.41, but over a third of the effects were negative. Therefore, they attempted to test for characteristics of the feedback interventions associated with positive change. They hypothesized that behavior is regulated by comparison of feedback to goals or standards, which are organized hierarchically, and only feedback-standard gaps that receive attention can participate in behavior regulation. Feedback at the middle level of the hierarchy (middle level of generality) draws attention to the most useful place to spur improvement. The amount of feedback should be enough to focus attention, not too much to overwhelm, at a middle level of generality.

Sadler (1989) discussed the activity of comparing one's work to a standard and directing one's attention to relevant criteria. He pointed out that most such comparisons involved more than one criterion, and for multi-criterion judgments,

"Which of the potential criteria are singled out for mention has less to do with what is detectable through the senses than with what is deemed to be *worth noticing*" (p. 133). For most classroom purposes, the priority would be the lesson's objectives or curricular learning goals.

Mode

Decisions about feedback mode are about choosing the method by which feedback message is conveyed (written, oral, demonstration). Recommendations include:

- Select the best mode for the message.
- Interactive feedback (talking with the student) is best when possible.
- Use written feedback on written work or on assignment cover sheets.
- Use a demonstration if "how to do something" is an issue or if the student needs an example.

There have been many studies of "written feedback." Several studies, going back 50 years, have investigated the effects of grades versus written comments on student performance. Page (1958) is the classic of this type of study. Page found that student achievement was higher for a group receiving prespecified comments instead of letter grades and higher still for students receiving free comments (written by the teacher). Writing comments was more effective for learning than grades. Other researchers replicated Page's study many times over the years, with an interesting result: sometimes these results replicated and sometimes they did not (Stewart and White 1976). More recent research has identified the problem: in these early studies about comments, the "feedback" was evaluative or judgmental, not descriptive. Page (1958) himself described the prespecified comments as words that were "thought to be 'encouraging'" (p. 180). Evaluative feedback is not always helpful.

The nature of "comment studies" changed as the motivation literature began to point to the importance of the functional significance of feedback: how does the student *experience* the comment, as information or as judgment? The section about functional significance of feedback takes up that discussion.

Some of the work done about written feedback probably applies to all verbal feedback, whether written or oral. Written feedback has the advantage – for older students – that it stays, so they can continue to use it as they revise work, for example. But for younger students, reading the feedback is sometimes more difficult than the work itself, if they can even read it at all.

Modeling and social learning theory provide a rationale for using demonstrations as feedback. For things that students need to learn how to do, modeling or demonstrating is a powerful way to show students how to do it. Any educational psychology textbook will make the point that students learn a lot of things by observing. This applies not only to physical skills like learning to tie shoes, but also to academic skills like learning how to revise a poem.

Audience

Decisions about the audience for feedback include deciding whether to give feedback to an individual student, to a small group, or to the whole class. Recommendations include:

- Give individual feedback to communicate, "The teacher values my learning."
- Give group or class feedback if most of the class missed the same concept on an assignment; this becomes an opportunity for reteaching.

The classroom management and differentiated instruction literature help teachers balance their obligations to individual students with their need to teach the whole class. Obviously, a teacher cannot operate as if he or she were a simultaneous tutor for each of the students in the class. Some individual instruction is required. In fact, in my own work, teachers who began learning about formative assessment found it necessarily assumed, required, and led to more differentiated instruction. There are ways to give feedback to both individuals and groups simultaneously; for example, passing back practice papers with individual written feedback on them and then going over commonly missed concepts in a mini-lesson.

The classroom environment is crucial, too, as Hattie and Timperley (2007) and many others point out. Formative assessment – especially corrective feedback – only works in a climate where correction is seen as "lighting the way forward" (Tunstall and Gipps 1996), and not as punishment or diminishment. Students can only strive for challenging goals in a climate where it is "safe" to fail or to need improvement.

Bloom (1984) described his research agenda, shared and advanced in the work of many of his students, summarized in an *Educational Leadership* article called "The Search for Methods of Group Instruction as Effective as One-to-One Tutoring." Tutoring effect size is approximately 2 standard deviations. Bloom devoted much of his career to searching for classroom methods that might approach that. It was in this research agenda that he developed mastery learning, which includes "feedback and correctives," procedures that look very much like the current formative assessment and feedback. For mastery learning alone, the effect size is about 1.00. Mastery learning and enhanced prerequisite skills, which is part of the "diagnostic" aspect now often subsumed under formative assessment, had an effect of 1.60. Thus, formative assessment that includes individual correctives can be carried out in classroom groups and can approach the effect of one-to-one tutoring, which is tailored to individual needs.

Focus

Decisions about the focus of feedback include whether to give feedback about the work itself, about the process the student used to do the work, about the student's internal regulation, or about the student personally. Recommendations include:

- When possible, describe both the work and the process, and the relationship between the two.
- Comment on student's self-regulation if the comment will foster self-efficacy.
- Avoid personal comments.

Hattie and Timperley (2007) reviewed feedback literature to synthesize a model of feedback that focused on its meaning. First, they summarized others' meta-analyses in a very comprehensive and clear way. Their review used the lens of formative assessment questions ("Where am I going? How am I going? Where to next?"), which they called "feedback questions." Thus, they recognized the importance of feedback in the formative process. Feedback can be the information that drives the process or it can be a stumbling block that derails the process.

Hattie and Timperley proposed a model of feedback that distinguishes four levels: feedback about the task (e.g., feedback about whether answers were right or wrong, or directions to get more information), feedback about the processing of the task (e.g., feedback about strategies used or strategies that could be used), feedback about self-regulation (e.g., feedback about student self-evaluation or self-confidence), and feedback about the student as a person (e.g., pronouncements that a student is "good" or "smart"). Their review found that the level at which the feedback is focused influences its effectiveness. Feedback about the qualities of the work and feedback about the process or strategies used to do the work are most helpful. Feedback that draws students' attention to their self-regulation strategies or their abilities as learners can be effective if students hear it in a way that makes them realize they will get the results they want if they expend effort and attention. Personal comments ("Good girl!") do not draw students' attention to their learning.

Crooks (1988) reviewed studies of the effects of both formative and summative classroom assessment on students. He concluded that feedback was most effective if it functioned to focus students' attention on their progress in mastering educational tasks. I commend his whole review to readers, for the explanation of a host of short-, medium-, and long-term effects of all sorts of classroom assessment practices.

Function

Decisions about the functional significance of feedback include whether to give feedback that the student will experience as descriptive or as judgmental/evaluative. The recommendation is to give descriptive, not evaluative, feedback for formative purposes.

Ryan et al.'s (1985) cognitive evaluation theory described perceptions of the environment that influence intrinsically motivated behavior. They offered three propositions: (a) if an action results in the experience of autonomy or agency (an internal locus of control), it increases intrinsic motivation to act in that way; (b) if an action results in the perception of competence, it increases intrinsic motivation to act in that way; and (c) events vary in functional significance. The same events that result in feelings of competence one day may another day be perceived as externally imposed. An event functions as informational if it leads to perceptions of competence; so, for example, feedback a student finds really useful for improvement might be perceived as informational. An event functions as controlling if it does not lead to feelings of competence; so, for example, a simple grade on a paper might be perceived as controlling. An event can also be amotivational, perceived to be absent of any information or intent to control. Formative classroom assessment by definition must be informational.

Butler and Nisan (1986) investigated the effects of grades (evaluative), comments (descriptive), or no feedback on both learning and motivation. They used two different tasks, one quantitative task and one divergent-thinking task. Students who received descriptive comments as feedback on their first session's work performed better on both tasks in final session and reported more motivation for them. Students who received evaluative grades as feedback on their first session's work performed well on the quantitative task in final session, but poorly on the divergent thinking task and were less motivated. The no feedback group performed poorly on both tasks in the final session and also was less motivated.

Black and Wiliam (1998) summarized a body of research and concluded, like Crooks (1988) before them and Hattie and Timperley (2007) after them, that feedback that draws student attention to the self rather than the task is likely to have negative effects on performance, while feedback that draws student attention to the task is likely to have positive effects on performance. The most effective teachers actually praise students less than average. So feedback should function to draw students' attention to the task, in a descriptive manner, rather than judging the student personally.

Comparison

Decisions about comparisons are decisions about what to use as the reference point for feedback. Criterion-referenced feedback compares a student's work to standards or criteria for good work. Norm-referenced feedback compares a student's work to the work of other students. Self-referenced feedback compares a student's work with his or her own past performance or to expectations based on his or her own past performance. Recommendations include:

- Use criterion-referenced feedback for giving information about the work itself.
- Use self-referenced feedback for giving information about student processes or effort.
- Use self-referenced feedback for unsuccessful learners who need to see how they are making progress, not how far they are from the goal.

Bangert-Drowns et al. (1991) did a meta-analysis using 58 effect sizes from 40 reports about the effects of feedback in instruction. The mean effect was 0.26, a small effect, and 18 out of the 58 effects were negative. However, when they compared the 30 effect sizes from studies with corrective feedback and no pre-search availability (no peeking ahead at answers) to the distribution of the remaining 28 effect sizes, they found that the former demonstrated strong positive effects. They wrote,

> If one were to use all four variables to divide the effect sizes into two groups, feedback effects could be shown to be even more positive. That is, studies that controlled for pre-search avail-ability, used corrective feedback, did not administer a pretest, and focused on text comprehen-sion or classroom testing produce an average effect size of 0.77 ($SE=0.08$, $N=16$). Studies that did not possess one or more of these characteristics demonstrated no effect for feedback ($M=0.07$, $SE=0.06$, $N=42$). Obviously, under optimal conditions, mediated intentional feed-back can be expected to produce very large achievement effects. (p. 229)

In this analysis, corrective feedback, which amounts to criterion-referenced feedback, is key.

Stiggins' work on the classroom assessment environment (Stiggins and Conklin 1992), and earlier work by sociologists on what they called the classroom structure (Rosenholtz and Rosenholtz 1981; Simpson 1981), particularly emphasized what kind of comparisons – normative or criterion-referenced – were made in class. Normative comparisons foster "winners and losers." They also foster a view of intel-ligence as fixed, which in turn makes attributions "stable and uncontrollable"; that is, students begin to believe that they cannot do anything about their intelligence and will be, for example, always "a C student." Covington (1992) and Ames and Archer (1988) in their reviews both point out that a classroom that fosters intrinsic motiva-tion uses criterion-referenced feedback. Covington also pointed out that such feed-back needs to be tailored to show students their success – what they can do – so self-referenced feedback delivered in a criterion-referenced manner (e.g., "here's what you did last time, and here's what your work is like now, and see how much better this time is") is appropriate for unsuccessful learners.

Valence

Decisions about valence are about the affective impact of feedback: positive or negative. Recommendations include:

- Use positive comments that describe *what* is well done.
- Accompany negative descriptions of the work with positive suggestions for improvement.

Tunstall and Gipps (1996) categorized types of teacher feedback into a typology in two dimensions: whether the feedback is descriptive or evaluative, and whether it is about what is right or what is wrong. Tunstall and Gipps pointed out that on the evaluative side, feedback can be positive or negative, rewarding correct or good work and punishing incorrect or poor work. The further you go toward the descrip-tive side, the more feedback all becomes positive in valence. Descriptions of what the student has achieved are, of course, positive. Descriptions of what the student should work on next address gaps or errors, but such criticism becomes "constructive criticism" or, in our terms, "formative." Teachers provide content and strategies for the student to use going forward.

Clarity

Decisions about clarity include decisions about how to make feedback clear to the student. This will, of course, differ for different students. Some will be able to comprehend more complex messages than others. Recommendations include:

- Use vocabulary and concepts the student will understand.
- Tailor amount and content of feedback to student's developmental level.

Regarding the importance of clarity, there's the obvious logical argument. Students cannot use information they do not understand, and students need to be able to feel like they understand information before they will have the confidence to go ahead and use it.

Sadler (1989) had some other interesting things to say about clarity more generally. He observed that for any piece of work that requires "multicriterion judgments" (that is, work of any complexity), there will be many more potential criteria than can reasonably support instruction and assessment. To make holistic judgments of quality about their work, students must select the most relevant criteria from among all possible criteria. To simplify this process and to insure that students and teachers both attend to the same criteria, many teachers use rubrics. Sadler (1983) suggested that it would be more satisfactory and less mechanical to consider the universe of criteria as of two kinds, manifest and latent criteria. Manifest criteria are consciously invoked during the production and assessment of work. Latent criteria are in the background, activated only when some aspect of the work deviates from expectation as, for example, when a paper exhibits exceptionally poor grammar and usage. So the manifest criteria are being learned, and the latent are ones that are assumed unless they are unexpectedly absent.

As students progress, criteria change from manifest to latent. Latent criteria can pop up when the qualities they represent are conspicuously absent. This ebb and flow of criteria is perfectly normal.

> The art of teaching for improvement is to generate an efficient and partly reversible progression in which criteria are translated for the student's benefit from latent to manifest and back to latent again. The aim is to work towards ultimate submergence of many of the routine criteria once they are so obviously taken for granted that they need no longer be stated explicitly (Sadler 1983, p. 73).

I think these points are worth making in an age when we have discovered clear rubric sheets work so well to focus student work (the proximal goal for classroom learning). Rubric sheets are a step along the way to internalizing and routinizing criteria (the distal goal of "education"). Rubric sheets do not comprise all possible criteria, only the manifest criteria for particular students working on particular goals.

Specificity

Decisions about specificity are decisions about how precise to be in providing descriptions, corrections, and suggestions for improvement. Recommendations include:

- Tailor specificity to the student and the task.
- Feedback should be specific enough that the student knows what to do, but not so specific that it is done for him/her.
- Identify errors or types of errors, but correcting every one (e.g., copyediting or supplying right answers) does not leave the student anything to do.

Literature supporting these recommendations has already been cited. Remember that Kluger and DeNisi (1996) found that feedback at a middle level of generality was most effective. Also, Sadler (1989) pointed out that the meaning of criteria requires concrete examples of things possessing them, and except for right/wrong-type things, a set of good examples is helpful. But he cautioned teachers to be careful not to let the examples completely define the criterion. He used art or literature as an example; no one novel or painting completely defines "good" novels or paintings. Sadler also pointed out that some of the deficiencies in a student's response may be because the student does not understand the task completely. So specific feedback can be needed that addresses (a) task definition, (b) match of work to criteria and/or explanation of what the criteria mean in this context, and (c) strategies for gap closure and/or opportunities for student self-monitoring and selection of strategies.

Tone

Decisions about tone include decisions about word choice and about the expressive quality of the feedback message. Recommendations include:

- Choose words that communicate respect for the student and the work.
- Choose words that position the student as the agent.
- Choose words that cause students to think or wonder.

Johnston (2004) pointed out that how we talk with students sets up expectations. "What are you noticing?" positions the student as someone who notices. "How are you going to approach this as a writer?" positions the student as a writer. The work of Allington (2002) and Johnston (2004) both suggest that primary reading teachers are more likely to treat good students this way than poor students. However, all students benefit from being approached in a respectful tone that attributes *agency* to students.

Covington (1992) introduced the idea of "motivational equity." He observed that while it is inevitable that some students will come to school with more cognitive abilities than others, and that students will vary in their interest and talent for particular subjects and tasks, there is no reason why every student should not have access to equally motivating instruction: instruction that fosters intrinsic goals, avoids competition, provides interesting assignments and access to resources, and enhances student belief in the connection between effort and outcome. As we have seen, these are all qualities of good teacher feedback in formative assessment.

Discussion and Implications for Practice

This chapter sought to answer a question of practice: What kinds of feedback are most effective? It differs from previous reviews of feedback literature (Bangert-Drowns et al. 1991; Black and Wiliam 1998; Brookhart 2004; Butler and Winne 1995; Crooks 1988; Hattie and Timperley 2007; Kluger and DeNisi 1996), the aim of which was to advance theory, in that this chapter's aim was to support practice.

The method the chapter used to accomplish this aim was to organize the feedback literature according to decisions teachers make when they give feedback. Recommendations about how to make those decisions were based on the research literature. Thus, one of the major contributions of this chapter is the classification of teachers' choices about feedback strategies and feedback content. Awareness of what choices are available is the first step toward making informed choices when giving feedback in practice. To summarize, teachers have these kinds of choices about the *strategies* they use to give feedback:

- Choices about timing – when and how often to give feedback
- Choices about amount – how many points to make, and how much to say about each
- Choices about mode – whether to give oral, written, or demonstration feedback
- Choices about audience – whether to give individual or group feedback

Teachers also have these kinds of choices about the *content* of their feedback.

- Choices about focus – whether to focus on the work itself, the process the student used to do the work, the student's self-regulation, or the student personally
- Choices about the functional significance of feedback – whether to use descriptive or evaluative language
- Choices about the reference against which to compare the work – to criteria for good work (criterion-referenced feedback), to other students (norm-referenced), or to the student's own past performance (self-referenced)
- Choices about the valence of the message – whether to be positive or negative
- Choices about the clarity of the message – clarity in this case meaning clear to the student
- Choices about the specificity of the message – whether to be too picky, just right, or overly general
- Choices about the tone of the message – to think about the implications of the feedback for what the student will "hear" about himself or herself

These insights about teachers' choices of feedback strategies and content have formed the basis of a book for practitioners (Brookhart 2008). That book contains many examples of how these choices might work themselves out in teachers' practice, in various subjects and levels: elementary reading, elementary and secondary writing, mathematics problem solving, content area reading, and content area projects.

If these categories are indeed the universe from which feedback choices arise, and if the recommendations in this chapter form a kind of tool kit for good practice, then the implication for administrators and policy makers is to ensure that practitioners are aware of these recommendations and follow them. Providing professional development to teachers to develop skills at giving good feedback will be important. Modeling good feedback in the supervisory role, following these same principles, will also be important. If I had to pick just one principle to lift up as the most important, I could not. But I could pick two: description and tone. Feedback that is provided as description of the work and description of what might be helpful next steps, delivered in a tone that communicates the learner is valued and capable and by inquiring after the learner's thinking, is the most effective feedback for formative assessment purposes. Both the literature and my experience as a teacher and researcher support this conclusion.

References

Allington, R. L. (2002). What I've learned about effective reading instruction from a decade of studying exemplary elementary classroom teachers. *Phi Delta Kappan, 83*, 740–747.

Ames, C., & Archer, J. (1988). Achievement goals in the classroom: Students' learning strategies and motivation processes. *Journal of Educational Psychology, 80*, 260–267.

Bangert-Drowns, R. L., Kulik, C. C., & Kulik, J. A. (1991a). Effects of frequent classroom testing. *Journal of Educational Research, 85*, 89–99.

Bangert-Drowns, R. L., Kulik, C. C., Kulik, J. A., & Morgan, M. (1991b). The instructional effect of feedback in test-like events. *Review of Educational Research, 61*, 213–238.

Black, P., & Wiliam, D. (1998). Assessment and classroom learning. *Assessment in Education, 5*, 7–74.

Bloom, B. (1984). The search for methods of group instruction as effective as on-to-one tutoring. *Educational Leadership, 41*(8), 4–17.

Brookhart, S. M. (2004). Classroom assessment: Tensions and intersections in theory and practice. *Teachers College Record, 106*, 429–458.

Brookhart, S. (2008). *How to give effective feedback to your students*. Alexandria, VA: Association for Supervision and Curriculum Development.

Butler, D. L., & Winne, P. H. (1995). Feedback and self-regulated learning: A theoretical synthesis. *Review of Educational Research, 65*, 245–281.

Butler, R., & Nisan, M. (1986). Effects of no feedback, task-related comments, and grades on intrinsic motivation and performance. *Journal of Educational Psychology, 78*, 210–216.

Covington, M. V. (1992). *Making the grade: A self-worth perspective on motivation and school reform*. Cambridge, UK: Cambridge University Press.

Crooks, T. J. (1988). The impact of classroom evaluation practices on students. *Review of Educational Research, 58*, 438–481.

Greene, J. A., & Azevedo, R. (2007). A theoretical review of Winne and Hadwin's model of self-regulated learning: New perspectives and directions. *Review of Educational Research, 77*, 334–372.

Hattie, J., & Timperley, H. (2007). The power of feedback. *Review of Educational Research, 77,* 81–112.

Johnston, P. H. (2004). *Choice words: How our language affects children's learning.* Portland, ME: Stenhouse.

Kluger, A. N., & DeNisi, A. (1996). The effects of feedback interventions on performance: A historical review, a meta-analysis, and a preliminary feedback intervention theory. *Psychological Bulletin, 119,* 254–284.

Page, E. G. (1958). Teacher comments and student performance: A seventy-four classroom experiment in school motivation. *Journal of Educational Psychology, 49,* 173–181.

Rosenholtz, S. J., & Rosenholtz, S. H. (1981). Classroom organization and the perception of ability. *Sociology of Education, 54,* 132–140.

Ryan, R. M., Connell, J. P., & Deci, E. L. (1985). A motivational analysis of self-determination and self-regulation in the classroom. In C. Ames & R. Ames (Eds.), *Research on motivation in education* (The classroom milieu, Vol. 2, pp. 13–51). Orlando, FL: Academic.

Sadler, D. R. (1983). Evaluation and the improvement of academic learning. *Journal of Higher Education, 54*(1), 60–79.

Sadler, D. R. (1989). Formative assessment and the design of instructional systems. *Instructional Science, 18,* 119–144.

Simpson, C. (1981). Classroom structure and the organization of ability. *Sociology of Education, 54,* 120–132.

Stewart, L. G., & White, M. A. (1976). Teacher comments, letter grades, and student performance: What do we really know? *Journal of Educational Psychology, 68,* 488–500.

Stiggins, R. J., & Conklin, N. F. (1992). *In teachers' hands: Investigating the practices of classroom assessment.* Albany, NY: SUNY Press.

Tunstall, P., & Gipps, C. (1996). Teacher feedback to young children in formative assessment: A typology. *British Educational Research Journal, 22,* 389–404.

Chapter 12
Using a Measurement Paradigm to Guide Classroom Assessment Processes

Sandy Heldsinger

Introduction

Much that has been written on educational assessment appears to set up dichotomies. A distinction is made between criterion- and norm-referenced assessment (Gronlund 1981, 1982; Hopkins and Antes 1990; Mckenna and Stahl 2003; Stiggins 2008). Pen-and-paper tests are set up in contrast to performance tasks (Chudowsky and Pellegrino 2003; Fischer and King 1995; Herman et al. 1992), and summative assessment is seen as being distinct from formative assessment (Brookhart 2003; Krause et al. 2006). Often, teacher judgments are valued, but there is hostility toward standardized testing (Abrams et al. 2003; Cizek 2001; Derewianka 1992; Snyder 2008). More recently, *assessment for learning* has been compared with *assessment of learning* (Popham 2006; Stiggins 2008). Perhaps the starkest dichotomy we create is the one between teaching and assessment (Heritage and Bailey 2006).

In much of the discussion of these dichotomies, it is apparent that areas of tensions arise because of a disjuncture between the conventions of measurement theory and the practicalities of classroom assessment. Brookhart (2003) made a case for new theoretical developments in the area of measurement in the classroom and argued:

> Instead of always beginning with the large-scale context and "applying" or transferring to the classroom assessment context—therefore systematically underemphasizing some things (like the formative feedback loop) and overemphasizing others (like sample size)—it is time to take what we know about how to "do" measurement theory and work intentionally with the classroom context. It is time, and it is important. We have a better chance of being relevant and of learning useful things if we study assessment in its habitat. (p. 11)

S. Heldsinger (✉)
University of Western Australia, Crawley, WA, Australia
e-mail: sandy@assessmentcommunity.com.au

C.F. Webber and J.L. Lupart (eds.), *Leading Student Assessment*,
Studies in Educational Leadership 15, DOI 10.1007/978-94-007-1727-5_12,
© Springer Science+Business Media B.V. 2012

In this chapter, I will extend Brookhart's argument. I draw on concepts inherent in the measurement paradigm to show that the dichotomies discussed in the assessment literature are not fundamental, but are rather a matter of emphasis. In doing so I hope to consolidate our understandings of the purpose and value of student assessment, be it as classroom teachers or as test developers. My overarching intention in this chapter is to show why teacher observation is at the heart of all our work in assessment.

Measurement Paradigm

We are all familiar with physical measurement, having measured and used measurements of such things as length, temperature, and mass in everyday life. In such contexts, however, we generally have no involvement in the construction of measuring instruments. Consequently, in these contexts we are users of measuring instruments, and measurement is merely an act in which an already constructed instrument is used to obtain measurement of an attribute such as length. We tend to forget though, that the scientists who helped standardize the units and devise the measuring instruments were outstanding researchers in their fields who labored long and hard to produce the scales we take for granted and the instruments on which we rely (Kuhn 1961).

In education, we have to construct our measuring instruments. Obtaining measurement, in the classical definition of the term, requires specialist knowledge, and teachers do not necessarily have either the expertise or the time to devise assessments that provide measurement. I, however, want to draw on concepts inherent to a measurement paradigm, to show how teachers can refine their assessment processes to obtain good information about student growth in learning.

The concept of a *continuum* is central to a measurement paradigm and we need to examine this concept in the context of student development (Andrich 2002a; Thurstone 1959). The other concept which is important and which I will discuss is that of *latent* and *manifest* ability. (For example, Chomsky's use of the terms *competence* and *performance*, Chomsky 1965.)

Continuum

The Collins English Dictionary (1979) defined a continuum as "a continuous series or whole, no part of which is perceptibly different from the adjacent parts" (p. 325). The emphasis needs to be on the word perceptibly. The adjacent parts on a continuum are different. Perceiving those differences on a very fine grained level is, however, difficult. "The continuum implies qualitative variation, and it may or may not also possess quantitative aspects" (Thurstone 1959, p. 50).

Consider the passage of time. Although time has passed in the last half an hour, it is difficult to discern changes in the quality of light over that same period.

But after a longer period of time has passed, the changes in light are more discernible. We can easily distinguish between mid-morning and noon (Andrich 2002a).

A teacher reaching the end of a year of teaching is acutely aware of how much progress the students have made, particularly when contemplating starting the next year with a new cohort of students. The progress made on a daily or weekly basis, however, is harder to discern. This is further complicated by the sense that students do not continually go forward, but that they sometimes appear to regress. Standing back, it is easy to appreciate the development made from the time students start school to the time they leave. Appreciating the development that takes place on a daily basis is more complex.

Although development or growth is conceptualized in many different ways, a general feature of the concept of development is that it is the process by which an individual builds upon previous learning in a progressive fashion. That is, growth is inherently cumulative, which is the basic feature of any quantitative attribute. It should be stressed that this does not imply that growth is simply a process of cumulative addition of skills and factual knowledge; however, it implies that learning builds upon and transforms the product of prior learning to form a greater cognitive capacity.

Increasingly, the terms *developmental* and *continuum* are used in education, but it has been my experience that we do not very often stop to consider the concepts from which the terms arise. This is an issue Thurstone (1959) identified when he observed,

> One of the most fruitful ideas we can give our students is that most of the functional relations in nature are continuous. There are exceptions here and there in which critical values appear with sudden discontinuities, but these are the exceptions. (p. 9)

I contend that when we use the term *developmental continuum* in education, we are referring to the very fine changes in student ability that occur as students build upon the products of prior learning to form a greater cognitive ability.

Latent and Manifest Ability

We now need to consider the concept of latent and manifest ability. I would like you to imagine Roger Federer in a situation where he is working on behalf of UNICEF. I do not think anybody would deny that in this situation Federer has tennis ability, but it is just that his ability cannot be observed—it is latent. Now, imagine watching Federer in a grand slam match. In this context, his tennis ability is clearly observable— it is manifest (Chomsky 1965; Styles 1999; Wood and Power 1987).

Teachers continually place students in situations that allow them to observe students' underlying or latent ability, that is, to make their ability manifest. They use a broad range of techniques from simply talking with or observing their students to questioning and probing their students' understandings, from providing short tasks or extended project work to administering standardized tests (Heritage and Bailey 2006; Mindes 2007; Rowntree 1987; Sadler 1998; Wiliam 2006).

The Concepts of a Continuum and of Latent and Manifest Ability in the Classroom Context

Now consider the concepts of a developmental continuum and manifest and latent ability in action in a classroom. The following is a description of an activity that may be typical of activities in many early childhood classrooms. It is taken from video footage collected during a study of growth in student learning in preprimary and year 1 in Western Australian government schools (Louden et al. 2008). The footage shows a period in the day when the teacher has just finished one activity and is waiting to start the next and she is using the time to quiz her students. She targets particular students (in a comforting early childhood way) and asks them to distinguish between short and long words, to say a word omitting its initial sound or its middle sound, to construct compound words, and to distinguish between sounds.

There is nothing arbitrary about the game the teacher is playing with her students. In my analysis of the activity, I would say she has a very good understanding of a latent developmental continuum of early literacy ability. She appreciates which skills and understandings precede others, and she is using the game as an opportunity to make manifest her students' ability and to check that ability in relation to those skills and understandings. She understands the relationships between skills. When a student drops a phoneme whilst constructing a compound word, she turns what is essentially an assessment exercise into a teaching opportunity. Wiliam (2006) appropriately describes a moment such as this:

> At this point, the teacher has created a *moment of contingency*—a point in the light of instructional sequence where the instruction can change direction in light of evidence about the students' achievement, thus allowing her to adapt the instruction to better meet their needs. (p. 285)

A moment of contingency, as described by Wiliam, is possible because of the teacher's understanding of the latent developmental continuum and because of her ability to interpret the manifestations of her students' ability.

The Concepts of a Continuum and of Latent and Manifest Ability in the Broader Educational Context

Consider the concept of a continuum and the concept of latent and manifest ability in relation to the range of documents we use in education and the range of assessment processes we use. Syllabus documents describe what students need to be taught to move them further along developmental continua. Outcomes frameworks describe what learning looks like at points or stages along these developmental continua. The full range of assessments that teachers use from observations to standardized tests are all attempts to understand a student's ability relative to the latent developmental continua. I imagine that our curriculum documents have largely arisen from teachers observing which skills and understandings precede others and by analyzing how learning builds on the products of prior learning. I would, however, caution that we do not have the language to capture the fine changes that happen on a day-to-day basis in student development and that no matter how carefully crafted our curriculum documents are, they can provide only relatively coarse-grained information.

When we view our work in education from the perspective of a latent developmental continuum, it becomes apparent that the dichotomy between curriculum and assessment is not a fundamental one. Similarly, whilst the distinctions we make between teacher assessments and standardized testing and between multiple-choice questions and performance assessment help us understand the different features of the assessment types, all assessments share a common purpose: to elicit information about students' positions on the underlying developmental continuum.

Formal Assessments

I would now like to look in detail at the more formal assessments we construct. I show that if we conceptualize student ability in terms of a continuum, and we devise assessment processes to represent as far as possible the ordering of the skills and understandings of the underlying developmental continuum, we are likely to obtain good information about student growth.

I will first take you through an idealized test of numeracy skills—the type of question and answer tests that we are all familiar with. I will then look at the assessment of written performances. In both instances, my overarching question is, *"How can teachers refine their assessment processes to obtain deeper understandings of the nature of student development and growth?"*

Question and Answer Assessments

The idealized numeracy test (see Fig. 12.1) consists of five questions. In devising the test, the teacher would be aware of the skill assessed by each item and would be able to describe those skills (see Table 12.1).

Let us say the teacher administers the test to five students and calculates their total scores (Table 12.2). The generally accepted interpretation of total scores is that the student with the highest total score is the most able, and the student with the lowest total score is the least able. The teacher arranges the test results to reflect this (Table 12.3). On this test, Tim is the weakest student. Clare is the strongest.

To obtain a better understanding of what the total score means in relation to the skills needed to obtain that total score, the teacher arranges the questions from the easiest question, the question most students answered correctly, to the hardest question, the question the least students answered correctly (Table 12.4). She then inserts into the table the descriptions of the skills needed to answer the question

Fig. 12.1 Idealized
numeracy test

Q1.   7 - 2 =

Q2. $\dfrac{2}{6} = \dfrac{}{3}$

Q3.   1 7
            $\times$ 3

Q4.   5 6
            $+$ 3 4

Q5.   1 4
            $+$ 1 3

Table 12.1 Skills assessed in the idealized test

Q1.	Subtract one-digit numbers
Q2.	Reduce a fraction by a factor of 2
Q3.	Multiply two-digit numbers by one digit
Q4.	Add two-digit numbers involving regrouping
Q5.	Add two-digit numbers involving no regrouping

Table 12.2 Results for five students

	Q1	Q2	Q3	Q4	Q5	Total
Clare	1	1	1	1	1	5
Kate	1	0	1	1	1	4
Matt	1	0	0	0	1	2
Sam	1	0	0	1	1	3
Tim	1	0	0	0	0	1

Table 12.3 Results ordered from the lowest to the highest total score for students

	Q1	Q2	Q3	Q4	Q5	Total
Tim	1	0	0	0	0	1
Matt	1	0	0	0	1	2
Sam	1	0	0	1	1	3
Kate	1	0	1	1	1	4
Clare	1	1	1	1	1	5

Table 12.4 Results ordered from the easiest question to the hardest question and from the lowest to highest total score

	Q1	Q5	Q4	Q3	Q2	Total
Tim	1	0	0	0	0	1
Matt	1	1	0	0	0	2
Sam	1	1	1	0	0	3
Kate	1	1	1	1	0	4
Clare	1	1	1	1	1	5
Total	5	4	3	2	1	

Table 12.5 Student results in relation to skills assessed

	Q1. Subtract one-digit figures	Q5. Add two-digit numbers involving no regrouping	Q4. Add two-digit numbers involving regrouping	Q3. Multiply two-digit numbers by one digit	Q2. Reduce a fraction by a factor of 2	Total
Tim	1	0	0	0	0	1
Matt	1	1	0	0	0	2
Sam	1	1	1	0	0	3
Kate	1	1	1	1	0	4
Clare	1	1	1	1	1	5
Total	5	4	3	2	1	

correctly (Table 12.5). In arranging the test results in this way, it becomes apparent that Tim can subtract one-digit numbers, but he cannot as yet add two-digit numbers. Clare, on the other hand, demonstrated that she has achieved all of the skills tested including the most difficult, which required her to reduce fractions by a factor of 2.

Obviously, this test is highly idealized and it is unlikely that a test would assess such a breadth of development or that a teacher would have the hardest question in the test as the second question. This example is, however, useful in demonstrating how a test can be constructed to reveal information about the underlying developmental continuum and information about students' ability in relation to that developmental continuum (Andrich 1985, 2002b; Guttman 1950, 1954).

The example also highlights that the dichotomies of *formative* and *summative* assessments, and of *criterion- and norm-referenced* assessment, are in fact simply a matter of emphasis. The teacher knows where Tim is at that point in time, but also has information about what needs to be taught next. The teacher could generate normative information such as the mean score for the five students, but she also has information about the skills the students demonstrated in order to obtain their total scores.

"How can teachers refine their assessment processes to obtain deeper understandings of the nature of student development and growth?"

My answer to the question in the context of this type of assessment is that teachers need to give careful consideration to the ordering of skills and understandings in the domain they wish to assess. In developing assessment tasks or items, they need to replicate that ordering as far as possible, and the long-standing advice about structuring a test from the easiest questions to the hardest questions should be interpreted as structuring the test from questions lower on the continuum to questions higher on the continuum (Styles 1999). Analyzing and describing the skills assessed by each question will assist in the process and will also help with the interpretation of the test results. The test should include questions that the least able students can answer as well as questions that only a few of the most able students can answer correctly so that information is provided for all levels of achievement.

Tests Where Several Score Points Are Allocated to Each Question

The scoring on the idealized test was dichotomous: right (1), wrong (0). In many instances, however, teachers devise tests where several score points are allocated to each question. It is therefore important to briefly consider the purpose of the score points.

It is not uncommon to hear teachers say that their test will count as 30% of the final mark so they will allocate 30 score points or that they follow the rule of a mark a minute, which will help their students manage their time more efficiently. If we accept that learning is cumulative, that student ability is latent, and that assessment provides the opportunity to elicit manifestations of students' latent ability, then the purpose of the assessment process is to try to replicate in some form the underlying developmental continuum and to assess each student's ability in relation to that continuum. It follows that the purpose of score points is to provide information about student ability relative to the underlying continuum. That is, a student with a higher score on a question is regarded as more able or is further along the developmental continuum than a student with a lower score. After giving careful consideration as to what constitutes development in relation to each particular question asked, a teacher has a fairly good knowledge of how to allocate score points so that each additional score point is associated with an increase in the quality of response.

Ensuring Score Points Provides Useful Information About Student Ability

To explain why it is important that each score point allocated to an answer provides meaningful information about an increase in the quality of response, I need to introduce the Rasch Measurement Model and the graphical displays that can be obtained when data are analyzed using the Rasch Model. These displays provide useful insights into the relationship between student ability and the demands of a test question and in particular the relationship between student ability and an answer with two or more score points (e.g., an answer scored 0, 1, 2 or 0, 1, 2, 3, etc.).

The Rasch model is a mathematical model that specifies the probability of a correct response on an item as a function of the difference between the ability of person and the difficulty of a question or test item (Andrich 1988; Rasch 1960/1980). In the Rasch model, the outcome resulting from the interaction between a student and an item is dependent on two aspects: the ability of the student and the difficulty of the item. At the point where the student ability equals the difficulty of the item, there is a 50% probability that the student will answer the item correctly.

Figure 12.2 shows the category probability curve for a question that is scored right (1) or wrong (0). The horizontal axis shows the abilities of the students on the test as a whole (expressed as logits—the Rasch terminology for these units), and the

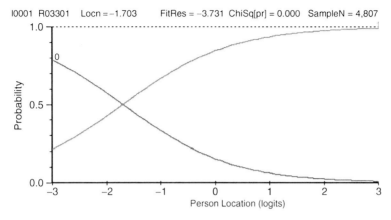

Fig. 12.2 Category probability curve for a question (scored 0, 1) that is easy relative to the ability of the students tested

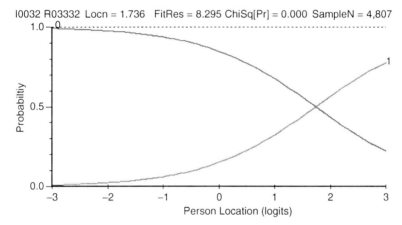

Fig. 12.3 Category probability curve of a question (scored 0, 1) that is difficult relative to the ability of the students tested

vertical axis shows the probability of the student answering the question correctly. The question displayed in Fig. 12.2 is easy relative to the ability of the students. Drawing on our idealized test, this curve could be for a question such as question 5. For a student like Tim, there is some probability that he will answer the question correctly because his ability, as determined by his total score on the test, is not quite as high as the difficulty of the question. On the other hand, for a student like Clare there is a very high probability that she will answer question 5 correctly as her ability (as determined by her total score on the test) is considerably beyond the difficulty level of the question. That is to say it is an easy question for her.

Figure 12.3 shows the category probability curve for a question that is hard relative to the ability of the students. Drawing on our idealized test again, this curve

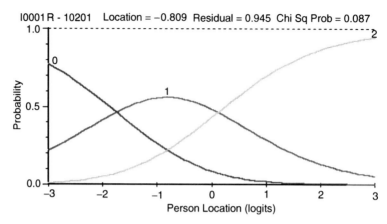

Fig. 12.4 Category probability curve for a question scored 0, 1, 2 in which each score point contributes meaningful information

could be for question like question 2. For this question, there is a very low probability that Tim will answer the question correctly, given his ability, but there is a higher probability that Kate and Clare will answer it correctly. Another way of describing this is that Tim is still learning to add two-digit numbers, and it is therefore highly unlikely that he can reduce a fraction.

Figure 12.4 is taken from an analysis of a question that has a maximum score of 2. As previously described, the curve shows the relationship between ability and the probability of a student being given a score in a given category—either 0, 1, or 2. It can be seen that for students in the lower range of ability, there is a higher probability of being scored 0 than 1 or 2; in the middle ability range, there is a higher probability of being scored 1 than 0 or 2; and in the top ability range, there is a higher probability of being scored 2 than 0 or 1. This is an example of a question in which each score point provides meaningful information about students' development in that each successive score indicates more of the latent ability being assessed. This situation results in the points between successive categories being ordered as the threshold between 0 and 1 is lower on the continuum than the threshold between 1 and 2. That is, the first threshold is at a location of approximately −1.7 logits and the second threshold at approximately 0.2 logits.

Figure 12.5 shows a question in which thresholds are not ordered as required; in fact, the threshold between 0 and 1 appears higher on the continuum (at approximately 2.2 logits) than the threshold between 1 and 2 (at approximately 0.8 logits). This means that there is no region in the ability range that students have a higher probability of receiving a score of 1 rather than a score of 0 or 2. In this instance, the score point of 1 is not providing any meaningful information. A range of factors may result in disordered thresholds, including the arbitrary allocation of score points, an incorrect hypothesis of qualitative differences among responses, or errors in or misunderstandings in marking.

The type of analysis and the resultant displays described here will not be possible for most teacher-devised assessments. However, even without access to software

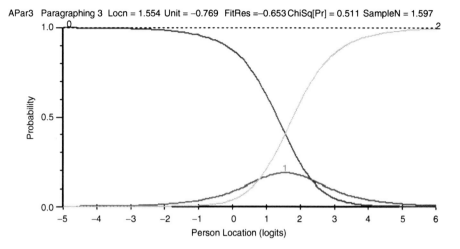

APar3 Paragraphing 3 Locn = 1.554 Unit = –0.769 FitRes =–0.653 ChiSq[Pr] = 0.511 SampleN = 1.597

Fig. 12.5 Category probability curve for a question scored 0, 1, 2 in which each score point does not contribute meaningful information

used in these examples, much can be achieved by careful consideration of what constitutes a higher order response and by teachers checking their marking criteria against student performances.

From my experience as a test developer, I would argue that all marking keys and rubrics can be developed only after careful scrutiny of the range of students' answers. I usually begin the marking process with a hypothesis of what constitutes a qualitatively better answer, and which will therefore be scored higher, but I then need to check this hypothesis against the student answers. (I need to check that my marking key allows me to distinguish between qualitatively different answers and that each score point is associated with an increase in the quality of the response.) If marking keys are developed in this way, then it is highly likely that all or nearly all score points will provide meaningful information increases in the quality of responses.

Rubrics

I would now like to look more closely at rubrics. Rubrics are an extension of this work as they articulate why one performance is better than another, which implies a student is further along the latent developmental continuum of interest. In recent years, much has been published about the use of rubrics, and there are strong advocates for their use. They are seen as a quick and efficient way of assessing students, of providing accountability for the allocation of grades, and for informing students about the standard of their work in qualitative terms (Andrade 2000; Perlman 2002; Taggart et al. 2001).

It is important at this stage that I recount a series of research studies my colleague, Dr. Stephen Humphry, and I conducted into the assessment of narrative writing. Our findings are central to the assessment of all performances, be they of written performances, performances in motion such as drama or sport, or of products such as a works of art. I will discuss these research studies in some detail as it is important I explain why I can say so confidently rubrics are not necessarily the panacea for all our assessment challenges. Importantly, our research shows why rubrics should be developed to be appropriate to specific tasks rather than from abstracted or more general notions of student development.

Research into the Assessment of Writing Performances

The research arose from the full-cohort testing program that was introduced in Western Australia in 1999 following a decision from the State and Federal Ministers of Education that all students aged approximately 7, 9, and 11 would be assessed in reading, writing, numeracy, and spelling. It was also agreed that the tests would be the responsibility of each of the eight states or territories in Australia.

Western Australia has a mandated *Curriculum Framework,* which includes an *Outcomes and Standards Framework* (OSF). The OSF describes the typical progress students make in each of eight learning areas. Learning in these areas is described in terms of eight stages, referred to as eight levels. With the introduction of full-cohort testing, a rubric for the assessment of narrative writing, an aspect of the English OSF, was created. This rubric consisted of nine criteria. Markers were required to make an on-balance judgment as to the level (1–8) of each student's performance overall, and then they were required to assess each performance in terms of spelling, vocabulary, punctuation, sentence control, narrative form of writing, text organization, subject matter, and purpose and audience.

The category descriptions within each criterion were derived directly from the OSF (shown in Fig. 12.6). That is, the description used to determine a score of 2 in spelling was taken directly from the description of level 2 performance in the OSF, the description for a score of 3 was taken directly from the level 3 description in the OSF, and so on. The number of categories for each criterion is shown in Table 12.6.

This marking rubric was very much liked by approximately 300 teachers who meet each year at a central location to mark the students' narrative writing. When the marking rubric was presented at teachers' professional development seminars, it was also well received. Dr. Humphry, however, identified issues relating to the psychometric properties of the data obtained from this assessment, the most tangible being the distribution of student raw scores.

Figure 12.7 shows the raw score distribution of year 3, 5, and 7 students in 2001, 2003, and 2004. It can be seen firstly that the distributions remained relatively stable over the period (2001–2004). This stability was achieved through the training of markers and in particular through the use of exemplar scripts, rather than by applying post hoc statistical procedures.

Second, and most importantly, the graph shows that although there is a large range of possible score points (1–61), the distribution clusters on a relatively small

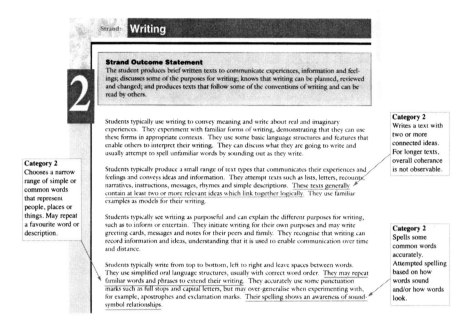

Fig. 12.6 Extract from the outcomes and standards framework showing how the Western Australian Marking Guide was originally derived

Table 12.6 Original classification scheme for the assessment of writing

Aspect	Score range	Aspect	Score range
On-balance judgment (OBJ)	0–8	Form of writing (F)	0–7
Spelling (Sp)	0–5	Subject matter (SM)	0–7
Vocabulary (V)	0–7	Text organization (TO)	0–7
Sentence control (SC)	0–7	Purpose and audience (PA)	0–7
		Total score range	0–61

subset of these (in particular scores around 18, 27, and 36). In effect, we were classifying students into three broad groups, as the predominant scoring pattern was all 2s, or all 3s, or all 4s across the nine criteria. I would like you to reflect on whether you have seen a similar pattern in your students' results when you have used a rubric to assess performances. Have you noticed a tendency for your students to cluster on a small subset of score points?

Initially, we were uncertain if the issue of clustering of performances related to the nature of writing development, itself, or if it was related to artificial consistencies introduced by the marking guide. To better understand this, we set up a series of studies in which we tested several hypotheses.

The first hypothesis was that the marking of all aspects of a piece of writing by a single marker generated a halo effect. For example, weak spelling influenced the judgments on all other criteria. The second hypothesis was that the structure of the

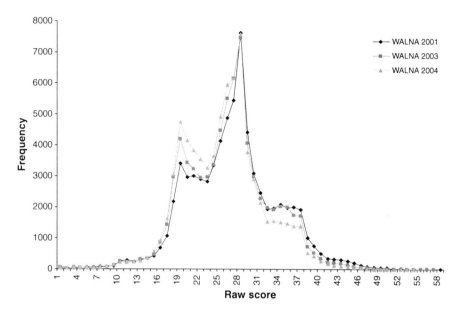

Fig. 12.7 The raw score distribution of year 3, 5, and 7 students narrative writing as assessed through the Western Australian Literacy and Numeracy Assessment in 2001, 2003, and 2004

rubric itself led to artificial consistencies in the marking. The third hypothesis was that the descriptions of the qualitative differences, as captured in the categories for each criterion, were relatively crude. We found that all three factors contributed to the clustering on a small subset of score points, and that these factors were interrelated. I will now discuss each of the research studies we carried out, as the work we did may alert you to issues with your own rubrics.

As I said, the first hypothesis was that the marking of all aspects of a piece of writing by a single marker generated a halo effect, especially in the context of the on-balance judgment of the level of performance. That is, the same judge would tend to give the same level on all aspects more than different judges would if they each marked a separate aspect. This hypothesis was tested by having each marker mark only one aspect of a performance (e.g., only spelling or only sentence control) and not allowing him or her to see how the other aspects of the performance were marked. The results of this study showed that a halo effect did, to some extent, cause artificial consistency in the marking.

Having removed the halo effect, yet still observing artificial consistency, we concentrated our studies on analyzing the rubric itself, and it became apparent that aspects of the rubric overlapped logically and semantically. Table 12.7 shows an extract taken from the marking guide, and it can be seen that a student who writes a story with a beginning and a complication would be scored 2 for the criterion *form of writing*. This student will necessarily have demonstrated some internal consistency of ideas (category 2, subject matter). Similarly, if a student who has provided a beginning and a complication, he or she has most probably provided a narrative that contains two or more connected ideas (category 2, text organization).

Table 12.7 Extract from the narrative marking guide shows semantic overlap of criteria

	Category 1	Category 2
Form of writing	Demonstrates a beginning sense of story structure, for example, opening may establish a sense of narrative	Writes a story with a beginning and a complication Two or more events in sequence May attempt an ending
Subject matter	Includes few ideas on conventional subject matter, which may lack internal consistency	Has some internal consistency of ideas Narrative is predictable Ideas are few, maybe disjointed, and are not elaborated
Text organization	Attempts sequencing, although inconsistencies are apparent	Writes a text with two or more connected ideas For longer texts, overall coherence is not observable

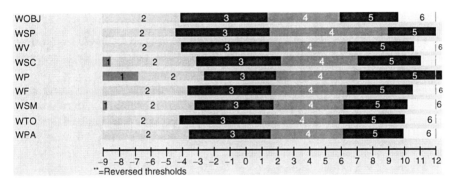

Fig. 12.8 Threshold map showing the relationship between ability and the probability of a score for each criterion

Based on this work, the marking rubric was refined by removing all semantic overlap. The results from this second series of studies showed that the semantic overlap did also to some extent cause artificial consistency in the marking.

A third source of artificial consistency was investigated—that of the relative crudeness of classification. As I explained earlier, the marking rubric was derived directly from the levels of performance described in the OSF. The explanations that accompanied the introduction of the OSF were that the average student would take approximately 18 months to progress through a level. The levels, therefore, do not describe and are not expected to describe fine changes in student development.

The statistical analysis of the data provides the opportunity to examine the relationship between levels (as depicted in the marking rubric) and student ability. Figure 12.8 is taken from the analysis of the writing data and shows that within a wide ability range, a student would have a high probability of being scored similarly on each criterion. For example, students within the ability range of −3 to +1 logits would have a high probability of scoring all 3s, whereas students in the ability range

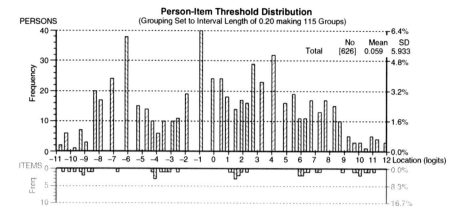

Fig. 12.9 Distribution of students in relation to the thresholds provided in the rubric

of +1 to +6 logits would have a high probability of scoring all 4s. Based on the mean scores of students of different age levels, these ability ranges equate to approximately 2 years of schooling.

Although the marking rubric contained many criteria, and therefore many score points, it provided only relatively few thresholds, or points of discrimination. Essentially, all the information about student performance was obtained from the overall judgment, the on-balance judgment of the student's level. All other judgments were replications of that judgment.

Figure 12.9 provides another way of looking at the data. The graph shows the distribution of persons (students) in relation to the thresholds (or points of discrimination between successive categories) provided in the rubric. The horizontal axis shows the distribution of persons (above) and the distribution of thresholds (below) on the same scale. You will notice that where there are gaps between successive thresholds, the student distribution tends to form clusters.

An analogy to timing a long-distance race may help in explaining this phenomenon. Imagine that you are timing students as they come across the finish line, but that your stop watch only records in minutes and not in seconds. Although students cross the line at varying times, you can only record that they took 3 min, 4 min, 5 min, and so on; thus, in drawing a distribution of students across times, there will be "clumps" of students at 3, 4, and 5 min and gaps between these time intervals.

This is what was happening with the rubric. Over and above the issues related to the halo effect and the semantic overlap, the marking rubric did not capture the fine changes that can be observed in student writing development. Although there were qualitative differences between the students' written performances, our markers could classify the students only into three or four relatively crude groupings.

Devising a Rubric to Obtain Fine-Grained Information About Student Growth

Before I go on to show how we addressed these issues, it is important to reflect on our findings in relation to the concept of a continuum and the concept of latent and manifest ability. You will remember that I gave the definition of a continuum as "a continuous series or whole, no part of which is perceptibly different from the adjacent parts," and explained that although the adjacent parts are different, it may be difficult to perceive those differences. The student performances are a manifestation of underlying student ability on the latent developmental continuum. The findings from our studies showed that the marking rubric provided only coarse descriptions of that latent continuum. As a result, student performances could be classified into only three or four score groups, with relatively large gaps between these scores. Having established this, we were still uncertain as to whether this finding was particular to writing development. Did writing ability only manifest as broad or wide qualitative changes in performance?

Based on an analysis of our findings, we hypothesized that the general level of description in the framework of how student learning develops did not provide the level of detail we needed for a marking rubric of students' narrative writing. The framework makes no mention of *character* and *setting* for example, and it does not articulate in fine detail how students' *sentence level punctuation* or *punctuation within sentences* develops. To test if this was in fact the case and that it was possible to devise a rubric that captured finer gradations in performance, we devised a new marking guide.

The new guide emerged from a close scrutiny of approximately 100 exemplars. These were exemplars we knew very well as they had been central in the training of markers on the old guide. We compared the exemplars, trying to determine whether or not there were qualitative differences between them and trying to articulate the differences that we observed. Not all of the criteria we trialed worked as we had intended. For example in weaker performances, we identified a difference between those performances that had a sense of an oral register and those performances that had successfully adopted a written register. This qualitative difference, however, was not borne out by the trial data.

We found it very difficult to adequately describe development in students' control and structuring of sentences. Theoretically, we classify sentences as simple, compound, and complex, but we found that this classification does not represent the qualitative differences between students' use of sentences. Immature writers may attempt to use complex sentences, but they make errors. More mature writers may use simple sentences to effect. We conducted a separate study to determine the underlying developmental continuum in relation to students' structuring and control of sentences.

I want to reiterate that the students' performances are manifestations of underlying developmental continua. The rubric emerged from the scrutiny of these performances and the descriptions of qualitative differences between the performances.

Table 12.8 Revised classification scheme for the assessment of writing

Aspect	Score range	Aspect	Score range
On-balance judgment	0–6	Punctuation within sentences	0–3
Spelling	0–9	Narrative form	0–4
Vocabulary	0–6	Paragraphing	0–2
Sentence structure	0–6	Character and setting	0–3
Punctuation of sentences	0–2	Ideas	0–5
		Total score range	0–46

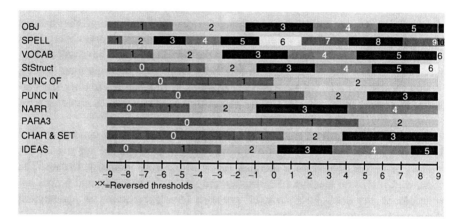

Fig. 12.10 Threshold map for the new guide showing the relationship between ability and the probability of a score for each criterion

We had no preconceived notion of how many qualitative differences there would be for each criterion or that there would necessarily be the same number of qualitative differences for all criteria; thus, the number of categories for each criterion varied depending on the number of qualitative differences we could discern.

For example, in *vocabulary* and *sentence structure,* there are seven categories because in a representative range of student performances from years 3 to 7, seven qualitative differences could be distinguished and described. In *paragraphing,* however, only three qualitative differences could be distinguished so there are only three categories. Table 12.8 shows this revised classification scheme.

The threshold locations from the analyses conducted using data derived from the new guide are shown in Fig. 12.10. You can see that a student, who was assessed in the on-balance judgment as being level 2, has a probability of being scored 3, 4, or 5 for spelling or being scored as either 2 or 3 for vocabulary, and so on. As the rubric has categories that were not aligned, we had removed the issues associated with the halo effect. More importantly, as each category describes empirical qualitative differences in performance, each score point provides meaningful information about student development.

The person/item distribution generated from marking with the new guide illustrates this point (Fig. 12.11). You will notice that the thresholds are distributed more

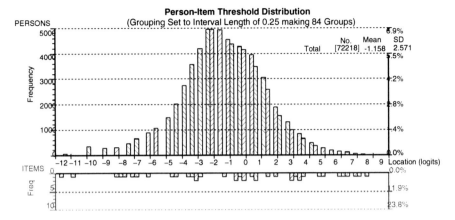

Fig. 12.11 Distribution of students in relation to the thresholds provided in the new rubric

evenly across the continuum, and as a result the person distribution is more continuously distributed without the same peaks or clustering as shown previously. The more even distribution of thresholds from the different aspects, which arose from the careful scrutiny and articulation of the qualitative differences among the student performances, provides precision of assessment along the continuum.

It may look as though we have created a more complex and more time-consuming way of marking. The opposite is in fact the case. The marking has become far quicker, less training is required, and there is greater reliability in the marking. After training, to check marker reliability, all markers are required to mark the same set of 20 scripts. The analysis of this marking shows that 85% of markers had correlations of over 0.90 with the average marks of all markers for those scripts. It appears that because we have captured well the way in which narrative writing develops, the decision-making process involved in assessing a performance has become considerably easier.

"How can teachers refine their assessment processes to obtain deeper under-standings of the nature of student development and growth?"

Earlier I indicated that in developing marking criteria for questions which are allocated several score points, I usually begin the process with a hypothesis of what constitutes a qualitatively better answer, and will therefore be scored more highly, but that I would check this hypothesis against the students' answers. The same applies in developing rubrics. It is also important that teachers examine their mark-ing to see if any performances which are significantly qualitatively different have been given the same score point. This may indicate that their rubric has not been able to distinguish between performances at a fine-grained level. If the assessment process is to provide valuable information about what students need to do, that is, what small improvements they can make, which will eventually lead to large improvements, then it is important that the rubric provides fine-grained information for both students and teachers.

Discussion

I began this chapter by posing the question, "Are the dichotomies we describe in education fundamental or are they merely a matter of emphasis?" This is not a new question. Bloom (1969) provided an answer when he explained that the same tests could be used for formative and summative purposes. Heritage and Bailey (2006) expressed surprise that in the twenty-first century, a distinction is made between teaching and assessment when John Dewey wrote in 1897,

> Education must begin with an insight into the child's capacities, interests and habits. It must be controlled at every point by reference to the same considerations. These powers, interests and habits must be continually interpreted—we must know what they mean. (cited in Heritage and Bailey 2006, p. 145)

In my own discussions with teachers, I have noticed a tendency for the dichotomies to be treated as fundamental. I hope that by drawing on concepts inherent in the measurement paradigm, the concept of a continuum and the concept of latent and manifest ability, I have demonstrated that the broad range of assessments used in education, from teacher observations to standardized tests, have a shared purpose: to elicit information about students' positions on the underlying developmental continuum and that teachers can use information from all assessments to obtain deeper understandings of student development and growth.

Very seldom are the concepts of a continuum and latent and manifest ability explicitly discussed in relation to teacher assessment, although the literature written for classroom teachers often refers to these concepts implicitly when discussing growth or development. (For example, see Andrade 2000; Mindes 2007; Perlman 2002; Stiggins 2008; Taggart et al. 2001.) This is, perhaps, not surprising because although the concept of a continuum is intuitive, the lack of understanding of latency of ability combined with the rudimentary nature of educational measures makes it difficult for us to fully appreciate the continuum. As Styles (1999) explained in regard to general intellectual functioning,

> Whether intellectual development appears continuous or discontinuous, increasing smoothly or in spurts, will depend on the size of the unit of measurement (that is, the scale) and the length of the time between successive measurements. Thus, using a large unit (usually associated with a more general measure) far apart in time will make learning look discontinuous compared with using a smaller unit (usually associated with a more specific measure) for measurements closer in time. (p. 23–24)

Returning to Brookhart's advice that "it is time to take what we know about how to 'do' measurement theory and work intentionally with the classroom context" (Brookhart 2003, p. 11), I advocate that by using a measurement paradigm to guide classroom assessment processes, it is possible to show how teachers can draw on their observations of students' performances to devise marking criteria and how they can refine their assessments so that they obtain good information about student growth in learning.

Acknowledgments I would like to acknowledge the contribution of my colleagues Professor David Andrich and Associate Professor Irene Styles at the Graduate School of Education, UWA, in shaping my thinking on assessment processes, and in particular, I would like to acknowledge the central contribution of Dr. Stephen Humphry.

I would also like to acknowledge the key contributions of Jocelyn Cook, Genevieve Palmer, Martina Bovell, Bronwyn Davies, Jan Brandreth, and the WALNA marking team leaders to the writing research.

References

Abrams, L. M., Pedulla, J. J., & Madaus, G. F. (2003). Views from the classroom: Teachers' opinions of statewide testing programs. *Theory into Practice, 42*(1), 18–29.

Andrade, H. G. (2000). Using rubrics to promote thinking and learning. *Educational Leadership, 57*(5), 13–18.

Andrich, D. (1985). An elaboration of Guttmann Scaling with Rasch models of measurement. *Sociological Methodology, 15*, 33–80.

Andrich, D. (1988). *Rasch models for measurement.* Beverly Hills, CA: Sage Publications.

Andrich, D. (2002a). A framework for relating outcomes based education and the taxonomy of educational objectives. *Studies in Educational Evaluation, 28*, 35–59.

Andrich, D. (2002b). Implications and applications of modern test theory in the context of outcomes based education. *Studies in Educational Evaluation, 28*, 103–121.

Bloom, B. S. (1969). Some theoretical issues relating to educational evaluation. In R. W. Tyler (Ed.), *Educational evaluation: New roles, new means* ((National Society for the Study of Education Yearbook, Part 2), Vol. 68, pp. 26–50). Chicago: University of Chicago Press.

Brookhart, S. M. (2003). Developing measurement theory for classroom assessment purposes and uses. *Educational Measurement, Issues and Practice, 22*(4), 5–12.

Chomsky, N. (1965). *Aspects on the theory of syntax.* Cambridge, MA: Massachusetts Institute of Technology.

Chudowsky, N., & Pellegrino, J. W. (2003). Large-scale assessments that support learning: What will it take? *Theory into Practice, 42*(1), 75–83.

Cizek, C. J. (2001). More unintended consequences of high-stakes testing. *Educational Measurement, Issues and Practice, 20*(4), 19–26.

Derewianka, B. (1992). *Language assessment in the primary classroom.* Marrickville, Australia: Harcourt Brace Jovanovich, Publishers.

Fischer, C. F., & King, R. M. (1995). *Authentic assessment, a guide to implementation.* Thousand Oaks, CA: Corwin Press.

Gronlund, N. E. (1981). *Measurement and evaluation in teaching.* New York: Macmillan Publishing Co.

Gronlund, N. E. (1982). *Constructing achievement tests* (3rd ed.). Englewood Cliffs, NJ: Prentice Hall.

Guttman, L. (1950). The problem of attitude and opinion measurement. In P. F. Lazarsfeld (Ed.), *Mathematical thinking in social sciences.* New York: Free Press.

Guttman, L. (1954). The principal components of scalable attitudes. In S. A. Stouffer et al. (Eds.), *Measurement and prediction.* New York: Wiley.

Hanks, P. (1979). *Collins Dictionary of the English Language.* Sydney, Australia: William Collins Sons & Co.

Heritage, M., & Bailey, A. (2006). Assessing to teach: An introduction. *Educational Assessment, 11*(3&4), 145–148.

Herman, J. L., Ashbacher, P. R., & Winters, L. (1992). *A practical guide to alternative assessment.* Alexandria, VA: Association for Supervision and Curriculum Development.

Hopkins, C. D., & Antes, R. L. (1990). *Classroom measurement and evaluation.* Itasca, IL: F.E. Peacock Publishers.

Krause, K. D., Bochner, S., & Duchesne, S. (2006). *Educational psychology for learning and teaching*. Sydney, Australia: Nelson Australia, Pty Ltd.

Kuhn, T. S. (1961). The function of measurement in modern physical science. *ISIS, 52*, 161–193.

Louden, W., Rohl, M., & Hopkins, S. (2008). *Teaching for growth*. Crawley, Australia: The Graduate School of Education, University of Western Australia.

Mckenna, M. C., & Stahl, S. A. (2003). *Assessment for reading instruction*. New York: The Guildford Press.

Mindes, G. (2007). *Assessing young children*. Upper Saddle River, NJ: Merrill Prentice Hall.

Perlman, C. (2002). An introduction to performance assessment scoring rubrics. In C. Boston (Ed.), *Understanding scoring rubrics. A guide for teachers* (pp. 5–13). Maryland, MD: Eric Clearinghouse on Assessment and Evaluation/University of Maryland. Retrieved October, 2006, from www.eric.ed.gov

Popham, W. J. (2006). *Mastering assessment: A self-service system for educators*. New York: Routledge Taylor & Francis.

Rasch, G. (1960/1980). *Probabilistic models for some intelligence and attainment tests*. (Copenhagen, Danish Institute for Educational Research), expanded edition (1980) with foreword and afterword by B. D. Wright. Chicago: The University of Chicago Press.

Rowntree, D. (1987). *Assessing students: How shall we know them?* London: Kogan Page.

Sadler, D. R. (1998). Formative assessment: Revisiting the territory. *Assessment in Education: Principles, Policy & Practice, 5*(1), 77–85.

Snyder, I. (2008). *The literacy wars. Why teaching children to read and write is a battleground in Australia*. NSW, Australia: Allen and Unwin.

Stiggins, R. (2008). *An introduction to student-involved assessment FOR learning*. Upper Saddle River, NJ: Pearson Education.

Styles, I. M. (1999). The study of intelligence – the interplay between theory and measurement. In M. Anderson (Ed.), *The development of intelligence*. Hove, UK: Psychology Press.

Taggart, G. L., Phifer, S. J., Nixon, J. A., & Wood, M. (2001). *Rubrics: A handbook for construction and use*. Lanham, MD: Scarecrow Press.

Thurstone, L. L. (1959). *The measurement of values*. Chicago: The University of Chicago Press.

Wiliam, D. (2006). Formative assessment: Getting the focus right. *Educational Assessment, 11*(3&4), 283–289.

Wood, R., & Power, C. (1987). Aspects of competence-performance distinction: Educational, psychological and measurement issues. *Journal of Curriculum Studies, 19*(5), 409–424.

Chapter 13
Putting the Focus on Learning: Shifting Classroom Assessment Practices

Sherry Bennett and Dale Armstrong*

Introduction

Ask non-educators what assessment means, and their response will likely be related to one or more of the following topics: testing, measuring, grading, or reporting. However, new directions in classroom assessment suggest that assessment has as much, if not more, to do with teaching and learning as it has to do with grading and reporting. The shift from curriculum, based on what teachers will do, to a more student-centered, constructivist approach to teaching and learning has corresponding implications for traditional testing, measuring, grading, and reporting processes.

Concurrently, educators have been presented with an increased focus on high stakes assessments, designed to measure student learning and gauge the effectiveness of the system. Many have quipped that weighing the pig more often does not make it fatter; hence, the solution to school improvement does not lie in more testing. In order to make a real difference in student achievement, educators must shift their focus from traditional views of testing, grading, and reporting, and embrace a more holistic view of classroom assessment.

This chapter will explore key issues that emerge when educators engage in the process of shifting classroom assessment practices from grading to a solid focus on student learning. Recommendations for action will be made to address the ongoing need to build classroom assessment capacity.

*Deceased

S. Bennett (✉)
Alberta Assessment Consortium, Edmonton, AB, Canada
e-mail: sherry@aac.ab.ca

Conceptual Framework

Figure 13.1 provides a schematic representation of the Alberta Assessment Consortium (AAC) research-based foundational beliefs and principles that guide conversations about effective classroom assessment practices. This framework highlights four key, distinct yet overlapping, elements of the classroom assessment cycle.

Learner Outcomes

Assessment begins with the learner outcomes. Several different terms are used to represent this body of knowledge, skills, and attitudes that students are to acquire. Depending on the context, learner outcomes might be referred to as curriculum standards, objectives, learning goals, or learner expectations. In Alberta, learner outcomes are identified within the Program of Studies, the legally mandated curriculum for students.

Planning

A planning cycle links the learner outcomes to assessment and instruction. Different from a traditional planning process that focuses on instructional activities, this

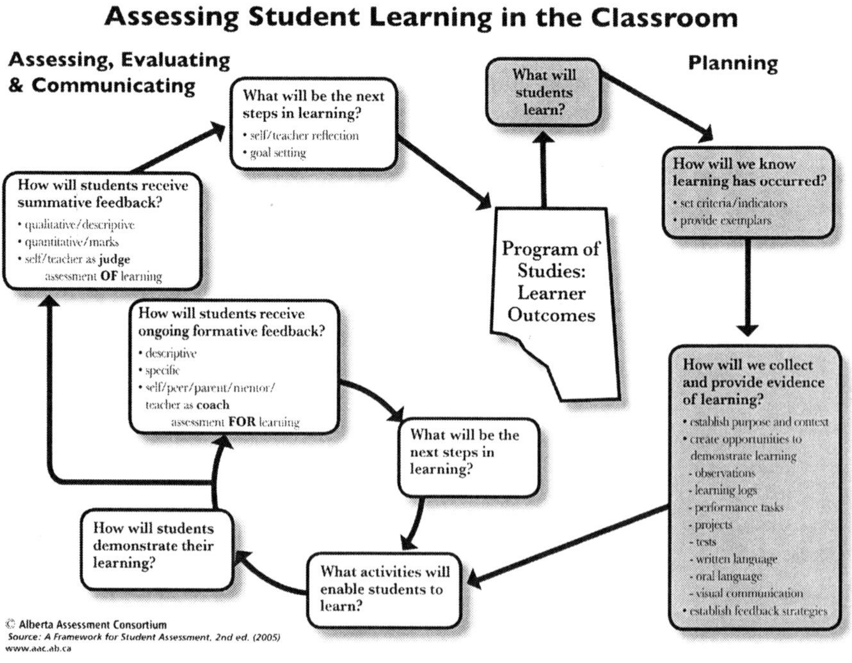

Fig. 13.1 Assessing student learning in the classroom

cycle is focused on planning for assessment. In the spirit of backward design (Wiggins and McTighe 2005), the planning cycle begins with a consideration of the end result of the learning process. In other words, what would it look like if students had successfully attained the learner outcomes? What knowledge would they be able to share through the vehicle of the skills and processes? In what ways would we gather that evidence? After careful consideration of answers to these questions, instruction is then designed to ensure that students will be successful in achieving the end goal.

Formative Assessment

The formative assessment cycle gives students permission to be learners without the fear of failure. A learning environment is created and opportunities provided for students to practice skills and receive specific and descriptive feedback designed to improve student learning. Formative assessment is most effective when it links to future learning opportunities, where students have a chance to integrate the feedback into a new learning context where they can demonstrate their improved skill and understanding. Formative assessment experiences are typically ungraded and not included in report card grades (O'Connor 2007).

Summative Evaluation

The summative evaluation phase follows the formative assessment cycle as a formal check to determine that learning has occurred. When students have been properly prepared through student-engaged instruction and formative assessment, summative assessment is an opportunity to celebrate student performance focused on what has been learned. Gardner (2000) suggested that culminating assessments can be "occasions of pleasure" (p. 132).

The AAC conceptual framework puts student learning at the core and provides a visual reminder of the key processes that guide the design of effective classroom instruction and assessment.

Rationale

The AAC is a not-for-profit organization dedicated to the enhancement of classroom assessment practices in the interest of improved student learning. AAC products and services are accessed through a highly practical website (www.aac.ab.ca) that includes an extensive online library of performance assessment tasks based on Alberta curriculum; models of formative assessment strategies spanning a variety of subjects and grade levels; tools and templates to assist teachers in creating classroom assessment materials; a collection of professional development modules covering a wide range of assessment topics; and an ongoing commitment to provide a variety of professional development opportunities for its membership.

A research study, commissioned by AAC (Alberta Assessment Consortium 2003), sought to examine "what classroom teachers in Alberta and the Northwest Territories know and do with respect to student assessment in order to attain the Teaching Quality Standard." The study also examined the shared responsibility of education partners in providing appropriate professional development to assist teachers in enhancing classroom assessment practices.

Subsequently, education partners in Alberta formally began a conversation in 2007 with the goal of developing a vision statement for building classroom assessment capacity to enhance student success. The resulting shared vision, as articulated by education partners in Alberta, is as follows:

> Student growth, understanding and engagement in learning are enhanced by quality classroom assessment practices focusing on the *Goals and Standards Applicable to the Provision of Basic Education in Alberta* and are supported by jurisdiction and ministry policies.

This vision requires:

- Support for the teacher's role and capacity as the primary agent in providing ongoing assessment of students' success in achieving provincial goals and standards.
- Proactive leadership in developing a shared vision and understanding of quality assessment among educators at all levels of the system, students, parents, and the community.
- A comprehensive approach to professional development that includes dedicated time to practice and share ideas.
- Sustained funding to build quality classroom assessment capacity.
- Coherent policies related to assessment, evaluation, and reporting (Alberta Education 2008a).

Based on this vision, a conditional grant was made available to the AAC to develop a project charter to begin to enact the vision statement. However, funding cuts at the ministry level in the spring of 2009 put the project on hold for an undetermined period of time. Notwithstanding the withdrawal of funding, the needs that led to the development of the vision statement remain.

Three key issues emerge that, with focused attention, provide a solid foundation on which to build classroom assessment capacity. Without a deep understanding of the principles contained therein, assessment-related initiatives are at risk of superficial treatment, thus negating the opportunity for achieving deep and lasting change.

Key Issue #1: Alignment of Curriculum, Instruction, and Assessment Is Essential

Curricular alignment is essential if assessment evidence is to yield valid interpretation of results. Curricular integrity is achieved when teachers are knowledgeable about their subject matter, instructional strategies are in keeping with the intent of the discipline, and assessment methods are intentionally selected to provide evidence of student learning in accordance with the legally mandated learner outcomes.

Key Issue #2: Assessment for Learning Must Move Beyond the Application of Generic Strategies

Assessment for learning strategies should be focused and specific. It is not enough to simply indicate in a lesson or unit plan that peer feedback will be used for a particular assessment task. During the planning stage, teachers anticipate where students will require additional scaffolding and build in formative assessment experiences that provide specific questions and coaching opportunities. Teachers observe during classroom discussions and conversations in order to diagnose learning needs on an ongoing basis and create formative assessment opportunities to address emerging needs.

Key Issue #3: Grading Practices Must Be Supportive of Learning

Appropriate design of assessment provides *all* students with the best opportunities to learn. Punitive grading practices that are focused on behavior management work against the goal of improving student learning. Alternate strategies can be employed to ensure the success of all students.

This chapter will examine these key issues and provide practical, research-based strategies that can be employed by teachers in the interest of improved student learning for all students. When policy makers, leaders, and teachers come to deeply understand the principles of quality assessment embedded within these issues, they create a framework for action.

Discussion

Key Issue #1: Alignment of Curriculum, Instruction, and Assessment Is Essential

Curriculum, instruction, and assessment must be aligned in order to have the greatest impact on student learning. As self-evident as this may seem, the synergy that comes from this alignment is not easily attained.

Curriculum

In order for learning and teaching to be meaningful, it is essential to look for the big ideas of the discipline, not just what is easy to measure. Facts and details that often make up a large proportion of traditional classroom assessments are rarely the big ideas. Knowledge is advancing so rapidly that the focus of teaching and assessment must be to help students learn to learn, learn to think, and to use their knowledge and understanding in real-world contexts. As Fisch (2007) so aptly pointed out, "We are currently preparing students for jobs that don't yet exist using technologies that haven't yet been invented in order to solve problems we don't even know are problems yet."

The front section of each Alberta program of studies contains the philosophical foundation on which the curriculum is based. Perusal of various programs of study reveals similar goals for students—citizenship, communication, problem solving, analysis, critical thinking, and so forth. Enduring understandings (Wiggins and McTighe 2005) develop from these key program elements and become the vehicle through which the content of each discipline is infused.

These program foundations have implications for classroom practice across subject areas. For example, development of active and responsible citizenship is a key program element in social studies. Students begin to experience these rights and responsibilities in the context of classroom citizenship where they have the opportunity to demonstrate those skills through participation in decision making and experience the consequences of their actions. Elements of citizenship are evident in other disciplines as well, as students "[d]emonstrate positive attitudes for the study of science and for the application of science in responsible ways" (Alberta Education 1996, p. B.2) and "become mathematically literate adults, using mathematics to contribute to society" (Alberta Education 2007, p. 3).

Another key program element that crosses subject areas is that of problem solving. Instead of a traditional approach to content through reading a chapter and independently answering questions, students are presented with situations that are truly problematic, requiring them to access and retrieve information and engage in authentic problem solving. Similar pedagogical processes are evident in a mathematics program where the emphasis is not on teaching specific procedures, but rather on having students explore and develop personal mathematical strategies and then critically evaluate the effectiveness and efficiency of their strategies. These higher level process skills are the ones that will endure long after the facts and details of the current topic of study have been forgotten.

Tremendous power exists when teachers work together to take collective responsibility for student learning. Instead of working within discrete subject areas, teachers working collaboratively to discover what common elements exist across disciplines will find that the effort devoted in one subject will pay dividends in other subject areas. When students are aware of such linkages, the potential exists for them to be more purposefully committed to their learning.

Program foundations unfold at each grade level through general and specific outcomes. Rather than being seen as separate entities, program foundations and grade level learner outcomes work together to provide a meaningful structure for student learning. The danger of working only at the big picture level lies in lack of focus; the corresponding danger of working only at the detail level lies in lack of purpose. Powerful learning opportunities exist when both are balanced. Enduring understandings that flow from the program foundations serve as "conceptual Velcro" (McTighe 2007) to which students can attach specific content information. When students understand the overarching structure, they are better able to access the content they require to solve problems and complete learning tasks.

Instruction

Instructional strategies must correspond with the intent of the curriculum. Hence, instruction moves away from a content delivery model and focuses on the development of process skills. Several terms are used in the literature to describe a process-based approach to learning with some of the most common being inquiry-based learning, project-based learning, problem solving, and critical thinking. While there are unique nuances to each term, a common element is a shift in how the roles of student and teacher are viewed. In a traditional model, teachers direct the learning process by providing content as background information and asking questions to check for understanding. Students are often most concerned with getting the correct answer as the teacher is seen as the audience for the learning and assessment tasks.

By contrast, in a process approach to learning, teachers create an environment of inquiry by asking thought-provoking questions and encouraging students to do the same. Students are presented with opportunities to explore and investigate open-ended problems or challenges. Meaningful learning follows as students access the information they require in order to solve the problem or challenge, have the opportunity to think critically and creatively, ask questions, challenge assumptions, make and test inferences, and engage in dialogue about their learning. Such an environment encourages students to take an active role to direct and focus their learning. In such contexts, teacher preparation includes a readiness to provide scaffolding and support for students who require extra guidance, but not to take over the responsibility for thinking for the students. In essence, the goal is to be critically thoughtful "about everything students do and study in school" (Alberta Education 2008b, p. 3).

When the decision is made to shift the instructional design, it is essential that students are aware of the new focus on process learning goals. Otherwise, they may be operating under an old paradigm believing the learning goal is "finding the answers to other people's questions for the satisfaction of the teacher" rather than seeing inquiry as a "process of being puzzled about something, generating their own questions and using information to satisfy their own interest and to develop their own knowledge" (Alberta Education 2004, p. 8).

Assessment

Clearly this shift in instructional design requires a corresponding shift in assessment practices. For students, assessment becomes less focused on documenting what has and has not been learned and more focused on charting the learning journey for continued success. This requires students to be active participants in their assessment. In essence, it creates a seamless transition between learning and assessment.

When teachers acquire the skills to read and interpret programs of study through the lens of assessment, they pose questions such as, "What evidence will I need to determine that the desired learning has taken place?" and "What will my students *do* to provide that evidence?" This focus on the verbs in the learner outcomes is in stark contrast to a more traditional way of viewing curriculum through the nouns, which essentially leads to a list of topics to teach. It is only by reading learner outcomes through the verbs that teachers are able to determine the appropriate level of cognition required for instruction and assessment.

Bloom's taxonomy can be a useful tool to assist teachers in determining the correct alignment. For example, if the learner outcome asks students to evaluate alternatives, then instruction and classroom assessment must lead the students to that process. If instruction and assessment remain at the comprehension level, the best planned lessons and teacher-created assessments will not help students achieve the skills necessary to be successful when confronted with assessment items that are aligned to the level of cognition. The verbs in the learner outcomes become directing words to guide instruction and assessment.

Consider examples from two Alberta programs of study. Within a Grade 2 science unit on buoyancy, a learner outcome asks students to "[d]evelop or adapt methods of construction that are appropriate to the design task" (Alberta Education 1996, p. B.9). The verbs "develop" and "adapt" suggest that the students need to do much more than merely construct an object of the teacher's design following a predetermined sequence of instructions. Clearly, the expectation is that even young learners can engage in higher level skills and processes. Students interact with the content in meaningful ways to help meet their project and learning goals. The assessment is not based solely on the ability to create a product, but must be designed to capture evidence of the development process and of the students' thinking as they make the adaptations to the design. These are complex processes where it is not always appropriate to assign a letter grade. Student self-reflection can be a credible way to gather evidence of learning.

In another example, a high school language arts outcome asks students to "[u]se production, publication and presentation strategies and technologies consistent with context" as they "experiment with various strategies to create rapport between the presenter and the audience" (Alberta Learning 2003, p. 57). The element of experimentation in this outcome clearly puts the responsibility on students for determining strategies and technologies that would be consistent with particular contexts. To do this, students need to set criteria for what constitutes audience rapport in various contexts and then evaluate the effectiveness of their selected strategies against the criteria. Caution must be taken not to turn this outcome into a teacher-directed list of strategies for students to incorporate in their work, but rather to keep the responsibility focused on the student for providing evidence of learning. The teacher's role is to design an engaging, thoughtful assessment that allows students to demonstrate their learning while honoring the element of student choice that is clearly inherent in the outcome.

As helpful as the taxonomy is in assisting with alignment, some have erroneously misused it as a ladder, expecting that students must move through all the levels in sequence. This is an incorrect application of the taxonomy which often results in an inordinate amount of time devoted to the memorization of facts and details. The language of the learner outcomes determines the appropriate level of cognition and the corresponding design of instruction and assessment. Careful reading and interpretation of the outcomes can maximize student learning and avoid an activity designer approach to instruction and assessment (Wiggins and McTighe 2005) that results from a cursory reading of the outcomes.

It is not enough, however, for teachers to be knowledgeable about the application of the taxonomy. *Students* need to become conscious of the processes in which they are engaged so they can become focused on meeting the learning goals. In the context of large-scale assessment, students need the skills to read and interpret the questions, and then evaluate their responses to ensure they are responding at the required level of cognition.

An understanding of the correct application of Bloom's taxonomy is essential in order to design an appropriate and balanced classroom assessment plan. Because multiple-choice items can only measure a portion of the learner outcomes, the addition of written response items is essential to provide a broader picture of student learning. However, some learner outcomes require actual demonstration of learning, in essence performance assessment, in order to gather evidence of student attainment of the full range of learner outcomes. As such, it is inappropriate for a classroom assessment plan to mimic the design of the large-scale exams. Figure 13.2 provides a summary of the strengths and limitations of various assessment strategies based on the framework of Bloom's taxonomy.

Consider the potential impact on student motivation and learning if teachers began their planning process by reflecting on the question posed by Stiggins (2001): "What assessments might you conduct next week that your students would not want to miss?" Aside from the benefit of student engagement, Darling-Hammond (2008) reported that when using performance tasks "[t]eachers and students come to understand the standards deeply, and they work continuously on activities and projects that develop skills as they are applied in the real world, as well as on the examinations themselves" (p. 271). Thus, "teachers do not have to choose between teaching well and getting good results" (Black et al. 2003, p. 29).

Key Issue #2: Assessment for Learning Must Move Beyond the Application of Generic Strategies

Assessment for learning or formative assessment has been at the forefront of educational reform for over a decade. Stiggins (2006), commenting on the results of the Black and Wiliam meta-analysis, indicated that consistent application of the principles of assessment for learning can lead to unprecedented gains in student achievement, between 0.5 and 1.5 standard deviations, with the largest gains realized by low

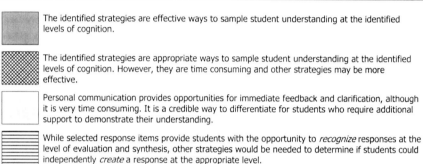

	Knowledge	Comprehension	Application	Analysis	Synthesis	Evaluation
Selected Response						
Written Response						
Performance Assessment						
Observation						
Personal Communication						

The identified strategies are effective ways to sample student understanding at the identified levels of cognition.

The identified strategies are appropriate ways to sample student understanding at the identified levels of cognition. However, they are time consuming and other strategies may be more effective.

Personal communication provides opportunities for immediate feedback and clarification, although it is very time consuming. It is a credible way to differentiate for students who require additional support to demonstrate their understanding.

While selected response items provide students with the opportunity to *recognize* responses at the level of evaluation and synthesis, other strategies would be needed to determine if students could independently *create* a response at the appropriate level.

Fig. 13.2 Preparing the way for valid results: linking levels of cognition with assessment strategies

achievers. With this potential, why then are we not seeing consistent gains in student achievement? The answer may very well lie in a misunderstanding of the relationship between strategies and principles.

Assessment for learning strategies, such as setting criteria with students, viewing exemplars, using descriptive feedback, peer coaching, student self-reflection, second chances, no zero policies, and so forth, have become the topic of conversation in the literature, within professional learning teams, and in formal professional development contexts. While strategies are easily accessible, readily transferred to classroom contexts, and have the potential to change practice in the short term, they lack the rigor on which to make long-term decisions regarding system level policies that impact classroom practice. Deep and lasting change can only occur when strategies are securely grounded in principles.

A misunderstanding of this relationship is evident in comments from educators who state that they "do assessment for learning" because they give second chances, but then ask how many second chances they must give to students. Others may state that they use assessment for learning because they do not give zeros, but then wonder how to get students to hand work in on time. Or they may wonder how to deal with students who do get assignments in on time and feel it is unfair not to dock marks from students who submit work late. Such comments reveal an incomplete understanding of the principles behind the strategies.

While individual authors may have slightly different definitions of assessment for learning, the following three principles seem to be consistently part of the literature base on the topic of assessment for learning:

1. Students are actively engaged in the learning/assessment process.
2. Teachers use the results of formative assessment to guide instruction.
3. Students use the results of formative assessment to improve work in progress.

These principles push against traditional grading practices and traditional roles of teacher and student. They require both a redefinition of policy as well as the informal social contracts within the classroom.

An example of the difference between a strategy and a principle is illustrated in the following vignette. In a social studies class, students are engaged in a performance task where they must analyze information and make a recommendation for action. The teacher has determined that peer feedback will be integrated into the project. While peer feedback is an appropriate strategy, its application to the classroom can be successful or not, depending on how and when it is incorporated into the assessment cycle. Peer feedback, in this example, can potentially be ineffective under the following conditions:

- Students are unclear as to the assessment criteria, resulting in feedback that lacks specific focus.
- Students are too new to the target skill and are unable to recognize its presence and/or to provide specific suggestions for improvement.
- The skill of providing feedback has not been modeled for students, nor have they been given the opportunity to practice this skill.
- Artificial quotas have been applied within the classroom grading structure, thus limiting student motivation to engage in peer feedback.
- Feedback occurs too late in the assessment cycle to allow students to make changes to their work based on feedback received.

While the strategy of peer feedback is sound, its application may not be appropriate and as such, its value toward improvement of student learning remains tenuous. A restructuring of the strategy of peer feedback in this example based on the *principles* of assessment for learning would reveal:

- Students actively engaged in conversation with the teacher and peers about the criteria.
- The teacher using the results of formative assessment to determine which students require additional support with the target skill, and then coaching and guiding these students toward improved demonstration of learning.
- Students who value the feedback process and are motivated to make the extra effort to adjust their work.

The potential for improved student learning increases when teachers use principles as the basis for making decisions about the integration of strategies into classroom practice.

Even when guided by principles, care must be taken to ensure that the assessment for learning strategies are focused on improving student *learning*, not simply improving student performance. Specific, descriptive feedback and second chances may raise student scores on a particular assignment, but unless the student is able to transfer the feedback from one learning context to another, the improved results remain locked within the assignment itself. Assessment for learning must solidly focus on learning, and teachers have a responsibility to help students see how the learning can be transferable to new learning contexts.

To accomplish this end, clarity must be attained as to the relationship between formative and summative assessment. While formative and summative assessments occupy distinct positions within the classroom assessment cycle based on their status as either graded or ungraded, merely identifying an assessment task as ungraded does not ensure that it meets the criteria for a true formative assessment experience. Black et al. (2003) remind us that "if the information is not actually used in altering the gap, then there is no feedback" (p. 15).

It is during the planning stage that teachers create the link between formative and summative assessment. Consider a high school social studies performance task where students take on the role of an elected government representative. Their task is to analyze the potential impact of a series of actions and present their findings to the decision-making body of their political party. In creating the assessment plan, the teacher includes opportunities for students to co-construct the criteria (Davies 2007), embeds opportunities for peer coaching and student self-reflection, and then provides time for students to make midcourse adjustments to their work prior to submitting it for final grading.

Co-constructing criteria is a shared responsibility between student and teacher. Students are not likely able to do this independently, as criteria ultimately must evolve from the learner outcomes. By inviting students into a discussion as to what effective analysis entails, students come to understand "what counts" (Gregory et al. 1997, p. 7). As students gain more experience with this process, the quality of their contributions will improve. Over time, students might be able to generate a list of elements that must be present in order for their analysis to be effective:

• Provide sufficient background information.
• Provide accurate information.
• Make connections among pieces of information.
• Predict impact and possible consequences of action/inaction supported by credible evidence.

Formative assessment opportunities are then designed as part of the assessment plan. Specific prompts are provided at various points during the administration of the task to guide peer coaching and self-reflection opportunities. Teachers monitor work in progress and are able to provide additional scaffolding to students who are experiencing difficulty. Some students may need a graphic organizer to help frame effective research questions; other students may be provided with a prompt that will serve as a model for identifying possible consequences and the evidence to support the inference. Questioning takes on a new purpose during instruction as teachers learn to ask the type of questions that will provide evidence of learning and assist in designing the next steps in instruction. Rather than using questions to check for content knowledge, or as a classroom management technique, good questions can be used to promote thinking and diagnose learning needs (Black et al. 2003).

In this example, learning continues even during summative assessment. The key is to create feedback that leaves the responsibility for learning clearly in the hands of the student. Typical red pen corrections of grammar, spelling, and so forth at the end of the assessment cycle will not facilitate improved student learning. "A focus on formative assessment does not just add on a few techniques here and there—it organizes the whole teaching and learning venture around learning" (Black et al. 2003, p. 79). When properly focused and positioned, formative assessment helps ensure that learning continues during the assessment process.

Key Issue #3: Grading Practices Must Be Supportive of Learning

Grades are supportive of learning when they

- Are congruent with beliefs about the purpose of teaching, learning, and assessment.
- Align with curricular outcomes, separating achievement from effort.
- Acknowledge that learning is cumulative and takes place over time, thus placing greatest emphasis on the most recent evidence of learning.
- Avoid punitive actions against students.

According to Alberta Education (2006),

The major purposes of student assessment and evaluation are to improve student learning and guide students, their parent/guardians, teachers, and others with a legitimate need to help students to acquire the knowledge, skills and attributes as stated in the programs of study. (p. 13)

If assessment is intended to improve student learning, then educators must see grading within a broader context of documenting and communicating what has been learned to date and what further learning is required, rather than using grading to simply perform a sorting and selecting function. School and jurisdiction mission statements invariably subscribe to the goal of success for every student. Yet, alongside such noble intents, we often find grading practices that have more to do with behavior management than with learning. According to O'Connor (2007), grades need to be consistent, accurate, meaningful, and supportive of learning. Grading practices that interfere with these criteria are broken and in need of repair.

Grading is inherently a subjective process. Some may argue that number crunching, the process of performing mathematical calculations on a set of numeric student marks, is an objective process. However, at several points along the way, teachers made decisions as to which curricular topics to emphasize during instruction, which questions to include or exclude on specific assessments, which marks to include in a grading period, what weighting to assign specific items and assessments, and so forth. Care must be taken not to equate quantitative information with objectivity. "The question is not whether it is subjective, but whether it is defensible and credible" (O'Connor 2007, p. 13).

To be credible, assessments must relate back to the big ideas of the discipline. It is incongruent to suggest that our goal as educators is to help students learn to think critically, solve problems and communicate, and then provide summative evaluation based on the ability to memorize facts and details. It is equally incongruent for classroom assessments to mirror the design of large-scale testing in an attempt to raise student scores on large-scale assessments. By design, large-scale testing can only measure a portion of the learner outcomes. Yet some would suggest that formative assessments

> are similar in design and format to district and state assessments so that students have opportunities throughout the year to practice responding to items that match in type, terminology, and rigor the items they will encounter on the state assessments. (Ainsworth 2007, p. 85)

Such an approach may lead to a "test prep" mindset at the expense of authentic learning and assessment.

By contrast, curricular alignment demands the use of a broad range of assessment strategies and a match between the assessment need and the appropriate strategy:

> Student knowledge might be assessed using completion items; process or reasoning skills might be assessed by observing performance on a relevant task; evaluation skills might be assessed by reflecting upon the discussion with a student about what materials to include in a portfolio. Self-assessment may help to clarify and add meaning to the assessment of a written communication, science project, piece of art work, or an attitude. (Centre for Research in Applied Measurement and Evaluation 1993, p. 4)

Alignment with curriculum also implies that grades reflect only student achievement, and that any references to effort are reported and/or communicated separately from the achievement grade. Teacher evaluations of student learning must be based on observable evidence, according to criteria derived from the learner outcomes and gathered through observations of learning processes, conversations with students, and examination of products that students create. This triangulation of evidence (Davies 2007), along with careful determination of criteria, increases both the validity and the reliability of the evaluation and the resulting grade.

Caution must guide the reporting of inferences about student behaviors. Often based on limited data, these report card comments and effort scale ratings form part of a student's permanent record. There needs to be a clear distinction between the need to share important insights about student learning and making judgments about student effort, worth, and potential, and a determination as to whether or not the report card is the place to be sharing such insights and observations. Care must also be taken to avoid "effort creep"—the invasion of effort into scoring rubrics under aliases such as neatness, workmanship, penmanship, creativity, appeal, and so forth. As Davies (2008) stated, "You can't see effort—you see the results of effort."

The delineation of learning into discrete grading and reporting periods sets the stage for misinterpretation of the teaching/learning/assessment cycle. Learner outcomes identify what students are expected to achieve by the end of the year of learning. It stands to reason that time is an essential component in this sequence. The demands of an arbitrarily imposed grading and reporting cycle may lead teachers to assign grades mid-year that indicate certain learning goals have not been met. However, it may be more correct to indicate that these goals have not been met "yet." Well-designed formative assessments provide teachers and students with information as to what has been learned and what still remains to be learned.

Rushed to submit grades on time, teachers sometimes feel they have no choice but to assign a mark of zero to students who have not submitted required work by the deadline. However, "if the grade is to represent how well students have learned, mastered established learning standards, or achieved specified learning goals, then the practice of assigning zeros clearly misses the mark" (Guskey 2004, p. 51). Reeves (2004) pointed out that the mathematical flaw in using zero within a 100-point scale "is to assert that work that is not turned in deserves a penalty that is many times more severe than that assessed for work that is done wretchedly and is worth a D" (p. 325). Rather, appropriate diagnosis must be made to determine the reason for the lack of required evidence of learning. Is it a time management problem, a lack of requisite background skill and knowledge, or a behavioral issue? Appropriate diagnosis and timely intervention assist in aligning good instruction with sound grading practices.

AAC advocates for sound assessment and grading practices. A notation on all AAC rubrics indicates that "[w]hen work is judged to be limited or insufficient, the teacher makes decisions about appropriate intervention to help the student improve." Thus, even within a summative assessment situation, the intent is that *all* students have the opportunity to meet at least the acceptable standard. Opponents may argue that this simply keeps teachers and students embroiled in a never-ending cycle of unfinished work.

> Certainly this structure challenges traditional notions about the purpose of grading and reporting as well as the roles of student and teacher. The intent of this system places student learning at the core of our work. As such, the teacher's primary role is to coach and guide and the student's role is to take an active role in his/her learning. Teachers anticipate which students will need additional support and put those interventions in place during the learning process, rather than waiting until the end of the grading cycle when realistically, there may no longer be sufficient time to make any adjustments.
>
> This system has implications for school and jurisdiction policies regarding students who have not completed sufficient work to allow teachers to make an accurate judgement about their performance. It also requires educators to deal with behavioural concerns separately from student achievement. These are complex issues that require thoughtful, informed decision-making on the part of school and jurisdiction learning communities. (Bennett and Mulgrew 2009, p. 25)

"Without doubt, changing the way students are graded alters what people associate with 'real school.' Consequently, one can expect opposition to new grading techniques" (Marzano 2000, p. 2). Grading is a largely "unexamined and private practice" (O'Connor 2007, p. 117), thus contributing to the challenge of system-wide improvement in grading practices.

Implications and Conclusions: A Call to Action

Assessment has been at the forefront of educational initiatives in Alberta for the past decade. Building on an extensive research and literature base, jurisdictions throughout the province are developing new policies on student assessment. As important as it is to have policy in place, policy alone will not change practice. It is incumbent upon policy makers at all levels to deeply understand this work and be prepared to support the development of quality classroom assessment within their sphere of influence.

Education partners in Alberta have identified a set of essential conditions that must be in place in order to support implementation of any initiative, policy, program, curricula, or priority (Alberta's Education Partners 2010). Framed within a shared responsibility and a culture of learning, these essential conditions include shared vision, leadership, research and evidence, resources, teacher professional growth, time, and community engagement. These essential conditions apply when considering the support necessary to see the desired growth in classroom assessment capacity. While teachers are the front line workers and bear a great deal of responsibility for the actual enactment of sound classroom assessment practices, shared responsibility at all levels is needed to provide the required support to impact this change.

Black and Wiliam (1998) spoke of the challenge teachers face to integrate even extensively researched and well-grounded principles into classroom practice, due to the complexity of their professional lives. In contrast, what they need "is a variety of living examples of implementation, as practiced by teachers with whom they can identify and from whom they can derive the confidence that they can do better. They need to see examples of what doing better means in practice" (Black and Wiliam 1998, p. 11). Thus, the challenge lies in creating opportunities to support the development of teacher leaders. This includes providing flexible timetables that allow these teacher leaders to remain in the classroom where they are able to implement the desired changes, while also providing them with enough flexibility to respond to opportunities to mentor their colleagues.

New structures are required to allow this teacher leadership to develop. A reallocation of budgets may actually provide a long-term solution as funding is redirected to support the development of local expertise. The fly-in consultant model will not change professional practice over the long term. Caution must be exercised, though, to ensure that the move to local leadership continues to include adequate support for a broad base of leadership development. Without adequate support and mentoring, professional learning teams can become little more than opportunities to perpetuate existing practice, which in the end will not achieve the desired results.

At the ministry level, it is essential that developers of curricula ensure that the programs of study are congruent with the desired end result. This requires a consideration of not only what is unique to each discipline, but also what skills and competencies are common across disciplines. The use of a consistent curricular framework and common language across subject areas supports teachers and students to see the learning targets. When curricula are written with assessment in mind, developers have a focused lens on what they might reasonably expect students to *do* to demonstrate their learning, thus avoiding vague student outcomes that state that students will "appreciate" or "know" or "experience" or "understand." These verbs are not specific enough to allow teachers to gather evidence of student learning. Effective curriculum design begins with assessment.

Support for curriculum implementation requires direct support for assessment by design, rather than as an afterthought. Appropriate classroom assessment expertise must guide the development of ministry produced curriculum and classroom assessment support materials, as well as the assessment component of publisher developed resources. Curriculum and classroom assessment cannot exist as independent silos; merging the work of these two departments has tremendous potential to impact teacher practice and ultimately student learning.

Equitable support throughout the province must be in place to ensure that *all* teachers have access to professional development opportunities to support and enhance the building of classroom assessment capacity. Large urban boards, simply by their size, have access to teams of consultants in curriculum and assessment that are not available throughout the rest of the province, where a single consultant might have responsibility for supporting all programs of study from K–12. Funding structures should not be created that inadvertently, yet surely create pockets of regional disparity.

Ministry also has a responsibility to ensure that large-scale testing follows the same principles of sound assessment practice (Centre for Research in Applied Measurement and Evaluation 1993) as is expected in the classroom. More than one measure must be used and the weighting commensurate with the breadth of learner outcomes that can reasonably be assessed in a large-scale exam. To provide an accurate representation of student learning, public reporting should reflect the full range of what matters most, not simply what is easy to measure.

Policy makers at the jurisdiction level need to be knowledgeable about what constitutes effective assessment practice and ensure that adequate funding and expertise exists to sustain the desired changes. It is important to view the results of large-scale assessment within the appropriate context, and proactively communicate with parents and the public about evidence of the *full* range of student learning, not only what is reported publically through large-scale provincial student achievement results.

Jurisdiction instructional leaders must possess the expertise to support school-based leaders as they implement the required changes in practice. Criteria for selection of administrators need to be focused on leadership qualities along with exemplary teaching practices. Professional development and coaching support are essential components for school-based leaders as they transition from a management model to a learning model. They require skills to understand and cope with the pace of curricular change in order to, in turn, provide that support for teachers to ultimately impact the learning of students.

The Alberta Principal Quality Practice Guideline states that the school principal "ensures that student assessment and evaluation practices throughout the school are fair, appropriate and balanced" (Alberta Education 2009, p. 5). Principals need to be first and foremost experienced and effective teachers; have expertise with curriculum, instruction, and assessment; be able to recognize effective classroom practices in action; and have the skills to support and mentor teachers during the change process. They have the opportunity to create the cognitive dissonance that will move the learning agenda forward in their schools and to work together with their staffs to create explicit goals for change. At the same time, they need to find a balance and set a tone that encourages teacher self-reflection and provides opportunities for collaboration.

In this new paradigm, teachers have the opportunity to examine their belief systems and look critically at their classroom assessment practices to determine ongoing goals for their own professional growth and development within school and jurisdiction initiatives. This requires courage to confront instructional and assessment practices that may no longer be in harmony with new curricula. In short, they cultivate a growth mindset (Dweck 2006) not only within their students, but also in regard to their ongoing professional practice.

Postsecondary institutions play a role in determining the type of assessment practices that exist in the Kindergarten through Grade 12 system. Consider the potential impact on teacher practice when students in education faculty programs not only have the opportunity to learn about quality classroom assessment practices, but see these modeled in their coursework. This has implications for traditional grading practices at the postsecondary level.

On a broader plane, a number of questions emerge in terms of the impact that postsecondary institutions have on current assessment structures. What role do university entrance requirements play in determining existing grading practices in high schools? How far down the system do these narrow grading practices extend? Beyond grades, what other evidence of student proficiency might postsecondary institutions use in selecting students for admission? These questions do not have easy answers and would best be considered within a broader consultation process involving Kindergarten through Grade 12 educators, business, industry, ministry, teacher professional associations and postsecondary institutions.

In a proactive way, research institutions could contribute greatly to the knowledge base of classroom assessment by undertaking a focused study of models of teacher leadership in classroom assessment, based on the previously described scenario advocated by Black et al. Additional research on the effects of formative assessment practices within the Alberta context would be a tremendous support in moving assessment initiatives forward.

In short, there are no quick and easy solutions to the complex work of building classroom assessment capacity. While the research base is solid and the language has become commonplace throughout Alberta schools, deep implementation has not yet occurred. Some of the explanation lies in the design of the 3-year Alberta Initiative for School Improvement cycle, which has led some teachers and leaders to simply wait out the current initiative, knowing that another focus is imminent. Given the potential impact that assessment for learning can have on student achievement (Stiggins 2006), Alberta educators can no longer look at the building of classroom assessment capacity as an optional endeavor. The shared vision (Alberta Education

2008a), articulated by the education partners cannot be achieved if educators are expected to work independently. It is essential that educators at all levels work together to take collective responsibility for student learning.

References

Ainsworth, L. (2007). Common formative assessments. In D. Reeves (Ed.), *Ahead of the curve: The power of assessment to transform teaching and learning* (pp. 78–101). Bloomington, IN: Solution Tree.

Alberta Assessment Consortium. (2003, January). *Power of assessment for learning* (Research report). Edmonton, AB: Author.

Alberta Education. (1996). *Science (elementary)* [Electronic version]. Retrieved December 14, 2009, from http://www.education.alberta.ca/media/654825/elemsci.pdf

Alberta Education. (2004). *Focus on inquiry: A teacher's guide to implementing inquiry-based learning*. Edmonton, AB: Author.

Alberta Education. (2006). *Effective student assessment and evaluation in the classroom: Knowledge and skills and attributes*. Edmonton, AB: Author.

Alberta Education. (2007). *Mathematics Kindergarten to grade 9*. [Electronic version]. Retrieved January 1, 2010, from Alberta Education: http://www.education.alberta.ca/media/645594/kto9math.pdf

Alberta Education. (2008a). *Alberta assessment consortium conditional grant*. Unpublished manuscript.

Alberta Education. (2008b). *Embedding critical thinking into teaching and learning*. Retrieved January 1, 2010, from Alberta Education: http://www.learnalberta.ca/content/ssocirm/pdf/embeddingcriticalthinkingintoteachingandlearning.pdf

Alberta Education. (2009). *Principal quality practice guideline: Promoting successful school leadership in Alberta*. Edmonton, AB: Author.

Alberta Learning. (2003). *English language arts (senior high)* [Electronic version]. Retrieved December 14, 2009, from Alberta Education: http://www.education.alberta.ca/media/645805/srhelapofs.pdf

Alberta's Education Partners. (2010). *A guide to support implementation: Essential conditions*. Edmonton, AB: Author.

Bennett, S., & Mulgrew, A. (2009). *Building better rubrics*. Edmonton, AB: Alberta Assessment Consortium.

Black, P., Harrison, C., Lee, C., Marshall, B., & Wiliam, D. (2003). *Assessment for learning: Putting it into practice*. Berkshire, UK: Open University Press.

Black, P., & Wiliam, D. (1998). Inside the black box: Raising standards through classroom assessment. *Phi Delta Kappan, 80*(2), 139–147.

Centre for Research in Applied Measurement and Evaluation. (1993). *Principles for fair student assessment practices for education in Canada*. Retrieved from http://www.education.ualberta.ca/educ/psych/crame/files/eng_prin.pdf

Darling-Hammond, L. (2008). Assessment for learning around the world: What would it mean to be internationally competitive? *Phi Delta Kappan, 90*(4), 263–280.

Davies, A. (2007). *Making classroom assessment work* (2nd ed.). Courtenay, BC: Connections.

Davies, A. (2008, April). *Collecting evidence of learning and reporting using symbols and percentages*. Workshop session presented for Southern Alberta Professional Development Consortium, Lethbridge, AB.

Dweck, C. (2006). *Mindset: The new psychology of success*. New York: Ballantine Books.

Fisch, K. (2007). *Shift happens*. Retrieved January 1, 2010, from http://www.youtube.com/watch?v=ljbI-363A2Q

Gardner, H. (2000). *The disciplined mind: Beyond facts and standardized tests, the K–12 education that every child deserves*. New York: Penguin.

Gregory, K., Cameron, C., & Davies, A. (1997). *Setting and using criteria.* Merville, BC: Connections.

Guskey, T. R. (2004). Zero alternatives. *Principal leadership (middle level edition), 5*(2), 49–53.

Marzano, R. (2000). *Transforming classroom grading.* Alexandria, VA: Association for Supervision and Curriculum Development.

McTighe, J. (2007, October). *Assessing understanding.* Keynote session presented at the annual conference for the Alberta Assessment Consortium, Edmonton, AB.

O'Connor, K. (2007). *A repair kit for grading: 15 fixes for broken grades.* Portland, OR: Educational Testing Service.

Reeves, D. (2004). The case against the zero. *Phi Delta Kappan, 86*(4), 324–325.

Stiggins, R. (2001). *Assessment for learning: A hopeful vision for the future [CD-ROM].* Portland, OR: Assessment Training Institute.

Stiggins, R. J. (2006). *New mission, new beliefs: Assessment for learning [DVD].* Portland, OR: Educational Testing Service.

Wiggins, G., & McTighe, J. (2005). *Understanding by design* (Expanded 2nd ed.). Alexandria, VA: Association for Supervision and Curriculum Development.

Chapter 14
The Ecology of Student Assessment

Charles F. Webber, Judy L. Lupart, and Shelleyann Scott

Reconceptualizing and Redefining Assessment

The value of student assessment lies in its capacity to improve and document the outcomes of teaching and learning. However, the impact of assessment data can be a two-edged sword. Desirable outcomes include the utility of assessment data to guide instruction, motivate students, inform parents and community members, and shape decision making by educational leaders and policy makers. Problematic outcomes of assessment may be defensive behavior, resistance to change, maintenance of poor assessment practices, confusion about school accountability, and reduced trust among stakeholders.

Borrowing from the field of biology, we suggest that the constructs of *evolutionary adaptation* and *homeostasis* can provide an interesting analogy for facilitating change in assessment practices within schools and educational systems. The application of biological terms to a social organization is not new. This was demonstrated in Buckley's (1968) classic paper called "Society as a Complex Adaptive System" which Schwandt and Goldstein (2008) described as:

> ...a useful bridge between the interests of complexity scientists and those of social entrepreneurs as they struggle to apply the concepts of complex adaptive systems to societal (social) change and innovation...in the context of social value creation and societal change. (p. 86)

C.F. Webber (✉)
Faculty of Human, Social, and Educational Development,
Thompson Rivers University, Kamloops, BC, Canada
e-mail: cwebber@tru.ca

J.L. Lupart
Faculty of Education, University of Alberta, Edmonton, AB, Canada
e-mail: judy.lupart@ualberta.ca

S. Scott
Faculty of Education, University of Calgary, Calgary, AB, Canada
e-mail: sscott@ucalgary.ca

C.F. Webber and J.L. Lupart (eds.), *Leading Student Assessment*,
Studies in Educational Leadership 15, DOI 10.1007/978-94-007-1727-5_14,
© Springer Science+Business Media B.V. 2012

Even earlier, Auguste Comte (1876), considered to be the "father of sociology" (Hudson 2000, p. 541), used biology as a filter to characterize society. He suggested that underpinning themes, such as "variability, conflict, and selection of the fittest," influence evolutionary social change (Hudson 2000, p. 540). Further, Hudson (2000) outlined two pervasive themes that emerged from Comte's work: "(i) the emphasis on conflict, especially competition for resources, status, or survival; and (ii) the identification of the origins of change as exogenous to the system of interest" (p. 540).

Homeostasis is the tendency of an organism to seek a constant state of equilibrium or, in the words of Claude Bernard, "la fixité du milieu intérieur" (Cooper 2008, p. 426). Homeostasis is characterized by the "regulation of states of the body through negative feedback mechanisms...on active stabilization of bodily states against disturbances from the outside..." (Cooper 2008, p. 419). A negative feedback mechanism is where a change is detected that results in action to correct the imbalance which then switches off the negative feedback loop once equilibrium has been achieved. Adolph (as cited in Cooper 2008) noted that homeostatic controls do not have to be learned or consciously monitored; rather, stability is achieved autonomously, that is, without conscious thought. Bernard described homeostasis as the capacity of an organism to "continually compensate for and counterbalance external variations" (Cooper 2008, p. 422) so that equilibrium is the result of compensation behaviors in order to maintain a sensitive balance within the organism. Buckley (1968) described the purpose of a homeostatic system as characterized by "its functioning to *maintain the given structure of the system* within pre-established limits... geared principally to *self-regulation* (structure maintenance) rather than adaptation (*change* of system structure)" [emphasis in original] (p. 490).

Although homeostasis can be a desirable state for continued good health of a cell or organism, when the analogy is applied to assessment practices within classrooms and schools, it demonstrates the maintenance of the status quo. In contrast, educational systems where assessment data are used to promote growth and improvement for all stakeholders manifest an evolutionary adaptation approach to change. Although it may appear that homeostasis and evolutionary adaptation are dichotomous constructs, *both* are necessary for system health, with homeostasis supplying stability and evolutionary adaptation facilitating growth. As Allport (1960) noted, equilibrium on its own is not a normal or productive state; indeed, "stability brings evolution to a standstill, negating both growth and cohesion" (p. 160).

At this juncture, it is important to highlight the underpinning values and assumptions embodied within this chapter. First, in addition to the need for homeostasis and evolutionary adaptation, assessment must attend concurrently to the learning needs of individuals within the micro setting of the classroom and the collective expectations of the larger community. Second, assessment often generates an emotive response within educational communities and, therefore, a *pastoral care* approach is important to adopt to ensure that all stakeholders have a safe environment that enables them to grow. As used in this chapter, pastoral care encompasses attention to the emotional, psychological, professional, and ethical well-being of all concerned. Third, this chapter endorses the international, multicultural, and global perspectives presented in previous chapters. We argue that it is only through respectful cross-cultural dialogue that each of our societies can achieve and sustain a civil democracy, which we contend is the ultimate goal of our education system. We acknowledge that the contentions made in this chapter may not be embraced in all cultural and political contexts. Nonetheless, our view is that every child deserves to learn within a morally and ethically sound educational environment so that they have the social capital necessary for successful, productive participation in a thriving democratic society.

Spectrum of Influence

The terminology used to discuss student assessment has shifted from formalized language, such as formative and summative, to include a welcome focus on "of learning" (traditionally conceptualized as summative), "for learning" (to inform teaching and learning), and "as learning" (student metacognition used as a learning tool) (Earl 2007). Differentiating among the purposes of assessment is a crucial skill that educators must have to make appropriate choices and to design meaningful instruction for students. As Earl (2007) correctly stated, "There is no 'one right way' to assess students…Assessment activities work best when the purpose is clear and explicit and the assessments are designed to fit that purpose" (p. 89).

Earl (2007) also noted that "It won't be a simple task to change assessment in schools" (p. 93). Our research supports this caution. That is, despite the best intentions of educators to engage with more effective assessment practices, there continues to be widespread confusion about the terms such as assessment "of," "for," and "as" learning (Webber et al. 2009). The apparently simple and straightforward terminology now being used widely has not resulted in greater clarity and understanding of good assessment. Indeed, the confusion actually impedes school and classroom improvement initiatives.

Understanding the complexity in assessment—for example, assessment in the classroom with students, assessment for the purposes of making judgments about curricula, and assessment and evaluation of the effectiveness of schools and school systems—makes it unsurprising that so much "prepositional confusion" persists. Perhaps, a broader view of the role of assessment is necessary, particularly in relation to its micro and macro influences (see Fig. 14.1). That is, different forms of assessment serve different educational aims. Understanding the different aims of assessment means that educators need to refrain from labeling one form of assessment as the only appropriate approach and appreciate the value of a balanced assessment portfolio. The dominant theme in much of the educational literature is that formative assessment is the most desirable form of student assessment. However, the dominance of this perspective has obscured the merit and utility of summative forms of assessment.

Student Context

Assessment serves very different purposes at various levels and in a range of contexts. At the micro level of society, the lives of individual students are influenced immensely by how classroom and external assessment is conducted (see Fig. 14.2)

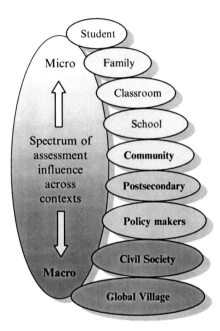

Fig. 14.1 Spectrum of assessment influence

and how the results are reported. Life-altering decisions are made on the basis of assessment data. For example, decisions are made about whether students will receive specialized support and, if so, how much, in what form, and for how long. Students' self-efficacy is shaped by the conversations that arise from assessment. In addition, assessment results determine the educational opportunities that students are able to access within the K–12 system and beyond.

Family Context

Assessment can be a powerful positive or negative influence in families. Assessment data that conform with parent perceptions of their children are viewed as valuable. Unfortunately, when there is a disconnect between school and parental perceptions and educational expectations, conflict may result. Further tension can ensue if assessment involving projects and homework interferes with extracurricular activities deemed to be valuable to children's holistic development. To present a balanced perspective, educative assessment can open positive conversations among children, parents, and educators in relation to students' understandings, skill development, and emotional maturation. From a parental decision-making perspective, assessment data can guide choices such as where children will attend school and what support services to access.

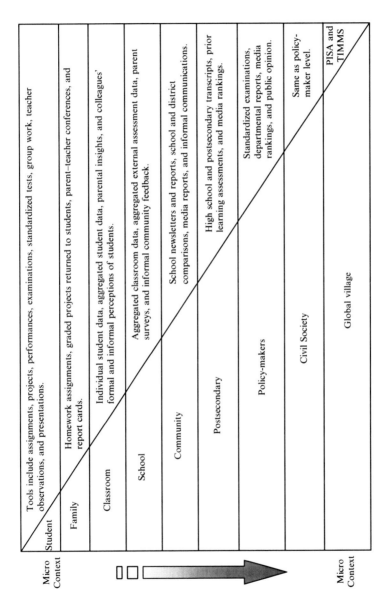

Fig. 14.2 The range of assessment tools—micro to macro contexts

Classroom Context

Teachers employ assessment to structure instructional experiences, select teaching materials, and make judgments about student learning. Teachers are expected to align assessment activities with the program of studies that they are required to follow. Teachers are held accountable for differentiated assessment to meet the varied needs of their charges. Assessments provide information that teachers can use to inform students, parents, and school administrators for their decision-making purposes. Ideally, assessment serves to engage and motivate students to learn, monitor their own progress, and set learning goals.

School Context

Assessment guides decisions about school goal setting, staffing, and resource allocation, plus student assignment to particular classrooms. It informs the design of professional development for teachers and principals. It influences administrators' decisions about school policy development and implementation. Moreover, assessment informs teachers and principals about the optimal types of communication with parents and community members. Assessment results shape administrators' perceptions of the viability of particular strategies for inclusion and teaching practices. In recent years, assessment data have a role in the marketing of schools and programs.

Community Context

Student assessment impacts community members' perceptions in many ways. Individual students and their families share opinions of teachers, schools, and programs in the multitude of informal conversations that occur in daily life, for example, in supermarkets, at sporting events, and over back fences. Formal communications from schools, in the form of report cards and newsletters, reinforce and challenge the veracity of ongoing informal conversations. News reports of school events constitute a form of assessment in that they are used to make judgments about the quality of teaching and development of responsible student behavior. The community itself can develop a reputation that reflects the events that occur in its schools and its environs. For example, school violence may suggest that particular communities are prone to criminal activity and populated by undesirables, and vice versa. Media reports of assessment data can influence the public perception of specific communities and the effectiveness of their schools. Because assessment is a powerful influence on public perception, it is important that school and community leaders understand what assessment data mean and how they can be used appropriately to optimize student achievement.

Postsecondary and Beyond

Student assessment data are used as gate keeping tools by employers and postsecondary institutions. The results of high school exit examinations, both teacher assigned grades and external marks, are accepted by much of society to be valid tools for screening and ranking young people. Institutions seek often to build their reputations on the basis of how selective they are with their admission criteria. That is, the higher the grades required for admission, the more prestigious the institution can claim to be in its marketing of reputation. Grades are used in the allocation of student scholarships and research grants. These practices occur in spite of the sometimes questionable accuracy and comprehensiveness of assessment data in representing the knowledge and skills of individual students.

Policy-Making Context

Policy makers need information to do their work at the more macro level. School district administrators and school boards develop policies that reflect their knowledge of individual schools and the school system in general. Moreover, they use assessment data to shape assessment policies such as reporting frequency and formats. Professional development policies and budget allocations are informed by the results of school and external assessments. Significantly, policy makers are influenced by the informal communications that occur within the educational systems they represent; the informal influences can be based on accurate and inaccurate perceptions, but they do shape how policy makers make decisions. At the broader provincial or state level, policy makers do not have full access to a range of individual student assessment data and, therefore, must rely on macro-oriented assessment summaries compiled by bureaucrats and on standardized testing programs to inform policy, curriculum development, and resource allocation. It is noteworthy that policy makers have multiple allegiances. For instance, they have a responsibility to support and enable the micro-level work of students and educators within their jurisdictions, albeit from a distance, while they concurrently are responsible for the stewardship of community resources and for meeting the multiple and politicized expectations of the electorate.

Civil Society Context

It is crucial that all stakeholders in educational systems understand their roles in the creation and sustenance of the larger society. That is, a generally accepted assumption within Western nations that an educated populace is essential in the establishment and maintenance of a thriving democracy. Therefore, it behooves participants at all levels of the educational spectrum to understand and use appropriately the assessment data that are both available and useful for the types of decisions they are responsible for making. In addition, if a civil society is to be enhanced, stakeholders must recognize the value of different forms of data for different types of decision making, spanning contexts that range from the micro through the macro. Further, participants in a civil society understand and accept that some stakeholders will make decisions that seemingly conflict with those made by other stakeholders. For example, it is necessary for provincial or state legislators to call to account school districts that, according to available assessment data, are failing to meet the needs of their communities. That well may mean that local school authorities are discomforted by interventions made by their legislative superordinates. Indeed, the dialogue that emerges from jurisdictional tensions can and should lead to public dialogue and transparent decision making, all in the interest of the collective educational good.

Global Context

Marshall McLuhan's (1964) vision of a "global village" has come to pass, and nations now exist in a milieu characterized by massive global migration of information, ideologies, and cultures. International competitiveness of individuals, groups, and entire nations is dependent on how data are used and harnessed. Societies and educational systems are judged, at the macro level, on the basis of student assessment data. These data include those resulting from the Organisation for Economic Co-operation and Development's (OECD) Programme for International Student Assessment (PISA) and the International Association for the Evaluation of Educational Achievement's (IEA) international assessment initiative called Trends in International Mathematics and Science Study (TIMSS).

International student assessment data are used by national governments and international organizations to portray the capacity of various societies to participate in the global village. The stakes are high at this level, and nations' educational currency is dependent on the assessment data collected at the micro level and collated to the macro level.

Figure 14.2 displays the range of assessment tools available to inform decision making from the micro (individual) through the macro (collective) levels. It is evident that the range of tools available at the individual student level is significantly greater than that found at the global level. It is important to emphasize that there are different tools serving different purposes. Educators must develop an appreciation for the different purposes these tools serve for other stakeholder groups in society. The impact of classroom-level assessment on individual students is direct and easy to observe, while the importance of aggregated tools such as PISA and TIMMS is easier to dismiss at the classroom level because the impact is predominantly at the governance and societal levels. This argument ought not to be interpreted as dismissing the importance of the individual learners, but it illustrates that the data required and recognized as significant by governments and social leaders are aggregated, comparative data due to their macro-focused responsibilities.

Educators who demonstrate a deep appreciation of the need to use different assessment tools for varying purposes are, in fact, manifesting an evolutionary adaptive state. This means that they perceive the importance of positive organizational change for the purposes of "growth and cohesion" (Allport 1960 p. 160).

Moderating Influences

Given our earlier argument for the value of both evolutionary adaptation and homeostasis, we move now to considering the moderating influences on educators in relation to student assessment. These include a wide range of personal, cultural, environmental, and temporal considerations that influence educators' capacity to change (see Fig. 14.3). For example, *the personal* encompasses individuals' knowledge, ability, levels of self-efficacy and resilience, responsiveness, risk

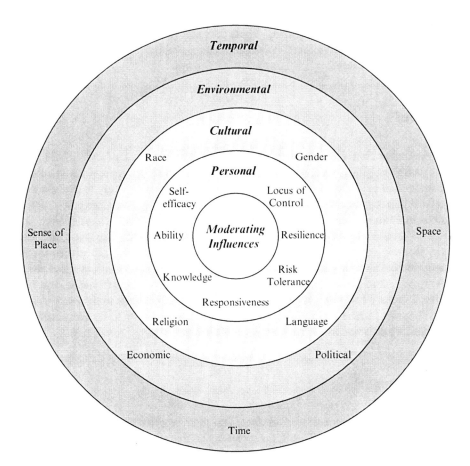

Fig. 14.3 Moderating influences

tolerance, and locus of control. *The cultural* involves factors such as race, gender, language, and religion. *The environmental* includes economic and political influences. *The temporal* dimension revolves around less tangible aspects of time, space, and sense of place.

Personal

Individual educators possess unique personalities that have been shaped by genetic and environmental influences. Cognitive and experiential differences account for at least some of the observable variations in professional understandings. However, deficits in teacher knowledge of student assessment can be addressed through effective teacher education and professional development, both of which can lead to increased levels of efficacy. In turn, high levels of efficacy lead to heightened internal loci of control and can promote personal resilience. Learning and transferring new assessment strategies into regular teaching repertoires require a responsive state of mind and an openness to risk taking. These personal attributes can inhibit or nurture professional growth and ultimately influence change initiatives focusing on improving student assessment.

Cultural

Western education systems serve diverse societies comprised of individuals and groups with origins from all over the world. When teachers are representative of the diversity that exists in their communities, then they are more likely to possess the cultural literacy necessary to navigate the nuances of difference. Conversely, variations in culture, race, and religion also can confound teachers' capacity to think beyond their personal cultural schema, particularly when they do not share the backgrounds of their students. Teachers' gender may impede the professional connections that they can make with students and families from cultures that have divergent customs concerning the roles of men and women. Educators who have the cultural literacy and interpersonal capacity to navigate solutions to the complexity that diversity in race and religion can present are more likely to be successful in establishing effective assessment practices for all students.

Environmental

The socio-economic contexts of students and their families clearly influence how students achieve in school. That is, the social capital that students accumulate because of travel, exposure to books and technology, and informed parenting increases the likelihood that they will prosper within traditional schools. Alternatively, students without similar social capital may struggle to achieve as well. Thus, teachers need to develop assessment and reporting expertise that overtly encompasses fairness and equity and that encourage school–community partnerships and communication regardless of socio-economic status. Educators who are able to utilize appropriate assessment tools and provide students with necessary assistive technology, for example, garner assessment data that accurately reflect students' knowledge and skills. However, compensatory assessment interventions require resourcing in the form of equipment, professional development, and time.

Support for students with deficits in social capital costs money and, therefore, funding decisions affecting assessment frequently are contentious and result in debate. This political dimension to assessment is exacerbated when there are additional competing power agendas within societies. Power struggles occur among stakeholders who compete for resources and control. If power struggles are not resolved or at least balanced then minority groups may remain oppressed and unable to participate fully as members of a functioning democracy. Therefore, economic decisions around assessment made by educators and those who support them must reflect the needs of all children in society.

Temporal

The context of assessment involves issues related to time, space, and sense of place. That is, assessment tools that worked well at one stage of a society's evolution may no longer be appropriate. Similarly, assessment tools that are appropriate for use in one part of a nation may be rejected in a different setting. In other words, educators' assessment practices must manifest a viable sense of time and place. Another dimension of time that is related to assessment is the amount of time required for educators to learn about and to develop educationally sound tools and practices. Time also is a consideration when seeking an appropriate balance among teaching, learning, and assessing. Importantly, the wasting of time engaged in unproductive political debates and power struggles causes untold frustration among educational stakeholders and can actively impede successful evolutionary adaptation.

The recent emergence of information and communication technologies (ICT) has created new configurations for time and space that previous generations of educators simply did not experience. For example, the synchronous and asynchronous nature of time is a factor in educators' ability to access and engage with professional learning communities. Online learning about assessment is commonly accessible, and this creates assessment networks that span time zones and political boundaries. An alternative perspective around the potential of ICT is its use in promoting flexible partnerships and communication between the school and its community. For example, schools can employ software that enables asynchronous communication with students and their families that facilitates the monitoring and reporting of student progress.

Educators' sense of place also entails their conceptualizations of their roles and responsibilities within a particular educational setting and system. Professional identity is formed in part through dialogue with colleagues, leaders, professional associations, and experts. These professional conversations can be constructive when they promote discernment and transparency in assessment practices. Alternatively, toxic enculturation and socialization can occur when educators are embedded within overly partisan interactions that fail to acknowledge the value of differing stakeholder perspectives.

Each of the moderating factors presented above has the potential to affect dramatically the capacity of educators in schools and systems to collect accurate, useful student assessment data. However, when the cumulative influences of the moderating factors are considered, then it is no wonder that student assessment is often a contested area of education that elicits strong and sometimes irresponsible stances. This means that educators must remain vigilant to the application of the principles of sound assessment and to the acquisition and expansion of their pedagogical and assessment skill set, regardless of prevailing cultural dynamics. Indeed, it is the personal responsibility of each teacher and educational leader to maintain an educationally sound assessment stance throughout their careers.

Making a Case for the Assessment Virtuoso

The essence of assessment as learning for teachers is akin to that of talented conductors holding the complete musical score in their heads, with a flair for improvisation. They must hear the nuances of each instrument, intuit the emotions of the players, allow them the freedom to experiment, and subtly guide and extend the talent and virtuosity of each of them in personal ways, by providing feedback and encouragement on a moment-by-moment basis. What better focus for professional development than teachers, working together and becoming virtuoso conductors of student learning, who know the targets, can see and hear the performances, and provide the guidance for students to get better and better.

(Earl 2007, p. 96)

The *assessment virtuoso* is an individual with a superior state of understanding that encompasses deeper conceptualizations of assessment from the micro to the macro context and appreciates the differentiation and importance of different assessment typologies for different purposes. With an understanding that assessment is contentious, but is also key to bringing about successful change within schools and systems, the virtuoso has the capacity to recognize when evolutionary adaption is needed for the health of the organization. Conversely, virtuosos understand when an organization needs to maintain a homeostatic state, at least temporarily, in order to embed sound assessment frameworks. Virtuosos can be seen in all educational roles. For example, they can be the insightful teacher, the perspicacious leader, innovative professional developers, sagacious and concordant union leaders, and boundary-breaking policy makers. Virtuosos are distinguishable based on their capacity to discern and empathize with individual stakeholder perspectives evident across roles, even when there are conflicting and biased agendas. Perhaps most important in the advancement of educational assessment, virtuosos can create cross-role synergies that lead to necessary evolutionary adaptation within schools and systems. The virtuoso is an active, not passive, role that leads to positive, responsible, and sustainable change. Educational virtuosos grasp the significant notion that stakeholders' normally will react to system feedback in ways that seek to maintain the status quo, or homeostasis. Moreover, virtuosos recognize that the tendency to maintain the status quo normally is an involuntary response that, when required for the sake of individual and organizational health, must be countered in thoughtful, diplomatic ways. Virtuosos also are adept at providing pastoral care to members of educational communities and systems engaged in improving student assessment.

Assessment virtuosos possess a heightened level of assessment literacy. They can interpret data and use it for knowledge creation and mobilization relevant to their educational roles. They comprehend the possibilities and limitations of various forms of assessment data. Virtuosos have a personal portfolio of refined professional skills. They are exemplary communicators encompassing written, verbal, and interpersonal skills. Their critical and creative thinking capacities incorporate sophisticated problem solving and decision making based on appropriate assessment-related data sets. To support critical and creative thinking, virtuosos must be skilled in accessing and strategically using information from a range of sources (information literacy). Increasingly, they need to possess information and communication technology skills that enable them to access and manage information at the local, national, and global levels. Finally, to exploit synergies across competing role groups, virtuosos demonstrate high-level team-working skills that support constructive collaborations.

Conclusion

Leading assessment can be a daunting task, rife with uncertainty and the potential for conflict among educational stakeholders. At times, assessment is seen by some as a control mechanism intended to deprofessionalize educators. Too often, the only desirable form of student assessment is perceived as that which allows educators to diagnose and address individual student needs; this perspective ignores or, at worst, denigrates the assessment information that senior educational leaders and policy makers must have to meet their macro-level responsibilities. Educational leaders are obligated professionally and morally to seek a virtuoso level of assessment literacy.

Educational leaders also must seek a vibrant and sustainable balance between homeostasis and evolutionary adaptation (Fig. 14.4). They must develop deep understandings of the wide array of forms and purposes of assessment and, importantly, appreciate the role-specific assessment interests of stakeholders. To create the educational contexts where assessment is valued and used well, effective leaders can identify and understand the moderating influences of personal, cultural, environmental, and temporal dimensions. Further, leaders must know how and when to ameliorate or exploit moderating influences on assessment, depending on their positive and negative effects.

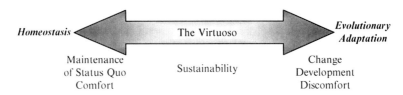

Homeostasis	The Virtuoso	Evolutionary Adaptation
Maintenance of Status Quo Comfort	Sustainability	Change Development Discomfort

Fig. 14.4 Virtuoso continuum

However, leading assessment is made more complex by the need for educational leaders to be mindful of more than just the local context and to facilitate assessment practices that recognize the demands of participating in the global village. Earlier, we posited that student assessment occurs in the context of diversity and that sound assessment contributes to a morally and ethically sound educational environment for every young person. This leads, we stated, to the development of individual and collective social capital that is necessary to sustain a thriving civil democracy. Clearly, the connections among teaching and learning, assessment, social capital, thriving societies, and the global village are complex, fragile, and fraught with power differentials. Nonetheless, their import makes it easy to argue for careful attention to the development of virtuoso-level dialogue and decision making in schools, systems, and societies. It is equally straightforward to state that the dangers and lost potential of barely functioning or failed societies are too disastrous to allow. Therefore, it is essential that educational leaders seek to realize the possibilities of sound policy and practice within the ecology of teaching, learning, and assessment throughout the global village.

References

Allport, G. W. (1960). *Personality and social encounter*. Boston: Beacon.

Buckley, W. (1968). Society as a complex adaptive system. In W. Buckley (Ed.), *Modern systems research for the behavioral scientist* (pp. 490–513). Chicago: Aldine Publishing Company.

Cooper, S. J. (2008). From Claude Bernard to Walter Cannon. Emergence of the concept of homeostasis. *Appetite, 51*, 419–427.

Earl, L. (2007). Assessment as learning. In W. D. Hawley (Ed.), *The keys to effective schools: Educational reform as continuous improvement* (pp. 85–98). Thousand Oaks, CA: Corwin.

Hudson, C. G. (2000). From social Darwinism to self-organization: Implications for social change theory. *Social Service Review, 74*(4), 533–559.

McLuhan, M. (1964). *Understanding media: The extensions of man*. New York: McGraw-Hill.

Schwandt, D., & Goldstein, J. A. (2008). Society as a complex adaptive system (classic paper section). *E:CO Issue, 10*(3), 86–112.

Webber, C. F., Aitken, N., Lupart, J., & Scott, S. (2009, May). *The Alberta student assessment study final report* (Report to Alberta Education), Edmonton, AB.

Index

CPSIA information can be obtained at www.ICGtesting.com
Printed in the USA
LVOW071525050613

337126LV00001B/1/P